DATE DUE

CULTURAL ENCYCLOPEDIA OF THE BODY

CULTURAL ENCYCLOPEDIA OF THE BODY

Volume 1: A–L

Edited by
Victoria Pitts-Taylor

GREENWOOD PRESS
Westport, Connecticut • London

Library of Congress Cataloging-in-Publication Data

Cultural encyclopedia of the body / edited by Victoria Pitts-Taylor.
    p. cm.
   Includes bibliographical references and index.
   ISBN: 978-0-313-34145-8 ((set) : alk. paper)
   ISBN: 978-0-313-34146-5 ((vol. 1) : alk. paper)
   ISBN: 978-0-313-34147-2 ((vol. 2) : alk. paper)

   1. Body, Human—Social aspects—History. 2. Body, Human—Social aspects—
Dictionaries. 3. Body image—Social aspects. I. Pitts-Taylor, Victoria.
   HM636.C85 2008
   306.4—dc22   2008019926

British Library Cataloguing in Publication Data is available.

Library of Congress Catalog Card Number: 2008019926
ISBN: 978-0-313-34145-8 (Set)
        978-0-313-34146-5 (Vol. 1)
        978-0-313-34147-2 (Vol. 2)

First published in 2008

Greenwood Press, 88 Post Road West, Westport, CT 06881
An imprint of Greenwood Publishing Group, Inc.
www.greenwood.com

Printed in the United States of America

The paper used in this book complies with the
Permanent Paper Standard issued by the National
Information Standards Organization (Z39.48-1984).

10   9   8   7   6   5   4   3   2   1

For Chloe

CONTENTS

PREFACE

This encyclopedia is organized by body part alphabetically, and body parts from head to toe, external and internal, are included. Readers can, of course, find entries of interest under the body-part section, but as many body parts are interconnected and overlap (for example, essays on the face and the mouth are found in separate sections in the encyclopedia, but the face can include the mouth), a perusal of the contents listing all of the entries is the best way to identify topics. Many of the body parts are examined in a lengthy entry identified as a cultural history of the body part; for example, there is a cultural history of the mouth, a cultural history of the skin, and a cultural history of the eyes. In addition, entries are included for issues or practices related to the individual body part. For example, under the heading skin, there are entries on body piercing, branding, cutting, scarification, skin lightening, stretch marks, subdermal implants, and tattoos.

Some body parts are subsumed under a broader category, such as the reproductive system. Under this heading, readers will find topics such as a cultural history of menopause, a cultural history of menstruation, fertility treatments, a history of birth control, a history of childbirth in the United States, and menstruation-related practices and products. Cross-references at the end of some entries alert readers to other essays of related interest.

Some entries have a United States-based focus; others are international. The coverage is sometimes contemporary, historical, or both. In addition to broad entries on a body part, a few entries focus on icons associated with the body part, such as the entries on Michael Jackson's face and French performance artist Orlan's facial surgeries.

Fascinating dates throughout history related to the body are found in a chronology. Each essay has a section on further reading, and a substantial selected bibliography enables more research. Historical and contemporary photos illuminate the entries.

ACKNOWLEDGMENTS

I would like to thank all of the writers from across the globe—the United States, Germany, Ireland, Scotland, Norway, England, and Australia—whose work is collected here for their careful research, imaginative writing, and diligence. I'd also like to thank Wendi Schnaufer of Greenwood Press for her role in developing this project. Professor Barbara Katz Rothman of the City University of New York aided me in finding authors, as did the Centre for Somatechnics at Macquarie University in Sydney, for which I am grateful. Queens College of the City University of New York gave me a sabbatical to accomplish this project. I thank Gregory Taylor for his willingness on numerous occasions to serve as an unofficial consultant on medical matters addressed herein. I'd also like to thank him for his patience, humor, and moral support. I thank my friends and family who have supported me in various ways and upon whom I leaned during the early days of being a working parent. Foremost, I acknowledge my daughter Chloe Isabelle Taylor, who was born during this project. In the first months of her life, she cheerfully shared her mother's attention during many hours of writing and editing. I dedicate these volumes to her.

ACKNOWLEDGMENTS

INTRODUCTION

This cultural study examines how bodies are understood, what they mean to society, how they are managed, treated, and transformed, and how they are depicted and represented. Describing such aspects of the body on an encyclopedic scale is an extraordinary challenge, as much a feat of imagination as of knowledge.

The Scope of the Corpus

An encyclopedia is an "exhaustive repertory of information" on a particular subject or branch of knowledge, according to the Oxford English Dictionary; however, the scope of cultural information on the body is boundless. All sorts of issues, including those that are environmental, political, geographical, and technological, can be related to the body. The entries in this encyclopedia address many disparate topics. They describe slavery and colonialism as relevant to the cultural study of the body. They also point to sex, beauty, and fashion. They raise issues of warfare and commerce, science and technological invention, birth control, childbirth and breastfeeding, epidemics and diseases, and supernatural beliefs and religion, among many others. The range of topics the entries address is vast, as are the representations of the body to which they refer. Human bodies are variously portrayed in poetry, painting, and sculpture, in plays and operas, in religious artifacts and cave drawings, in novels and self-help books, on television, and in other popular media. Although reading them is a hermeneutical practice rather than a scientific one, these representations may suggest some of the symbolic meanings of bodies in various cultures and time periods. The entries also draw from many disciplines that are concerned to some degree or another with human bodies, including anthropology and archaeology, sociology and political history, philosophy, art history, literary studies, and medicine.

This volume is not a medical encyclopedia of the body, but the contributors draw on the history of medicine, along with the other aforementioned disciplines, as knowledges that concern the ways in which we live in and experience the human body. The history of medicine is so complex that one might be tempted to leave medicine out of a cultural history of the body altogether, drawing a line between scientific interests in the human body and interests that are socially scientific, philosophic, and artistic. But such a division is unfeasible, partly because the lay or non-medical history of the human body has been deeply influenced by the practices and theories of physicians since the time of Hippocrates. The ancient medical theories of Greek and Roman physicians, as well as those from India and the Arab world, shaped understandings of bodily workings and activities for centuries. In addition, medical understandings of the body cannot always be easily separated from other knowledges about the body, like philosophy. Although the *Hippocratic Corpus* demarcated medicine as a distinct profession, physicians have long concerned themselves with philosophical matters. Debates over the physicality and location of the mind and soul, for example, persisted from antiquity through the seventeenth century, until they were overshadowed by discussions of the brain.

A cultural study of the body cannot discount medicine, then, or any of the other disciplines interested in humans and bodies. This encyclopedia addresses many topics and themes of cultural interest in the human body, including many cultural practices from around the world and across epochs. This encyclopedia should be read as a set of suggestions for framing a cultural perspective on the body. It might inspire what the famous sociologist C. Wright Mills called the "sociological imagination," or the ability to see beyond the individual body or person to the broader cultural context and social structure that shapes her or his experience.[1]

Cultural Accounts of the Body

A cultural account of the body is really a method, a way of imagining how the body carries symbolic significance in social life, and how people experience their own bodies and the bodies of others as socially or culturally significant objects. For example, ideals or norms reflect how a whole society thinks about bodies, such as what characteristics constitute a "fat" body, or which term is used to describe such a body. It is common knowledge that societies change their views about the attractiveness of particular body sizes and shapes, as any stroll through the Metropolitan Museum of Art can attest. And the terms people use to describe size also vary in meaning. The word "corpulence," for example, has a different set of historical associations than "obesity," with the former linked to wealth and leisure, and sometimes even to health, and the latter to medicalized notions of disease, risk, and addiction. How important the size of the body is to a society also varies. Consider, for example, that standardized measurements of what is viewed as fat weren't really in vogue until the mid-twentieth century, with the development of the height/weight table in 1943 and, later, the Body Mass Index.

A cultural account of the body can examine other physical differences, particularly those that seem to be important to any given society or community, such as those assigned to groups based on gender, race, ethnicity, class, citizenship, or sexual practices. A cultural approach considers how bodily differences come to be seen as group differences, rather than just simply as variations, and considers the mechanisms and methods by which societies and communities make efforts to detect, investigate, measure, chart, or categorize bodily differences. For instance, craniometry, which is the study of the shape of the face and skull, represented efforts in the physical anthropology of the eighteenth and nineteenth centuries to categorize differences between racial groups. Pieter Camper's investigation of the facial angle and Samuel Morton's work on cranial capacity were part of a larger history of scientific interest in racial attributes. Camper, Morton, and others sought to prove the existence of significant physical differences in social groups, and to theorize the implications for intelligence and other characteristics. Rather than dismissing these forays into the human body simply as scientific missteps, one can consider how they were related to social, political, or economic concerns of their time, or ponder how their research was received and utilized. It appears that "scientific racism" was used to fuel eugenics and fascist movements of the twentieth century and played a major role in justifying colonialism and racial discrimination in earlier periods. The differences of bodies, then, cannot be taken for granted; rather, a society's efforts to generate, frame, or measure differences in ways that correlate with social groupings—and usually social hierarchies—needs to be investigated.

A cultural inquiry into the body needs to be, to some extent, comparative, because bodily practices and norms are constantly changing and differ between groups and time periods. Standards of hygiene, for instance, are among the bodily norms that diverge greatly over time and place. Bathing has been religiously ritualized, organized for public socializing, and sometimes discouraged as decadent or inauspicious. Variations on bathing can reveal something about the different kinds of attitudes toward nudity and clothing, sexuality, gender roles, menstruation, and other sex differences, and what counts as sacred and profane in a society. Changes in bodily standards and practices can have social and sometimes even political significance. Practices can also reflect considerable divergence in perspectives between communities; a custom that is widespread in some areas may be abhorrent in others, such as female genital cutting across northern Africa and in other parts of the globe, the wearing of permanent neck rings among the ethnic Burmese in Thailand, or the widespread popularity of breast implants in the United States and elsewhere. Each of these practices violates the taboos of other societies or other generations and induces significant critiques. A practice can also change in a single community across generations. For example, the rise of the Afro hairstyle in the 1960s created considerable generational conflict among African Americans, many of whom had been straightening their hair since at least the latter part of the nineteenth century.

A cultural study of the body can consider how any part of the body is treated, represented, or transformed. Hair might seem like a superficial topic until one considers that hairstyles can be symbolically connected to social issues such as race and gender, and to social and historical matters like slavery, colonialism, and religion. Through one's hair a person might display her social status as a member of the aristocracy or the royal court, as a follower of a particular religion or sect, or as a slave or a criminal. One might be encouraged to dye her hair blond if she were a prostitute in ancient Rome, or might be inspired to dye it red and pluck out any hairs on her forehead if she were a member of the court of Elizabeth I. If a woman's hair is curly and members of the dominant culture have straight hair, she may believe that straightening her hair is more beautiful or acceptable, as did many immigrant and African American women in the first half of the twentieth century. A practice such as hair straightening can be seen as a symbol of assimilation, and new hairstyles can be preferred by radicals and revolutionaries, such as the black activists of the 1960s who embraced the Afro as a symbol of black pride. A religion may ask or demand that a woman wear wigs after marriage (sometimes shaving her hair first), as in some Orthodox Jewish sects, or cover one's hair during religious services, as do Muslims, Jews, and, until recently, many Christians. Veiling may be banned or officially discouraged, as it was in Iran, Turkey, and Egypt in the late nineteenth and early twentieth centuries, or it may be mandatory or brutally enforced, as in Iran after the 1979 revolution. Veiling might be seen as a symbol of women's oppression, as many feminists have contended, or as a matter of religious expression, as immigrant communities have argued recently in France, or as a sign of anti-colonial nationalism, as in the movement for Algerian independence.

An inquiry into almost any other part of the human body from a cultural perspective can be equally multifaceted. Hair is more visible and easily transformable than skull shape, but the latter is also culturally interesting. From the widespread use of trephination, the drilling of a hole into the skull, in pre-Incan cultures, to the nineteenth-century investigations of the head and skull in craniometry and phrenology, the head and skull have had interesting roles in human culture. Likewise, the nose: from the piercing of the left nostril of women on the Indian subcontinent, to the measuring of noses in racial typologies, to the rise of rhinoplasty among ethnic minorities as a tool of assimilation, the nose is variously symbolic in matters of reproductive health, beauty, and racial hierarchies, among others. The hands, mouth, heart, and bones have equally interesting cultural significance.

The genitals of both women and men are immensely fascinating from cultural perspectives. The cultural history of testicles leads one to antiquity, when the castration of slaves was common in the Persian empire and eunuchs were employed in the royal palaces of ancient China, and to Renaissance Europe, when *castrati* were used in church choirs and celebrated in music halls. The penis is a matter of intense cultural investment in many cultures, and has been modified in numerous ways. A brief recitation of penis modifications includes not only circumcision, but also infibulation, subincision, and the piercing named after Prince Albert, Queen Victoria's husband. There are also various methods to curb masturbation, a matter of great concern in the eighteenth and nineteenth centuries, and contemporary surgeries undertaken by male-to-female transsexuals. From the overt worship of the phallus in ancient Greece to its role in Freudian theory in the early twentieth century, the penis is symbolically varied but culturally ubiquitous.

Female genitalia and reproductive organs are also deeply inscribed with symbolism. The vagina, depending on one's culture, is variously a place of physical underdevelopment, shame, secrecy, a source of supernatural power, or a space of liberation and feminist reclaiming. In Western philosophy and medicine, female genitalia were considered underdeveloped or interior versions of male genitalia until the nineteenth century, and were referred to as "secret places" or "shameful parts" in various translations of the *Trotula*, a collection of gynecological writings from the twelfth century. The vagina was also considered a passive vessel for reproduction. But in many traditions, including in the Marquesas Islands of Polynesia, female genitalia have been seen as powerful, and are displayed to fend off evil supernatural spirits. Many myths surround female genitalia, including the *vagina dentata*, Latin for "vagina with teeth," and the medieval chastity belt, which is supposed to have been widely used in medieval Europe to block entrance to the vagina. A contemporary myth in South Africa and elsewhere holds that sex with a virgin can guard against contracting the AIDS virus, echoing earlier stories about the vagina in relation to syphilis. The other female genitalia are equally controversial. The very existence of the clitoris, first scientifically "discovered" in 1559 by anatomist Realdo Columbus, has been debated for centuries, and its role in the physiological processes of female orgasm was a major concern of psychoanalysts, psychiatrists, sexologists, and women themselves in the twentieth century. The clitoris is subject to surgical reduction or removal in female genital cutting, a practice that has ancient origins but which currently affects more than 100 million women and girls worldwide. The clitoris is directly implicated in religious and cultural attitudes about female sexuality. Currently the female labia are undergoing surgical transformation in new practices of gynecological cosmetic surgery in many western societies.

Unique or rare differences in body parts can culturally matter, too, and exceptional bodies and body parts have been both celebrated and scorned. The so-called Hottentot Venus, who was actually an African slave named Saartjie (Sarah) Baartman, was taken to London in 1810 and displayed as part of an ethnological exhibit, held up as a spectacle for the size of her buttocks. In the age of scientific racism, she was used as an example of the supposed primitivism of non-Westerners. During the 1830s, women from the Burmese *Padaung* tribe, who wear neck rings that compress the shoulders and make the neck look dramatically longer, were taken to England and paid to be put on display in the Bertram Mills Circus as ethnological freaks. The reception of intersexed individuals, born with ambiguous genitalia, has varied widely and ranged from fascination and honor to scorn and stigmatization. *Hijras* in Hindu society, who are born either with ambiguous genitalia or are biologically male but live as transsexuals, are frequently members of the lower castes, but they have important roles in rituals and ceremonies related to fertility. American Navajo *nadles*, born intersexed, have been celebrated, but in Western traditions, intersexed people have been highly stigmatized. In medicine they came under the scrutiny of teratology—from *tera*, Greek for monster—dedicated to the study of anomalous bodies and birth defects.

The contributors to this encyclopedia have also pointed to contemporary forms of body modification that have created spectacular bodies. Within the realm of cosmetic surgery, the French performance artist Orlan has generated considerable controversy. The face of contemporary singer Michael Jackson has been endlessly fascinating to the media, partly because his cosmetic surgeries appear to defy both racial and gender expectations. The tragic fate of Lolo Ferrari, a popular French figure who held the world's record for having the largest breast implants, has been widely understood as a sign of the decadence of cosmetic surgery. There are also non-surgical forms of body modification, many of which are borrowed from indigenous groups, that are popular among youth and subcultures of body artists or body modifiers in the West. These include tattooing, body piercing, and scarification, which have been widely practiced as rites of passage in indigenous societies. Practices like scarification that are unremarkable in some cultures can be shocking in others, and may be interpreted as a sign of rebellion or social disaffection.[2]

A cultural study of the human body describes in part how the body changes throughout time and place, both affecting and affected by historical, political, scientific, and philosophical transformations. Culturally speaking, the human body is a moving target, morphing alongside changing ideas of gender, sex, race, religion, community, and belonging, among other matters. One significant implication of this view regards the natural body.

The Natural Body Versus the Socially Constructed Body

The concept of the body as "natural" frames it as a biological constant, fixed across culture, time, and place. As sociologist Chris Shilling summarized in *The Body and Social Theory* (1993), naturalistic theories of the body view it as "the pre-social, biological basis on which the superstructures of the self and society are founded."[3] Such views of the body are to varying degrees deterministic, emphasizing biology as a blueprint for human behavior and culture. Importantly, they also use a model of the body that is more or less universal, leaving bodies and bodily behaviors that differ from this model to be considered abnormal, pathological, or less developed in some way. Shilling suggests that naturalistic theories have dominated our understanding of the body, the self, and society since the eighteenth century. Naturalism continues to dominate medical and psychiatric approaches to the body, and naturalistic views of human bodies and behaviors are buttressed by recent developments such as the human genome project and the invention of neuroscientific technologies to view the brain (PET scans). Genetic and physiological maps of human bodies seem to point firmly to biology (to genes and hard-wiring in the brain) to explain many aspects of human life and embodiment.

But while the naturalistic body is still the preferred model of medicine and the hard sciences, we are also witnessing the emergence of a widespread interest in what might be called the cultural body, the body as seen from sociological and cultural perspectives. This can be linked to a number of recent developments. The rise of "biopsychosocial" theories in medicine in the 1980s pointed to the significance of psychological and social factors in health and illness. Transformations in biotechnology, such as the rise of in vitro fertilization procedures and genetic engineering, have ushered in an awareness of the malleability of the physical body. The rise in the visibility of the body in social and cultural practices, particularly in postmodern cultures like the contemporary United States, has highlighted the body as a resource for identity formation and social values, and has also generated interest in more traditional and indigenous body practices and rites. In addition, the rise of feminism, postmodernism, multiculturalism, and postcolonial theory in academic, artistic, and philosophical spheres has underscored the body as a site of significant political, social, and cultural activity.

Generated largely in opposition to naturalism, cultural theories have instead argued for culture's influence on the body, especially but not exclusively in terms of the its meanings and significance. Theoretical perspectives such as social constructionism, multiculturalism, and feminism have argued that the body is inscribed by culture. Here the body is understood as a surface to be read and coded by social relations. Unlike a naturalistic body, this cultural body is vulnerable to history and is semantically malleable. The cultural body is a place where social relations are manifested and sometimes are literally rendered visible. This body is also, as the philosopher Michel Foucault has outlined, subject to forces like normalization and medicalization, wherein bodies are defined as normal or pathological.

The existence of a "natural" body is called into question by the theory of social constructionism. Social constructionism is a perspective that argues that, "things are not discovered but actually produced."[4] If the body is socially constructed, then social forces define, influence, shape, and produce the body. Fat, then, would be socially produced; what counts as fat in any given society depends upon the social relations and social institutions of that society. This does not deny the physiological existence of adipose tissue that constitutes fat, but suggests that its meaning is highly social. From a social-constructionist perspective, sex is also socially produced. The physical differences between men and women may include genetic and hormonal variations, but the meanings of those differences, and the translations of those differences into gender roles, are social affairs. Even the idea that there are two sexes is a matter of interpretation. The one-sex theory, that the female body represented an incomplete version of the male body, lasted from antiquity until the nineteenth century in Western traditions. And while we now have a two-sex model, some societies recognize a third sex, based on the existence of intersexed individuals who are born with ambiguous genitalia. Further, the feminist biologist Anne Fausto Sterling has argued for the existence of five sexes, and contemporary medical textbooks can provide evidence of even more variations. From a social-constructionist perspective, how many sexes there are depends upon the cultural work of organizing, classifying, and interpreting the body.

Feminist scholarship and feminist politics have been enormously influential in highlighting the body as a major site of culture. Feminist theory has been deeply interested in the social construction of gender relations, and much feminist work assumes that gender roles do not follow biological, but rather social, imperatives. Feminist scholarship on the body has focused on, among other issues, the influence of gender norms on the ways in which the physical body has been framed, including in religion, medicine, and the law; the ways in which experiences of embodiment are shaped by gender roles, from how people adorn themselves to their physical shapes and comportment; the use of the body in developing and maintaining social hierarchies; the oppression of women and girls via their bodies; and violence against female bodies. However, feminists have disagreed over the role of the natural body. Radical feminists have embraced a naturalistic view of the body, stressing "the embodied nature of sexual difference"[5] and insisting that there are essential differences between men and women based in part on biology. They have also pointed to some of the practices outlined in this encyclopedia, like female genital cutting, footbinding, and cosmetic surgery, as examples of violence against women, and, implicitly, violations of the natural body. The radical feminist defense of the natural body also underlies some criticisms of other kinds of body modification, as well as of medicalization, or the processes by which the human body comes under the purview of medicine. Thus the feminist position on the natural body is ambivalent, with some championing the natural and defending it from cultural assaults, and others viewing embodiment as fluid and socially constructed.

Multiculturalism and postcolonial theories have also contributed to the view of the body as socially constructed. Multiculturalism urges sensitivity to diverse viewpoints and cultural practices, and rejects universalistic ideas of self, body, and society. A multicultural view points out that bodily practices vary widely across cultures. One implication is that the dominant conceptions of the "natural" body may in fact reflect culturally specific norms. In addition, postcolonial theorists have described how colonialism and cultural imperialism have generated hierarchies of race, binary notions of "civilization" and "primitivism," and ethnocentric ideas about the body and the self. Applied to considerations of the body, these perspectives argue for examining the power relations inherent in knowledge about different kinds of bodies, cultures, and bodily practices. These viewpoints are related to, but not identical to, cultural relativism, which argues that the norms and moral standards by which we judge human behavior are always culturally specific, and thus limited in their applicability to the behaviors and practices of others. Cultural relativism asks us to suspend our judgment about the practices and beliefs of people who are different from us.

Despite the flourishing of cultural perspectives on the body, the "natural" body remains a powerful concept that is sometimes used as a moral measure. Some body modifications and practices, for example, are said to violate nature, and some anomalous bodies have been considered "unnatural." This has happened regularly in the histories of medicine, psychiatry, and sexology, and such criticisms are also found in contemporary political debates over the body. But this encyclopedia rejects the "natural" body in favor of exploring the fluidity of the body, including the varieties of bodies, the kinds of ways people have lived their embodied lives, and the variability of our knowledges about the physical body. Even aspects of the physical body that appear to be essential or unchanging, like the basics of human reproduction, are subject to varying interpretations over time and place. For example, as Lisa Jean Moore describes, the thirteenth-century theologian

Thomas Aquinas saw a moral importance to the ejaculation of seminal fluid that would not meet the scrutiny of scientific reasoning today, and descriptions of sperm since the invention of the microscope in the seventeenth century have been highly subjective. But even contemporary medical descriptions of the roles of sperm and egg are not culturally neutral; instead, they are saturated with metaphoric language that imbues them with social meanings. In addition to looking at the variations between and among bodies, a cultural study of anatomy examines bodies at this level of discourse and representation.

There are limits to a social-constructionist perspective. Importantly, the treatment of the body at the level of narrative or text has tended to overshadow explorations of the physicality or materiality of the body in social-constructionist accounts. For example, the phenomenological experiences of embodiment have been under-examined in social-constructionist theories. This encyclopedia embraces a social-constructionist perspective without assuming that alone it can be comprehensive. The knowledge gathered herein is offered in part as evidence for the changing character of the human body, and of the cultural relativity of bodily norms and standards. But importantly, a cultural perspective is not simply a corrective to a wholly biological view of the body, and does not depend upon proving naturalistic views to be wrong. Rather, a cultural view opens up the body to new ways of thinking that are fascinating in their own right, and that can be seen to both complicate and complement naturalistic approaches.

Cultural Relativism and Human Rights

A cultural inquiry into the body leads one to consider the wide variety of human bodies and bodily practices, and to question any fixed idea of a proper way to live in, adorn, and treat the body. From the accounts collected here, for example, it appears that one would be hard pressed to find *any* culture that does not modify the body in some way. The pristine body, left alone, cannot therefore serve as a measure against which we might judge bodily practices. The ethical implication might be that physical norms are simply culturally relative, and that value neutrality is the only appropriate response to the scope of the diversity of human bodies and practices.

Cultural relativism, while not unproblematic, is a useful perspective to employ in a cultural study of the body. Cultural relativism can be thought of as a method of trying to see the practices of people through their own eyes, which is vital to understanding the cultural significance of bodies. Many of the practices outlined in this book are commonplace in one culture, but considered unnatural or bizarre in another. The practice among Aboriginal Australians of slicing the underside of the penis has been considered mutilation by outsiders, as have the customs of filing the teeth, wearing neck rings, footbinding, and circumcision that have been undertaken in various cultures across the globe. The essays here generally avoid the term "mutilation" to describe these practices, because as it is currently used, the term is normative rather than descriptive. It is important from a culturally relativistic viewpoint to attempt to see the subjective, culturally specific value of these practices, a task made impossible by their immediate condemnation and dismissal. It is also clear from the diversity of bodily practices that mutilation is a highly subjective, culturally biased term often applied only to those practices violating the body that are unfamiliar, rather than to those which are commonplace and widely accepted. As we use it here, cultural relativism can be considered a method that requires a suspension of such immediate value judgments in order to increase the richness of understanding of the body's meanings.

Yet it is difficult, and perhaps even undesirable, to sustain value neutrality in a cultural inquiry of bodies, partly because it is the relations of power and inequality expressed in body practices that make them important to study from cultural perspectives. The power relations of sex and gender, race and ethnicity, class and so on are primary forces in the social and cultural shaping of human bodies. The roles of slavery, colonialism, racism, class dominance, and gender dominance in producing culturally meaningful human bodies are profound, and these are not ethically neutral matters. Bodies vary greatly, but variations in bodily comportment, adornment, and experience are not always due to the voluntary agency of embodied selves. Force and coercion are sometimes directly involved in bodily practices, and hierarchies of power can generate troubling ethical concerns. Further, some of the practices described herein have been determined by observers to violate human rights. While it is true that universal notions of human rights are in fact culturally limited and specific, concerns for human rights are nonetheless important to contemporary societies around the world.

While a culturally relativist approach might try to suspend biases, critical awareness of power relations cannot not be wholly removed from consideration in a cultural account of the body. Rather, the social context of body practices, including the social hierarchies, power relations, and politics of bodily practices, should be seen as deeply significant to any cultural understanding of them. The social context is useful for generating subtle understandings of body customs. For example, any practice of castration could be condemned by contemporary readers as equivalent mutilations that are wrong or pathological because they appear to violate a "natural" body. But a perspective that balances a culturally relativist approach with concern for power and inequality might complicate this interpretation. One might see the forcible castration of slaves in the Persian empire in a different light than the voluntary castration of Roman *Galli*, priests of the ancient cult of Cybele. While from the naturalistic point of view the practices all amount to removing the testicles, from the perspectives employed here, they vary in meaning because the social relations that shape the practices are different. The cultural study of the body does not concern itself with defending an ideal of the natural body, then, but rather concerns how bodies are meaningful for the people whose they are.

Human rights regarding the body are currently a matter of considerable global concern and disagreement. A cultural study of the body needs to consider issues of human rights while acknowledging that understandings of human rights are themselves culturally relative. Among the many practices now under global review are those that constitute female genital cutting, also commonly called female genital mutilation, or FGM. Female genital cutting practices are widespread and deeply controversial. They raise significant worries about individual agency and consent, in part because they are usually performed on children, and because of the considerable risks they appear to pose. A cultural account of female genital cutting practices can examine their cultural relevance, the meanings they have for the people who use them, the power relations between men and women (and adults and children) that influence them, and the historical, religious, and political contexts that shape them. Such an approach is likely to offer a more nuanced understanding of female genital cutting than a purely naturalistic account. While by itself such an account does not answer the ethical dilemmas posed by the practices, a nuanced cultural understanding is vital for developing a relevant ethical critique.

Body Parts: Organizing the Corpus

What makes up the body is not self-evident or purely a matter of empirical investigation. Rather, the organization of the body into various parts is a practice of cultural interpretation. Which organs and components are identifiably distinct, how they are identified and labeled, and to what larger groupings they belong has been the outcome of an historical, contested social process of producing medical and lay knowledge about the body. Body parts have variously been "discovered" and contested, they have waxed and waned in significance, and they have been seen as distinct or subsumed under other parts or systems. In this sense, the parts of the body are socially constructed.

This encyclopedia is an example of the social production of body parts. It represents a selective process of naming and organizing. To begin with, the parts chosen for consideration here represent only some of those that could be named. In addition, among the organs, systems, and parts named here, some are subsumed under broader categories. The fingers are discussed as part of the hands; the toenails are considered together with the rest of the feet. Neurons are not discussed independently, but rather as part of the brain, while the head is treated distinctly from the brain, since its cultural significance does not seem to be exactly reducible to it. Body parts are also joined to or separated from other components. There are many ways to categorize the vagina: on its own, as part of the reproductive organs, and as part of the female genitalia. The vagina is listed separately here, as is the clitoris, but the labia minora and majora are considered together. Finally, the kinds of parts listed vary. Some are organs (the skin, the heart), some are systems or parts of systems (the reproductive organs, the muscles), some are groupings (male and female genitalia), some are bodily fluids (blood, semen), and others are none of the above (the waist).

This cultural study of the body should inspire a certain kind of imagination, a way of looking at the body. A cultural approach opens up the body to the investigation of meanings and values, metaphors, attitudes and beliefs, and positions the body as a central site of cultural investment. The diversity of lived bodies is astonishing, and the body remains a vast territory for cultural exploration and discovery.

Notes

1. C. Wright Mills, 2000 [1960]. *The Sociological Imagination*. 40th Anniversary Edition. Oxford: Oxford University Press.
2. Victoria Pitts, 2003. *In the Flesh: The Cultural Politics of Body Modification*. New York: Palgrave Macmillan.
3. Chris Shilling, 2003. *The Body and Social Theory*. London: Sage, p. 37.
4. Bryan S. Turner, 2004. *The New Medical Sociology*. New York: W.W. Norton, p. 40.
5. Janet Price and Margrit Shildrick, eds., 1999. *Feminist Theory and the Body: A Reader*. New York: Routledge, p. 5.

Further Reading

Fausto-Sterling, Anne. *Sexing the Body: Gender Politics and the Construction of Sexuality*. New York: Basic Books, 2000.

Foucault, Michel. *An Introduction*. Vol. I of *The History of Sexuality*. Trans. Robert Hurley. London: Allen Lane, 1979.

Moore, Lisa Jean. *Sperm Counts: Overcome by Man's Most Precious Fluid*. New York: NYU Press, 2007.

Pitts, Victoria. *In the Flesh: The Cultural Politics of Body Modification*. New York: Palgrave, 2003.

Price, Janet, and Margrit Shildrick, eds. *Feminist Theory and the Body: A Reader*. New York: Routledge, 1999.

Shilling, Chris. *The Body and Social Theory*. London: Sage, 1993.

Turner, Bryan S. *The New Medical Sociology*. New York: W. W. Norton, 2004.

Victoria Pitts-Taylor

CHRONOLOGY

ca. 24000–22000 BCE.	Carving Venus of Willendorf, a limestone figurine of a female, is thought to suggest early ideals of beauty and fertility. The figure has rounded and prominent breasts, belly, vulva, and buttocks.
ca. 10000 BCE.	Evidence of tattooing within the heterogeneous Jomon culture in Japan.
ca. 10000–5000 BCE.	Earliest known efforts at trephination, or drilling a hole in the skull, often to cure various ailments.
8000–1000 BCE.	Oldest specimens of deliberately mutilated or modified teeth found in North America.
5300–4000 BCE.	Earliest forms of body piercing including ear piercing in ancient China, nose piercing in the Middle East, and lip piercing in the Aleutian Islands.
4000–3500 BCE.	Figurines from Egypt depict tattoos.
3500 BCE.	Ötzi the "Iceman," the frozen mummy found in Italy in 1991, is adorned with tattoos.
3100 BCE–31 BCE.	Egyptian elite shave all of their hair and wear wigs. Lips are painted with henna and other plant extracts, and archaeological evidence points to further uses of cosmetics. Henna is used to mark the fingers and toes of pharaohs in preparation for the afterlife. Tattoos on Egyptian female mummies date to 2000 BCE. During the New Kingdom (1559–1085 BCE), stretched earlobes become fashionable.
2000 BCE.	Early Mayans practice simple forms of tooth modification, sharpening them to a point. By the end of the first millennium CE, the practice becomes more elaborate, including the use of jade and pyrite inlays.
2000 BCE.	Trephination is widely practiced in pre-Inca Peru.
2000 BCE.	Founder of the Xia dynasty, Da Yu, marries a woman rumored to have tiny "fox" feet. This begins the history of footbinding. However, footbinding is infrequent until the end of the eleventh century CE.

2000–1400 BCE.	Minoan women on the island of Crete paint their faces or wear makeup of some kind, and wear cloths wrapped around the waist under the breasts, which remain exposed.
1810–1750 BCE.	Assyrian Law Code of Hammurabi makes references to eunuchs.
700s BCE to 1911 CE.	Castration is practiced in China.
600s BCE.	First Olympic games held in Olympia, Greece, lasting until the fourth century CE.
612–330 BCE.	Persian Empire dominates Mesopotamia. Widespread castration of males performed, usually on slaves and prisoners of war to serve in the ruling courts.
ca. 580–ca. 500 BCE.	Life of Pythagoras, the pre-Socratic philosopher and mathematician and the first to explicitly theorize that beauty consists of three components: symmetry, proportion, and harmony. He considers these to be natural properties, intrinsic to all beautiful things.
551–479 BCE.	Life of Confucius, Chinese philosopher. His ideas about the heart are central to Confucian thought.
400s BCE.	Sushruta, famous Indian physician, practices surgery and medicine. Often regarded as the father of surgery, he is credited with early otoplastic techniques and rhinoplasty. He also describes a procedure for piercing and stretching the earlobes of children.
400s BCE.	Female genital cutting first achieves widespread popularity among the Phoenicians, Hittites, and Ethiopians.
ca. 490–ca. 430 BCE.	Life of the classical Greek sculptor Phidias, who creates widely admired sculptures which conform to the "golden ratio" of facial size and symmetry. *Phi*, an irrational number almost equivalent to 1.68, is named after him.
ca. 460–ca. 370 BCE.	Life of Hippocrates of Cos, known as the father of Western medicine. The *Hippocratic Corpus*, a collection of medical writings by early followers of Hippocrates, was profoundly influential in the development of Western medicine.
384–322 BCE.	Life of Aristotle, Greek philosopher. Aristotle determines the heart to be the center of the human body and its most important organ.
264 BCE.	First gladiator competitions are held in Rome; slaves and war captives fight against each other, sometimes joined by lions and other large animals.
ca. 250 BCE.	Andean regional development tradition in South America practice facial scarification, which is possibly used to express one's ethnic origin or socioeconomic status. In Mexico, the Veracruz tradition practices scarification in the first millennium CE.
204 BCE.	Cult of Cybele is officially adopted in Rome. Known as *Galli*, the priests of this cult castrate themselves.

200s BCE.	Human dissection comes into use in Alexandria. Before this, interior human anatomy can be explored only through indirect means.
ca. first century BCE–**1600s** CE.	In Mayan cultures of South America, bloodletting is a sacred practice.
ca. 129–ca. 200.	Life of Galen, Greek physician. Galen's treatise *On the Usefulness of the Parts of the Body* is highly influential in the development of anatomy and cardiology, and asserts that the heart is directly connected to the soul.
100s–500s.	*Kama Sutra*, a compendium of writings on love, is collected in its present form sometime during the Gupta period in India. Written in Sanskrit by the philosopher Mallanaga Vatsyayna, the text describes a variety of ways to make oneself attractive to the opposite sex, including the use of makeup, and methods to enhance pleasure, including sexual positions and the use of genital piercings.
570–632.	Life of Muhammad, the Prophet of Islam. During this time, veiling is not a religious practice, but a diffuse cultural practice throughout the Arabian Peninsula. Although Muhammad forbids castration, eunuchs guard Muhammad's tomb in Medina until the 1920s.
ca. 965–1039.	Arab or Persian scholar Ibn al-Haitham, or Alhazen, writes that eyesight may be improved with a ground optical lens. He is regarded as the father of optics.
900s.	Caucasian women begin removing their body hair after Crusaders return from the Middle East. This lasts until the 1500s, when the queen of France, Catherine de Medici, calls for such practices to stop.
1000s.	Footbinding starts to spread throughout China. By the end of the Song dynasty in 1125, footbinding is extensively practiced.
1100s.	Mughals are thought to have introduced the practice of mehndi, elaborate henna paintings on the hands and feet, to India.
1224.	Francis of Assisi, a Catholic saint, is usually credited as the first reported case of stigmata.
ca. 1225–1274.	Life of philosopher and Catholic theologian Thomas Aquinas, who posits that the flesh is the instrument of the soul.
ca. 1284.	Salvino D'Armate is credited with pairing two lenses to create wearable, corrective eyeglasses.
1200s–1400s.	Numerous texts on palmistry are written in Latin; earlier texts written in Arabic are brought to Europe by returning Crusaders.
ca. 1400.	An early model of the corset debuts in Spain.
1400s.	Eyeglasses are worn with darkened lenses in China as early as 1430 by judges in the courtroom to hide the expression of their eyes.

1452–1519.   Life of Leonardo da Vinci, artist, anatomist, and illustrator. He is deeply interested in anatomy and anatomical illustration.

1500s.   The corset emerges as a garment of choice in French and English high society.

1500s–1700s.   Handfasting is considered the equivalent of marriage in the British Isles, Germany, and America. In Scotland, handfasting persists until the early twentieth century.

mid-1500s–   During the European colonial slave trade, the use of branding is common, though
1830s.   not universal.

1533–1603.   Life of Elizabeth I, Queen of England from 1558–1603. Known for ostentatious dress, Elizabeth's tastes in fashion include high ruffs, puffy sleeves, wide skirts, and decorated bodices. She removes her hair at the hairline, which is thought to make her appear intelligent.

1559.   Realdo Columbo, an Italian anatomist, claims to have "discovered" the clitoris as the "seat of women's delight."

1578–1657.   Life of English doctor William Harvey, the first to conceive of the heart as a pumping mechanism.

1596–1650.   Life of philosopher Rene Descartes, who first poses the so-called "mind-body" problem in its modern form.

1597.   Earliest illustrated record of rhinoplasty, in the book *De Curtorum Chirurgia*.

early 1600s.   The development of obstetric forceps by the barber-surgeon Peter Chamberlen marks the start of male involvement in live births.

1620.   Thomas Venner's work *Via Recta* first uses the term "obesity," describing it as an "occupational hazard of the genteel classes."

1628.   English physician William Harvey first describes the circulation of blood throughout the body.

1629.   One of the first recorded cases of an intersex individual being persecuted in a court of law on American soil is documented. Thomas/Thomasine Hall, an adult living as a man, is investigated for dressing in women's apparel.

1630.   Flemish artist Peter Paul Rubens marries sixteen-year-old Hélène Fourment, who serves as his muse in many paintings, which are now famous for their idealization of the voluptuous, fleshy female body.

1642.   Royal decree to end footbinding in China. Despite the ban, footbinding peaks during the Qing dynasty (1644–1911).

1666.   The first known blood transfusion involving a human recipient and an animal donor takes place.

1677.   Dutch microscopist Anton van Leeuwenhoek identifies sperm by examining semen under a microscope.

1693.	Philosopher John Locke, in his treatise *Some Thoughts Concerning Education*, decries the use of children's corsets.
1705.	Introduction of the idea of "blood quantum" in the United States to measure racial status.
1707–1778.	Life of Carolus Linnaeus, Swedish physician and biologist who divides *Homo sapiens* into four racial groups—*Africanus, Americanus, Asiaticus,* and *Europeanus*. He is credited with developing and popularizing the major classification/taxonomic system still used by biologists today.
1710.	The first known monograph on menopause is written by Simon David Titius.
1722–1789.	Life of Pieter Camper, Dutch anatomist and anthropologist. Camper's theory of the facial angle is used by Charles Darwin as proof of his theory of evolution.
1724–1804.	Life of philosopher Immanuel Kant, who argues against the attempt to use physical science to understand questions properly belonging to philosophy.
1750.	Medical profession in Europe begins a crusade against the corset.
1758–1826.	Life of Franz Joseph Gall, the father of phrenology.
1762.	In *Émile*, his treaty on education, philosopher Jean-Jacques Rousseau (1712–78) argues passionately against the wet-nursing of infants.
1765.	French court hairdresser Legros de Rumigny institutionalizes the education of hairdressers.
1769.	Captain James Cook's first voyage to the South Pacific. Tattooing is largely reputed to have been reintroduced to European culture as a result of his voyages.
1789.	French Revolution. Wigs go out of style, as do other ostentatious signs of wealth and status. The corset is replaced for a short time in France by a cloth brassiere.
1794–1847.	Life of German surgeon Johann Friedrich Dieffenbach. He lays claim to inventing modern rhinoplasty, which he performs without anesthetic.
late 1700s.	Lives of Hamadsha saints Sidi Ali ben Hamadsha and his servant, Sidi Ahmed Dghughi. It is believed that the practice of head slashing among the Hamadsha originates with them.
1800s.	Craniometry is an important part of the physical anthropology.
1810.	Saartjie Baartman, a Khoi slave from what is now South Africa, is taken to London to be displayed as an ethnological curiosity. She is also called Hottentot Venus.
1812.	French physician C. P. L. de Gardanne coins the term menopause (*ménèspausie*) in his dissertation on the subject.
1820–1906 CE.	Life of Susan B. Anthony, American feminist, who decries the corset as an impediment to women's equality.

1820s.	English astronomer Sir John Herschel suggests methods for grinding and molding glass lenses to be placed directly upon the cornea.
1825.	Clitoridectomy is first formally reported as a viable medical treatment in an edition of the British medical journal *The Lancet.*
1827.	Karl August Weinhold, German physician and scientist, advocates mandatory infibulation for all those deemed unfit to reproduce. In the nineteenth century, infibulation is also promoted as a cure for masturbation.
1827.	Scientists discover the existence of the ovum, the female egg.
1830s.	Padaung, "long-necked" women from Burma, are taken to England and paid to be displayed as ethnological freaks in the Bertram Mills Circus.
1830s.	Modern photography invented.
1830s.	Development of the first minstrel shows, consisting of a variety of skits designed to mock African American stereotypes, from demeanor to appearance.
1832.	Jean Werly, Swiss tailor, establishes the first factory to weave seamless corsets, making them distinctly less expensive and thus more popular with the working classes.
1832.	George Catlin, painter and ethnologist, carries out the first detailed study of the O-Kee-Pa, a chest suspension ritual of the Native American Mandan tribe.
1832–1837.	Publication of *Histoire générale et particulière des anomalies de l'organisation chez l'homme et les animaux* by French anatomist Isidore Geoffroy Saint-Hilaire. It establishes teratology, the study of anomalous bodies and birth defects.
1846.	Development of anesthesia.
1862.	American corsetiere Luman Chapman secures the earliest recorded patent for a breast supporter. Bras become known as "emancipation garments" because they are less constricting than the corset.
1863.	Publication of William Banting's pamphlet, *A Letter on Corpulence Addressed to the Public*, recommending reducing consumption of starch and sugar.
1867.	Antiseptic is developed.
1870s.	Scientists discover the fertilization of the egg by sperm.
1870s.	Voluntary-motherhood movement in the United States argues that, by practicing abstinence or *coitus interruptus*, women can control their fertility and gain more dignity rather than be subjected to the sexual will of their husbands.
1870–1965.	Life of Helena Rubenstein, the founder of one of the early mass-produced lines of cosmetics.
1873.	Legal prohibitions against contraception arise in the United States with the passage of the anti-obscenity Comstock Act.
1874.	The Medical Act of 1874 mandates that all doctors in Japan be trained in Western medicine.

1875.	Electrolysis is invented in St. Louis, Missouri.
1881.	American physician Edward Talbot Ely records the first cosmetic otoplasty in medical literature.
1882.	Another royal decree to end footbinding in China.
1883.	Debut of Pinocchio, the wooden puppet with a nose that grows longer and longer the more lies he tells, in the novel by Carlo Collodi (1826–1890).
1893.	First documented fat injection procedure is said to have taken place in Germany by Franz Neuber, on a patient with a sunken cheek caused by a tubercular illness.
1894.	Unbound Foot Association founded in China, eventually collecting more than 10,000 supporters.
1896.	The first commercial menstrual pad in the United States is manufactured by Johnson & Johnson.
1896.	The first Asian blepharoplasty (eyelid surgery) was performed in Japan by a doctor named K. Mikamo on a woman who had been born with one "double" and one "single" eyelid.
1897.	Austrian doctor Felix von Luschan (1854–1924) publishes his method of classifying skin color, the Luschan scale.
1897.	Publication by Havelock Ellis (1859–1939), British physician and sexologist, of *Sexual Inversion*, the first English-language medical textbook on homosexuality. Ellis also wrote a multivolume study of sexual psychology as well as many other texts on sexuality.
1899.	The first documented abdominoplasty was performed by American surgeon H. A. Kelly.
1899.	The ruler of Egypt, Qasim Amin, calls for an end to veiling and other practices identified as misogynistic.
1901.	First modern antiaging facelift. German surgeon Eugen Hollander (1867–1932) performs a rhytidectomy on a Polish woman.
1901.	First modern bodybuilding competition is organized in London by Eugen Sandow.
1905.	Madame C. J. Walker's invention, the hair cream "Madame Walker's Wonderful Hair Grower," is first marketed to the masses. Walker, an African-American woman, becomes a millionaire.
1906.	The first formally recorded Western attempt to end the practice of female genital cutting began in colonial Kenya.
1907.	The fashion magazine *Vogue* popularized the French term brassière to describe a group of undergarments becoming increasingly implemented to support women's breasts.
1907–1927.	American surgeon Charles C. Miller performs numerous rudimentary eye lifts for cosmetic purpose on female patients.

1908.   Sigmund Freud (1856–1939) introduces the psychoanalytic concept of penis envy in his article entitled "On the Sexual Theories of Children." In 1905, he describes the erotic qualities of the breast in his *Three Essays on Sexuality.* Freud's work is highly influential in theories of sexuality, including his understanding of the Oedipus complex and female orgasm.

1914.   Birth control activist Margaret Sanger (1879–1966) is charged with violating the Comstock Act when she publicly urged women to limit their pregnancies in her socialist journal *The Woman Rebel.*

ca. 1916.   The remains of Saartjie Baartman, the famous so-called "Hottentot Venus," are dissected by French anatomist George Curvier. Her genitals, along with her skeleton and brain, are stored in formaldehyde and placed on display in the French Musée de l'Homme until the 1970s.

1917.   The Catholic Church mandates that women veil in church, but officially reverses the custom in 1983.

1919.   Walter Dandy injects air, as a contrast agent, into the skull of a living person and is able to produce some of the first x-rays of the brain.

1920.   "The Prophylactic Forceps Operation," by Joseph B. DeLee of Chicago, is published in the *American Journal of Obstetrics and Gynecology*, DeLee's procedure for a routine, normal birth requires sedating the mother through labor and giving ether during the descent of the fetus.

1920.   *The Correction of Featural Imperfections*, by Charles Conrad Miller of Chicago, first describes early platysmaplasty techniques.

1921.   Margaret Sanger establishes the American Birth Control League, later Planned Parenthood of America.

1921.   Vittorio Putti invents the Osteoton, which increases interest in limb-lengthening procedures.

1926.   Patient Shima Kito has facial surgery—including a rudimentary blepharoplasty—to "Westernize" his Asian features. This is one of the first Asian blepharoplasties in the United States.

1932.   S. H. Camp and Company introduces A, B, C, and D cup sizes for bras.

1932.   Publication of Aldous Huxley's novel *Brave New World*, which depicts babies born with genetically engineered traits.

1933.   Publication of *Natural Childbirth* by Grantley Dick-Read, an English obstetrician, influences the rise of a natural childbirth movement.

1935.   Doctors António Egas Moniz and Almeida Lima perform the first lobotomy; Walter Freeman and James Watts bring the procedure to the United States.

1936.   Reza Shah Pahlavi of Iran forcibly outlawed the veil and enforced Western dress, as did his son who followed him as shah.

1936.	Tampax tampons go on the market.
1943.	Metropolitan Life Insurance Company develops height/weight tables to try to standardize ideal body size.
1948.	First Mr. Universe competition for body builders.
1949.	Discovery of the use of botulinum toxin to block neuromuscular transmission and paralyze or weakens muscles. (In 2002, Botox is approved for use in treatment of facial lines.)
1950s.	Rise of the civil rights movement in the United States.
1950s.	Chlorpromaze (Largactil, Thorazine) is one of the first drugs used to treat schizophrenia, and antidepressants use begins.
1953.	Alfred Kinsey (1894–1956) publishes *Sexual Behavior in the Human Female*. Among other revelations, Kinsey identifies the clitoris as the primary site of women's orgasms, counter to Freudian notions.
1953.	The first issue of *Playboy* magazine is published, with Marilyn Monroe on the cover.
1954.	Once common throughout the Malay Archipelago, tooth filing, tattooing, and other bodily rituals are banned after Indonesian independence.
1960s.	Development of weight-loss surgery.
1960s.	Rise of the disability rights movement, the "second wave" of the feminist movement, and the black liberation movement in the United States.
1960s.	The Afro hairstyle becomes identified with the black liberation or Black Pride movement. In the 1970s, the hairstyle is widely popular in African American communities.
1960.	Founding of Lamaze International, an organization to promote the childbirth method of Fernand Lamaze (1891–1957).
1960.	First Overeaters Anonymous group is founded in Hollywood, California.
1960.	The U.S. Federal Drug Administration approves the first oral contraceptive for use as a birth control method.
1963.	Silicone breast implants are developed. They become the most widely used and controversial breast implant material, and are banned in 1992 but reintroduced a decade later.
1965.	First Miss Universe competition for female body builders.
1965.	U.S. Supreme Court decision in *Griswold vs. Connecticut* effectively legalizes contraceptives throughout the United States.
1968.	First appearance of the Afro on the cover of the popular black magazine *Ebony*.

1968.   Protesters at the Miss America pageant in Atlantic City infamously burn bras, but historical accounts suggest that bras weren't actually burned, but put into the trash. Also in protest of the pageant, the National Association for the Advancement of Colored People stages the first Black Miss America pageant.

1969.   William Fabrey founds the National Association to Aid Fat Americans, now the National Association to Advance Fat Acceptance.

1970s.   John Money, a Johns Hopkins psychologist, and his team of colleagues advocate the surgical "correction" of intersexed individuals.

1977.   Liposuction first used by French plastic surgeon Yves-Gerard Illouz.

1978.   Birth of Louise Brown, the world's first baby fertilized in vitro, in England.

1978.   Psychotherapist Susie Orbach publishes her landmark text, *Fat Is a Feminist Issue.*

1979.   The chador, a full-body cloak, is reinstated as required dress for women in Iran when the Ayatollah Khomeini comes to power and installs an Islamic theocracy.

1980.   Publication of African American poet Audre Lorde's (1934–1992) *Cancer Journals.*

1983.   American Jenny Craig cofounds her highly successful weight-loss company.

1990.   French performance artist Orlan announces she will use plastic surgery as art.

1990s.   World Health Organization (WHO) officially recognizes obesity as a "physiological disease."

1996.   Death of the last Chinese royal eunuch, Sun Yaoting (born 1903). He was castrated in 1911.

2000.   Lolo Ferrari, French porn star who held the world record for the largest silicone-enhanced breasts, dies under suspicious circumstances.

2000s.   United Nations describes breast ironing in southern Cameroon as a form of violence against women.

2002.   France returns the remains of Saartjie Baartman to her homeland of South Africa after international pressure.

2003.   African Union adopts Protocol on the rights of Women in Africa, which among other issues calls for an end to female genital cutting, to supplement the African Charter Human and Peoples' Rights.

2007.   American College of Obstetrics and gynecology publishes a warning against genital cosmetic surgeries, including so-called "vaginal rejuvenation', in the journal *Obstetrics and Gynecology,* arguing that they are not medically indicated nor are they documented to be safe or effective.

2007.   V-Day, an organization founded by Vagina Monologues writer Eve Ensler and UNICEF launch a campaign to stop rape and torture of girls and women in the Democratic Republic of Congo.

2008.   Turkey repeals ban on veiling in universities and other public institutions.

Abdomen

Abdominoplasty

Often known by its colloquial name, the "tummy tuck," abdominoplasty is a major surgical procedure in which skin and fat are removed from the middle and lower abdomen and the abdominal muscles are tightened. Complete abdominoplasty involves the removal of more extensive amounts of skin and fat; the operation often lasts from two to five hours. The procedure begins with the surgeon making an incision from hip to hip above the pubis. An incision is then made around the navel, and the skin of the abdomen is peeled back. The abdominal muscles are then pulled together and sewn into place to tighten them. The skin is then stretched back over the abdomen, "excess" skin is removed, and the navel is resituated. A partial abdominoplasty (sometimes marketed as a "mini-tummy tuck") is less extensive and requires less time, usually no more than two hours. Only the lower abdomen is affected and the navel is not removed. Both operations may be performed under either general or local anesthesia. Depending on the surgeon, abdominoplasty may be an outpatient procedure or may involve a stay in the hospital.

The first documented abdominoplasty was performed by American surgeon H. A. Kelly in 1899. The first major innovation in this procedure was the removal and replacement of the navel, which was first performed in the mid-1920s. Since the 1990s, abdominoplasties have increasingly involved suction-assisted lipectomy (SAL) as a means of fat removal. SAL can be combined with either a complete or a partial abdominoplasty. Although exact statistics are not available, it appears that abdominoplasty rates grew continuously throughout the twentieth century. By 1967, Brazilian physician I. Pitanguy claimed to have performed the operation on 300 patients, and it has become increasingly popular in the past few decades. According to the American Society of Plastic Surgeons (ASPS), the tummy tuck was the fifth most-popular cosmetic surgery procedure in 2005, with a total of 135,000 surgeries performed in the United States. Ninety-five percent of these patients were women.

Abdominoplasty endeavors to "correct" two conditions: a supposedly excessive amount of skin and fat in the abdominal region, and loose abdominal muscles. Cosmetic surgeons present abdominoplasty as the solution to

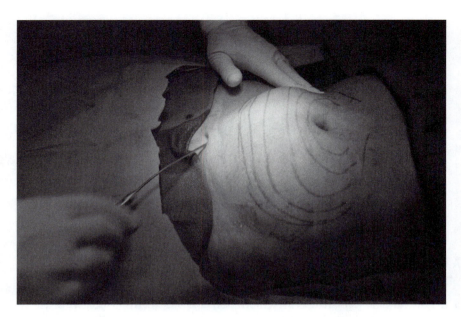

Woman getting liposuction on her stomach. (AP Photo/Lauren Greenfield/VII)

increased abdominal girth and muscular flaccidity after pregnancy. The abdomen changes during pregnancy and often does not regain its shape after childbirth. Multiple pregnancies further alter the shape and consistency of the abdomen, meaning that more extensive surgery is usually performed on women who have had many children. In addition to mothers, the other group of patients who are seen as ideal candidates for abdominoplasty are those who have lost large amounts of weight, but have skin and tissue that did not retract after their weight loss. This hanging skin is sometimes referred to as an "apron," which is said to cause physical discomfort in the form of chafing. Abdominoplasty also attracts those who have a regular regime of healthy diet and exercise that has not resulted in a flat stomach. Marketing materials target these potential patients, describing them as people for whom the abdomen is a "problem area."

The ideal body shape that surgeons and patients aim to achieve through abdominoplasty has a flat abdomen with a firm (toned or muscular) appearance. The "before" and "after" photographs used to advertise this procedure emphasize the flatness of the postoperative abdomen. The flat stomach was not always an aspect of the ideal female form. Idealized women's bodies in artistic representations tended to be symmetrical. However, rounded or fleshy (rather than flat or muscular) abdomens were the norm in ancient and Renaissance art. Contemporary art, advertising photography, and other representations (such as those in comic books or video games) have rejected this ideal in favor of flat stomachs, which may or may not be accompanied by large busts. A more athletic model of feminine beauty has also arisen in the late twentieth and early twenty-first centuries; images of women with muscular abdomens, including the defined muscle cluster colloquially known as a "six pack," have become more common.

Associations of plastic surgeons do not collect information on racial or ethnic variations in abdominoplasty rates. However, according to the ASPS, abdominoplasty is the fifth most-popular cosmetic surgery procedure in the United States, but it is not among the top three procedures chosen by African American, Asian American, or Hispanic patients. These statistics suggest that patients of color choose to undergo abdominoplasty at equivalent or lower rates than Caucasians. The physical conditions that abdominoplasty addresses would appear to affect people of all racial and ethnic groups equally, although it is obvious that more women than men opt for this procedure.

Abdominoplasty is now perceived by doctors and patients as an established and routine procedure. It entails risks similar to those of other cosmetic surgery procedures, including the possibility of infection, excessive scarring, and the dangers of general anesthesia. Abdominoplasty is not recommended for women who plan to become pregnant in the future, as the abdominal skin is stretched during pregnancy and this may at least partially reverse the results of the tummy tuck. It is generally agreed, however, that pregnancy and childbirth after abdominoplasty do not pose any risks to the health of the fetus.

One area of some controversy surrounding this surgery is the advisability of combining abdominal liposuction simultaneously with the abdominoplasty, a common practice. Although recent studies claim that there is no increase in patients' death rates when liposuction (SAL) is performed during the abdominoplasty, some surgeons prefer not to combine cosmetic surgery procedures. They sometimes suggest that patients' desire to undergo multiple surgeries at the same time is influenced by "makeover" shows on television, and that this may be unnecessarily dangerous. Other doctors claim that too much liposuction during the abdominoplasty can negatively affect circulation.

Further Reading: Bordo, Susan. *Unbearable Weight: Feminism, Western Culture, and the Body* (Tenth Anniversary Edition). Berkeley: University of California Press, 2004; Gimlin, Debra. *Body Work: Beauty and Self-Image in American Culture*. Berkeley: University of California Press, 2002.

Erynn Masi de Casanova

Blood

Bloodletting

Bloodletting—phlebotomy or venesection in technical terms—refers to a process in which a vein (or occasionally an artery) is deliberately opened and blood is allowed to flow out of the body. It has been practiced from ancient civilizations to recent history and is integral to medical, spiritual, and (gendered) cultural practices.

Bloodletting's extended history as a medical practice can be traced to early Egyptian and Greek cultures. In European cultures, the practice became popular and most extensively used from the late Middle Ages up until the nineteenth, and in some areas the early twentieth, century. The medical practice of bloodletting stems from humoral theory, in which the body was believed to contain four humors, of which blood was the most paramount. Mental, physical, and emotional illnesses were believed to be caused by an imbalance of the humors, which bloodletting could restore. Thus, inmates of asylums were bled to restore their sanity and pregnant women were bled to prevent their babies from becoming too big, or to prevent too much bleeding at birth. Bleeding was thought to remedy fevers, infections, wounds, injuries, coughs, colds, headaches, a patient's final dying hours, and even the complaints of infants as young as two months old. Initially bloodletting was prescribed solely as a treatment for a wide range of conditions, often in conjunction with lunar phases and astrological charts, but by the eighteenth century, it had become a popular way to maintain general well-being, and regular bloodletting, or "breathing a vein," was recommended as a part of an overall healthy regime.

Specialized equipment for bloodletting was an essential tool of the bloodletter's trade, and included a range of cutting and piercing instruments to enable blood flow, as well as receptacles to contain, measure, and analyze the blood. Indeed, the journal of the British Medical Society, *The Lancet*, takes its name from a long-bladed instrument used to open veins. Leeches were also a popular means to draw blood, and were initially harvested from the wild and sold through pharmacists—briefly facilitating a new rural economy. However, their popularity was such that wild stock quickly depleted, and by 1800 leech farms had opened across Europe. The burgeoning market in leeches inspired William Wordsworth's tale "Resolution and Independence," originally titled "The Leech Gatherer." In well-to-do households, special bleeding bowls were crafted from fine materials, including gold and silver, and became valuable family heirlooms.

Bloodletting has also enjoyed a high status as a spiritual practice in many parts of the world. In Mayan culture, which existed in South America from the first century BC to the seventeenth century, bloodletting was an honored ritual and sacred practice. The Mayan king ritually bled himself from the tongue and penis, performing a sacred, trance-inducing dance that enabled him to communicate with the spirit world. His shed blood had manifold significance and was offered on behalf of all of his people to ensure the fertility of the maize crop and to repay the blood shed by the gods to create human beings. His blood was caught on paper which was then burnt in order to release the blood into the spirit realm, and the receptacles used for this were elaborate and highly prized ornaments. Men in rural areas also practiced bloodletting, but as a protection rite which did not extend beyond their immediate families. Women also occasionally performed bloodletting, but only from the tongue. For Mayan people, then, blood was a powerful interlocutor between the human and spirit worlds, and its shedding had powerful material and symbolic implications.

During the Middle Ages, bloodletting practices were also popular among Christians, who focused on the sacrificial blood shed by Jesus during his torture and crucifixion. They believed that if the blood of Jesus was shed to wash away the sins of the world, then, likewise, shedding their own blood could purge them of their sins. Self-flagellation became particularly popular among religious orders, with nuns the most devoted practitioners. At times of mass upheaval, such as during the bubonic plague across Europe, troupes of self-flagellating Christians toured the infected areas, shedding their blood in the hope of purging the sins which must undoubtedly be the cause of such a scourge. Spontaneous bloodletting—stigmata— also has a long history in the Christian faith. Here, without any stimulation, individuals shed blood from parts of the body that resemble the wounds of Jesus.

Anthropologists also have noted the significance of bloodletting as a cultural practice that establishes gender roles and power in many small-scale societies. For example, bloodletting is used within rites of passage in which boys become men by ritually and symbolically separating themselves from their mother's blood and the female realm. In many cultures, males are thought to be weakened by contact with female blood, either directly during gestation and birth, or by a woman who is menstruating, as well as symbolically through maternal contact and particularly breastfeeding. Thus, male bloodletting rituals act as a symbolic rebirth into masculine power and culture. Cultures which adopt these practices are often patriarchal, and the apparent links between male blood shedding—through bloodletting, sacrifice, and symbolism—and female oppression have been considered by a number of feminists to be highly significant for understanding dominant world religions and cultures in which reverence for male blood shedding through sacrifice, power, war, violence, and death triumphs over "natural" female blood shedding, reproduction, and its life-affirming associations.

In contemporary Western cultures, bloodletting has a predominantly negative status, associated with self-mutilation and pathology. However, bloodletting has become a recognized sexual practice, called "blood sports" among some sexual aficionados, such as those who participate in sadomasochism, as well as a spiritual experience for those who practice ritualized body modification.

Further Reading: Bradburne, James M., ed. *Blood: Art, Power, Politics and Pathology.* New York: Prestel, 2002; Meyer, Melissa, L. *Thicker Than Water: The Origins of Blood as Symbol and Ritual.* New York: Routledge, 2005; Starr, Douglas. *Blood: An Epic History of Medicine and Commerce.* New York: Warner Books, 2000.

Kay Inckle

Cultural History of Blood

Blood is a fluid that runs through the veins and arteries and carries oxygen, amino acids (nutrients), and antibodies (natural disinfectants) through the organs of the body. The average human body contains ten pints (five liters) of blood and can lose 10 percent of its capacity without serious problems. However, at 20 percent blood loss, ill effects begin, and at 30 percent blood loss, the brain starts to cease functioning. Blood is a vital fluid in the human body, but also, due to its presence at birth—and (often) death—as well as its striking color, it has had a profound impact on people throughout the ages, becoming invested with powerful symbolism and beliefs. Blood has been connected with the soul or the "essence" of a person; punishment and salvation; family ties and relations; and nobility, national identity, racial categorisation, and racism. And, because it is both deeply symbolic and essentially mortal, blood is also the crux of many overlapping, contradictory, and antagonistic belief systems. It is simultaneously seen as the vital life force, intrinsically divine, yet also the transmitter of death, danger, and pollution, particularly in racial and gender terms. Blood is medical, magical, spiritual, social, and political.

Blood, Magic, Gods, and Science

Early human civilizations, including the ancient Egyptians and the early Greeks, demonstrated great reverence for blood. It was not only a corporeal fact of human existence, but it was also perceived as a vital essence containing a deeper life force and an individual's characteristics and spirit. As such, the blood of a person with desirable traits was believed to transmit curative and regenerative potential. Thus, to maintain youth and vigor, the Egyptians recommended bathing in the blood of young men or women, while the Romans believed that drinking the fresh blood of a powerful gladiator could not only invigorate the imbiber, but could also cure illnesses such as epilepsy. In parts of northern Europe, the blood of a beheaded criminal was believed to cure epilepsy, tuberculosis, and hydrophobia; while in the Balkans, an enemy's blood was consumed to ensure longevity and power. Indeed, drinking the blood of strong young people remained a popular remedy up until the fifteenth century, when the doctor of the ailing Pope Innocent VIII prescribed him the blood of three ten-year-old boys in order to extend his life. However, the pope rejected the remedy, and he quickly died.

It is not merely blood itself that has been revered as a vital force, a protector and giver of life. Symbolic representations of blood have been held in equally high esteem. Red charms, red ochre, red palm oil, red paint, and "dragon's blood"—a red tree resin—have been used across China, Africa, Europe, and Australia in order to improve protection and healing. In Hinduism, women marry in red, while in other cultures a wedding ring is worn on the third finger of the left hand because this finger is believed to carry blood directly to the heart.

In other areas, blood and its shedding, particularly menstrual blood, has been associated with danger and pollution that must be monitored and contained in order to avoid ill consequences. Indeed, many societies (for example in Papua New Guinea) believe that male and female blood is intrinsically different, and that women have more blood than men. In parts of southern England, blood shed on the earth was believed to make a field barren, while in other cultures, blood shed during ritual has to be carefully contained and protected because of its potential powers. In Europe, it was extensively believed that blood shed from a violent death would create a permanent stain, and that the corpse of a murder victim would bleed in the presence of the guilty party. Indeed, this often led to cadavers being placed before the accused to ascertain their guilt or innocence.

In Christianity, the blood of Jesus has profound significance for believers, and the celebration of the Eucharist involves the consumption of red wine from a sacred chalice that, according to some denominations, transforms into the actual blood of Jesus through a process called transubstantiation. The Eucharist also involves the consumption of ceremonial wafer or bread, "the host," which likewise symbolizes, or transforms into, the flesh of Jesus. At particular periods in Christian history, particularly during the Middle Ages, the phenomena of the "bleeding host" was frequently reported, when the ritually blessed or consecrated bread or wafer would begin to shed blood. This was often believed to result from an assault upon it by a Jew, and incited a number of massacres of Jewish people. As Christianity flourished, the connection between blood and the spirit or soul of a person became established in European culture, reflecting beliefs that were prevalent in many other communities in the world.

Because of human blood's perceived connection with the soul, humans have had a complex relationship not only with it, but also with blood of animals. For example, Cherokee hunters follow protocols set down in a sacred myth which describes how upon killing a great bear, in reverence to the animal's spirit, the hunters carefully drained its blood on the ground and covered it with leaves before carrying the carcass away. The spirit of the bear then reconstituted itself from the blood, and lived on. Likewise, in both Jewish and Islamic traditions, an animal must be bled carefully and ritually in order to fully respect the escaping life force of the animal. Muslim doctrine also requires prayer offered by an Imam as the animal dies in order to comply with halal protocol; in Judaism, keeping kosher requires that the meat subsequently be stored and be prepared separately to milk based products.

In other traditions, however, blood is a delicacy and is consumed with great enthusiasm. The Masai in Africa drink fresh lion's blood in order to ingest its strength, while in Ireland and the north of England, bovine blood is collected and mixed with milk (in a ratio of three parts blood to one part milk), poured into an animal intestine, and boiled to create a sausage. "Blood sausage," "black pudding," "blood pudding," or "pudding," as it is known—"disheen" in County Cork, Ireland—is sliced, fried, and consumed with bacon and eggs as part of a traditional breakfast.

Scientific interpretations of blood have coexisted with cultural and spiritual beliefs, sometimes in contrast to them, and at other times with more compatibility. The most prevalent theory of blood, which survived from the early Greek period through to the nineteenth century, even withstanding the discovery of circulation, was humoral theory. This was based on the idea that the body contained four humors—melancholy (black bile), blood, choler (yellow bile), and phlegm (lymph)—which corresponded to the four elements that made up the natural world (earth, air, fire, and water). Humors were believed to ebb and flow through the body like the tides, and good health stemmed from their correct proportional balance. Thus, various forms of purging and bloodletting were prescribed as curative remedies and, indeed, "humor" is still associated with temperament and condition today. Of all the humors, however, blood was the most paramount, not only because it contained the vital force, the spirit of a person, but also because it appeared to contain all four elements or humors. The fourfold composition of blood was documented by early medics, who noticed that as (drained) blood coagulated, it separated into four layers which corresponded in both color and consistency to the four humors. Humoral theory, and the related bloodletting and purging treatments, dominated medicine—despite the discovery of circulation—until well into the nineteenth century, and was only finally dispensed with following the scientific revolution.

Blood as Cure and Danger

The modern era of science and medicine may suggest an end to some of the mystical associations between blood, purity, and danger. Nonetheless, these notions have persisted throughout medical history, and the history of blood transfusion is testament to the enduring symbolic and political properties of blood.

The curative potential of blood was widely endorsed from early human history, but until the discovery of veins, arteries, and circulation, blood was *ingested* or *applied* rather than *transfused*. The first blood transfusions took place in Europe in the 1660s and were initially between animals. However, in 1666, the first transfusion involving a human recipient and an animal donor took place. The rationale behind cross-species transfusion was that since characteristics, traits, and temperaments were contained in the blood, humans could benefit from animal blood. For example, the blood of a calf could calm the turbulent and violent exactions of a madman. Indeed, the first transfusion apparently proved this and the patient, after going into deep trauma, did display increased passivity and "sanity." (It is likely that he was suffering from syphilis and the shock created by the alien blood caused a brief remittance to impact of the virus.) The immediate success of the treatment was widely reported, and other animal-to-human transfusions occurred. However, the majority of transfusions resulted in ill health and death—also the eventual fate of the original recipient. A flurry of hostility was whipped up among more conservative medical practitioners, as well as their Christian counterparts, who were highly suspicious of both the curative potential and moral legitimacy of the practice, and legislation quickly outlawed it. Even today, Jehovah's Witnesses still refuse blood transfusions on religious grounds.

It was almost two centuries later that the procedure—now human-to-human—was revived in Europe, and not until 1908 that it was practiced in the United States. The transfusions in Europe sparked the cultural imagination rather than religious condemnation, and the mythical vampire, a demonic creature who sucked away the human life force by drinking blood from the throats of his helpless victims, appeared in popular literature.

In the 1920s, knowledge of the different blood groups enabled blood transfusions to have much more predictable outcomes. Transfusing blood had radical impacts on a whole range of illnesses, injuries, and life-threatening circumstances, and was widely adopted as an almost miraculous treatment. World War II provided motivation to rapidly develop technologies for the transfusion and storage of blood. However, this technical progress also enabled some of the more troubling beliefs regarding blood and humanity, purity, and pollution to resurface.

Since ancient times, blood has been associated with family lineage and descent, and has been of special importance to nobility. Indeed, European royals were often believed to be of "blue blood," a divine trait that distinguished them from the lowly masses. Their blue blood was apparent in the visibility of their veins through their soft, white flesh, and royals often accentuated both the whiteness of their skin and the blueness of their veins with colored (and often quite toxic) cosmetic applications. Throughout Europe, and in particular within the Germanic and Russian dynasties, close intermarriage was encouraged as a means of ensuring the purity of royal bloodlines.

Meanwhile, the discovery of the "New Worlds," and the subsequent enslavement and colonization of indigenous peoples, was legitimized by the evolutionary theories of the time—which posited the northern European (male) as the most evolved and superior of all the "races." And not only were the physical, mental, and emotional characteristics of the "races" perceived to be determined by evolution, but also the blood. Thus, in 1705, in the American colonies, the Virginia Black Code introduced the idea of "blood quantum" in order to measure racial status, a concept which remained in legislative use for more than two and a half centuries. By 1866, a person deemed to be of one quarter "Negro" or "Indian" blood was classified as a member of that race and denied the status, rights, and privileges enjoyed by "white" people. Later still, the idea shifted to the "one-drop rule," meaning that the smallest trace of "non-white" heritage would be enough to define—and lower—the individual's racial status.

In twentieth-century Europe, Adolf Hitler was the one of the most vocal proponents of the idea of racial blood. He believed in maintaining the purity of the Aryan nation through careful measurement and control of racial heritage and bloodlines. Early in his regime, he enacted harsh penalties for those who married outside of Aryan bloodlines, and his fear of "racial contamination" was so great that he quickly prevented Jewish doctors from practicing. (This was later rescinded toward the end of war years, when their expertise was desperately needed in an ailing Germany). Yet, in a horrific irony, these ideas about blood and racial purity were being replicated among some of the very nations fighting the Nazis. During the war, blood transfusion and donation had become a huge part of the European (and later the world) war effort. Donating blood was portrayed an act of national pride and identity—a vital and patriotic service to the troops on the front lines. However, in the United States, where racial segregation was still in operation, panic arose at the possibility of "black blood" being transfused into white soldiers. (There were never such concerns for possible black recipients of "white blood.") Thus, a policy was adopted by the major blood collecting and distributing agencies, including the Red Cross, that blood was to be labelled by racial category in order to prevent such "pollution" occurring. This practice was not fully eradicated until the 1960s.

In other countries, such as India, not only did racial categories provide a source of anxiety for those handling and receiving blood donations, but further complications were added by the caste system, as well as discomforts regarding the exchange of blood between Muslims and Hindus. Thus, it seemed that human blood was not only capable of restoring life, but also of causing intolerable pollution. Interestingly, while in many smaller societies, bloodletting rituals and menstrual taboos are practiced to prevent gender contamination through blood, no such gendered concerns have been provoked in Western cultures by blood donation and transfusion.

In the latter half of the twentieth century, technology and treatments involving blood and its products developed rapidly, creating a massive global industry. In many European cultures, blood donation retained its wartime status as an altruistic gesture for the good of the nation or humankind. Elsewhere, including in Japan and the United States, blood was regarded as a commodity; blood donors were paid for their services, and collection companies traded with hospitals and medical institutions. Indeed, in 1998, a barrel of crude oil was worth $13, while the same quantity of blood would fetch $20,000. However, this commodification of blood spurned a number of public health and ethical concerns. Buying and selling blood for profit commonly meant that the poor and destitute quickly became the main donors. Blood was also widely taken from prison inmates, since collectors could harvest large amounts of blood for little outlay. Blood harvesting also was exported, and many parts of the world that had been ravaged by war, corrupt governments, or the legacy of colonialism became rich pickings for those trading in blood—"red gold."

Other groups of donors were more fortunate. These included those who had developed immune antibodies to hepatitis, or women who were rhesus negative (a rare blood group that can cause a mother's blood to "attack" a rhesus positive fetus she is carrying). Their blood was highly prized, and donors were paid handsomely. In one case, a rhesus-negative woman was reputed to have earned up to $80,000 per year for her donations.

However, paying for blood was not universally welcomed. Many groups, including religious and charitable organizations, opposed it on ethical grounds, while others drew attention to the health risks—for donors and recipients involved in drawing blood from vulnerable members of society. But it was not until outbreaks of hepatitis in the 1970s and HIV in the 1980s among recipients of blood donations that more serious questions were asked about the policies, practicalities, and risks of collecting blood. Blood shifted from a giver of life to a harbinger of death. This time, the threat of contaminated blood was not just established on racial lines, but also in terms of sexuality. Gay men, as well as Africans, those who had travelled to Africa, and Haitians, were among those depicted as the most likely carriers of the HIV and were quickly prevented from donating blood, regardless of their actual health and lifestyle. Indeed, HIV was portrayed by some fundamentalist groups as a scourge upon gays and sexually "promiscuous" people, who contaminated "innocent" recipients with their poisoned blood. Despite medical, technological, and scientific advances, blood continues to carry powerful symbolism that is often linked to politicized fears of purity and pollution, contamination and danger.

Blood symbolism continues to predominate the contemporary cultural imagination. Post 1960s political art movements made extensive use of blood symbolism, and feminists in particular have used blood in performance art to make provocative statements about the oppression and status of women in contemporary culture. Vampire myths and legends abound in Hollywood movies, and continue to fascinate contemporary audiences. Language remains rich with blood symbolism and metaphors: "bloody," an eighteenth-century term for vigor and prowess, is now a disparaging adjective; "bad blood" causes angst; "blood brothers," or one's own "flesh and blood," denote extra-special bonds; while "blood on your hands," "blood money," and "bloody mindedness" are most definitely to be avoided. *See also* Bloodletting.

Further Reading: Bradburne, James M, ed. *Blood: Art, Power, Politics and Pathology.* New York: Prestel, 2002; Favazza, Armando, R. *Bodies Under Siege: Self-mutilation and Body Modification in Culture and Psychiatry.* 2nd ed. Maryland: The Johns Hopkins University Press, 1996; Hackett, Earle. *Blood: The Paramount Humour.* London: Jonathan Cape, 1973; Hewitt, Kim. *Mutilating the Body: Identity in Blood and Ink.* Bowling Green: Popular Press, 1997; Inckle, Kay. *Writing on the Body? Thinking Through Gendered Embodiment and Marked Flesh.* Newcastle-Upon-Tyne: Cambridge Scholars Publishing, 2007; Meyer, Melissa, L. *Thicker Than Water: The Origins of Blood as Symbol and Ritual.* New York: Routledge, 2005; Starr, Douglas. *Blood: An Epic History of Medicine and Commerce.* New York: Warner Books, 2000.

Kay Inckle

Brain

Cultural History of the Brain

The cultural history of the brain follows the historical relationship between changing concepts of the self and different representations of the brain as a physical organ. In the West, this history takes the form of an extended debate about the physicality of the mind and the soul. Currently, an understanding of the brain is inseparable from any scientific investigation of reason, memory, imagination, mental illness, or any other capacity associated with the mind. But this is a comparatively recent phenomenon. Prior to the seventeenth century, these were questions asked of the soul, not the brain.

The concepts of soul and mind were first defined in ancient Greece. For Plato, there was a distinct difference between the mortal flesh and the immortal rational soul. Aristotle, on the other hand, believed that the soul and matter were intimately related. The implications of this debate were tremendous. The Western concepts of free will, morality, and individuality originate in an understanding of the nature of the soul. Well into the medieval ages, representations of the brain were a battleground for these disputes. The seventeenth century marked the rise of mechanical philosophy, in which the body was viewed as a machine. René Descartes (1596–1650), the most influential philosopher of this period, has had a double legacy for the cultural understanding of the brain. First, following Plato, his absolute distinction between mind and body was the first modern expression of what is commonly called the mind-body problem. Second, by exploring the body as a soulless machine, he laid the groundwork for further mechanical explorations of the brain.

In the nineteenth century, the scientific understanding of the brain came into direct conflict with the legacy of the soul. Scientists looked to the anatomy of the brain to answer philosophical and moral questions. Explorations into the nature of free will moved from the church to the laboratory. Many of the nineteenth-century thinkers held an "identity" view of the brain and the mind, which contends that there is no meaningful distinction between the two. In the twentieth and twenty-first centuries, imaging technologies

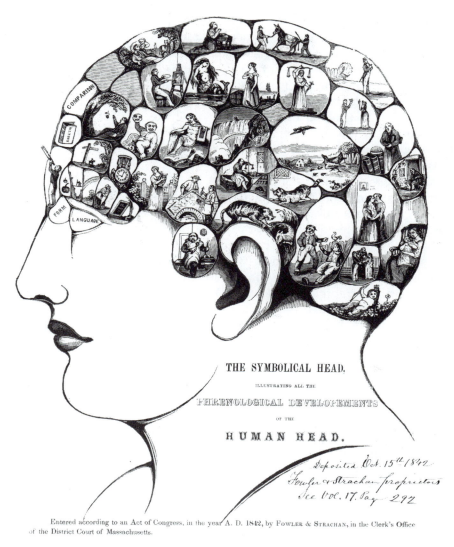

Illustration of all the phrenological symbolic meanings of the human head, ca. 1842. Courtesy of Library of Congress, LC-USZ62-100747.

such as MRI and PET scans increased our understanding of the brain tremendously. Brain researchers make far-reaching claims about the type of knowledge they will be able to produce with these tools. They use images of the brain to explore memory, trauma, character, and other issues of the mind. Although these claims are couched in medical terms, they depend upon a long tradition of philosophical and religious arguments for their coherence.

Ancient Greeks and the Middle Ages

Greek philosophy, drama, literature, and medicine set the terms for the Western world's conception of the brain. Their major disputes, particularly between Platonic dualism, the belief in a division between the soul and body, and the Aristotelian insistence on their inseparability continued to dominate the West well into the seventeenth century.

Homer, the poet of *The Iliad* and *The Odyssey*, made a distinction between two different kinds of souls. On the one hand, he described the psyche, which had no exact location in the body but represented the essence of the person as a whole. The psyche was immortal and continued its existence in Hades after the death of the body. On the other hand, he described body-souls, which had a specific location within the body and perished with it.

In Plato's philosophy, there was also a distinction between a physical body and a transcendent soul, and man was composed of these two elements. Plato further divided the soul into three parts: the Logos, the Theymos, and the Epithymetikon—each with a hierarchy of its own. The soul, being reality and truth, was called upon to tame the subservient body, which was part of the illusionary world of appearances. Plato's map of the body incorporated this philosophical system. The Logos was the soul of rationality and immortal. It resided in the head, the most divine part of the body, and ruled over the rest of it. Plato did not assert that the brain was the mind; rather, he explained that the rational soul was housed in the brain. The other parts of the soul were also located in specific areas of the body. The Thymos, the source of emotion, was located in the chest. The Epithymetikon, the soul of desire and passions, resided below the diapragm, separated from both the Thymos and the Logos.

Plato's body/soul dualism was a major influence in the cultural history of the West, but Aristotle challenged it in fifth-century Greece. Aristotle's rejection of Plato's dualism followed from his assertion that form or soul was inseparable from matter or flesh. Aristotle further rejected Plato's map of the body in which the head and brain held a privileged position. While Aristotle's own model of the soul was complicated, incorporating both a rational and irrational component, its principle legacy was as a challenge to the dualism of Plato.

The Greeks had two major theories to explain the origin and processes of thought in relation to the body—what we would call cognitive theory today. The first was encephalocentric theory, the idea that the brain occupied a privileged place in thinking, and the second was cardiocentric theory, which placed the heart at the center of consciousness. Plato, along with Pythagoras, Hippocrates, and Galen, were the major theorists in the encephalocentric school, while Aristotle and the Stoics were the defenders of the cardiocentric school. It is one of the oddities of Greek science that Aristotle was the first to use systematic dissection in his analysis while at the same time he identified the heart as the rational center of the body.

Plato's dualism was to have a lasting impact on Western culture. First, the distinction between soul and body became a central tenant in Christian theology and later in Descartes' philosophy. Second, the hierarchy of the brain over the body posited that logic, lodged in the brain, ruled over the emotions and desire, both of which were relegated to the lower parts of the body. Aristotle's challenge to Plato's dualism remained the subordinate position throughout the Middle Ages. The notable exception was the work of St. Thomas Aquinas in the thirteenth century, which posited that the flesh was the instrument of the soul. This stands in contrast to the Christian form of the Platonic position, which viewed that the body was the dungeon of the soul.

Descartes and the Origin of the Modern Mind-Body Problem

From the time of the Greeks until the seventeenth century, the more general relationship between the body and the flesh overshadowed the cultural history of the brain. It was not until the seventeenth century that the brain began to take a more central role in the discourse around the body. The central figures in this transformation were René Descartes and Thomas Willis.

Descartes' philosophy first posed the body-mind problem in its modern form. Descartes believed that the mind was made of an entirely different substance than the brain and the body. As two different elements, the body and the mind operated according to different laws. This view, following on Plato, was termed "substance dualism." It was a radical position. In Descartes' philosophy, the properties of the mind, such as reason, imagination, and will, were estranged from the body. Physical stimuli, not human will, produced the movements of the body. He depicted the nerves, which passed though the brain, as a pulley system allowing one part of the body to react to stimuli from another. (In his later work, Descartes famously suggested that the pineal gland was the site where the soul and the body interacted. Descartes did not identify the soul with the pineal gland; the soul had no existence in the physical world, but rather was able to interact with the body via this gland. By severing the soul from the body and making it king, Descartes transformed the body into a machine. Previous depictions of the mind coexisted with the lesser souls, or animal souls, that animated the body and explained the appetites and emotions. However, for Descartes, the spilt between mind and body was absolute.

The central problem for Descartes, and those who followed him, was to explain how these two different substances of mind and body interacted. In the world described by Descartes, what did it mean to have free will and responsibility when the body was beyond the control of the mind? Descartes created a world in which mortality and humanity in general existed only in the mind. Equally important, he set the stage for others to develop the opposite conclusion. If the body were only a machine, then it could be explored as a machine. Other thinkers, who did not accept Descartes' dualism, examined the physicality of the brain in order to explain the mind. Thomas Willis took the lead in this search.

Thomas Willis (1621–75), an English medical doctor and a professor at Oxford, was a follower of William Harvey, who in 1628 first described the circulation of blood through the body. Willis performed many dissections and experiments in his study of the brain. If Descartes' work marks a clear break with the classical tradition, than Willis has a foot on both sides of this gap. Willis developed the idea of the corporal soul, which he located both in the blood and in the fluids of the nervous system. In essence, this was the old soul of Aristotle bought into the mechanical age. Rather then rid the body of the soul, like Descartes, Willis transformed the soul to fit into the mechanical idea of the body. Among his other efforts, which included contributions to the anatomy of the brain and nervous system, Willis sought to explain the mechanical rules of the soul.

The Rise of Scientific Medicine

The contemporary scientific understanding of the brain emerged at the end of the eighteenth century and throughout the nineteenth century. It was at this time that medical and scientific language began to dominate discourse about the brain.

The rise of scientific medicine still wrestled with the legacy of Descartes and Willis. On the one hand, there was the church-sanctioned, dualist tradition, which presented the problem of the brain as the search for the seat of the soul in the body. For these scientists, the problem was to reconcile a scientific understanding of the brain with the moral legacy of the soul. They asked, for example, how free will is possible if the mechanics of the brain explained the consciousness of the mind. This tradition approached the science of the brain from an explicitly moral and philosophical perspective.

As late as 1796, scientist Samuel Thomas Soemmerring (1755–1830) located the organ of the soul in the "fluid of the cerebral ventricles." For Soemmerring, the exploration of brain anatomy was no different than religious speculation on the nature of the soul. Soemmerring's research on the brain was assailed from two directions. The first attack was a dispute over the physical location of the mind. Franz Joseph Gall (1758–1826), the father of phrenology, argued that the mind is located in the cerebral cortex, rather than the fluid. The second assault, from the philosopher Immanuel Kant (1724–1804), who ironically wrote the introduction to Soemmerring's work, argued against its attempt to use physical science to understand questions properly belonging to philosophy, since Soemmerring's goal was to link metaphysics and brain anatomy.

Soemmerring's argument for this link marked a central turning point in the cultural history of the brain. Two key questions arose from this dispute: first, whether the scientific exploration of the brain speaks to questions of the soul, and second, what discipline is best prepared to discus the nature of the soul. Kant's rejection of Soemmerring argument is a defense of philosophy. Kant was skeptical that a brain anatomist could add anything to an understanding of the soul, and argued that the soul cannot search for itself outside of the soul, in the physical world. Explorations of the soul therefore should be reserved for philosophers.

Franz Joseph Gall's phrenology explicitly rejected both Soemmerring and Kant. Phrenology was a science of the brain which asserted the following: first, that the brain was the organ of the mind encompassing both thought and will; second, that different sections of the brain, called personality organs, corresponded to personality characteristics; and third, that the size of these different organs related directly to the propensity of their characteristics. Gall further believed that differences in size were visible as bumps on the head. The range of phrenology's claims was impressive. Different regions of the brain were identified for such diverse attributes as destructiveness, hope, wonder, time, individuality, tune, and causality, among others. Gall essentially argued that he could answer questions of philosophy and religion by exploring brain anatomy. His work is the most explicit example of the soul being directly mapped onto the brain.

Phrenology to some extent was a scientific fad. It claimed the ability to identify both criminals and the mentally ill by exploring the bumps on the head. But in the eighteenth century, scientific explorations of the brain began to shy away from philosophical claims. The language of the soul began to recede from medical discourse. The default position of brain science was the identity view, which asserted that there is no meaningful distinction between the brain and the mind. This, of course, is a philosophic position in its own right.

Pierre Flourens (1794–1867), for example, countered the arguments of phrenology through a series of experiments in 1824 that demonstrated a more holistic understanding of brain function. The question of brain localization became a central point of dispute in brain research during the latter part of the nineteenth century. By the end of the nineteenth century, arguments over the cortical localization of brain function spoke in a medical language unknown to philosophers and theologians who had previously addressed the soul.

Mental Illness

Representations of the brain are at the center of mental illness. The Greek understanding of the soul discussed above forms the basis for the two models of mental illness in antiquity. On the one hand are psychological explanations that rely upon the biography and social interactions of the disturbed individual. These psychological explanations find their best expression in classical Greek art and theater such as the Oedipus cycle of Sophocles. The other tradition, drawn from Hippocrates and Galen, the famous doctor of antiquity, stressed the physical basis of mental illness. Both somatic and psychological theories of mental illness incorporated a theory of the brain.

In the Middle Ages in Europe, the ancient explanations of madness inherited from Galen and others merged with Christian concepts of morality. The Catholic church, for example, associated madness with the devil possessing the body. The body was a battleground for the religious contest between good and evil. At the same time, an almost opposite concept emerged—the holy fool. This idea linked madness with spiritual insight. In this model of disease, it is impossible to isolate the disease from the morality.

In the seventeenth century, care of the insane moved away from communities and families and toward confinement in large institutions increasingly sponsored by the state. This was especially true in France, and many contemporary scholars, particularly Michel Foucault, have linked the "great confinement" of the mentally ill to the rise of the absolutist state (Foucault, 1965). The physical separation of the mentally ill demonstrated the increasingly complex relationship between the state's power to control and confine and the ability of medical experts to assert definitions of madness. Asylums provided the new doctors of madness with subjects to examine, and those confined in asylums were now medical subjects of the state.

In 1799, James Hadfield was tried for the attempted assassination of King George III. The court ruled that he was not responsible for his actions due to insanity. This was one of the first examples of the insanity defense, which strongly linked questions of mental illness, the brain, and free will. Brain researches now spoke directly to questions of guilt and innocence, volition and criminality. The Hadfield case is a good illustration of how issues associated with madness moved from the church to the state via the expertise of the medical profession. Madness was no longer outside of rationality, expressing the will of devils and gods, but rather confined within human reason itself. As part of this transformation, religious explanations of the soul gave way to medical explanations. The medical expert, not the priest, was now called upon to explain questions of the soul—evil, volition, and guilt—in the courtroom. But it would be wrong to state this conclusion too forcefully. Many non-medical experts continue to assert their domain over the soul to this day.

In the nineteenth century, the meaning of brain research was still in doubt. The debate between J. C. A. Heinroth (1773–1843) and Wilhelm Griesinger (1817–68) illustrates how the medical profession at the turn of the nineteenth century still relied upon the religious history of the soul. Heinroth argued that mental illness was a voluntary expression of free will. Griesinger disagreed and explained that, "mental illnesses are brain disease." Heinroth's religious conviction informed his medical research. He tried to demonstrate that brain research or the exploration of the soul in the physical body was complementary to his moral beliefs. For Heinroth, the physical exploration of the brain was an extension of the moral exploration of the soul. This debate occurred at a moment when the distinction between religion, morality, and medicine was not clear.

Another strand of thought in the nineteenth century held that mental illness was not only physical but also hereditary. This idea was referred to as degeneration theory. French psychiatrists J. Moreau de Tours (1804–84) and Benedict Augustin Morel (1809–73) are associated with this theory. According to their model, both somatic and moral factors explained individual and family decline over generations. With the work of Valentin Magnoan (1835–1916) and Cesare Lombrosos (1836–1909), these theories were linked to evolution and criminal pathology. Degenerates were cast in an evolutionary light as less developed. In 1881, defense attorneys tried to demonstrate that Charles Guiteau, the assassin of President James A. Garfield, was a degenerate. Again, as in the Hadfield case, medical experts were called upon to explain Guiteau's soul. By the late nineteenth century, degenerative arguments fueled calls for sterilization and confinement in the United States.

Recent developments return to the brain as the central explanation of mental illness. António Egas Moniz and Almeida Lima performed the first lobotomy in 1935, and Walter Freeman and James Watts brought the procedure to the United States. In the late 1940s, Freeman, a neurologist, began performing transorbital frontal lobotomies without the assistance of a neuro-surgeon. Following Freeman's work, the procedure became both easy to do and exceptionally common as a way to treat a variety of psychological symptoms. The efficacy of the procedure was questionable, however, and the accuracy of the collected statistics describing success rates was often in doubt. Lobotomies were popular during a time when doctors and the public felt particularly powerless to address issues of the mentally ill. The decline in lobotomies seems to correlate with the rise of chlorpromazine, a pharmacological treatment for mental illness.

In the 1950s, chlorpromazine (Largactil, Thorazine) was one of the first drugs used to treat schizophrenia. In the same decade, antidepressants began being used. The current use of psychopharmacological drugs provides a strong cultural context to argue for the organic causation of mental illness, and the tremendous rise in the varieties and uses of psychotropic drugs affected a compelling move to physicalism, which relates the mind to the physical workings of the brain. The use of such drugs relies on what has been termed a new science of brain identity. The identity view posits that mental phenomena are related to physical processes of the nervous system. Explorations of the mind therefore become physical explorations of the brain.

Brain Imaging

In addition to the success of drug intervention for mental illness and brain diseases, the most important evidence for the identity view of the brain comes from the new representations of the living brain through imaging technology. Prior to technological images of the living brain in the twentieth century, representations of the brain were either anatomical drawings or picture of a dissected animal or human brain. The new image of the brain was to have a profound effect on how society understood the relationship between the brain and the mind.

When World War I ended, the brain was still referred to as the "dark continent" of the body. Whereas X-ray technology illuminated other organs and systems in the body, the brain remained beyond the reach of the new imaging technology. But in 1919, Walter Dandy injected air, as a contrast agent, into the skull of a living person and was able to produce some of the first X-rays of the brain. At first this technique worked only on infants because of their soft skulls. Finally, Dandy hit upon the technique of injecting air into the spinal column until it rose and filled in the space around the brain. It was incredibly painful. Dandy became famous and the living brain became visible.

In the 1980s, technology emerged that allowed the living brain to become more clearly visible than ever before. Chief among these were PET scans and, later, fMRI (functional MRI) imaging technology, which allowed a more detailed examination into brain function by exploring the relationship between localized activity in the brain and blood flow. In addition to becoming key instruments of medical diagnosis, functional images of the working brain provided a powerful cultural representation of the brain that has impacted how society views both the mind and the soul. Chugani, Phleps, and Hoffman, for example used PET scans of the brain to create a visual encyclopedia of normal brain function throughout life. Images of the living brain raise the question of how functional representations of the brain, as opposed to philosophic, artistic, and religious representations, affect the concept of self.

Witnessing the living brain produced great optimism for curing diseases and understanding the nature of intelligence and knowledge. The 1990s were declared the "decade of the brain" by President George H. W. Bush. Brain research, it was hoped, would lead to cures for neurological and degenerative diseases, and address other problems such as addiction and personality disorders. New fields such as neuromarketing were invented. Many old questions that concern the nature of the individual were brought under the purview of brain research. Almost any difference imaginable between two groups of people, from gender to political views, has been examined and explained with reference to brain activity. For example, recent studies used functional MRIs to examine how the brains of Republicans and Democrats respond to pictures of candidates in the 2004 presidential election (Kaplan, 2007.) A whole range of social and psychological issues are now brought under the auspices of brain science, and researchers are looking for the "neural basis of social behavior."

Further Reading: Crivellato, Enrico, and Domenico Ribatti. "Soul, Mind, Brain: Greek Philosophy and the Birth of Neuroscience." *Brain Research Bulletin* (2007): 327–36; Gardner, Howard. *The Mind's New Science: A History of the Cognitive Revolution.* New York: Basic Books, 1985; Hagner, Michael. "The Soul and the Brain Between Anatomy and Naturphilosphie in the Early Nineteenth Century." *Medical History* 36 (1992): 1–33; Harrington, Anne. *Medicine, Mind, and the Double Brain: A Study in Nineteenth-Century Thought.* Princeton, NJ: Princeton University Press, 1987; Kaplan, Jonas, Joshua Freedman, and Marco Iacoboni. "Us Versus Them: Political Attitudes and Party Affiliation Influence Neural Response to Faces of Presidential Candidates." *Neuropsychologia* 45.1 (2007): 55–64; Kevles, Bettyann. *Naked to the Bone: Medical Imaging in the Twentieth Century.* Reading, MA: Addison-Wesley, 1998; Mashour, George, Erin Walker, and Robert Martuza. "Psychosurgery: Past, Present, and Future." *Brain Research Reviews* 48:3 (2005): 409–419; Porter, Roy. *The Greatest Benefit to Mankind: A Medical History of Humanity.* First U.S. edition. New York: W. W. Norton, 1998; Porter, Roy. *Flesh in the Age of Reason.* First U.S. edition. New York: W. W. Norton, 2004; Young, Robert M. *Mind, Brain, and Adaptation in the Nineteenth Century: Cerebral Localization and Its Biological Context from Gall to Ferrier.* New York: Oxford University Press, 1990; Zimmer, Carl. *Soul Made Flesh: The Discovery of the Brain—and How it Changed the World.* London: Heinemann, 2004.

Andrew Greenberg

Breasts

Breast Cancer Awareness

Breast cancer is a common disease that women have often suffered in silence. Although the risk of developing it has increased since the 1940s, breast cancer remained stigmatized, privatized, and did not become public until the 1970s. Although there were at least 1,000 women's health movement organizations in the 1970s, almost no one had heard of breast cancer support groups or an organized breast cancer movement until a decade later. Today, breast cancer is an embodied experience women often explore collectively, a visible problem for scientific investigation and pharmaceutical development, and a site of diverse feminist activism.

Demographics and Diagnosis

Breast cancer is the most common cancer among women except for skin cancer and it is the second leading cause of cancer deaths after lung cancer. More than 2 million U.S. women are living with breast cancer. In 2007, 178,480 women were diagnosed with breast cancer and 40,460 died. Men, too, can develop breast cancer, and in 2007, 2,030 of them were diagnosed with the disease. The lifetime risk of developing breast cancer for women born today is 1 in 8 (statistically, "lifetime risk" means that if every woman lived to the age of eighty-five, 1 in 8 of them would develop breast cancer); for women born in the 1970s, the lifetime risk was 1 in 10. The lifetime risk estimate is calculated based on all women in the United States and does not take into account differences in age, race/ethnicity, and family history. The risk varies according to age—for women ages thirty to thirty-nine, the risk is 1 in 233 and for women ages sixty to sixty-nine it is 1 in 27. White women are more likely to develop breast cancer than Latina, Asian American, or African American women, but African American women are more likely to die from the disease than women in other racial/ethnic groups. The difference may result from the broad effects of institutional racism, such as African American women's exposure to toxins in the environment (they are more likely to reside in communities that are contaminated by toxic waste and other chemical pollutants), being diagnosed when breast cancer is more advanced, and/or racial disparities in treatment.

More than half of all cases of breast cancer develop in women who have no identifiable risk factors other than age. Between 5 and 10 percent of breast cancer cases are linked to inherited mutations of BRCA1 and BRCA2, the "breast cancer genes." A screening mammogram (an X-ray of the breast) is used to detect breast changes for women who have no signs or symptoms of breast cancer. There is considerable debate about its use among premenopausal women. A diagnostic mammogram is conducted after a breast lump or other sign or symptom of breast cancer (pain, discharge, or a change in breast size or shape) has been found. Treatment depends on the size or extent of the tumor, and whether it has spread to lymph nodes or to other parts of her body, from Stage 0 ("carcinoma in situ," in which abnormal cells are confined in the ducts or lobules of the breast) to Stage IV (cancer has spread to the bones, liver, lungs, or other organs). After the process of "Staging," treatment is determined, consisting of combinations of surgery (breast conserving surgery such as lumpectomy, or "mastectomy," removing the breast), radiation therapy, chemotherapy, and/or hormone therapy. Tamoxifen (also called tamoxifen citrate and Nolvadex) is a hormonal treatment for breast cancer. At first prescribed for women with advanced breast cancer, in 1990, tamoxifen was approved by the U.S. Food and Drug Administration for women diagnosed with early stage breast cancer and became the world's most frequently prescribed breast cancer treatment. Of women diagnosed with breast cancer 5 years ago, 89 percent are still alive.

History, Politics, and Rise of a Social Movement

There are many reasons for the transformation and growth in breast cancer awareness and politics. As with 1970s women's health movement strategies more generally, early activists focused on medical decision-making, the authority of medicine, and support networks. Large numbers of individual women, such as journalist Rose Kushner (1975), questioned why the one-step procedure of diagnosis followed by radical (Halsted) mastectomy—removing the affected breast, underarm lymph nodes, and both chest wall muscles—was the standard therapy for breast cancer. At the time Kushner developed breast cancer, physicians exercised sovereign power by making decisions that patients were expected to follow. Kushner refused. The dominant story of breast cancer was that full recovery is possible or at least the appearance of full recovery. Postsurgical use of a prosthesis (worn in a bra) or breast reconstruction sustained the story and enabled one-breasted women to "pass."

Often inspired by the civil rights and women's movements, activists sought to make breast cancer visible and audible: after her mastectomy, Deena Metzger bared her tattooed chest for a widely reprinted photograph ("The Warrior") and poet Audre Lorde wrote *The Cancer Journals* in 1980 describing her resistance to covering up her chest with a prosthesis and to remaining a silent and isolated breast cancer patient. Activists within the medical profession such as physician Susan Love took issue with the standard therapy, and some U.S. biomedical scientists turned toward making science more democratic.

By the late 1970s and early 1980s, women founded organized breast cancer groups, including the Susan G. Komen Breast Cancer Foundation (1982)—now Susan G. Komen for the Cure—that sponsored its first "Race for the Cure" in 1983. In 2005 it drew more than 1 million people into the largest series of 5K runs/fitness walks in the world. One of the first breast cancer organizations with an explicitly political agenda, Breast Cancer Action (BCA), was founded in 1990 by Barbara Brenner and other breast cancer survivors and their supporters to make breast cancer a public issue, empower women and men in decision-making, and direct attention to changes in state and federal legislation favorable to breast cancer prevention and treatment. In 2002, BCA began to ask women to "Think Before You Pink," questioning the large number of pink ribbon products and promotions and why companies both promote the pink ribbon campaign and manufacture products that are linked to breast cancer.

In 1991, a coalition of professionals, lay people, and establishment and grassroots breast cancer organizations formed the National Breast Cancer Coalition (NBCC) to promote research, improve access to screening and care, and increase the influence of women with breast cancer in policy. NBCC has effectively lobbied for the 1990 National Breast and Cervical Cancer Early Detection Program as well as the Breast and Cervical Cancer Prevention and Treatment Act of 2000 that provide financial assistance to low-income women for screening of breast cancer (but there as yet are few securely funded treatment programs). A unique contribution of the NBCC is Project LEAD (Leadership, Education and Advocacy, Development), a four-day science education program to prepare breast cancer activists to participate in determining research and funding priorities as members of grant review panels.

Another focus of organized resistance is on environmental causes of breast cancer. An increasing body of evidence indicates that exposure to both radiation and toxic chemicals in the environment is contributing to the increased incidence of breast cancer. The Silent Spring Institute (SSI), founded in 1994 by breast cancer activists in Massachusetts in response to reports of elevated rates of breast cancer on Cape Cod, has brought together an alliance of scientists, activists, physicians, public health advocates, and public officials to develop multidisciplinary research projects aiming to identify links between environmental pollutants and women's health, especially breast cancer. Whereas SSI focuses on transforming the science of breast cancer, other activist groups challenge the connection between breast cancer and toxins in the environment from a different direction. The Toxic Links Coalition (TLC) organizes an annual tour in San Francisco's financial district, stopping to protest at the corporate offices of polluters during its Cancer Industry Awareness Month, and to expose the questionable ethical and environmental practices of AstraZeneca and other companies in the cancer establishment.

Because they rely on a personal awareness and understanding of living with breast cancer to frame their organizing efforts, and challenge standard practices in breast cancer research and clinical medicine, breast cancer activists and organizations make up an "embodied health movement." Breast cancer activists introduce their subjective experiences into debates about prevention, treatment, and breast cancer science. Sharing experiences and raising consciousness among group members are as central to the work as redirecting funds and transforming biomedical science.

Today, public awareness has provided both support and sustenance for women living with breast cancer. Annual federal funding for breast cancer research and treatment in the United States is more than $800 million. Professional norms and breast cancer informed consent legislation separate diagnosis from treatment of breast cancer. Funding agencies have mandated the inclusion of breast cancer advocates at every stage of the research funding process, first in California (California Breast Cancer Research Program, 1993) and then nationally (Department of Defense Breast Cancer Research Program, 1993). Pink ribbons symbolizing efforts to find a cure for breast cancer, breast cancer walks and runs to raise funding and awareness, and free mammograms are familiar parts of today's landscape. There are hundreds of personal Web sites by women with breast cancer; published stories and memoirs; and plays, films, and art exhibitions by and about women with breast cancer. In these forums, women share experiences, raise consciousness, speak in the language of embodied experience, and give and receive support locally.

The transformation from silence to speech, invisibility to visibility, and victim to survivor in breast cancer awareness has not come without struggle and division among breast cancer activists. Controversy surrounds Breast Cancer Awareness Month, initiated in 1985 by Imperial Chemicals Industry (ICI), identified by some breast cancer activists as a member of the "cancer establishment." Among other products, ICI manufactures plastics, pesticides, and pharmaceuticals, including tamoxifen. Currently, tamoxifen—and Breast Cancer Awareness Month—is sponsored by one of the largest multinational pharmaceutical companies in the world, AstraZeneca. Some activist groups (BCA, Toxic Links) refuse to accept funding from industry, arguing it would produce a conflict of interest, whereas others rely on industry support. Susan G. Komen for the Cure is a leader in Breast Cancer Awareness Month and is criticized for accepting funds from and maintaining ties with pharmaceutical interests.

Breast cancer groups continue to struggle with ways to make their messages clear to diverse groups of women, to separate out the difference between real prevention and diagnosis, and to focus attention "upstream" to where the causes of breast cancer are created.

Further Reading: Aronowitz, Robert. *Unnatural History: Breast Cancer and American Society.* New York: Cambridge University Press, 2007; Braun, Lundy. "Engaging the experts: Popular Science Education and Breast Cancer Activism." *Critical Public Health* 13 (2003): 191–206; Breast Cancer Action, http://bcaction.org/; Brenner, Barbara A. "Sister Support: Women Create a Breast Cancer Movement." In Kasper and Ferguson, eds. *Breast Cancer: Society Shapes an Epidemic.* New York: St. Martin's Press, 2000, pp. 325–353; Brown, Phil, Stephen Zavestoski, Sabrina McCormick, et al. "Embodied Health Movements: New Approaches to Social Movements in Health." *Sociology of*

Health & Illness 26 (2004): 50–80; Kasper, Anne S., and Susan J. Ferguson, eds. *Breast Cancer: Society Shapes an Epidemic*. New York: St. Martin's Press, 2000; Klawiter, Maren. *The Biopolitics of Breast Cancer: Changing Cultures of Disease and Activism*. Minneapolis: University of Minnesota Press, 2008; Kushner, Rose. *Breast Cancer: A Personal History and an Investigative Report*. New York: Harcourt Brace Jovanovich, 1975; Lerner, Barron H. *The Breast Cancer Wars: Fear, Hope, and the Pursuit of a Cure in Twentieth-Century America*. New York: Oxford University Press, 2001; Lorde, Audre. *The Cancer Journals*. Argyle, New York: Spinsters, Ink, 1980; National Cancer Institute. "Breast Cancer." http://www.cancer.gov/cancertopics/types/breast; Potts, Laura K. ed. *Ideologies of Breast Cancer: Feminist Perspectives*. London: Macmillan, 2000; Radley, Alan, and Susan E. Bell. "Artworks, Collective Experience and Claims for Social Justice: The Case of Women Living with Breast Cancer." *Sociology of Health & Illness* 29(2007): 366–390; Silent Spring Institute: Researching the Environment and Women's Health, http://www.silentspring.org/.

Susan E. Bell

Breastfeeding

Discussions about breastfeeding date back millennia, referenced literally and figuratively in religious texts such as the Bible, the Torah, and the Koran. Breastfeeding was an ordinary aspect of family life during biblical times. References to the length of time a woman should nurse her child as well as the health of breast-fed children also abound in antiquity. The Koran urges mothers to breastfeed for two years. At least one Jewish rabbi has interpreted the Torah to suggest that women should nurse with their left breasts, evoking imagery about closeness to the heart. The frequent referencing in religious sources to nursing and its association with birthing a child considerably normalized this mode of feeding a baby into toddler development.

Breastfeeding for financial or other gain dates back to at least to 2000 BCE with the Code of Hammurabi—the Babylonian Empire's legal code, which included wet-nursing rules. Wet-nursing usually refers to an individual other than the biological mother providing nursing services, and often for pay or a form of consideration of some kind. Wet-nurses would be banned from further use of their breasts for wet-nursing if an infant in their care died for any reason. Breastfeeding was the site at which life was affirmed, but also became subject to market forces and social considerations in the form of wet-nursing.

Religion and Breastfeeding

Nursing one's own child was, of course, far more common. However, wet-nursing evolved as a persistent presence in early religious and fictional literature. For example, the book of Exodus reveals perhaps the most famous instance in nursing. Written at about 1250 BCE, Exodus describes the story of a wet-nurse being hired for Moses, and unbeknownst to the employers, the nurse happens to be Moses' mother. What is clear during this period is that nursing occupied a space beyond mother and child, one that had community, political, and spiritual dimensions.

U.S. Government poster promoting breastfeeding, ca. 1936, WPA Federal Art Project. Courtesy of the Library of Congress, LC-USZC2-5325.

Abundant milk during lactation could be interpreted as a blessing. Consider this passage from Genesis (49:25): "Because of your father's God, who helps you, because of the Almighty, who blesses you with blessings of the heavens above, blessings of the deep that lies below, blessings of the breast and womb." On the other hand, dry, unyielding breasts were considered a curse. Consider this lament from Hosea (9:14), "Give them, O Lord—what will you give them? Give them wombs that miscarry and breasts that are dry." Breastfeeding then, in biblical times, was a contested space, not as to its acceptance or appropriateness, but rather carried metaphorical meanings about nurturing, power, and even politics.

There are references to power, wealth, and divinity in Isaiah (60:16): "You will suck the mil of nations, and suck the breast of kings; then you will know that I, the LORD, am your Savior and your Redeemer, the Mighty One of Jacob." Nursing was as much a political metaphor as a one for health, well-being, and bonding between mother and child.

Much can be inferred from early literary references to nursing, including those derived from biblical sources. In the nursing references to Moses, in Exodus, it is made clear by his adoptive mother that she will provide wages to the woman who breastfeeds her new infant. This perhaps is one of the earliest introductions to a system of labor or pay associated with breastfeeding. This reference also illuminates cross-nursing, the practice of nursing one's child and occasionally someone else's infant as well. However, cross-nursing, wet-nursing, and even breastfeeding have been controversial, especially in modern times.

Between the period marked by references to Jesus on earth and the fifteenth century, breastfeeding remained important. However, questions of wealth, social status, and class determined who was to breastfeed children. For example, in Sparta during the fourth century BCE, elite women were required to nurse their eldest sons, but subsequent siblings could be suckled by wet-nurses. Regular women had to nurse all of their own children.

Race and Class

At the height of the Roman Empire, wet nurses were slaves, supposedly well-kept by presumably loyal mistresses and masters. Depending on one's perspective, the slaves were provided room and board or forced to live with families and nurse their children. Thus, while the importance of what breastfeeding might convey or provide to a child was likely obvious, that the source need not be the child's mother also seems evident. Choosing to breastfeed sent a signal as well as electing not to do so.

In succeeding centuries, breastfeeding took on different meanings and, most notably, conveyed information about wealth, social status, and maternal priorities. By the sixteenth century, affluent European mothers rarely nursed their infants. Instead, these infants were handed over to wet-nurses, to return home when weaned, if they survived. Wealthy mothers were not expected to nurse. Instead, breast milk, social bonding, and social status could be purchased in the form of wet-nurses.

Class, race, and even fashion shaped social attitudes about nursing. Clothing designed for wealthy women rendered nursing impractical and inefficient. Corsets, for example, were an essential part of affluent women's social uniforms. However, the use of corsets resulted in bruised breast tissue and nipples, broken ribs, and crushed diaphragms, thereby making breastfeeding very painful. Yet, even if mothers were willing to withstand the pain of breastfeeding, the nearly dozen feedings per day might have been considered a severe inconvenience. Disrobing multiple times per day was not an issue taken lightly in the sixteenth and seventeenth centuries.

Corsets required pulling leather or cloth threads (usually with the aid of an assistant) to tightly bind the waist, torso, and breasts. This rise in fashion consciousness, however, proved to be at conflict with breastfeeding culture. Perhaps fashion won.

Breastfeeding took on new meanings during the periods marked by European and North American slavery. Breastfeeding's racial dimensions were revealed in the U.S. antebellum south. Enslaved black women became charged with the responsibility to nurse the babies of their wealthy, white owners. Slave owners considered placement of slave cabins and babies in order to increase production. It has been posited that 20 percent of mistresses used wet-nurses. This wet-nursing dynamic complicated the social constructions of slavery that were at least partially grounded in pseudoscience. In other words, slavery proponents justified that vertical hierarchy by promoting the pseudoscience of racial differences and the inferiority of blacks. In particularly, ascribed to black women were the characteristics of hypersexuality, laziness, and lack of intellectual acumen. It is curious that, given these deeply entrenched racial dynamics, white families used black wet-nurses. This dynamic has yet to be fully studied and thus understood for its rich contours.

Technology, Industry, and Twentieth-Century Social Movements

By 1850, infant formula became available and reduced reliance on wet-nurses. In 1853, condensed milk was first developed. The introduction of milk formulas expanded feeding options for recent mothers and their families. By using formula, women could feed their children without hiring wet-nurses. Equally, because of high rates of maternal mortality during childbirth, alternatives to breastfeeding were in demand. Formula revolutionized infant feeding by providing a reasonable, affordable, and safe alternative to breast milk.

By the early twentieth century, the social contours of nursing morphed again, but this time technology and women's employment shaped U.S. breastfeeding dynamics. Breastfeeding rates dropped during World War II as women went to work. In 1956, the steady decline in breastfeeding rates prompted the formation of La Leche League International, an organization devoted to promoting the use of breastfeeding.

According to the National Alliance for Breastfeeding Advocacy, breastfeeding rates fluctuated during the twentieth century. For example, despite studies documenting the health and emotional benefits of breastfeeding infants, breastfeeding rates plummeted between the 1970s and 1990, to only 50 percent. These declines can be attributed to several social movements. First, as women's lives were increasingly defined outside the borders of home, breastfeeding was perceived as less efficient and pragmatic for a growing population of new mothers. Second, in the last quarter of the twentieth century, the presence of women increased in the workforce across the employment spectrum. These jobs ranged from blue-collar employment in factories to law firms and hospitals. Third, the quality of formulas improved as well as the diversity of formula options available to recent mothers. Fourth, breasts became sexualized, and thus defined outside the function of nursing and providing benefit to infants.

By the late twentieth century, breasts were no longer the exclusive site of feeding infants, but rather the subject of sexualized media, restaurant, and even airline themes. This period became marked by greater mobility among women, but hostility rose toward public breastfeeding. In this same period, conservative movements politicized the proper role of women and their responsibilities toward their children. To combat hostility toward breastfeeding, state legislatures enacted laws to promote the right to breastfeed in public places, work environments, and public accommodations. In 1992, the U.S. Congress passed the Breastfeeding Promotion Act.

Breastfeeding is no longer viewed as the only way of feeding infants. Nor is traditional reproduction perceived as the only way to have children. Foreign adoptions and assisted reproduction (buying sperm and ova, and renting wombs) demonstrate the range of options available to parents who want to raise children and build families. Yet, these options necessarily limit breastfeeding as a possibility for feeding one's child.

Social dynamics give some indication as to why new mothers might choose not to breastfeed. The question is raised about what is best for the child, to breastfeed or not? Studies demonstrate that breastfed babies tend to be healthier, more responsive, and less prone to childhood illnesses. However, eating habits, environment, and exercise will be far more significant factors than breastfeeding in influencing health later in life.

Breastfeeding continues to be a deeply contested issue among new mothers. Some decide to nurse after their babies are born, and others find the increased predictability and efficiency of formula a far better fit for their families.

Further Reading: Center for Disease Control and Prevention. www.cdc.gov/cancer/breast/statistics.

Michele Goodwin

Breast Ironing

Breast ironing is a body-modification practice whereby the breasts of a young, prepubescent girl are flattened by pounding them and ironing them with hot objects. Breast ironing is most often performed in the Republic of Cameroon, though other neighboring nations such as Chad, Benin, and Guinea-Bissau also take part in this practice. Breast ironing is an attempt to make girls appear breastless, younger, and thus less sexually available. It is believed that breast ironing prevents rape and premarital sex. Breast ironing is quite controversial, pitting supporters of the practice who believe it is an important cultural tradition against those who believe it to be mutilation, akin to female circumcision.

Prevalence and Rationale

Cameroon is located on the western coast of Africa. It is a very geographically and culturally diverse nation of almost 18 million people, with a mix of rural farmers and urban dwellers. Both English and French are spoken, as well as numerous other dialects. Many in Cameroon practice a number of traditional rites of passage, such as circumcision and scarification. In addition to these practices, it is estimated that 26 percent of girls and women in Cameroon, both in rural areas and in towns, have had their breasts ironed. In some regions, more than half of the female population has undergone breast ironing. Islam, Christianity, and animism are practiced in Cameroon, with breast ironing most often occurring in the southern part of the country where Christianity is more prevalent. Incidences of breast ironing are much more rare in the Islamic northern part of Cameroon. Estimates suggest that in Muslim parts of Cameroon, only 10 percent women have had their breasts ironed. One reason for the lower incidence in Muslim providences of Cameroon may be the stricter Muslim codes regarding male and female sexuality.

The development of breasts is often seen as the marker of the development of female sexuality; breasts are seen to distinguish women from girls. Practitioners of breast ironing believe that as long as girls have yet to show signs of puberty, they will be less sexually appealing. Breast ironing will make girls appear younger and thus protected against a range of unwanted sexual advances as well as consensual premarital sex. According to the Child Rights Information Network, more than half of breast ironing is undertaken by mothers, intended to protect daughters from sexual advances, distractions from their studies, early pregnancy, or other problems associated with puberty. Traditionally, women are expected to remain virgins until marriage. A girl's breasts may be ironed in order to attempt to ensure her virginity. Incidences of rape are quite high in Cameroon, as are rates of HIV/AIDS and other sexually transmitted diseases. In some cases, breast ironing is also performed by girls themselves to protect against arranged early marriages, which can occur once a girl enters puberty.

Procedure

Breast ironing is most often performed by mothers on their daughters and takes place over a period of time. The father is often unaware of the procedure. Breast ironing most often occurs among pubescent girls who are beginning to develop breasts as early as age nine. Breast ironing refers not only to the literal ironing of the breasts; it also consists of beating, massaging, and binding the breasts in order to flatten them. This is most often done with stones, flattened rocks, banana peels, and coconut shells, as well as a wooden pestle used for grinding grains into flour. These objects are heated over hot coals. The developing breasts are massaged and pressed with these heated tools in order to flatten the breasts.

Objections

Breast ironing is not as widely practiced as female circumcision, and is often done in secret by a mother on her daughter. As a result it has not received as much attention as female circumcision. However, in recent years it has come under international scrutiny, and is now identified by the United Nations as a form of gender-based violence.

Critics of breast ironing see it as a form of bodily mutilation. The body is permanently altered through breast ironing. Breast ironing is a very painful procedure that takes place over a period of time. There is not a lot of research as to the long-term effects of breast ironing on the body, but there are some known results. The body is burned and scarred, and there is also a large amount of tissue damage that can result in near disappearance of the breasts. The breasts can lose their symmetry and become uneven in size. Ironed breasts can be unable to produce milk while breastfeeding. There is a risk of developing infection. There are also fears that breast ironing puts women at a higher risk for breast cancer, as cysts often develop as a result of the ironing procedure. Finally, critics fear that there are significant psychological risks to girls.

In addition, many mothers (and even girls themselves) iron breasts in the hope of protecting against pregnancy and other sexually transmitted diseases. There is some concern that people may see themselves as immune against pregnancy or other sexually transmitted diseases, including HIV, if they have their breasts ironed. Anti-ironing activists feel that these women may be more likely to participate in unsafe sexual practices. In addition, research conducted by those who work to prevent this practice have found that these girls are not less likely to participate in early sexual behavior.

One anti-ironing activist group known as the Association of Aunties has called for stronger legislation to protect young girls from this practice. In Cameroon, breast ironing is only prosecuted if a girl's breasts are deemed to be damaged from the practice. In these instances, practitioners can face up to three years in prison. However, partly due to the young age of victims, breast ironing is rarely reported, and as a result, few people have faced jail time. Therefore, governments have turned to campaigns in an effort to educate women about the dangers of breast ironing.

Further Reading: Child Rights Information Network, "Millions of Cameroon Girls Suffer 'Breast Ironing,'" http://crin.com/violence/search/closeup.asp?infoID=9218; United Nations Population Fund, www.unpfa.org; Varza, Roxy. "Breast Ironing in Cameroon: Women in Africa Bear a Painful Tradition," http://www.theworldly.org/ArticlesPages/Articles2006/September06Articles/Cameroon-Ironing.html.

Angelique C. Harris

Cultural History of the Breast

The historical, social, and psychological legacies of the breast reveal a stunning and profound complexity. In late modernity, breasts are increasingly contested sites, often subjected to both ridicule and fetishization, traversed by anxieties around fluidity, pollution, nature, health, technology, femininity, sexuality, motherhood, the role of women in the public and the workplace, and the politics and economics of race, class, and domesticity. In this Western cultural context, the breast is a highly treasured feminine attribute, obviously present in the wallpaper of our hypervisual world, and yet turns out to be a complex and symbolically rich object.

Anatomy and Physiology

The breast is a term used to refer to the upper ventral region of a mammal's torso. Human beings are members of the class of creatures called *mammalia* (or mammals). This term was taken from the Latin word for breast, *mamma*, by the Swedish Enlightenment botanist and physician Carolus Linnaeus (1707–78), who meticulously surveyed and divided plants and creatures into categories according to their defining characteristics. One of the characteristics could be found in animals whose offspring rely upon suckling mother's milk after birth. Linnaeus' work was not produced in a cultural vacuum—it formed part of a wider framework of an eighteenth-century male fixation with breasts and breastfeeding. On the female mammal, breasts have mammary glands that produce milk for their offspring (the process is called lactation). The milk is then directed into the nipple through the lactiferous ducts, with their characteristic tree- or root-like appearances. Human females are the only mammals with a more-or-less protruding breast shape. The reason for this has been subject to much speculation by evolutionists and biologists, but no consensus has been reached.

Developing breasts is a diverse process, which plays a fundamental part in the socialization of girls into women. Breasts develop through puberty and grow over time. Growing breasts is the initiation of a process that will continue throughout the life cycle. Beginning with puberty, there are monthly fluctuations in size and feeling and sometimes premenstrual tenderness and pain. Lumps and bumps may appear, and throughout life, there may be changes through weight gain and loss, pregnancy, lactation, and aging. During sexual excitation, a woman's breasts can increase in size by up to 25 percent, while the skin on the neck and breasts might flush with a red rash.

Lactation is a process triggered by the hormones of pregnancy and birth (oxytocin and prolactin) and is therefore almost exclusively reserved for the female of the species. The human male has breasts that are nearly homologous to the female's in terms of structure, if not size. Newborn babies of both sexes sometimes have swollen breasts in the first few days after birth because they have been exposed to the mother's hormones in the womb. Occasionally, newborns' breasts emanate what is colloquially termed "witch's milk." Men can occasionally lactate. This is sometimes caused by medication, tumors, or hormonal abnormalities. Prolactin is central to milk production and is usually stimulated by pregnancy and birth, but can also be induced by suckling. With their duct deficiencies, men have relatively little capacity for storing milk in their breasts and would therefore make a minimal contribution to infant feeding. Lactation aside, in both sexes the nipple can become erect when cold or through sexual arousal and/or stimulation, like sucking. A circular area of pink or dark brown skin called the areola surrounds the nipple. The rest of the breast is made up of fatty tissue, connective tissue, and ligaments.

Masculinity and the Breast

In a Western cultural context, it is highly unusual for a man to identify himself as breasted, despite an increase in the condition called gynecomastia—

the diagnosis for boys or men who grow breasts, either caused by a hormonal imbalance or as a consequence of obesity. When we hear the term "breast man" in popular parlance, the inference is not that he is a man with breasts, but rather that he is a male who identifies himself according to his love for women's breasts—they are what he desires in the feminine body. Despite such linguistic identifications with the female body, discussions of the male breast are rare, a silence that suggests that, in an operational sense, men do not have breasts in our culture. Men's nipples can of course also be sensitive to touching or kissing (and men can also get breast cancer). One of the few accounts which describes this taboo of masculine heterosexuality is by the Mexican artist Frida Kahlo (1907–1954), who referred lovingly both to the feminine character of her sizeable husband, the painter Diego Riviera, and to the beauty of his sensitive breasts. Studies of sexual behavior have indicated that homosexual men feel freer to express this side of their physical eroticism.

The Breast Vocabulary

English-speaking cultures have produced an extensive *lingua franca* (slang) for women's breasts. Many of these breast euphemisms are literal puns or carry oral connotations of food, eating, and drinking, like "melons," "cupcakes," and "jugs." Euphemisms are often put into use in order to neutralize socially precarious issues, like sex and bodily processes. The ballooning breast of Western popular culture is often a laughing matter. But historically and globally, the breast suggests a far more solemn status because of its crucial role in reproduction.

The more conventional etymological heritage of the word "breast" suggests multiple meanings, not all tied to anatomy or specific to the female body. For one thing, breasts have not always been so highly eroticized. Suckling has sometimes been the main focus of women's breasts. It is however quite clear that in contemporary Western cultures today, breasts have come to figure as the primary symbols of femininity, even more so than female genitals. Pornographic images of the breast are ubiquitous, and the phenomenon of surgical breast implants reflects a sexual fetishization of breast size.

The breast, chest, or bosom, is the part of the body where the heart is located, beating its vital rhythm and pumping blood throughout the organism. Hence, the breast is also often thought of as the symbolic source of identity—the place where one points to indicate self. It is also the area where one might put one's hand to indicate sincerity, emotion, and honesty. This is evident in art history, where bared breasts have symbolized virtues such as charity, chastity, hope, and justice. The breast is also sometimes where one places one's hand to take a pledge or to symbolize allegiance.

Breastfeeding: Between Nature and Culture

In contemporary culture, breastfeeding is frequently referred to and thought of as a natural phenomenon, in contrast to bottle-feeding. Breastfeeding ties the human species to other animals whose young are nourished in this way. However, the history of breast and infant feeding reveals an immense diversity of practices through times and different cultures. There is hardly a uniformity or natural law which governs all mothers and the ways they feed their babies. Rather, infants have been fed through various means and at different intervals, weaned at different stages, suckled sometimes by their mothers, and sometimes by other lactating women—for commercial or altruistic reasons. We also now know that breastfeeding is not purely instinctual (even among primates) but is a practice which must be learned both for mother and child—hence the expression, "the art of breastfeeding."

The Breast from Ancient History to the Renaissance

There is a continuum of breast representations through the ages. Take the case of the so-called Venus of Willendorf (20,000–18,000 BCE) from Northern Europe, whose dainty hands rest gently on top of her large, pendulant breasts. Historians are still debating whether this voluptuous feminine representation served as Paleolithic porn, or a portable fetish object invested with special powers. Some claim that there could have been an even more sacred function: human hands manufactured the Venus as a humble depiction of the great goddess. Perhaps the truth lies in the middle ground: Venus or goddess figures illustrate how ancient people viewed reproductive power and sexuality as two sides of the same coin.

It seems appropriate to continue the journey by quickly tracing the milky way through the vast two and a half million years of human presence on earth. Suckling a breast (or its symbolic representative, the bottle) is a universal prerequisite for membership in the human species. Today, many people may not have ever had breast milk as infants, but this is only a recent phenomenon: throughout past millennia, the majority of the world's population gained sustenance from the maternal breast, thus imbibing the breast-mother's qualities.

The earliest historical details of practices of breastfeeding date from around 3000 BCE, and emerged from the civilizations that populated Egypt, the Levant, and Mesopotamia. The records show that the people of these diverse locations had a similar approach to feeding their infants: babies were breastfed as a matter of routine, usually until the recommended age of weaning at between two and three years old. Babylonian, Hebrew, Egyptian, Ayurvedic, and Islamic texts testify to the importance placed on breastfeeding as the best means of nutrition for infants. But this emphasis on breastfeeding does not automatically reflect our modern investment in the emotional bond between biological mother and child. Rather, it was the quality of the milk and not necessarily the bearer of the breast per se which was the essential agent for infant well-being. Wet-nursing, paid and unpaid, was prevalent, and many infants were suckled and cared for (fully or in part) by women other than their biological mothers. Both Moses and Mohammed were suckled by wet-nurses. Moses, though, was unknowingly suckled by his actual biological mother, posing as a wet-nurse to the Pharaoh's daughter. Islamic cultures accommodated this practice through the concept of milk-kinship: children suckled by the same woman (not necessarily her biological offspring) were related to each other through the shared milk. A boy and girl suckled by the same woman would therefore be prevented from marrying each other.

Alongside written documents about breastfeeding are an abundance of breast-themed artifacts that were made in these regions during roughly the same historical period. These form only a fraction of a wide-reaching and trans-historical appreciation of breasts in symbolic form. Some of these objects can now be found in the collections of Western museums, such as the British Museum in London. Here one can find figurines of naked or semi-naked females, often cupping or bidding out their breasts with their hands, like the painted terracotta figurine with protruding breasts found in Syria (5000 BCE). Another example is a stone sculpture of a large-breasted feminine form found in Turkey (4500 BCE). Other breasted figures emerge from Egypt (from 4000 BCE), the Greek islands (from 2800 BCE), Iran (1400–1200 BCE), Mesopotamia (800 BCE), and Sicily (500 BCE). Mexican and Indian cultures produced similar representations, privileging the appearance of the figure's breasts (second century CE). There is also the Egyptian representation of Isis suckling her son Horus (Late Period), believed by art historians to be the prototype for the later images of the suckling Madonna, characteristic of later Judeo-Christian art. The same suggestion has been made about the suckling Mesopotamian goddess Ishtar. Later Hindu religion presents another variation on the theme through Krishna's mythic mother Jashoda, the suckler of the world. The sacred pair is depicted in an early fourteenth century bronze sculpture from the Vijayanagar period in India.

This visual investment has probably partly been a manifestation of the breast's powerful meaning as a symbol of maternity. Unlike the mysterious processes, which took place inside a woman's body during pregnancy and could not be seen (before the relatively recent invention of ultrasound scans), suckling provided a more tangible view of female fecundity.

The Madonna's Breast

The nursing Madonna (or Madonna *Lactans*) is a repeated motif in the art of continental Europe from the Middle Ages to the Renaissance. Here, Mary is venerated as the son's idealized mother: the mortal one who feeds the divine infant from her breast. One typical example of such a painting is Leonardo da Vinci's (1452–1519) *Madonna and Child* (*Madonna Litta*), probably painted around 1482. The naked baby Jesus is held in his mother's arms—as he turns away from her and looks toward the viewer, Mary's head is looking downward, gazing in tender admiration at her child. With his plump hand, Jesus clutches her breast, protruding from a slit in the red dress she is wearing. This Madonna exists because of her son—in a reversal from the natural order of things, when the child exists because of the life-giving powers of the mother.

In fifteenth-century Florence, when images of the *Madonna Litta* flourished, wet-nursing was prolific among the middle and upper classes. In a spiraling chain of suckling relations, wet-nursing also spread to lower classes, including that of the wet-nurse (or *bàlia*) herself: she would often have to hire a less-paid wet-nurse to feed her own baby—thus creating a hierarchy of wet-nurses. The quality of care provided by wet-nurses was not always of the highest standard, and many infant deaths have been attributed to them. There have been speculations about the possible links between this social phenomenon and the countless representations of the nursing Madonna in the same period. Art historians have interpreted the breast-baring Mary as an amalgamation of erotic and spiritual desires—a kind of sanitized pornography. Others believe she fit into the elaborate construction of a psychic myth, as a means of restoring the maternal bond in a culture that may have had, at least to our modern eyes, an unstable attachment to both the concept and person of the "mother." Yet another theory posits the nursing Madonna as a symbol of endless maternal reassurance and good nourishment in a time of political and religious upheaval, repeated epidemics (including the Black Death), crop failure, and an unreliable supply of food. In one sense, we could say that Florentine society resorted to a cultural mothering of its citizens through the images of the comforting and restoring Madonna. In any event, the nursing Madonna raises interesting questions about the relationships between the breast in historical representations, and the lived historical breasts of women—how art both reflects and reinforces moral concerns, as well as religious and reproductive politics.

Where Hunger and Love Meet

The psychoanalytical intervention in the late nineteenth and early twentieth centuries shook the moral foundations of the family: the idealized mother represented by the virginal Madonna *Lactans* was pushed aside by Sigmund Freud's assertion of the maternal breast as the instigator of infantile sexuality. Psychoanalysis is the therapeutic practice that situated sexuality at the center of the family. Freud introduced to the Victorians the idea that the key to sexuality is to be found in the relationship between parents and child. Freud described how the mother instigates and literally feeds sexuality into the infant, and argued that the force of libido (a sexual life energy) comes precisely from its propping (German: *anlehnung*) on a function essential to life itself, namely suckling. The breast is where the two drives for love and hunger meet: the soft cradle of sexuality. It is in a sense, also a meeting place, a propping, of nature and culture.

In *Three Essays on Sexuality* (1905), Freud provided a theoretical account of the timeless erotic qualities of the breast. For the developmentally immature and vulnerable newborn who is completely dependant on other beings for its survival, the first social encounter takes place through suckling in an undifferentiated sphere of symbiotic unity with the mother. The breast provides nourishment and psychic visions that gradually build a sense of self and other. It is important to clarify that, in psychoanalysis, the breast has different aspects. The "breast" refers to the breast as an idea and the breast as an organ, with the nourishing milk that comes from it. Moreover, it refers to the mother, or primary caregiver (wet-nurse or other) and the totality of care received by the infant from those around it. The infant merges all of these qualities into one psychic symbol. This is because it does not yet know how to differentiate between the internal and external, nor between things and people (it has no real comprehension of "I" and "you"). The ego (or sense of self) forms out of the infant's subsequent loss of the breast through weaning, and is propelled into action by a deep desire to recreate the paradise lost, represented in the unconscious fantasy of total plenitude in a mother-child symbiosis. It does so by seeking out other means of satisfaction from, say, intellectual and artistic pursuits. Human cognition and agency emerge out of an irreparable loss; endlessly seeking to replace what is missing through symbolic substitutions. Hence, perhaps, the many odes to the breast in art, music, literature, and philosophy.

The conjunction between the child's and the mother's desire of and in the other is explored by Freud almost solely from the infantile position rather than the mother's. This omission has been the invitation for other psychoanalysts (like Melanie Klein) and feminist thinkers to introduce the agency of the mother into this founding relation. Breastfeeding offers reciprocal pleasures between the giver and the receiver—a fact that in past times was openly acknowledged in medical texts and other documents, but which today has become associated with considerable taboo. It is safe to assume that this is because mother-infant sensuality threatens the heterosexual conjugal bond. Freud had of course scrutinized the rivalry between the infant and its father in his early work. For him, it is precisely the tense and jealous relation vis-à-vis the woman's bosom that prematurely prepares the stage for the Oedipal drama, when the child must face the daunting realization that the mother is already taken. The ensuing conflict between paternal authority and infantile omnipotence ensures that the child must come to accept a severance of the pre-linguistic symbiotic tie to the mother's body (and breasts). Instead of being reliant on its mother to regulate all needs and desires, the child now ventures into the wider social world, and gradually gains a subjectivity regulated by patriarchal language and social laws.

Breasts for Hire: Wet-Nursing

Wet-nursing, as a straightforward exchange of favors between women, has been going on since the beginning of time, both as a form of occasional assistance and in more substantial ways in cases when a mother could not provide nourishment for her child through death, abandonment, or illness. The European history of commercial wet-nursing reveals shifting notions of mothering which might surprise the modern reader. Before the Industrial Revolution, the wet-nurse was often a respectable, married countrywoman. Sometimes, she was a mother who had lost her own baby, leaving her with milk that could be used to feed other infants. The woman would either provide the suckling services in her own home, or be hired to work in the household of her employer. Wet-nursing could offer good money for her, at times higher than a laborer's wage, sometimes even securing retirement funds for her old age.

First introduced by the Romans, wet-nursing was gradually adopted by wealthy and noble European families, becoming well and truly established in medieval times (around 1150–1400 CE). As in previous times, poorer women continued to suckle their own infants. The rise of the commercial wet-nursing industry is intimately attached to the politics of reproduction and class. The growth of the European upper classes and the aristocracy from the medieval period onward appears to have been fuelled by the breast milk of less well-to-do wet-nurses. The key to this claim lies in the contraceptive effects of breastfeeding and the release of prolactin, which can repress ovulation for a considerable time after birth, a phenomenon called lactational amenorrhoea. The wet-nurse played an obvious role in the reproduction of her own household (sustaining her own children while spacing births), but was also indirectly involved in the procreative life of her employers, in that she enabled them to breed at much shorter intervals. In the Middle Ages and Renaissance, aristocratic women could, through passing on their babies to wet-nurses, produce up to sixteen or eighteen children in a lifetime, compared to women in sustenance cultures (historic and present) who often nurse their infants for two to four years and usually end up bearing a total of only four to six children throughout their lives.

The rationale behind the wet-nursing practice was twofold. On the one hand, it was thought to strengthen the husband's bloodline and ensure the family's future wealth and status by producing the maximum amount of progeny at a time when infant mortality was high. On the other hand, wet-nursing created a way around a cultural taboo that discouraged men from having sexual intercourse with a lactating woman. Both of these aspects reflect that, historically, since the abolition of mother-right and the rise of what has been called the "reign of the phallus," breastfeeding was not so much a woman's choice as it was that of her husband. Any decision in the matter was more likely to be based on social norms and expectations than on the woman's preference.

The regulation of maternity and childrearing continued to be dispersed from the Middle Ages through a variety of religious discursive formations, culminating in a divide between Catholics, who were tolerant of wet-nursing, and Protestants who condemned the practice as unnatural and detrimental to infant health.

Enlightenment and the Breast

From the mid-eighteenth century, a new trend emerged: in the bourgeois family, the role of the biological mother was reinforced and invested with intense emotions and increased powers. The mother was now seen as the moral foundation of the family, and women were therefore urged by clergy, doctors, and philosophers alike to selflessly devote themselves to caring for and educating their own biological offspring. It was no longer considered de rigueur to hire a wet-nurse to take care of a suckling babe. This changing attitude has its roots in several influential Enlightenment discourses, of which philosopher Jean-Jacques Rousseau's (1712–78) *Émile* (1762) is one example. In his treaty on education, Rousseau argues passionately against the wet-nursing tradition, seen as the cause of most social ills, and in favor of the maternal duty to breastfeed one's own progeny. Throughout written history, moralists and doctors have bemoaned the potentially damaging effects of a wet-nurse on her nurslings, and she frequently became a convenient scapegoat for a child's behavioral or medical problems. *Émile* provides a powerful example of a moral rhetoric, which fed into the general discourse on breastfeeding at the time and further, informed the promotion by church and government of the domesticated lactating mother. Enlightenment starts at the mother's breast, a view that transplanted itself into the ideological backbone of the French Revolution and Republicanism, when maternal breastfeeding was seen to provide the only acceptable nourishment for the new citizens of France. Correspondingly, breasts were put to use as the very symbols of newfound freedom and the goodness of equality. In France after the Revolution in 1789, the message was now that a woman's breasts could not be bought. Breasts loomed large in the public domain despite the exclusion of women from the right to vote and their peripheral role in Republican politics. Breastfeeding in public became a woman's blatant signal of support and loyalty for the Republic, and her only means of political participation.

The moral crusade against wet-nursing is linked to modernity's flagships for social improvement and the preservation of infant health: the medicalization of birth and infancy; the introduction of sweeping public regulations; and the nations-state's increased concerns about population control and productivity. Rousseau's rhetoric came to fuel French popular opinion—an intervention that signaled the demise of wet-nursing and subsequently opened the door for a new industry of artificial breast-milk substitutes.

From Breast to Bottle

The only viable alternatives to breastfeeding have a short history. Louis Pasteur's (1822–1895) discovery of bacteria and their role in the spread of disease meant that, from the early 1890s, animal milk could be pasteurized, thus offering a more hygienic alternative than had previously been available. Eventually, toward the end of the nineteenth century, efforts were made to create products specifically intended for feeding infants, in particular the many foundlings who were filling hospitals and institutions across Europe and North America. Prior to this, a foundling's best hope of survival would have been a wet-nurse's breasts—any other method of feeding (unpasteurized animal milk, pap, broths, etc.) would have greatly endangered its chance for survival. Despite this progress, wet-nursing continued to be a common method of feeding ailing or abandoned infants in U.S. hospitals and institutions right up to the 1930s and 1940s. To this day, infant formula continues to be a dangerous alternative in places where illiteracy, unclean water, and fuel shortages make the preparation of a safe bottle difficult. It is worth noting that, in a global context, breastfeeding remains the norm in infant feeding. Wet-nursing still exists, albeit in a somewhat transmuted manner: many hospitals around the world today have milk banks where women can donate or sell their milk, which can then be given to premature or sick infants who are unable to suckle their own mothers. There are also contemporary instances of noncommercial wet-nursing wherein a woman suckles the child of another as a matter of practicality or favor.

In the United States, bottle-feeding became popular in the two decades after the Great Depression of the 1930s, when efforts were directed at boosting consumer spending in order to get the economy back on its feet. The housewife became the target of many cutting-edge inventions aiming to make domestic chores easier and more glamorous. The marketing of infant formula to new mothers promised a great scientific innovation; formula was claimed to be far better for babies than breast milk. The transformation from breast to bottle was aided by the medical establishment, which initially endorsed formula as the ultimate choice in infant nutrition. Bottle-feeding would allow for predictable and regimented feedings at four-hour intervals, freeing up the mother's time for other work in the home. It also emancipated women's breasts from the drudgery of their functional role and turned them instead into luxury items for the entertainment and consumption of the heterosexual male.

Counter to the rising use of formula in the 1950s, the Catholic founders of the La Leche League believed staunchly in the emotional and physiological benefits of breastfeeding and created an expanding network of woman-to-woman self-help groups to support struggling mothers. A similar organization called the National Childbirth Trust was established in Britain, and Ammehjelpen emerged in Norway in the late 1960s to counteract what had become a bottle-feeding hegemony in maternity wards. Ammehjelpen is widely accredited as having done the legwork behind Norway's reversal in infant feeding: today Norwegian mothers are crowned the world champions of breastfeeding.

Colonialism and the Breast

In the American colonial setting of the seventeenth to the nineteenth centuries, wet-nursing was generally less widespread than in Europe. Some Northern women employed poor white wet-nurses, whereas Puritan women dutifully breast-fed their own babies as a matter of religious piety. However, in the colonies in the antebellum South, plantation owners frequently used African slave women as wet-nurses. Although many white women in the Southern colonies suckled their own babies, slave women were sometimes forced to abandon their own infants in order to serve as wet-nurses to the white offspring of their owner. Ellen Betts, a Texan, was one such women who was constantly put to work suckling the babies of fellow slaves, as well as those of her white oppressor; first the six boys her owner had by his first wife, and then the resulting offspring of his second wife. Betts described her experience:

> With ten chillen springin' up quick like dat and de cullud children comin' 'long fast as pig litters, I don't do nothin' all my days, but nuss, nuss, nuss. I nuss so many chillen it done went and stunted my growth and dat's why I ain't nothin' but bones to dis day. (Fildes, 1988: 143)

The painful legacy of slavery is revisited in current debates around some African American women's resistance to breastfeeding.

Posed against this chilling history is one astonishing story of courage and dignity, when the former slave, anti-slavery, and women's rights activist Sojourner Truth (1797–1883) stood up to a group of racist white men who had challenged her womanhood and suggested she show her breasts to the white women in the audience so they could approve or disapprove of the state of her femininity. According to *The Liberator* of October 15, 1858:

> Soujourner told them that her breasts had suckled many a white babe, to the exclusion of her own offspring; that some of those white babies had grown to man's estate; that, although they had suckled her colored breasts, they were, in her estimation, far more manly than they (her persecutors) appeared to be; and she quietly asked them, as she disrobed her bosom, if they, too, wished to suck! (quoted in Yalom, 1998: 124)

Mammary Madness

Some scholars see the breast's sexual allure as being culturally and historically specific. They cite anthropological evidence that there are societies in which the female breast does not function as sexual object. Erotic breast fascination then, is not a given universal phenomenon. There are cultures in the world that privilege other regions of the female body as especially erotic, such as the buttocks (Latin America, Africa, and the Caribbean), the feet (China), or the neck (Japan). One may also speculate that in cultures where women's breasts are normally bared, their sexual allure is decreased. But these casually exposed breasts could soon become a thing of the past. The historical, economic, and technological changes that have triggered and accompanied Western industrialization enables an unprecedented mass distribution of images through various media, a process of visual proliferation that has become particularly dominant in late capitalism. Globalization puts these kinds of cultural differences under the threat of extinction, as Western values and aesthetics are exported to every part of the globe.

In Western cultures at least, social anxieties about bodies, identity, health, reproduction, masculinity, and femininity are frequently managed through an obsession with viewing breasts. In opposition to the historical importance of breasts, which associated them primarily with their function in lactation, today Western breasts figure principally as a visual phenomenon. Breasts have an outstanding capacity to grab the look and generate attention. One example to cite is the moral outcries and media furor over singer Janet Jackson's alleged "wardrobe malfunction" at the Super Bowl in 2004, when her right breast was spectacularly revealed (complete with a star-shaped nipple shield/piercing), not only to the stadium audience but, within seconds, to viewers around the world. The incident exemplifies the paradoxical place of the breast in U.S. culture: at once highly visible and overly sexualized, yet tightly regulated by moral discourses on decency and the policing of nakedness in the public sphere.

The U.S. breast obsession, now exported across the globe, seems to have erupted during World War II, when soldiers were equipped with copies of magazines like *Esquire*, featuring a new and charming character: the pinup girl. Created by artists such as Alberto Vargas, she was a long-legged and large-breasted vision of perfect femininity, sent to troops in order to boost morale, promising a busty reward for the men who survived and returned home to the waiting women. Servicemen would sometimes even decorate their airplanes and bombs with beautifully breasted girls. Meanwhile, the busty women back home had been busy working, replacing the male labor that was lost to the war effort. Having served the needs of a nation at war, filling the jobs of their drafted men, when peace came, American women were expected to return to their prewar roles in the home. This re-domestification of women corresponded to a growing cultural obsession with big-breasted, curvy women: the dawn of "mammary madness."

The United States of the 1950s presented to the world copious cultural exports that fused capitalism and sexuality, and in which breasts featured prominently. The theme of money and sex became particularly evident in the movie *Gentlemen Prefer Blondes*, which was released in 1953, the same year that the film's female star, Marilyn Monroe, posed nude on the cover of the first edition of *Playboy* magazine. The novelty of this particular publication was that it had mass appeal and managed to detach itself from social stigmas surrounding the consumption of conventional pornography. The king of play-boys, editor Hugh Hefner, made selling sex, epitomized by the busty center-fold girl, seem like respectably clean, good fun, catering to the needs of men in addition to a whole new generation of American teenagers.

Not surprisingly, given its breast-obsessed popular culture, the 1950s also introduced the surgical procedure of breast augmentation for purely aesthetic reasons (commonly known as a "boob job"). Until then, having small breasts simply was not considered a medical or psychological issue, certainly not a problem that merited invasive surgery. Breast augmentation was first performed in the 1890s as a remedy for women who had already undergone other types of breast surgery, usually treatments for cancer (such as lumpectomies or mastectomies). The medicalization of small or normatively inadequate breasts went alongside a growing cultural fascination with the buxom woman. Small breasts were now diagnosed as a "disease" which was seen to cause some women severe psychological pain. The belief was that, by making the breasts bigger on the outside, one could make the woman feel better on the inside, and thereby cure the psychic disorder. Breasts were now seen as the ultimate feminine attribute.

Reclaiming the Breast

In daily life, Western women are expected to keep their breasts not only covered but tightly pressed and molded into the alphabetical-sized cups of standardized undergarments—neatly divided into two symmetrical globular shapes, lifted high on the chest, with nipples padded and shielded from the potential gaze of others. Free bouncing breasts and nipples that protrude from clothing are considered somewhat of a sexual provocation. The history of fashion and undergarments suggests how beauty ideals have changed through the centuries, and breasts have been rigorously disciplined accordingly: bared, partially or wholly concealed by décolletages, restrained or liberated, squeezed together, lifted high, shaped into globes or pointed bullets, bound flat against the chest, and so forth.

There is a special relationship between feminist activism and bras, which dates back to the No More Miss America demonstration in Atlantic City, New Jersey, on September 7, 1968. Feminists threw what were considered the tools of female oppression (makeup, curlers, wigs, women's magazines, and restrictive underwear like girdles and corsets) into a symbolic "freedom trash can." Incidentally, brassieres were also part of the inventory of constricting items discarded by the demonstrators, members of the women's liberation movement. For some unknown reason, the media reporting from this demonstration subsequently misrepresented what had happened, suggesting that bras had been not only been thrown away but moreover set alight. Bra burning was quickly seen as the feminist version of the U.S. pacifists' burning of draft cards during the Vietnam War. It caught the public imagination and, as a result, feminists are still referred to as bra burners—despite the somewhat mythic origins of this term.

Feminist critics point out that phallocentric culture has deep anxieties about the perceived multiplicity, softness, and fluidity of women's bodies, which are especially evident in the ambivalence expressed around breasts. This anxiety is not rooted in the breast as an organ, but rather in the cultural concepts around femininity and containment of fluidity with which breasts are associated. For example, in the United States since the 1950s, it has been common for pubescent girls to wear training bras (the purchasing of which is akin to a coming-of-age rite), even though their breasts are often still too small to actually require a support garment. Similarly, it is quite common for girls to be made to wear bikini tops long before the onset of puberty, at a stage when their breasts are anatomically identical to those of boys. These practices reveal not just the results of commodity culture that creates a product for every situation, but also the subtle workings of the social construction of gender identity. Juvenile breasts must be trained, and a girl has to learn to become "breasted"—it is not something she is born into.

Feminists did more than throwing a few bras in the bin. They actively challenged the degrading sexual objectification of the female body aptly represented by Hefner's Playboy Bunnies (or in Britain, the Page Three Girl, a topless soft-porn feature in some tabloid newspapers), where the breasts feature as a magnet for hetero-masculine attention. Instead, breasts became the subject for explorations about mother-daughter relationships, the mother's experience of breastfeeding, women's relationships with their own breasts from puberty to old age, and so on.

The French-born artist Louise Bourgeois (1911–) has had a lifelong dialogue with the breast in her work, which started in the 1930s. For example, in a performance from 1980 entitled "A Banquet/A Fashion Show of Body Parts," Bourgeois dressed in a costume with several pudding-like globular shapes attached to the front of her body. The work clearly plays with the ancient Greek sculptural representation of the many-breasted Artemis, but also raises associations with the relation between breasts and food, women and food, or women as food: the banquet of body parts.

Breast cancer, once an unspeakable condition and a social stigma, has turned into a productive area for women's self-expression. There is a plethora of literature made by women who have received this diagnosis, of which the lesbian African American poet Audre Lorde's (1934–1992) Cancer Journals is an example. First published in 1980, Lorde's journals provide a defiant articulation of the pain and grieving, the despairs and hopes of a breast cancer patient. Through the breast, Lorde expresses the unbreakable bond with her children, as well as her love for other women. Her breast is a mother's breast, and a lesbian breast: hence, she speaks from inside and outside the conventions that regulate these feminine attributes. Lorde's breast cancer narrative, despite its dark facets, became a vital sign of sexual liberation in the latter part of the twentieth century.

When the British photographer Jo Spence (1934–1992) was first diagnosed with breast cancer, she felt herself not only confronted with a new sense of corporeality, but also subjected to a medical machinery in which she had little or no control over her body. The experience of living with breast cancer, although physically and mentally debilitating, provided Spence with ideas for new projects—encouraging women's breast experiences as a platform from which to explore notions of sexual identity and social pressures. Spence turned her experience with breast cancer into one of critical analysis and resistance, documenting her trials and tribulations all the way to her deathbed. *See also* Breasts: Breastfeeding.

Further Reading: Ayalah, Daphne, and Isaac J. Weinstock. *Breasts: Women Speak About Their Breasts and Their Lives.* London: Hutchinson, 1979; Devi, Mahasweta. *Breast Stories.* Transl. Gayatri Chakravorty Spivak. Calcutta: Seagull Books, 1997; Fildes, Valerie. *Wet Nursing: A History from Antiquity to the Present.* Oxford: Basil Blackwell, 1988; Freud, Sigmund. *The Standard Edition of the Complete Psychological Works of Sigmund Freud. Vol. 7: A Case of Hysteria, Three Essays on Sexuality and Other Works (1901–1905).* Trans. James Strachey. London: Hogarth Press, 1953–1974; Golden, Janet. *A Social History of Wet Nursing in America: From Breast to Bottle.* Columbus: Ohio State University Press, 2001; Leopold, Ellen. *A Darker Ribbon: Breast Cancer, Women, and their Doctors in the Twentieth Century.* Boston: Beacon Press, 1999; Maher, Vanessa. *The Anthropology of Breast-Feeding: Natural Law or Social Construct.* Oxford: Berg Publishers, 1992; Olson, James S. *Batsheba's Breast: Women, Cancer, and History.* Baltimore: The Johns Hopkins University Press, 2002; Palmer, Gabrielle. *The Politics of Breastfeeding.* 2nd ed. London: Pandora Press, 1993; Spiegel, Maura, and Lithe Sebesta. *The Breast Book: Attitude, Perception, Envy and Etiquette.* New York: Workman Publishing, 2002; Yalom, Marilyn. *A History of the Breast.* London: Pandora, 1998; Young, Iris Marion. *On Female Body Experience: "Throwing Like a Girl" and Other Essays.* Oxford: Oxford University Press, 2005.

Birgitta Haga Gripsrud

History of the Brassiere

The fashion magazine *Vogue* popularized the French term "brassiere" in 1907 to describe a group of undergarments becoming increasingly used to support women's breasts. It was not until the 1930s, however, that the abbreviated word "bra" gained wider currency. Although a variety of garments for breast adjustment appear throughout the history of fashion, the

Member of the Women's Liberation Party drops a brassiere in the trash barrel in protest of the Miss America pageant in Atlantic City, New Jersey, 1968. (AP Photo).

development of the bra as we know it today coincides historically with the rise of women's liberation movements in the second half of the nineteenth century. Feminst groups advocated the undergarment as a means with which to provide the body greater movement in contrast to the more constrictive corset. As the bra gained broad consumer appeal in the first half of the twentieth century, it became closely tied to the frenetic paces of fashion and could both influence and conform to the silhouettes of women's attire. Caught up in fashion's commodity-driven cycle, the women's movement of the 1960s railed against the bra for forcing the body into consistency with restrictive, and often uncomfortable, standards of beauty. Even so, the bra has remained a popular female undergarment that, throughout its history, has been potently implicated within the changing cultural understandings of women's bodies.

Precursors to the Modern Bra

Devices to modify women's breasts have existed since ancient times. Women in Minoan Crete tied bands around their torsos, just beneath their breasts, to lift their bosoms and cause them to protrude exposed from their bodices. Female athletes of Crete also wore a bikini-like garment to support their breasts. Likewise, ancient Greek and Roman women bore tied cloth bands over their breasts, with or without straps, when exercising. Ancient Roman women also cinched their bosoms with strips of cloth, or fascia, which were thought to inhibit breast growth. Bodices and corsets, however, dominate the history of dress for centuries. The corset, having been closely associated with aristocratic women of the ancient régime in France, was replaced for a short time by a cloth brassière in the wake of the French Revolution at the end of the eighteenth century. Beginning in the Ming Dynasty, the Chinese popularized the lasting vogue for the *dudou*, or belly cover, which is created from a frontal bodice with fabric ties fastening around the neck and the back.

"Emancipation Garments"

Although earlier precedents exist, the origins of the modern bra date to the second half of the nineteenth century, when a series of American and European patents were taken out for a variety of devises assisting breast adjustment and support. In addition to the "breast supporter," or "bust bodice," there are also early examples of bras intended to enlarge the bosom that were termed "bust improvers." Popular as early as the 1880s, these undergarments contained pockets into which padding could be inserted. The American corsetiere Luman Chapman made the earliest recorded patent for a breast supporter in 1862. Chapman designed the undergarment as an alternative to the corset, which can chafe the breasts since it supports from below. Moreover, health risks, ranging from constrained breathing to rib compression, had become linked to the corset. But the uncorseted female body frequently carried libertine associations that would prove hard to dispel. In its fight against the corset, the Victorian reform dress movement propagated early bras, along with bloomers, as types of "emancipation garments." Olivia Flint, a Boston dressmaker, patented another breast supporter in 1876 that gained broader demand among women mindful of dress reform.

The bra's popular appeal arose as women gained new voices and expanded social roles as they moved out of the home and into the public sphere in the early decades of the twentieth century. The corset would become broken down into multiple components to permit greater freedom of movement. Early advances in bra technology were developed to cope with women's increased participation in athletics by supporting the breasts to prevent painful jiggling, which, moreover, associated the bra with proper bodily hygiene. As women's social migration into the workforce became noticeably forceful during World War I, when the draft depleted male workers, women gained new employment opportunities, requiring undergarments that provided ample comfort, allowed their bodies to move freely, were affordable, and could sustain repeated washings during the workweek. The bra also became more discreet under the suits, blouses, and tailored dresses associated with a professional and stylish appearance required for the workplace. Manufacturers met these new demands by standardizing bra components to cater to diverse customers with varied body types. Cups were introduced with adjustable contours, straps became thinner or disappeared entirely, and resilient fabrics such as rayon and rubber were utilized.

The Female Body and Fashion

As the bra won appeal for its practical applications in women's daily attire, it also figured into the ways in which women came to represent themselves in the public sphere. The bra became a central component facilitating new fashions according to changing cultural and social paradigms. The flapper of the 1920s, with her slender and narrow body associated with a youthful and liberated lifestyle, promoted a flat-chested ideal. Contributing to the trend, bras were developed to strap down and flatten the bosom. Even though a woman's skimpy silhouette remained fashionable through the 1920s, her bounded breasts did not. The cinch of her waist and curve of her bosom again became noticeably popular by the decade's end. During the Great Depression, Hollywood would offer fantastical and affordable reprieves from a failing economy, and the fashions popularized on the silver screen garnered mass appeal. Female viewers emulated the fuller, pointed breast popularized in films with the aid of cone-shaped bras.

The brassiere grew ever more popular into the 1930s, when the abbreviated term "bra" gained wide currency. At this time, the bra became firmly entrenched in the fashion system, with its vast apparatus of specialized manufacturers, retailers, and advertisers. Early bras had been typically custom made to fit individual women and, therefore, had to purchased from a custom dressmaker or sewn at home froom pattern books. In the 1930s, however, manufacturers worked in concert with retailers to increase sales in order to make the item more widely available. At this time, department stores typically sold bras within corset departments. Corset fitters who worked in such departments also began to fit brassieres in the 1930s. Both department stores and representatives of bra manufacturers trained bra fitters. With the increased role of bra fitters in the sale of the undergarment, bra tailoring became an ever-more precise undertaking. Bra bands and shoulder straps became increasingly varied, underwires began to be employed, and new synthetic materials such as nylon and latex provided increased elasticity. While stretchable cups initially adjusted to fit different breast shapes and sizes, the manufacturer S. H. Camp and Company introduced A, B, C, and D cup sizes in 1932. Although the Warner Company soon emulated this sizing method in 1937, only in the 1940s did this system gain wide usage in the United States and Europe.

In the 1940s, World War II hastened material shortages and stunted the manufacture of civilian goods as industrial production was redirected in service of the war effort. Many American bra manufacturers, including Maidenform, turned their energies toward the cause. Garment production was curtailed and clothing became simplified in response to limited materials. Bras, likewise, were made ever more efficient and marketed for women putting on uniforms and taking factory jobs. At the same time, pinup girls and actresses such as Lana Turner popularized the "sweater girl," with her torpedo, or bullet, bra made from a circular stitch creating a pointed cup. Not all bras, however, responded to changing fashions. With the increased diagnosis of breast cancer in the middle of the twentieth century, manufacturers also developed bras for women forced to undergo mastectomy operations. Although by the late 1910s bras had already been developed with prosthetics, in the 1940s and 1950s, the bra industry introduced more "natural" looking breast alternatives for mastectomy patients.

The rise of economic prosperity after World War II required manufacturers to develop a greater variety of bras to meet the market demands of a rapidly expanding consumer culture. Some advances sought to increase women's standards of living. With rising birthrates, for example, maternity and nursing bras were improved with waterproofing and zippered cups to ease breastfeeding. More often, however, bra technologies serviced the rapidly changing trends and fashions that burgeoned in the strong economy. The fashion for voluptuous curves, exemplified by such actresses as Marilyn Monroe and Brigitte Bardot, created a greater demand for foam padding in the 1950s and permanent, removable, or even inflatable pads made a full bosom available to every woman. No longer in shortage after World War II, metal wiring also became widely used to lift and support the bra cup to further accentuate a woman's curves.

Since the 1930s, bra manufacturers marketed lightly structured bras, or training bras, to female preteens and teens. This trend mirrored a broader practice among retailers and manufacturers that targeted these age groups and built a lucrative consumer base around them. The explosion of youth culture in the 1950s only galvanized the social and consumer influence of young women who sought to emulate the fashions and cultural practices of more mature women. At this time, the purchase of the training bra became a right of passage among many young women to prepare them for a future of bra wearing throughout their adult lives.

Bra Politics and Victoria's Secret

By the end of the 1950s, the bra appeared as an accessory required to achieve a new curvaceous ideal. However, in the 1960s and 1970s, feminists challenged popular standards of beauty. They argued that such norms, generated by a patriarchal status quo, reduce women to sex objects. As the bra was increasingly worn to emphasize the bosom, feminists targeted the bra as a major instrument of women's objectification. The widely reported incident of bra burning in protest of the 1968 Miss America pageant in Atlantic City became a benchmark moment in the history of feminism. However, historical accounts suggest that in fact, bras weren't actually burned, but put into the trash can. The feminist rejection of the bra was part of a broader cultural turn that brought about the popularization of the "natural look" among women. Bra manufacturers, intent on maintaining high revenues, began marketing less-structured bras with sheer and nude materials. In the United States, the undergarment industry also began targeting new demographics to maintain sales. Black Americans offered a customer base that had not been previously exploited. The constant prodding of inventive advertising and marketing strategies as well as the implementation of new technologies, colors, and patterns, however, insured the bra's continued popularity among a range of consumer groups.

In the 1970s, bra manufacturing underwent a dramatic reorganization that reflected broader economic currents as well. Earlier in the century, bra manufacturing had been the privy of individual companies. The acquisition of smaller firms by larger corporations dramatically changed bra production. Because bra manufacturing is quite labor intensive, requiring the assembly of a multitude of parts, corporations sought out more cost-effective methods of production. American manufacturing became increasingly outsourced to Third World nations, while Western European bra manufacturing was sent to Eastern Europe. To make bra production evermore efficient, bra making became increasingly mechanized; bra design became computerized in this period, as well.

By the 1980s, the ease with which bras could be manufactured created an increasingly lucrative market that was further propelled by the exploitation of new consumers. The rise in popularity of bodily maintenance through fitness and diet regimes helped promote a new demand for sportswear. The sports bra, made increasingly elastic by the development of synthetic materials such as Lycra, provided an efficient means of breast support for the female athlete. At the same time, this vogue also helped foster the fashion for underwear as outerwear, a style that was popularized by pop star Madonna's famous cone-breasted bustier designed by Jean-Paul Gautier. In the 1990s, lingerie companies such as Frederick's of Hollywood, which had been in business since the 1940s, found increased competition from new contenders such as Victoria's Secret, founded in the early 1970s. The push-up bra, which creates the appearance of a fuller bosom, also fed into increased focus on the eroticized body. The Wonderbra, which was designed in 1964 and purchased by Sara Lee in 1993, became a prominent contender in the bra market. Eroticized bra fashions in the 1990s provided feminists with a new platform for discussions of the female body. Feminists debated whether the scantily clad body merely perpetuated the female stereotype of the sex object or if it empowered women by taking charge of their own sexuality. In these ongoing controversies, the bra remains a major force in the cultural figuration of the female body.

Further Reading: Cook, Daniel Thomas, and Susan B. Kaiser. "Betwixt and be Tween: Age Ambiguity and the Sexualization of the Female Consuming Subject." *Journal of Consumer Culture* 2 (2004): 203–27; Cunnington, C. Willett. *The History of Underclothes.* London: M. Joseph, 1951; Farrell-Beck, Jane and Colleen Gau. *Uplift: The Bra in America.* Philadelphia: University of Pennsylvania Press, 2004; Fontanel, Béatrice. *Support and Seduction: The History of Corsets and Bras.* New York: Harry N. Abrams, 1997; Thesander, Marianne. *The Feminine Ideal.* Reaktion Books: London, 1997; Walsh, John. "Breast Supporting Act: A Century of the Bra." *The Independent* (29 August 2007), http://news.independent.co.uk/uk/this_britain/article2864439.ece (accessed September 2007); Yalom, Marilyn. *A History of the Breast.* New York: Alfred A. Knopf, 1997.

Sean Weiss

Lolo Ferrari's Breasts

Lolo Ferrari (1962–2000), born Eve Valois in Clermont-Ferrand, Puy-de-Dôme, France, was an erotic dancer, porn star, would-be pop diva, and queen of British Channel 4 television show *Eurotrash*. She died in suspicious circumstances. But more particularly, Lolo, whose chosen name is allegedly derived from the French slang word for breasts, holds the world record for the largest silicone-enhanced breasts. While actresses Chelsea Charms, Maxi Mounds, and Minka reportedly have larger surgically enhanced breasts than Ferrari, theirs were achieved through the use of string implants rather than silicone. Along with a large number of surgical procedures to accentuate her cheekbones, remodel her nose, endow her with "bee-stung" lips, enhance her eyes, smooth out and plump up her forehead, and suck fat from her belly, Ferrari underwent repeated operations to increase the size of her breasts. At the final count, Ferrari's (in)famous "airbags" as they are sometimes referred to, measured 130 cm (size 54G).

Lolo Ferrari at the Cannes Film Festival in 1996, four years before her death. © Stephane Cardinale/CORBIS SYGMA.

This latter modification involved the insertion of increasingly bigger silicone prostheses, the largest of which contained just over three liters of saline, are said to have weighed 2.8 kg each, and were designed by an aircraft engineer and expert in plastics.

What is perhaps most interesting about Ferrari's breasts is the many and varied ways in which they have been appropriated by others. In this sense, her breasts could be said to make explicit the feminist claim that in contemporary Western culture, female breasts are constituted as public property: they are scrutinized, objectified, fetishized, commodified, disciplined, and made meaningful in accordance with historically and culturally specific ways of seeing, knowing, and being. For example, in the context of pornography, Ferrari's breasts were no doubt associated with sexual licentiousness, and were probably highly prized (both by Ferrari herself as well as by the producers and consumers of the porn films in which she appeared). For Ferrari, some would argue, the ability of her gigantic breasts to draw the gaze of the viewer may well have furnished her with a sense of sexual power. Some may even claim that Ferrari's drive to excess ruptures the parameters of the normalizing gaze, turning it back on itself, denaturalizing it, exposing it for the disciplinary practice that it is. However, since her untimely death, a number of journalists, social commentators, and feminist theorists have divined from these now-perished but nevertheless spectacular orbs what they regard as the truth of Ferrari's life, her death, and her psyche. For example, *Boggle Box* reporter Colin Murphy described her breasts as "a testament to their owner's dangerous mental instability." Her surgical metamorphosis, he claims, "was actually a long, slow, painful suicide." Alison Boleyn, author of the tellingly entitled article "Lolo Ferrari: Death by Plastic Surgery," determined—not from interviewing her, but rather, from interpreting her body, and in particular her breasts—that Ferrari was "a textbook case of body dysmorphic disorder, a psychological condition in which the sufferer is irrationally convinced [that] their body is disgusting." Australian journalist William Peakin claims that Ferrari's self-image was negatively affected by her mother's self-hatred and her projection of this onto her daughter, whom she allegedly accused of being stupid, ugly, and fit for nothing better than emptying chamber pots. Furthermore, according to Peakin and others, Ferrari's father deprived his children of attention, openly cheated on his wife, and was supposedly guilty of a darker crime against Ferrari, the exact nature of which remains elusive. But for Sheila Jeffreys, who argues that the kind of woman-blaming evident in accounts such as Peakin's veils a large-scale system of exploitation, Ferrari's breasted embodiment serves as a grave example of the sadism and (self)mutilation associated with and effected by patriarchal institutions and practices such as pornography, cosmetic surgery, and heterosexuality.

What one finds in accounts such as those mentioned is an understanding of Ferrari's breasted-body as the textual expression of her inner turmoil, and of the injustices and childhood abuse that caused it. Despite their different political agendas, then, each of these commentators (re)inscribes Ferrari's breasts as evidence of her incompetence, lack of agency and/or intelligence, and impropriety; as all that she was, or ever would be (at least in the phallocentric culture which, according to feminists such as Germaine Greer and Jeffreys, was ultimately responsible for her construction and her demise). Consequently, these accounts and the different stories they tell could be said to function to diminish the complexities of the subject once animated in and through that dead flesh, and thus to be complicit in the objectification, fetishization, and commodification of both Ferrari's breasts, and of (female) breasted embodiment more generally.

Further Reading: Boleyn, Alison. "Lolo Ferrari: Death by Plastic Surgery," *Marie Claire* (Australia), March 2, 2001, p. 261; Jeffreys, Sheila. *Beauty and Misogyny: Harmful Cultural Practices in the West*, London: Routledge, 2005; Millstead, Rachel, and Hannah Frith. "Being Large Breasted: Women Negotiating Embodiment." *Women's Studies International Forum* 26:5 (2003): 455–65; Murphy, Colin. http://www.rte.ie/tv/blizzardold/8boggle.html (accessed April 20, 2002); Sullivan, Nikki. "Incisive Bodies: Lolo, Lyotard and the 'Exorbitant Law of Listening to the Inaudible.'" In Margret Grebowicz, ed. *Gender After Lyotard*. Albany: State University of New York Press, 2007, pp. 47–66.

Nikki Sullivan

Surgical Reduction and Enlargement of Breasts

Although the breast has never been divorced from its connotation as a symbol of femininity, the beautiful or perfect breast has a size and shape that varies according to culture and time period. Since the development of breast surgery, or mammaplasty, the breast has been seen as malleable for female improvement, but styles of surgical body modification are reflective of culturally varying standards and ideals. Breast surgery has largely involved two types of patient: the woman who is looking to restore breast symmetry or appearance following a mastectomy, and the woman who wants to enhance her beauty through elective breast modification. In both cases, cultural ideals of normalcy and beauty are relevant. In terms of aesthetic concerns, both the "too-large" and the "too-small" breast were medicalized, or defined as a medical problem, in the nineteenth and twentieth centuries. Women's psychological well-being has been invoked as one of the primary reasons for the surgical modification of the breast.

The "Too-Large" Breast

As far back as 1669, an English doctor, William Durston, pathologized the drooping breast and treated it as one would treat a tumor, with dramatic surgical removal that left unsightly scars. Even the first approaches of the nineteenth century failed to take aesthetics into consideration; removal, not reduction, became the method for dealing with breasts deemed as "deformities" for their size. It wasn't until the 1880s that surgery to reduce the "overly large breast" incorporated aesthetic sensitivity. Alfred Pousson performed the first modern reduction mammaplasty in 1897. The patient was a young woman whose breasts hung down to her thighs when she was seated. While the procedure alleviated her back pain, the surgery was in fact "aesthetically mediocre." Even so, Pousson's results catalyzed the formation of a new surgical ideal: one that transformed breast reduction surgery into aesthetic surgery. "Happiness," it was said, was linked an unscarred body with an erotic, "natural"-looking breast.

The modified breast that could pass for "natural" was initially defined as one that was overtly unscarred and had a functional (lactating) nipple. This definition, however, overlooked the role of the nipple in the erotic stimulation of a woman's body. German plastic surgeon Jacques Joseph (1865–1934) first proposed a two-stage procedure that would enable the preservation of the areola's vascularization. At this point, a new ideal emerged: a breast reduction surgery that, in addition to improving the aesthetic of the breast and maintaining the breast's maternal function, protected the nipple's ability to be stimulated (that is, its erotic function).

Although the medical preoccupation with breast reduction addresses the back pain sometimes caused by large breasts, it also reflects the turn-of-the-century notion of the ideal breast as smaller and round. As with concurrent surgeries designed to reduce the size of the nose, breast reduction was laden with race politics. "Virginally compact" breasts were considered the ideal and associated with white and Asian women, while large, pendulous breasts were seen as low class, negatively erotic, and associated with black and Jewish women. These associations gave the breast significance as an indicator of race and class in addition to beauty. By the 1930s, pendulous breasts were seen as damaging to self-esteem, and reduction surgery began to be linked to psychological treatment. That surgery could help resolve anxieties of race and class identity fueled its popularity and made the breast a site of both racial indication and racial concealment.

The current surgical trends of women in Brazil are illustrative of a racially driven desire to conform to ideals of whiteness and the upper classes, or even to "pass" as members of these categories. It has been suggested that a woman who wanted to decrease her breast size in Brazil would likely wish to increase the size were she in the United States. While well-off American women might be tempted to increase their breast size, breast reduction surgery has become a common rite of passage for upper-class, Brazilian teenage girls. The Brazilian upper class is interested in drawing a distinction between itself and the lower classes, which are often racialized as more "black." By ensuring that their own or their daughter's breasts are not "too big," upper-class women are maintaining what is considered an important set of social distinctions. In this way, racial and class distinctions are corporealized.

The "Too-Small" Breast

In the United States, the mid-twentieth century saw a transition from concern with the overly large breast to that of the too-small one. The large breast, once racialized and thought primitive, became eroticized and replaced the small breast as the new ideal. Breast augmentation saw its beginnings as early as 1887 when, following attempts at breast reduction, Viennese surgeon Robert Gersuny (1844–1924) became concerned with the postoperative body of the mastectomy patient. Although there was some interest in Gersuny's methods at the time, it wasn't until after World War II that breast enlargement began to replace breast reduction as the primary interest of the aesthetic surgery patient. During the postwar period, when gender boundaries were being reasserted after women's participation in the war effort, femininity found its articulation in larger breasts. As with the "too-large" breast, the "too-small" breast, as well as the sagging breast, were pathologized. The so-called pathology of too-small breasts became known as hypomastia. Historian Sander Gilman writes, "Small breasts come to be seen as infantilizing, and the sagging breast as a sign of the ravages of age. All these signs can be read as 'natural,' in which case any changes are seen as nonmedical, or they can be turned into pathologies of the body, in which case all interventions are medical" (1999, 249).

The "too-small" breast was given over to medicalization partly by linking it to unhappiness. Breast augmentation was now a cure for a psychological problem: self-esteem. Psychological theories about self-esteem, including Austrian psychologist Alfred Adler's (1870–1937) notion of the inferiority complex, were marshaled to support the new field of cosmetic surgery. Psychological interpretations of cosmetic surgery justified the practices, assuaging the social and medical discomfort with vanity and asserting the procedure's necessity. In his cultural history of aesthetic surgery, Gilman emphasizes that the surgeon had a lot to gain from the pathologization of aesthetic concerns. "Vanity demeans the surgeon, who is put in the place of the cosmetologist. With an emphasis on the alteration of the psyche, a new medical rationale is provided for precisely these procedures" (1999, 249).

To trace the history of the medical breast is to begin to understand how women learned to think of their bodies as sites on which to build their happiness, or rather, to think that happiness was attainable through the "perfect" body. In the ideology of cosmetic surgery, happiness became entangled with beauty and became corporeal.

Feminist Critique

Cosmetic surgery has aroused a tremendous stir from feminists, and the list of grievances against breast surgery is long. Their critiques represent the diversity of feminist thinking and consist of several, sometimes opposing, viewpoints. Some feminists have focused on the medicalization of the breast and criticized the pathologization of women's bodies based on beauty ideals. From this perspective, when beauty is defined as a medical issue, and breast implants are promoted as medical treatment, the line between "desire" and "need" becomes blurred. Feminist critics have pointed to the subjectivity of definitions of beauty, linking them to gendered and racialized prejudices, and have raised concerns about safety and risk. They have been especially critical of plastic surgeons' opinions about and FDA approval of silicone breast implant materials. They have also pointed to the highly gendered nature of the cosmetic surgery industry, wherein predominantly male doctors target primarily women as patients. Although the cosmetic surgery industry has claimed that breast implants contribute to female agency and empowerment, some feminists, like Sheila Jeffreys, view cosmetic surgery as a form of violence against women, and women's desires to undergo cosmetic surgery as self-mutilative. For Jeffreys, cosmetic surgery is never a freely made choice. Rather, beauty is a "most important aspect of women's oppression" (2005, 2), and the decision to have a surgery like breast augmentation is a forced one, made under the pressures of misogynistic attitudes.

However, there has been great disagreement among feminists over the question of women's agency and choice in regard to beauty practices such as breast augmentation surgery. Some, like medical sociologist Kathy Davis, have insisted that the decision to undergo cosmetic surgery is a rationally made choice. While Davis acknowledges that beauty ideals can be oppressive to women, she argues in her book *Reshaping the Female Body* that women who choose cosmetic surgery are able to empower themselves by taking an active part in negotiating how their bodies look and are perceived. Cosmetic surgery "can be a way, if a problematic one, for women to take their lives in hand" (1995, 12).

Some of the most rigorous feminist critiques have addressed the breast implant controversy through the framework of commodification. The commodification of the body conflates ideas of self-improvement with the virtues of consumerism; this has, in turn, raised the bar with regard to what women will do, or perhaps even feel they must do, to be beautiful and successful. Beauty has become "technologized," and women who reject high-tech procedures such as surgery can be "double-pathologized." While the consumerization and commodification of the body are now ubiquitous, the controversy over the risk of silicone implants has made women feel vulnerable with regard to their roles as informed consumers. The silicone implant controversy has raised important questions regarding scientific, medical, and governmental regulation and authority over people's bodies and their access to knowledge; likewise, it has catalyzed an interrogation of what is meant by informed consent.

The Silicone Controversy

Silicone implants, developed in 1963, became the most widely used and controversial breast implant material. Breast implant patients experienced a number of short- and long-term complications, including discomfort, skin tightness, hematoma and infection, silicone bleed, autoimmune disease, polyurethane toxicity, and implant rupture and leakage. In fact, these complications became such a significant concern that in 1992, the FDA banned silicone gel implants, limiting their use to controlled studies. In 1999, however, the Institute of Medicine released its report on the safety of silicone, resulting in an eventual lift of the ban. The study concluded that silicone did not provide a basis for health concerns, that silicone breast implants did not leak into breast milk, and that there was no relationship between silicone implants and breast cancer.

The breast implant controversy of the 1990s laid the groundwork for the largest product-liability settlement in U.S. history and fueled a complicated public debate. As the controversy took over the headlines, it became clear that all sides were divided. There were women with cosmetic implants who proclaimed that implants afforded them physical, emotional, and sociocultural benefits, and those who decried the coercion that influenced their participation in dangerous body-modification practices. There were postmastectomy cancer patients who felt strongly about reclaiming their femininity through reconstructive breast surgery, and those who felt insulted that they should be expected to put themselves (and specifically their breasts) at risk again following cancer. There were claims that surgeons were colluding with implant manufacturers to suppress important information regarding risks, and there were claims that cosmetic medicine was co-opting feminist rhetoric and conflating issues of women's health with issues of choice and physical autonomy.

One side of the debate worried that the FDA would limit women's ability to make their own choices about their bodies. Others argued that the FDA had been negligent with regard to addressing the dangers of breast implant surgery. Between the large corporations who manufactured breast implants and doctors who had the chance to profit greatly from them, there was a sense that information about their safety had been omitted or manipulated to be ambiguous. *New York Times* columnist Anna Quindlen noted at the time that, "breast implants had been held to a negative standard—'not unsafe'—rather than to the affirmative standard that women deserved ... Even those who opposed regulation acknowledged that the FDA had been guilty of inconsistency: it had not cared sufficiently about the health of American women to require that breast implants be routed through the testing and approval system it had set up to oversee the health-care industry. To many commentators, the traditional belief that female vanity deserves what it gets seemed to explain why it was this particular case the FDA had chosen to ignore" (Haiken, 230).

Critics of breast augmentation surgery have asserted for decades that it can cause illness. However, for a patient population that invests so much hope in breast surgery, unsuccessful procedures can be devastating. When breast surgery causes unhappiness, it is a particularly striking reversal of the psychological benefits its proponents trumpet. Women made ill by breast implants who spoke out during the silicone implant controversy helped transform public opinion about the practice. "The somatic experiences of a minority or patients who spoke out in public fractured the uniform assumptions of health and happiness held by women with breast implants. They could no longer 'pass' as erotic, and the antithesis of the erotic is the ill" (Gilman, 248).

The controversy brought feminist concerns about breast implant surgery to the fore. However, during the 1990s, women continued to get breast implants made of saline rather than silicone, and by 2005, close to 358,000 women in the United States were undergoing breast surgery annually. In 2005, silicone breast implants were reintroduced to the market.

Breast Cancer and Breast Reconstruction

The ban on silicone contained a caveat that caused great controversy: while aesthetic improvement could no longer justify surgery, the use of silicone implants in post-mastectomy reconstruction was still allowed. A line had been drawn between breast reconstruction and breast augmentation, with the former being seen as more justifiable than "vanity-based" augmentation. To the FDA, it was worthwhile risking long-term health dangers from silicone gel implants only if the patient had been deformed by cancer surgery. As Gilman put it, "Only a greater good could permit such a procedure" (1999, 243).

However, not all breast cancer survivors embraced breast reconstruction, and some women with breast cancer rebelled against its automatic use for post-mastectomy recovery. Some breast cancer survivors thought of their scars as prideful emblems of their survival. The poet Audre Lorde, for example, who had a mastectomy in 1979, refused reconstruction as well as a prosthesis, arguing that the visibility of breast cancer survivors is important to combat the stigma of the disease. In 1993, the fashion model Matuschka famously displayed the results of her mastectomy on the cover of the *New York Times Magazine*. She stated how she was thought the procedure, including removal of twenty-four lymph nodes, was unnecessary but was happy to help to publicize the epidemic of breast cancer.

The Psychology of Cosmetic Breast Surgery

Female cosmetic surgery patients have been considered psychologically suspect for decades. Not only did early cosmetic surgeons criticize their own patients' vanity and superficiality, but they proposed that some of them might be psychologically unwell. In the mid-twentieth century, Freudian psychoanalysis influenced psychotherapeutic views of cosmetic surgery patients, and presumed that a patient's desire for cosmetic surgery was a symptom of underlying neurosis. In the 1960s, psychiatric studies linked the majority of cosmetic surgery patients to unhealthy psychiatric diagnoses such as personality disorders.

However, as the popularity of cosmetic surgery has increased and its stigma has decreased, it is perhaps unsurprising that recent studies find a much lower rate of psychopathology among cosmetic surgery patients. In addition, the notion that women can use breast augmentation as a method of psychological treatment for low self-esteem and body-image dissatisfaction is now a standard argument in cosmetic surgery literature. Cosmetic surgeons now point to studies which suggest that cosmetic surgery leads to psychological improvements in at least three areas: body image, quality of life, and depressive symptoms.

However, as breast augmentation surgery is now aggressively marketed directly to prospective patients, there is concern that women's expectations are unrealistic. Further, some psychiatrists have recently suggested that cosmetic surgery patients ought to be screened for body dysmorphic disorder (BDD), defined as a preoccupation with an imagined or slight defect in appearance that leads to significant impairment in functioning. A person with BDD is thought to overuse beauty treatments such as cosmetic surgery and dermatology, and clinical reports have found that they do not typically benefit from them. Some clinicians and researchers propose that those with BDD should not be given cosmetic surgery, but rather cognitive-behavioral psychotherapy and psychiatric treatment. The relationship of BDD to cosmetic surgery is not yet well understood, however, and feminist critics from a diversity of viewpoints have challenged the association between BDD and cosmetic surgery.

The Trans Breast

The cultural obsession with the breast bears heavily on the way that femininity is defined and reflects the tendency to characterize and represent one's sexuality in the language of body parts. Breast surgeries have been part of a set of practices used to transform one's sex, in cases of transsexuality, and to resolve sexual ambiguities in cases of hermaphrodism. For some transsexuals and hermaphrodites, the transformations that cosmetic surgery offers are seen as psychological cures, alleviating the suffering caused by feelings of being trapped in the wrong or abnormal body. Critics of such surgeries argue that they pathologize bodily differences and equate biological attributes with gender. As for other breast surgery patients, body modification comes to bear the weight of responsibility for the "happiness" and "unhappiness" of its participants.

Further Reading: The American Society of Plastic Surgeons and the American Society for Aesthetic Plastic Surgery, Inc. "FDA approves return of silicone breast implants." ASPS Special Joint Bulletin, November 17, 2006, http://www.plasticsurgery.org/medical_ ?professionals/publications/loader.cfm?url=/commonspot/security/getfile.cfm&PageID=21590 (accessed September 6, 2007); Blum, Virginia L. *Flesh Wounds: The Culture of Cosmetic Surgery.* Berkley: University of California Press, 2003; Davis, Kathy. *Reshaping the Female Body: The Dilemma of Cosmetic Surgery.* New York: Routledge, 1995; Gilman, Sander L. *Making the Body Beautiful: A Cultural History of Aesthetic Surgery.* Princeton, NJ: Princeton University Press, 1999; Haiken, Elizabeth. *Venus Envy: A History of Cosmetic Surgery.* Baltimore, MD: The Johns Hopkins University Press, 1997; Jeffreys, Sheila. *Beauty and Misogyny: Harmful Cultural Practices in the West.* New York: Routledge, 2005; Morgan, Kathryn Pauly. "Women and the Knife: Cosmetic Surgery and the Colonization of Women's Bodies." In *The Politics of Women's Bodies*, Rose Weitz, ed. Oxford: Oxford University Press, 1998, pp. 147–163; Nash, Joyce D. *What Your Doctor Can't Tell You About Cosmetic Surgery.* Oakland, CA: New Harbinger Publications, 1995; Pitts-Taylor, Victoria. *Surgery Junkies: Wellness and Pathology in Cosmetic Culture.* New Brunswick, NJ: Rutgers University Press, 2007; Sarwer, David B., Jodi E. Nordmann, and James D. Herbert. "Cosmetic Breast Augmentation: A Critical Overview." *Journal of Women's Health and Gender-Based Medicine* Volume 9, Issue 8 (2000): 843–56; Yalom, Marilyn. *A History of the Breast.* New York: Alfred A. Knopf, 1997.

Alana Welch

Buttocks

Cultural History of the Buttocks

The human buttocks are largely composed of muscles used to stabilize the hip and aid in locomotion. In humans, females tend to have buttocks that are more rounded and voluptuous, as the presence of estrogen encourages the body to store fat in the buttocks, hips, and thighs. Evolutionary psychologists posit that rounded buttocks may have evolved to be desirable characteristics because they serve as a visible cue to a woman's youth and fecundity. Due in part to their proximity to the sexual organs, the buttocks have been highly eroticized by varying populations at different points in history. The fetishization and eroticization of the female buttocks was taken to the extreme in colonial contexts, especially in regard to the aesthetic lens through which African bodies were viewed. African women with exaggerated buttocks were, in many ways, thought to be exemplary of the shrewdness, ugliness, and hypersexuality of African bodies. The bodies and buttocks of women of color are, to some degree, still a large part of aesthetics and popular culture today.

Physiology of the Buttocks

Human buttocks are the fleshy prominence created by the gluteal muscles of the upper legs and hips. The gluteal muscles are separated into two halves (commonly known as "cheeks") by the intermediate gluteal cleft. The anus is situated in this cleft. The muscles of the human buttocks primarily serve to stabilize the hip joint, and serve several locomotive functions as well. The largest of the gluteal muscles is the *gluteus maximus*, which is Latin for "largest in the buttock."

The presence of estrogen tends to make the body store more fat, especially in the buttocks, hips, and thighs. The presence of testosterone, on the other hand, discourages fat storage in these areas. Thus the buttocks in human females tend to contain more adipose tissue than the buttocks in males, especially after the onset of puberty, when sex hormones are first produced in large quantities. Evolutionary psychologists and biologists hypothesize that rounded buttocks have evolved as a desirable and

Lithograph of a caricature of an Englishman and an African comparing buttocks from the late eighteenth century. © Historical Picture Archive/CORBIS.

attractive characteristic for women in part because this rounding clearly signaled the presence of estrogen and sufficient fat stores to sustain a pregnancy and lactation. Additionally, the buttocks (as a prominent secondary sex characteristic) are thought to have served as a visible sign or cue to the size and shape of the pelvis, which has an impact on reproductive capability, especially in women.

Humans have been preoccupied with the hips and buttocks as signs of feminine fertility and beauty since early human history. Statues and figurines such as the infamous Venus of Willendorf, which features exaggerated buttocks, hips, and thighs (among other excessive features) and is estimated to have been created as early as 24,000 BCE, seems to reflect this fact. Given that pronounced buttock development in women begins at menarche and that both buttock and breast volume tend to decline slightly with age (especially after menopause), full buttocks and breasts have long been a visible, palpable physical signal of youth and fecundity.

Eroticism and Aesthetics

In Western thought, the buttocks have been considered an erogenous zone for centuries—especially the buttocks of women. This eroticization of women's buttocks, however, is very heteronormative in its leanings. The presumption is that female buttocks are sexy and erogenous because of their proximity to and association with the female reproductive organs. Such a description of the female buttocks was laid forth in *Studies in the Psychology of Sex*, a multivolume work by late nineteenth and early twentieth century British physician and sexual psychologist Havelock Ellis (1859–1939). In this work, Ellis describes the butt as a highly fetishized secondary sexual characteristic, especially among Europeans. According to his analysis, this fetishization occurred in part because of the buttocks' proximity to the genitals and its historic/evolutionary associations with female fecundity.

Perhaps because of its fetishization and association with sexuality, the act of spanking—striking the bare buttocks with an open hand, paddle, or other blunt object—was a quite popular erotic pastime in Victorian Great Britain. Spanking was also a cornerstone of Victorian pornography. Depictions and descriptions of spankings and spanking enthusiasts were eagerly consumed during this era. "Lady Bumtickler's Revels" and "Exhibition of Female Flagellants" are two examples of such popularly consumed spanking-based Victorian erotica.

Spanking and the eroticization of buttocks is not exclusive to the female body. Men's buttocks have been eroticized in various ways throughout history. While women's buttocks are often eroticized in heterosexual erotica, men's buttocks are similarly eroticized in gay male circles. Although not its exclusive focus, much of gay male sexuality centers around anal penetration and intercourse. As such, male buttocks are eroticized in gay sexuality for their proximity to both the genitals and the anus. Interestingly, it is this very proximity to the anus (and its associated excretory functions and products) that makes speaking about or exposing the buttocks dirty or taboo for many.

The taboo associated with the anus certainly extends to anal sex, be it between men or between a man and a woman. Larry Flynt, publisher of the popular and controversial pornographic magazine *Hustler*, has made great use of the taboo around the anus and buttocks in his work. *Hustler*, known for being risqué and edgy in regards to content, regularly emphasizes the closeness of the anus to sex organs and other orifices, and the taboo pleasures of heterosexual anal sex. Although controversial from its outset, *Hustler* corners more than one-third of the male-oriented heterosexual pornographic magazine market.

Taboos and pleasures relating to the anus and buttocks were also of great import to famed psychoanalyst Sigmund Freud (1856–1939). Freud theorized that all successfully socialized human beings had to pass through three stages—the oral, the anal, and the genital. Human infants and children, he argued, related to the world and their surroundings primarily through their relationship with each of these orifices/parts at varying stages. According to Freud's theories, one could not pass to a subsequent stage without successfully navigating the challenges and lessons of earlier stages. As such, one could become "fixed" at either the oral or anal stages, thus evincing stifled development later in life. The descriptive terms "anal retentive" and "anal expulsive" (often abbreviated simply as "anal") stem from this Freudian system of psychoanalysis, indicating problems (such as being uptight and extremely controlling or unpredictable and rebellious, respectively) that stem from the existence of unresolved problems experienced during the anal stage. According to Freud, being "fixed" or "stuck" in the anal stage leads to a lasting focus on and eroticization of the anus rather than on the genitals. For him, this was the root of homosexual behavior.

Regardless of the reasons for doing so, the buttocks have been and continue to be eroticized and fetishized by many the world over. In fact, the pursuit of the perfect bottom has turned itself into quite a lucrative industry. For decades, butt lifts—surgical procedures to tighten, lift, and firm the buttocks—have been popular procedures performed by licensed plastic surgeons. Brazilian aesthetic surgeon Ivo Pitanguy developed one of the first widely used butt lift procedures during the 1970s, elements of which are still broadly used today. Early liposuction procedures—the removal of fat using a suction tube inserted through a tiny incision—were honed largely on butt lift patients who wanted perfectly toned bottoms without scars. And in recent history, butt implants and other augmentations have gained in popularity. Beginning in the late 1990s, American women began to seek, en masse, to enlarge, round, or otherwise surgically accentuate their hindquarters. This trend is credited in part to the Latina pop culture boom that arguably began in the United States with Latina actress/singer Jennifer Lopez. Fat transfer procedures, injections, and use of silicone or saline implants (such as those used with breast augmentation) are all popular options for buttock augmentation procedures. For those who choose not to go under the knife to enlarge their buttocks, a variety of pads that can be inserted into undergarments or stockings—or padded undergarments and stockings themselves—are widely available. Such temporary butt augmentation options tend to be popular among female impersonators and drag queens who wish to temporarily give their male physiques a more feminine touch.

The Buttocks, Race, and the Colonial "Other"

Beginning around the time of European colonial expansion, Western thought was rife with the drive to chart and classify the world, along with all its flora and fauna. As European explorers ventured out to see more and more of the world around them, they continually encountered new people, places, and artifacts. A part of this exploration and discovery included classifying these new discoveries—be they land, plant, or animal—into groups. This is particularly true of the bodies of those indigenous to the lands these colonial explorers encountered. While such peoples were often described according to their cultural customs, styles of governance, and the like, they were most frequently described and classified according to observable physical features. Along with skin color, noses, lips, eyes, and hair, buttocks became one of the features used to distinguish between "normal," "beautiful" European bodies and racial others. Excessive buttocks (just as with other exaggerated fleshy features) were thought to be analogous to an underlying primitive or animal nature, thereby serving as a justification for capture, enslavement, and the forced subjugation of colonialism. Specifically, buttocks that appeared excessive or exaggerated when compared to the European standard were thought to equate to an exaggerated sexuality, something both feared and fancied by Europeans.

Steatopygia

Steatopygia can be simply defined as the "excessive" development of fat on the buttocks and the surrounding area, namely the hips and thighs. More specifically, however, steatopygia was once considered a maladaptive, debilitating medical condition—something one suffered from and that set one apart from the acceptable standard. This term was developed particularly to describe the full-figured buttocks and thighs of African women, and was considered to be an especially prominent genetic characteristic of the Khoi Khoi peoples of southern Africa. Steatopygia was used as a justification for framing the bodies of African women as different from those of Westerners, and making numerous assertions about the ugliness and deviance of African bodies vis-à-vis the normalcy and beauty of European ones. In fact, women who were said to suffer from extreme cases of steatopygia were used to represent the grossness and savagery of the African in the European mind. Perhaps the most glaring example of this phenomenon can be seen in the "Hottentot Venus."

Hottentot Venus

The very moniker of "Hottentot Venus" speaks to the underlying assumptions that were placed upon the bodies of the women who exemplified this term. "Hottentot" is a word that Europeans used to describe a particular tribe of people native to the southernmost part of Africa—namely, those known as the Khoi Khoi. This term came to elicit African savagery and raw sexuality in the minds of many Europeans. Venus, on the other hand, is the Roman goddess of love, sensuality, and all things beautiful and refined. The juxtaposition of these terms, then, elicited the grotesque fascination of Europeans with the supposed shrewdness, crudeness, and raw sexuality inscribed upon the bodies of African women.

Perhaps the most famous person to physically embody the Hottentot Venus is Saartjie Baartman. Saartjie (aka Sara) Baartman was a Khoisan captive of Dutch South African colonists in the early nineteenth century. Official records suggest that, during her captivity, she attracted the attention of a man named Hendrik Cezar, who was fascinated by her large, shelf-like posterior and intrigued as to whether or not she possessed the elongated inner labia (which came to be known as the "Hottentot Apron") supposedly possessed by Khoisan women with steatopygia. Recognizing the market value of an exotic curiosity that had the power to both disgust and intrigue the European mind, Cezar entered her into a contract that would split profits with her if she agreed to be taken on tour and be placed on display. It is important to note that no substantiation of this story exists in her own words. The fairness, legality, and noncoerciveness of this contract are disputed by scholars, as Baartman died penniless, with no assets, only five short years after her 1810 London debut.

A huge hit in both in London and Paris, she frequently was showcased alongside with other people and objects commonly considered freaks and curiosities. Baartman was the object of both fascination and disgust. Her person was the subject of many jokes and satires in both France and Great Britain, including a French play that jokingly urged Frenchmen to refocus their lusts and curiosities from the likes of the Hottentot Venus back to the bodies of white French women, lest the state fall to ruin.

The fascination with the Hottentot Venus did not end with Sara Baartman's death. After she died in late 1815 or early 1816, her body was given to leading French anatomist Georges Cuvier. Her body was immediately dissected. The findings were written up in both "Notes of the Museum d'Histoire Naturelle," and "Histoire Naturelle des mammifères," the latter being a volume on the study of mammals. Baartman was the latter's only human subject. After the dissection, Baartman's genitals—the famed "Hottentot Apron," which she never allowed to be viewed during her lifetime—were stored in formaldehyde and placed on display in the French Musée de l'Homme along with her skeleton, brain, and a plaster cast of her buttocks. These items remained on display until the 1970s, when they were moved to storage. They remained in storage until 2002, when they were ceremoniously returned to her homeland of South Africa after much international pressure.

Racialization and Contemporary Pop Culture

Debating and Reclaiming the Black Booty

Feminists have long criticized the fascination with and sexualization of the bodies of women, including racialized treatments of women's bodies first seen in the colonial era. Contemporary debates now surround the representations of black women's bodies in popular culture. Some feminist thinkers are angered by what they consider the blatant objectification of the bodies and buttocks of women of color in music videos, movies, advertisements, and music. Many anthems are sung to voluptuous bottoms in music genres such as dancehall, hip-hop, and booty bass (supposedly so named because of its explicit lyrics, thematic focus on ample buttocks, and the fact that it was designed for an erotic style of dancing that places emphasis on the female butt). For some, the acceptance and display of full-figured bottoms is a cause célèbre. Among many black women, the visibility and purposeful display of ample backsides is an agentic strategy to reclaim the black body, to challenge dominant conceptions of what is beautiful or acceptable versus what is lewd, and to upend postcolonial notions about black female sexuality. Lauded by some for celebrating bodies and body parts that were once considered subhuman, unmentionable, and ugly, such depictions of the female backside are derided by others for potentially reproducing the same subjugation of female bodies of color evident during colonialism and slavery.

Notable Figures

Given popular culture's infatuation with the buttocks, it would come as no surprise that some people have risen to celebrity or have gained notoriety and acclaim for being in possession of exemplary or desirable buttocks. For example, Janet Jackson, younger sister of pop mega-icon Michael Jackson and a pop diva in her own right, is at least as famous for her body as she is for her voice. Her rear end has been one of her most notable features. Particularly during the days of her *Control* and *Rhythm Nation* albums, Jackson was known for having a rather large bottom—fuller than what was "acceptable" among most mainstream female entertainers at the time. She later confessed that brother Michael had given her a hard time over the size of her buttocks throughout her childhood, taunting her with nicknames such as "fat butt." Although she admits to having had a complex about her body at varying points, she never shied away from dancing or attempted to minimize or deemphasize her buttocks. By the time of her *janet.* album in 1993, the climate had changed such that she was frequently cited for her sex appeal and beautiful body—rear end and all.

Once an everyday girl from the Bronx, Jennifer Lopez has become a household name. Her derrière is partly to thank. Once a "fly girl" on the hit variety show *In Living Color* and a back-up dancer for Janet Jackson, Lopez's buttocks have garnered her perhaps as much attention as her acting, music, and dancing careers combined. Lopez is notable for celebrating—even emphasizing—her voluptuous backside during a time when many American women were trying to shed pounds and otherwise deemphasize their buttocks. Lopez's booty had become such a great media asset that it was even rumored that she had her buttocks insured for upwards of $100 million (some sources have quoted the amount to be $1 billion). The truth behind her butt insurance policy remains unclear.

London Charles (aka Deelishis) has been featured on the popular U.S. reality show *Flavor of Love* on the music channel VH1. Her real claim to fame, however, has been her large backside. Since her debut on *Flavor of Love*, Deelishis has been a favorite for covers and spreads of black men's magazines and urban ad campaigns. Charles touts her butt proudly, openly calling it her "greatest asset." She even released a single about herself (and women with similar physiques) in 2007, aptly called "Rumpshaker." Charles is also spokesperson for a line of jeans specially designed for women with curvier figures.

Ode to the Derrière

Numerous popular songs from various genres are dedicated, in whole or in part, to the sexiness, beauty, and desirability of ample buttocks. One of the first modern songs to be openly dedicated to the buttocks was "Fat Bottomed Girls," by British rock band Queen in 1978. In 1988, the Washington, D.C.-based go-go band E.U. released the hit single "Da Butt," which became a popular club crowd pleaser and was later used in the Spike Lee film *School Daze*. In 1992, the now-classic "Baby Got Back" by rapper Sir Mix-a-Lot was released. Arguably one of the most popular songs sung in celebration of ample backsides, "Baby Got Back" topped the U.S. Billboard charts for five weeks and won Sir Mix-a-Lot a Grammy for Best Rap Solo Performance. In 2001, Houston-based rhythm and blues group Destiny's Child released the song "Bootylicious," in which they celebrate the attractiveness of their own backsides. The song was their fourth number one hit in the United States. Since the early 2000s, songs about the beauty of the female buttocks have proliferated, and references to the backside are featured in innumerable songs—especially in the hip-hop, reggae/dancehall, and R&B genres. Such songs often make use of or even coin new monikers for the female buttocks. Some recent examples include "My Humps" by Black Eyed Peas and "Honky Tonk Badonkadonk" by country music singer Trace Adkins.

Further Reading: AskMen.com. "Janet's Fat Butt," http://www.askmen.com/gossip/janet-jackson/janet-fat-butt.html (accessed December 2007); Barber, Nigel. "The Evolutionary Psychology of Physical Attractiveness: Sexual Selection and Human Morphology." *Ethology and Sociobiology* 16 (1995): 395–424; BBC News. "Lopez: I'm No Billion Dollar Babe," http://news.bbc.co.uk/2/hi/entertainment/554103.stm (accessed December 2007); Bossip. "Deelishis," http://www.bossip.com/categories/deelishis/ (accessed December 2007); Cant, John G. H. "Hypothesis for the Evolution of Human Breasts and Buttocks." *The American Naturalist* 11 (1981): 199–204; Gilman, Sander. *Making the Body Beautiful: A Cultural History of Aesthetic Surgery.* Princeton, NJ: Princeton University Press, 1999; Hobson, Janell. *Venus in the Dark: Blackness and Beauty in Popular Culture.* New York: Routledge, 2005; Kipnis, Laura. "(Male) Desire and (Female) Disgust: Reading Hustler." In Raiford Guins and Omayra Zaragoza Cruz, eds. *Popular Culture: A Reader.* London: Sage Publications, 2005; Midnight Adventure Erotica. "Vintage Erotica and Nude Photos at Midnight Adventure," http://www.midnightadventure.com/vintage-erotica-female-flagellants.html. (accessed December 2007).

Alena J. Singleton

Surgical Reshaping of the Buttocks

The most common surgical procedures performed on the buttocks are buttocks enlargement (through implants, injections, or fat grafting) and "contouring" with liposuction. Buttocks enlargement or augmentation aims to increase the size and alter the shape of the buttocks, whereas liposuction of the buttocks aims to reduce their overall size and change their contour or shape. Buttocks augmentation is marketed primarily to women wishing for larger and rounder buttocks; liposuction of the buttocks targets primarily women who wish to reduce the size of their buttocks.

The implants used for buttocks augmentation (also known as gluteoplasty) are generally made of solid silicone. They may be either round or oval-shaped, smooth or textured. In implant surgery, incisions can be made either at the top of the buttocks on either side, underneath the buttock on each side where the cheeks meet the upper thighs, or a single incision can be made in the center of the buttocks crease along the sacrum. The implant can be inserted either above or below the gluteal muscle. Implant surgery is generally an outpatient procedure that takes approximately one to three hours. The addition of liposuction to the procedure tends to add at least one hour to the total time of the surgery. General anesthesia is most common with this procedure, although some surgeons may perform buttocks implantation with local anesthesia in combination with a sedative. Although this surgery has been the subject of recent media attention in the United States, the American Society of Plastic Surgeons (ASPS) estimates that only around 600 buttocks implant surgeries took place in the United States in 2005. According to a recent ASPS report, 90 percent of these patients were women.

Aside from implants, other methods exist for increasing the size of the buttocks. One of these procedures is called fat grafting or fat transfer, in which fat is removed from other areas of the body such as the abdomen or thighs and injected into the buttocks. During this operation, vacuum liposuction is used to "harvest" fat, which is then carefully inserted into predetermined sites in the buttocks. The procedure takes from one to four hours and may be done on an outpatient basis or may require an overnight hospital stay. Anesthesia may be general, local, or epidural. The fat-grafting procedure requires that the patient have sufficient fat to be removed and inserted into the buttocks. Unlike implant procedures, fat grafting is sometimes repeated, as fat cells tend to die once removed from their original location and may simply be absorbed into the surrounding tissue, reducing the mass of the buttocks. The fat-grafting procedure is sometimes colloquially referred to as a "Brazilian butt lift." Some South American surgeons perform buttocks augmentation by injecting chemical substances, such as a polyacrylamide and water mixture (hydrogel) or collagen, directly into the buttocks. These procedures are considered nonsurgical, and are performed on an outpatient basis under sedation. Such procedures are not well-known in the United States and are promoted as a reason to undertake cosmetic surgery tourism to Venezuela or Brazil.

For patients desiring smaller rather than larger buttocks, liposuction is the most common procedure. The time required for this procedure and whether or not it involves a hospital stay both depend on the extent of the liposuction (the quantity of fat to be removed). Liposuction involves a small incision, into which is inserted a needle and tube (or cannula). Powered by either a vacuum pump or a syringe, the cannula is repeatedly inserted and removed from the tissue in order to break up and remove fat cells.

According to the International Society of Aesthetic and Plastic Surgeons, the first buttocks "lift" (using liposuction) was performed by Brazilian surgeon I. Pitanguy in 1967. The first buttocks augmentation procedure is credited to Mexican surgeon M. González-Ulloa in 1977. This procedure is thus a fairly recent addition to the cosmetic surgery repertoire. Despite the small number of buttocks augmentation surgeries performed in the United States, this figure is apparently growing, reportedly due to a more full-figured ideal of feminine beauty. Some surgeons claim that weightlifters and bodybuilders favor buttocks implants to achieve a more muscular appearance. Liposuction of the buttocks is more popular in the United States than buttocks augmentation. Although statistics specific to buttocks liposuction are not available, liposuction is currently the most popular cosmetic surgery procedure in the United States, according to the ASPS, with 324,000 liposuctions performed in 2005.

In recent years, social scientists and other scholars have drawn attention to divergent ideals of feminine beauty with regard to the buttocks, pointing out different ideals among white, black, and Latina Americans and differences across countries and cultures. It is commonly found that both men and women of color favor larger buttocks in women, whereas the Caucasian ideal of beauty found in media is thinner, with smaller buttocks. Surgeons who perform buttocks augmentation claim that Latina, African American, and Caribbean patients most often request the procedure. Some journalists claim that buttocks augmentation is inspired by the rise of ethnic models of beauty represented by African American and Latina celebrities such as Beyoncé Knowles and Jennifer Lopez.

Large buttocks have historically been part of stereotypical representations of women of color, and especially women of African descent. During European colonialism, African women came to be associated with large buttocks, which were interpreted as an outward sign of primitive and irrepressible sexuality. One extreme example of this colonial portrayal of "other" bodies as exotic, animalistic, and oversexed was the exhibition of a young African woman named Saartjie Baartman. (known as the "Hottentot Venus") in Europe in the early 1800s. Baartman's naked body was displayed as a sideshow attraction in England and France, with particular attention paid to her large buttocks, thought to be typical of her Khoi Khoi people of South Africa. The branding of black women's bodies and sexuality as abnormal and uncontrollable has varied over time, but large buttocks have consistently symbolized this racist stereotype.

Buttocks augmentation is reported to be most popular in South America, especially Brazil. Brazilian ideals of feminine beauty place more importance on the buttocks (or in Brazilian Portuguese slang, the *bunda*) than on the breasts or other parts of the female body. Recent reports of Brazilians, in particular transgendered prostitutes, using industrial-grade silicone injections to increase buttocks size have caused public-health concerns regarding the dangers of underground procedures. The reputations of nations such as Brazil, Colombia, and Venezuela as centers of cosmetic surgery (for both domestic and foreign patients) is growing, and beauty queens from these countries have publicly acknowledged their cosmetic surgery experiences. Their reputation for having high rates of cosmetic surgery and more full-figured ideals of beauty lead to the association of these and other Latin American countries with buttocks augmentation.

Further Reading: Kulick, Don. *Travesti: Sex, Gender, and Culture among Brazilian Transgendered Prostitutes*. Chicago: University of Chicago Press, 1998; Negrón-Muntaner, Frances. "Jennifer's Butt." *Aztlán—A Journal of Chicano Studies* 22 (1997): 181–195.

Erynn Masi de Casanova

Cheeks

Surgical Reshaping of the Cheekbones

The cheekbone is the common name for the zygomatic or malar bone. The cheeks are the soft, fleshy parts of the face that spread from the eyes down to the mouth; their shape and appearance are largely influenced by the position and size of the cheekbones. Cheeks may look high or low, shallow and gaunt, or full and plump. High or prominent cheekbones are often associated with youth and beauty, and many contemporary actors and fashion and beauty models boast high cheekbones. Some biologists suggest that high cheekbones are an indication of both youth and a low testosterone/estrogen ratio, making women with high cheekbones more sexually desirable. However, in Japan studies have shown that high cheekbones are not considered beautiful, so their desirability in the West may be better attributed to cultural than biological tendencies. Faces with prominent cheekbones have a greater variation of light and shade in photographs and on film, which may partly account for their popularity in the entertainment industries.

Cosmetic surgery may be used to augment or diminish cheekbones, or to reduce cheekbone asymmetry. During World War I, plastic surgeons reconstructed the faces of many injured soldiers, including their cheeks and cheekbones, but cheekbone-specific cosmetic surgery is a relatively new procedure. The first published account of a malar implant was by Spanish plastic surgeon Ulrich Hinderer (1924–2007) in 1965, and the first reduction malarplasty was described by Japanese surgeon Takuya Onizuka in 1983.

Augmentation Malarplasty

Cheek implants can be inserted through incisions made just inside or below the eyelids, or most commonly through incisions inside the mouth (the intra-oral method), near the upper lip on the inside of the cheek. Tunnels through the flesh are created and the implants are maneuvered to sit on top of, or just beneath, the cheekbones. They are sometimes secured with tiny titanium screws. Dissolvable sutures are usually used to close the incisions. The intra-oral method carries a significant risk of infection (up to 6 percent) because the mouth contains large amounts of bacteria, so surgeons often prescribe antibiotics after surgery as a precaution. The operation usually requires a general anesthetic and takes one to two hours to complete.

Cheek implants come in many different sizes and shapes. The most common material used is silicone, which can be purchased in solid blocks and then carved into customized shapes. Expanded polytetraflouroethylene (ePTFE) is also popular. This is a nontoxic polymer that, unlike silicone, is porous. It allows tissue to grow into the implant itself, making it more secure, but also more difficult to remove later if complications arise or if the patient chooses to have more surgery. Bone taken from other parts of the body also can be used to augment cheekbones, and bone cement (hydroxyapatite cement) can be used instead of an actual implant.

Augmentation malarplasty is often performed in conjunction with other cosmetic surgeries, especially rhinoplasty, facelifts, and chin augmentations. In these cases, implants can be inserted from other already-open places on the face and extra incisions are not needed. Side effects from augmentation malarplasty are rare, but can include scarring, infection, facial nerve injury, postoperative bleeding, blood clots, and severe swelling. Asymmetry can occur if one implant shifts due to swelling or internal scarring.

Another way to make the cheeks appear higher or fuller is via fat transfer, in which fat is removed from another part of the body and injected into the cheeks. This is a less-permanent result and the effects are often more subtle. A newer cheek augmentation procedure, not yet widespread, can be conducted in conjunction with a facelift (rhytidectomy). Small sections of the patient's own subcutaneous musculoaponeurotic system (SMAS) that are usually discarded during a facelift are instead folded up beneath the skin and used to raise or project the cheekbone.

Cheek implants can give the face a fuller and therefore younger and healthier appearance. Some of the antiviral treatments for HIV-positive patients create a side effect called lipodystrophy, which causes a form of facial wasting. The cheeks often become very gaunt and sunken, giving a skeletal look and making the person identifiable as having HIV. They sometimes seek cheek augmentation, and may choose implants or fat transfers to improve their appearance and reduce the possibility of stigma and discrimination.

Reduction Malarplasty

Reduction malarplasty is often used to "feminize" the face. In Southeast Asia, where a heart-shaped face is considered very beautiful, wide cheekbones are not thought to be attractive, especially in women. In Korea and Japan, prominent zygoma can cause problems because they are sometimes associated with bad luck and negative personal characteristics. This may lead to difficulties in finding a spouse or to discrimination in the workplace.

To reduce the size or projection of the malar or zygomatic bones, an incision is made inside the mouth and a tunnel is created over the bones. The cheekbone is then made smaller by grinding or burring it down or cutting out parts of bone. This operation is performed under general anesthetic and takes about two hours. Cheek reduction can also be performed by working only on the soft tissues. "Buccal fat" is the name for cheek fat, and people with large amounts of this sometimes suffer because they are considered childish. Large cheeks can also give the impression that a person is overweight when they are not. To diminish buccal fat, a small incision is made inside the mouth, near the molars. Tissue layers are separated and the fat is then cut out. The operation can be performed with intravenous sedation or under general anesthetic.

Male-to-female transsexuals sometimes seek reduction malarplasty as part of their facial feminization surgery (FFS). Women's cheekbones are often smaller and more forward-projecting than men's, so cheek reduction procedures can add to the suite of cosmetic surgery procedures used to transform bodies from male to female.

Representation of Cheekbone Cosmetic Surgeries

Like almost all cosmetic surgery procedures, cheek implantation and reduction are advertised and promoted as a means to achieve a more youthful, beautiful, and masculine or feminine appearance. Sometimes low or non-prominent cheekbones are medicalized and described as "underdeveloped," as if they are a medical condition, when in fact they have no effect on a person's health. Many photos of models and actors have had the cheekbones enhanced with makeup or digital airbrushing, which creates unrealistic ideas of how normal cheekbones should look. Celebrities such as Michael Jackson, Farrah Fawcett, and Cher are suspected of having malar augmentation, and the French performance artist Orlan is famous for having cheek implants inserted into her forehead. *See also* Face: Michael Jackson and Face: Orlan.

Meredith Jones

Chest

O-Kee-Pa Suspension

The O-Kee-Pa (or Okipa) was an annual religious ceremony of the Mandan tribe of Native Americans who inhabited the banks of the Missouri River in areas now within the states of North and South Dakota. The four-day ceremony had three principal purposes: first, it was believed necessary to ensure an adequate supply of buffaloes, the tribe's principal food source; second, it was intended to prevent the repeat of a catastrophic global flood which the Mandan believed had befallen the earth in the distant past; and third, it was a coming-of-age ritual of sorts that presented the young men of the tribe with a physical ordeal. The ritual suspended them above the ground from ropes attached to thorns pierced into their chests or backs. It is this practice that is of interest here.

While the Mandan had been encountered by explorers as early as 1738, explorers and traders had described only cursorily their religious rituals. The first detailed study of the O-Kee-Pa's many intricacies was carried out by painter and ethnologist George Catlin (1796–1872) in 1832. It is his account which remains the most authoritative and comprehensive, principally due to the fact that the Mandan population was almost totally decimated by a small-pox outbreak in 1837, rendering further documentation basically impossible. There has been some controversy concerning the veracity of certain parts of Catlin's account, and the few members of the tribe who survived into the twentieth century variously disagreed with some small details. However, independent verification of the rituals themselves does exist, and it is indubitable that the salient features of the ritual narrative he describes are accurate.

Of particular note in Catlin's writings are his vivid descriptions of what he termed the O-Kee-Pa's "torturing scene," called the *pohk-hong* by the Mandan. This ritual was seemingly intended to engender a sense of spiritual communication, to prepare the tribe's adolescents for an arduous future, and to allow the tribe's elders to determine which of their young men were the strongest and most able to lead in the years to come. When the middle of the fourth day of the O-Kee-Pa arrived, several young men, having eschewed food, water, and sleep for the entirety of the ceremony, assembled at the village's medicine lodge. They took up a position in the center of the building and presented their bodies to two masked men, one wielding a knife and the other a handful of sharpened splints. Two incisions were made in the men's

O-kee-pa depicted in the 1970 film *A Man Called Horse*. Courtesy of Cinema Center Films/Photofest. © Cinema Center Films.

shoulders, two on their chests, one above and below each elbow, and one above and below each the knee. The men impassively submitted to the knives without a wince or a flinch. Splints were then pushed into each of the wounds. Buffalo skulls were hung from cords tied to the leg and arm splints, while those in the shoulders or the chest were fastened to rawhide cord attached to the lodge's roof. The young men were then hoisted aloft, their weight supported only by these piercings.

Once suspended, the men were spun around; slowly at first but ever quicker. They would begin to wail, chanting a prayer to their deity the Great Spirit, pleading him to help them endure their ordeal. Eventually, they fainted, and were carried away.

Following the smallpox epidemic, which reduced the Mandan to fewer than 200 people, the practice of the O-Kee-Pa ceased. Nevertheless, the descriptions in Catlin's book, as well as discussions in *National Geographic* of similar flesh-hook practices of certain Hindu sects in India, are influential to contemporary groups who are interested in reviving tribal bodily practices. Notably, a young South Dakota boy named Roland Loomis (1930–) began attempting to recreate certain aspects of the ritual. In secret, Loomis, later to assume the name Fakir Musafar after a twelfth-century Sufi mystic, carried out and documented numerous procedures that aped traditional ethnographic body practices, including the Mandan's O-Kee-Pa suspensions. In 1977, he began to publicly demonstrate these procedures, and quickly gained a public profile. By the middle of the 1980s, a loose movement known as "modern primitivism" had emerged, coalescing around Musafar's ideologies.

Adherents of modern primitivism subscribed to a philosophy that advocated the appropriation for their own ends of body practices they saw as primitive and spiritual. Although modern primitivism as a pure and distinct movement was fairly narrow and short-lived, its effects on the body-modification subculture were profound. The movement in general, and more specifically a number of body performers, body piercers, and others trained directly by Musafar, brought practices such as suspension to a wide audience. Today, there are many collectives of individuals engaging in suspension all over the Western world.

At the same time Musafar was clandestinely hanging from the ceiling of his garage, on the other side of the globe, Australian artist Stelarc also was experimenting with suspensions, although for entirely different reasons. First beginning to suspend himself in 1970, Stelarc's ideology was far removed from that of the modern-primitives movement. Instead of reviving indigenous rituals and seeking to bring the body to its most "primitive" and spiritual state, Stelarc used suspensions to illustrate what he termed the body's "obsolescence." Unlike Musafar, for whom suspensions were a deeply reverential and quasireligious experience, Stelarc's suspensions were purely artistic in intention, and explored the technological possibilities of the human body. He pioneered a number of novel suspension positions, and undoubtedly influenced the wave of suspension groups that have sprung up since the 1990s.

In contemporary body-modification circles, O-Kee-Pa suspension has come to refer to the specific practice of hanging the human body from two hooks pierced into the chest. Suspendees now approach suspension for a myriad of personal reasons beyond the appropriative spiritualism of the modern primitives and the visually theatrical art of Stelarc. While they may suspend from the chest, it is also common to suspend from the back or knees, or to hang with the body suspended horizontally rather than vertically. The specific suspension configuration appropriated from the Mandan is now more commonly called a "two-point vertical chest," and the associated ritual practices are often less pronounced.

Further Reading: Catlin, George. *O-Kee-Pa: A Religious Ceremony and Other Customs of the Mandan*. New Ed. Lincoln: University of Nebraska Press, 1976; Falkner, Allen. Suspension.org, http://www.suspension.org; Musafar, Fakir, and Mark Thompson. *Fakir Musafar: Spirit + Flesh*. Santa Fe, NM: Arena Editions, 2002; Paffrath, James D., ed. *Obsolete Body/Suspensions/Stelarc*. Davis, CA: J. P. Publications, 1984; Powell, J. H. "'Hook-Swinging' in India. A Description of the Ceremony, and an Enquiry into Its Origin and Significance." *Folklore* 25/2 (1914): 147–197.

Matthew Lodder

Pectoral Implants

A cosmetic surgical procedure generally performed on men, pectoral implants involves the insertion of silicone implants into the chest to simulate large or pronounced pectoral muscles. Although this procedure has generated increasing notoriety in the media in recent years, pectoral implantation is characterized by the American Society of Plastic Surgeons (ASPS) as a "fringe" cosmetic surgery procedure that has received more attention than is merited by its small numbers. (According to the ASPS, only 206 such procedures were performed in the United States in 2005.) The desire for pectoral implants among men implies acceptance of a masculine ideal of physical perfection based on large muscles and, more specifically, a broad chest.

Pectoral implant surgery in the United States was pioneered by M. Bircoll in the late 1980s. He is said to have popularized the procedure, using it first for reconstructive surgeries and then for patients requesting implants for cosmetic reasons. Rates of pectoral implants have grown slowly, and the procedure is still not widely used. In fact, breast reduction is more common among men than pectoral implantation, with more than 16,000 procedures in 2005. The ASPS refers to breast reduction as a reconstructive procedure, whereas pectoral implantation is portrayed as an uncommon cosmetic procedure. Despite this distinction and the relatively low numbers of men choosing pectoral implants, journalists and social scientists point to the existence of pectoral implant surgery as a sign that men are increasingly concerned with their physical appearance and more likely to choose surgical intervention.

The pectoral implantation procedure is similar to breast implant surgery (which is performed almost exclusively on women) in that it involves the insertion of silicone implants under the pectoral muscle, a process known as "subpectoral implantation." In pectoral implant surgery, the implants are usually inserted through incisions in the armpits. The surgery takes one to two hours, during which the patient is under general anesthesia. Surgeons may use up to three separate implants in each procedure, mimicking the layered structure of natural pectoral muscles.

In the early 1990s, many of the men undergoing pectoral implantation were involved in the world of male bodybuilding, either as amateurs or professionals. This is not surprising, as the ideal of the male body common in bodybuilding emphasizes well-defined chest muscles. Pectoral implants allow bodybuilders to achieve a larger and more muscular-looking chest than possible through exercise and weight training, potentially giving them an edge in competition. Surgeons report that increasingly, non-bodybuilders are opting for the surgery, including businessmen, actors, and models. No statistics are available on the race or sexual orientation of men opting for pectoral implantation, although some surgeons say that they have many gay clients. Pectoral implants are marketed to men who are dissatisfied with the appearance of their chest, are not candidates for breast reduction, and have not succeeded in achieving the desired look through exercise.

Western cultural ideals of masculinity as being symbolized by a large chest are not new, although perhaps modern media allow these ideals to be disseminated more easily than in the past. Muscular, rippling chests and torsos are clearly visible in much ancient Greek art. This ideal is immortalized in the well-known sculpture of Laocoön and his sons, created possibly as many as 100 years BCE. Muscular chests were only slightly less pronounced in ancient Roman art, and the breastplates of Roman warriors resembled sculpted, prosthetic chests with bulging pectoral muscles.

During the Renaissance and Elizabethan periods in Europe, the male chest became deemphasized in art and fashion, which highlighted opulent dress and stockinged legs. The cultural mores of the time linked masculinity to a cultivated intellect rather than to a chiseled body. With the beginnings of rationalist philosophy in the 1600s, the mind and body were seen as two separate entities, with the activities of the mind being seen as superior to the functions and appearance of the body. European men were encouraged to develop their minds, whereas women were associated with the body. Despite the masculine shunning of fashion and vanity, dress and appearance continued to be important for upper-class and elite men.

Victorian ideals of masculinity touted the importance of athleticism and physical health, yet social norms of modesty tended to keep the male chest covered. There were exceptions to this taboo, such as the well-known male nude sculpture *The Sluggard* by Frederic Lord Leighton. In Leighton's depiction, the male form is long and lean rather than bulky, yet the pectoral muscles are symmetrical and defined. In the early twentieth century, an athletic appearance, including a muscular chest, was popularized by entrepreneur and self-proclaimed fitness expert Charles Atlas (born Angelino Siciliano in Italy in 1892). Atlas shot to fame in 1922 after winning a contest in New York City to find "The World's Most Perfectly Developed Man." He went on to develop and distribute an exercise program designed to help men develop muscle strength. He claimed that his exercise plan had turned him into a muscular man from a "ninety-seven-pound weakling," and that the program could do the same for other "scrawny" men. In photographs, Atlas is generally depicted as shirtless and often flexing his pectoral muscles.

In contemporary portrayals, large and muscular pectorals have also been associated with dominant, even heroic, masculinity. The original television Superman, George Reeves, wore a suit with a generously padded chest and biceps. In more recent films, the chiseled chests of actors playing heroic characters, such as Arnold Schwarzenegger and former wrestling star Dwayne "The Rock" Johnson, have been featured prominently.

In the twenty-first century, the male body is increasingly subjected to public and private scrutiny, and the idealized, muscular male form is ever more visible in popular culture, including movies, television, and advertising. In the early 1980s, American fashion designer Calvin Klein began using nude or semi-nude male models to advertise underwear. Twenty years later, it is not uncommon to see shirtless men in advertisements or in mainstream television and film. Some have argued that this trend toward objectifying the male body, and specifically a toned figure and defined chest, is an outgrowth of gay male culture and gay body aesthetics.

Despite their cultural origins, these ideals have become part of mainstream heterosexual culture, and men of all sexualities report anxieties related to their looks. Some scholars and journalists have linked pectoral implants to body dysmorphic disorder (sometimes referred to as "bigorexia"), an unhealthy obsession among men with becoming larger and/or more muscular. Very little research has been done on this connection, which is often mentioned in media accounts of pectoral implants. Despite the assumptions surrounding men's body image and mental state, the cultural links between large, muscular chests and masculinity are clear.

Further Reading: Bordo, Susan. *The Male Body: A New Look at Men in Public and in Private*. New York: Farrar, Strauss and Giroux, 2000; Luciano, Lynne. *Looking Good: Male Body Image in Modern America*. New York: Hill and Wang, 2002; Moore, Pamela L., ed. *Building Bodies*. New Brunswick, NJ: Rutgers University Press, 1997; Pope, Harrison G., Katharine A. Phillips, and Roberto Olivardia. *The Adonis Complex: The Secret Crisis of Male Body Obsession*. New York: Free Press, 2000.

Erynn Masi de Casanova

Chin

Surgical Reshaping of the Chin

Plastic surgery procedures on the chin that include but are not limited to chin implants are dubbed "mentoplasty," which is derived from the Latin words *mentum*, for chin, and *plassein*, to shape. Chin augmentation is not a popular procedure compared to other cosmetic surgeries. According to the American Society for Aesthetic Plastic Surgery, the average cosmetic surgeon performs just 2.7 chin augmentations per year.

Beauty Ideals of the Chin

The aim of mentoplasty (and most other cosmetic surgeries) is to create a sense of balance, proportion, and symmetry in the face. Historically, a long chin has been associated with strength and power, while a short chin has suggested weakness. The shape of the chin is also significant. A ptotic chin, or "witch's chin," also has negative connotations. Cosmetic surgery of the chin is usually justified as an attempt to avoid these adverse social perceptions.

The size of the chin is perceived relative to that of the nose and forehead. For this reason, most mentoplasties are performed in conjunction with rhinoplasty and cosmetic forehead surgery. "Rhinoplasty" simply means plastic surgery of the nose. The size of the jaw also affects the appearance of the chin. Hence, mentoplasty is usually performed on adult patients whose teeth are fully developed and whose jaws have grown into, or is close to, adult size.

A number of techniques have been developed to express the ideal chin shape and measure a patient's actual chin in relation to the ideal. The relation between the ideal chin and specific facial features conforms to the ratio *phi*, also called the "golden ratio." Phi is an irrational number almost equivalent to 1.618. Phi was named after the classical Greek sculptor Phidias (ca. 490–ca. 430 BCE) whose widely admired sculptures conformed to this ratio. The ancient Greek philosophers Socrates, Plato, and Aristotle also expressed the idea that proportion and harmony were essential to beauty in different ways. During the Renaissance, Leonardo da Vinci applied phi to the human face in an illustration in his text *De Divina Proportione*. Art historians speculate that da Vinci used phi in his portrait the *Mona Lisa*. Today, most cosmetic surgeons use phi as a guide to construct the ideal chin.

Microgenia

"Microgenia" means abnormal smallness of the chin. To diagnose microgenia, the surgeon may drop a plumb line from the nasal spine to the chin projection. If the line does not graze the chin, the patient is likely to be diagnosed with microgenia; surgeons suggest mentoplasty to correct it.

Patient Profiles

Despite the fact that both sexes experience chin "deformities," the American Society of Plastic Surgeons reported that, in 2002, 69 percent of American mentoplasty patients were women and only 31 percent were men. Mentoplasty is also performed on people of Asian descent, in which case the procedure is specified as "Asian mentoplasty." This is a controversial distinction because it raises questions concerning the medicalization of racial features (other than Anglo-European features) and the unequal relations of social power that sustain these practices. The critical race theorist Eugenia Kaw has written about racism and "Asian" plastic surgery. Kaw and other critical race theorists argue that dominant ideals of facial beauty are products of their cultural and historical contexts. They argue that Anglo-European features are not intrinsically or objectively more attractive than, say, Asian or African features, but rather that Anglo-European ideals are privileged in nations where there is a history of Anglo-European colonization. Specifically, Anglo-European ideals of beauty become dominant norms in a number of ways, including through their treatment as medical issues.

Mentoplasty Procedures

Mentoplasty can be divided into two main categories, reduction and augmentation. Chin reduction surgery is performed in one of two ways. The surgeon will either shave down the bone tissue with a surgical saw in a procedure called "osteotomy" or perform what is termed a "sliding genioplasty." The sliding genioplasty technique involves removing a horseshoe-shaped piece of the chin bone and repositioning it. Sliding genioplasty may be used to augment the chin by moving the bone forward, or to reduce it by moving the bone backward. If the patient's chin is too small to accept an implant, or if the "deformity" is more complex, sliding genioplasty is preferred over a chin implant.

Chin implants have a number of advantages over the sliding genioplasty technique. Chin implants are a faster and technically easier procedure, and they do not put the mental and inferior alveolar nerves at risk. The implant procedure is also less expensive. Chin implant surgery can be performed under either local or general anesthesia. The procedure usually takes a little less than an hour. The surgeon makes an incision either inside the mouth along the lower lip or in the skin that lies just beneath the chin. A pocket is created in front of the mandible (lower jawbone). This pocket must not be deep enough to expose the mental and inferior alveolar nerves. Once the surgeon has bleeding under control, the pocket is flushed with a topical antiseptic solution. An implant that has been selected to create the desired size and shape is inserted into the pocket, which is then closed with sutures. Dissolving sutures are used for incisions inside the mouth, and ordinary sutures close the external incision. During healing, the chin is generally taped up to provide support and reduce swelling. Patients are usually given a short course of antibiotics. If the interior incision technique is used, the patient will be given a hydrogen peroxide mouthwash to keep the wound clean.

Historically, a wide variety of material has been used to fashion implants for insertion into the chin and other areas of the face. These include ivory, bovine bone, and a variety of alloplasts. An alloplastic material is an inorganic material, such as polytetrafluoroethylene (PTFE) or silicone, which is designed for insertion into living tissue. Biocompatibility is an important factor in selecting the appropriate material for the implant. An implant must not provoke chronic inflammation or foreign-body reaction from the immune system and must not be a known carcinogen. It must not degrade over time, yet it must be malleable. Today, chin implants are usually made from a silicone polymer (silicone chemically combined with oxygen) that can either be carved during the operation or molded preoperatively. After implantation, a capsule of dense fibrous tissue forms around the silicone, helping to keep the implant in place.

Chin implant surgery is considered a low-risk procedure. However, the same risks apply to chin augmentation as to all surgical procedures. Possible complications specific to chin augmentation include infection, skin changes, bone changes, and displacement of the implant or muscle tissue surrounding the implant. Displacement can result in a particularly poor aesthetic outcome. A further risk is erosion of the mandible. *See also* Face: History of Beauty Ideals of the Face.

Further Reading: Doud Galli, K., Suzanne, and Philip J. Miller. "Chin Implants," http://www.emedicine.com/ent/topic628.htm (accessed March 2007); Grosman, John A. "Facial Alloplastic Implants, Chin," http://www.emedicine.com/plastic/topic56.htm (accessed March 2007); Kaw, Eugenia, "Medicalization of Racial Features: Asian American Women and Cosmetic Surgery." *Medical Anthropology Quarterly* 7 (1993): 74–89.

Gretchen Riordan

Clitoris

Cultural History of the Clitoris

Definitions of the clitoris are constrained by social and political forces. For some Western scholars who have written about female bodies and sexualities, the clitoris is a very elusive, dangerous, and complicated organ. There is no universal or stable definition of the clitoris, and many of the definitions reveal anxieties about women's bodies and sexualities. The clitoris has many competing and contradictory narratives that vary depending upon personal, cultural, political, and historical circumstances. Based on who is defining the clitoris, it can be classified as an inverted and diminutive penis, a small erectile female sex organ, a love button, an unhygienic appendage to be removed, a site of immature female sexual expression, a key piece of evidence of sexual perversion, a vibrant subject of pornographic mediations, or a crucial region of female sexual orgasm.

Many anatomists, psychoanalysts, sexologists, activists, and pornographers have established their professional reputations by claiming expertise about the clitoris. Different male anatomical explorers dispute the "scientific" discovery of clitoris. In 1559, Realdo Colombo wrote of his discovery of the clitoris, "the seat of women's delight;" he called it "so pretty and useful a thing'" in his *De re anatomica.* But anatomists Kasper Bartholin, Gabriel Fallopius, and Ambroise Paré were also making claims to parts of women's bodies and challenged the crediting of Colombo with the clitoris. These male anatomists explored women's bodies as domains to be "discovered," dissected, and named, much like the terrain of the earth. Before the mid-eighteenth century, scientific explanations of men's and women's genitalia were based on a one-sex model whereby women's genital anatomy was an inverted male. The clitoris and uterus were internal or inverted versions of the penis and scrotum, respectively. Women's bodies were understood only through reference and comparison to the male body.

In biomedical textbooks of the 1900s through the 1950s, the clitoris was depicted and described as homologous to the penis, that is, it is formed from the same evolutionary structure, but is also considered inferior to the penis. Many anatomists appear preoccupied with the small size of the clitoris compared with the penis, and indicate this size is evidence of women's sexual inferiority. In 1905, Sigmund Freud, the father of psychoanalysis, published essays that argued for a differentiation of clitoral and vaginal orgasms. Freud argued that as children, the erogenous zone for girls was the clitoris, and through healthy sexual maturation, women become vaginally oriented. In other words, clitoral orgasms were considered immature. Proper socialization to heterosexuality meant that women would experience the "mature" orgasm in their vaginas.

Sexologists of the 1930s and 1940s, notably Havelock Ellis and Robert Latou Dickinson, read female genital physiology as evidence of their sexual experiences. As Heather Miller describes, sexologists like Dickenson often cited an enlarged clitoris as proof of prostitution or lesbianism. "Whether she chose under examination to reveal her 'sins' verbally or not, a woman's genitalia revealed her confession to the sexologist, her confessor. Her sex practices alone or with others, with men or women, in a normal or abnormal manner, thus entered the realm of the scientifically knowable. On the examining table, literally wide open under his scrutiny, Dickinson's subject could not hide her sexual secrets from him" (Miller 2000, 80). In this context, the clitoris can reveal a woman's transgression against patriarchal sexual norms. Beyond sexology, the control of women's sexual expression and so-called "perverted desires" is evident in other academic disciplines as well.

During the 1930s, art criticism of Georgia O'Keeffe's flower paintings, famous for their resemblance to genitalia, generally dismissed her artistic contribution and wrongly attributed her paintings to male genitalia rather than female. As one male critic wrote, "much of her earlier work showed a womanly preoccupation with sex, an uneasy selection of phallic symbols in her flowers, a delight in their nascent qualities" (cited in Mitchell 1978, 682). This interpretation suggests how difficult it might be to see clitoral imagery, as people have been so primed to celebrate phallic totems transhistorically and cross-culturally.

In 1953, Alfred Kinsey published *Sexual Behavior in the Human Female*, which was comprised of 5,940 interviews with women. Kinsey and his colleagues interpreted these data to define the clitoris as the locus of female sexual sensation and orgasm. The extensive research by Kinsey and his associates led him to assert that only a minority of women reach orgasm exclusively through coitus, and that a majority of women required direct stimulation of the clitoris. Building on Kinsey's work, in the 1960s, William Masters and Virginia Johnson, famed for conceiving the four-phase female sexual response cycle, presented data that claimed there was only one kind of orgasm. Their scientific research purported that clitoral stimulation was necessary for women to achieve orgasm. Instead of the psychoanalytically influenced theory of clitoral and vaginal orgasms, Masters and Johnson described that the sexual response cycle usually involved the clitoris. The clitoral shaft increases in size, then the clitoris withdraws from the clitoral hood and shortens in size, and finally afterwards it descends.

Despite this scientific evidence culled from women's own voices, the practice of labeling and describing the function of the clitoris was abandoned in anatomical textbooks from the 1950s through the 1970s.

Importantly, a survey of lay and medical dictionaries found that definitions of the clitoris refer to the male body as a template or norm from which the female body is somehow derived. This definition often implies that the clitoris is inferior to the penis. If one based one's knowledge exclusively on historical anatomical rendering and dictionary definitions, it would be possible to believe that the clitoris is small, purposeless, and subaltern to the penis.

Many groups of feminists began to focus on issues of women's health in late 1960s, rebelling against the medical hegemony that mystified and alienated their own bodily functions. Throughout the 1970s, consciousness-raising groups of women equipped with plastic vaginal speculums, mirrors, and flashlights taught one another how to explore their sexual and reproductive organs. These women fueled the feminist self-help health movement and created fertile ground for feminist reformation of anatomical texts. The feminist self-help health movement enabled women to look at one another's genitals, discuss genital functioning, and observe the wide range of variation in female anatomy.

The self-examinations and group meetings revolutionized existing descriptions and renderings of the clitoris. It has been noted that, "from minor homologue it is transfigured into the *raison d'être* of other organs. Deliberate, self-conscious effort is made to present the clitoris as a 'functioning integrated unit'" (Moore and Clarke 1995, 280). Such effort was buttressed by the Hite Report on Female Sexuality, published in 1976 by the feminist sexologist Shere Hite. The report was based on data from 3,000 anonymous questionnaires distributed to American women between fourteen and seventy-eight years old. Although many questioned the methodological rigor of this study, the project amassed significant and compelling data about the importance of clitoral stimulation for female orgasm.

These feminist insurgencies met great resistance from mainstream anatomical practices. The grassroots movement was threatening to the traditional allopathic biomedical enterprise and treated as dangerous. For example, the Feminist Women's Health Center in Los Angeles was raided by the police; women were arrested for practicing medicine without a license for the crimes of treating yeast infections and retrieving lost tampons. Anatomists throughout the 1980s and 1990s reasserted women's sexual response as linked exclusively to reproduction, not sexual pleasure. Certain anatomical texts of this time seem to purposefully render the clitoris as useless or unnecessary.

Throughout the 2000s, videos, CD-ROMs, and Web-based anatomies have emerged as new modes of viewing genital anatomy. These new ways of accessing images and descriptions of the clitoris do not necessarily change the definition of the clitoris. Notably, feminists still participate in research on women's genital anatomy. For example, Rebecca Chalker, a pioneer of the self-help health movement, has established that the clitoris is made up of eighteen distinct and interrelated structures. Further, biometric analysis of a diverse sample of female genitals has suggested that there is a great range of variation in women's genital dimensions, including clitoral size, labial length, and color. Further, urologists in Australia have provided evidence that the clitoris is continuously misrepresented by medical dissectors and anatomists. Instead of identifying the clitoris as being solely the glans, an accurate rendering of the organ in its totality would mean that the clitoris is larger than most adult penises.

The relationship between genital anatomy and sexuality has led Western women use elective cosmetic surgery on the vaginal labia and the clitoral hood to beautify the genitalia and enhance clitoral sensitivity. However, Western feminists have condemned ritual genital cutting in Africa. While some African feminists have been working to eliminate female circumcision, others have claimed that Westerners see only cultural oppression and the subordination of women in these practices, calling them instances of mutilation, whereas they themselves are not so condemnatory. The management of the clitoris figures prominently in international human rights through debates about female genital cutting (FGC). (The practice is sometimes also referred to as clitoridectomy, or female genital mutilation, FGM.) According to the United Nations, "FGC/FGM refers to all procedures involving partial or total removal of the external female genitalia or other injury to the female genital organs for cultural or other non-medical reasons." According to the Center for Reproductive Rights, it is estimated that 130 million women worldwide have experienced FGC. While generally presented as a practice that is exclusively performed by non-Western cultures, according to Sarah Webber (2003), some women in the United States were circumcised in the nineteenth century to treat masturbation and nymphomania. Understanding the form and function of the clitoris can also assist women to receive treatment for unsatisfactory sexual responses. According to studies reported by the American Medical Association, more than 40 percent of women in the U.S. report experiencing some form of sexual dissatisfaction, ten percent higher than men report. However, historically less attention has been paid to 'female sexual dysfunction' than to male. Hormonal fluctuations and physiology can account for some "female sexual dysfunction." Recent scientific studies have been conducted to understand variations in the clitoris' sensitivity and clitoral erection. Although there are no estimates of its overall prevalence, the condition known as clitoral phimosis affects women's clitoral functioning. This condition refers to the case of an extremely tight hood of skin surrounding the clitoris, or cases in which there is no opening in the skin for the glans of the clitoris to protrude for stimulation. Women who have clitoral phimosis report difficulty in achieving orgasm.

Pornography is another realm from which individuals get information about human genitalia that contributes to the confusion and mystique about the clitoris. In *Men's Health* (2000:54) magazine, an article called "Sex Tricks from Skin Flicks" provides advice for readers from forty X-rated films. For example: "You know her clitoris needs attention, especially as she nears climax. But it's hard to find such a tiny target when both your bodies are moving. Use the flat of your palm to make broad, quick circular motions around the front of her vaginal opening. That way, you're sure to hit the spot." Clearly, some men and women are viewing pornography as instructional aids in their genital and sexual exploration.

Whether it is print, film, or online media, the clitoris, or "clit" as it is referred to almost exclusively in porn, has been depicted with great attention to detail and celebration of diversity of shape, size, and color. That is not to say all renderings of the clitoris are intentionally feminist or particularly instructive. In the 1972 film history *Deep Throat*, directed by Gerard Damiano, the actress Linda Lovelace's clitoris is purported to be nine inches down her throat. The only way for her to experience orgasm is to have her throat stimulated repeatedly with a long, erect penis. Contemporary films also feature the clitoris, such as director Jack Remy's *Pleasure Spot* (1986), plotted around a clitoral transplant, and *Papi Chulo Facesitting* (2005), which presented the main character Luv positioning her clitoris over the nose of Tom. Pornographic series such as *Tales from the Clit*, *Terrors from the Clit*, and *Pussy Fingers* offer a variety of shots of the clitoris as part of female genital anatomy and female sexual expression.

Adorning the clitoris with jewelry is practiced through clitoral piercings. More commonly than the glans, which is not often large enough for a ring, the clitoral hood is pierced with surgical steel, titanium, or other precious metals. Anecdotal reports suggest that there is increased sexual stimulation through clitoral piercings. Additionally, some women report that there is a stigma associated with their genital piercings among medical professionals.

Clearly, mapping, representing, excising, celebrating, and defining the clitoris constitute controversial and even political acts. As a result, the clitoris has many competing and contradictory narratives that vary depending upon personal, cultural, political, and historical circumstances. In contemporary Western and biomedical settings, the clitoris is commonly described as less than two centimeters long and comprised of three parts, the glans, shaft, and hood, with more than 8,000 nerve endings. Still, many sex surveys report that many men and some women cannot identify the clitoris on a woman's body. Based on who is defining the clitoris, it can be classified as an inverted and diminutive penis, a small erectile sex organ of the female, a love button, an unhygienic appendage to be removed, a site of immature female sexual expression, a key piece of evidence of sexual perversion, or a vibrant subject of pornographic mediations. These different definitions of the clitoris depend upon the historical, social, political, and cultural contexts, including who is representing the clitoris, for what purposes, and under what conditions.

Further Reading: Braun, Virginia, and Kitzinger, Celia. "Telling it Straight? Dictionary Definitions of Women's Genitals." *Journal of Sociolinguistics* 5, 2 (2001): 214–233; Chalker, Rebecca. *The Clitoral Truth: The Secret World at Your Fingertips.* New York: Seven Stories Press, 2002; Colombo, Realdo. *De Re Anatomica*, 1559; Federation of Feminist Women's Health Centers. *A New View of the Woman's Body.* New York: Simon and Schuster, 1981; Freud, Sigmund. *Three Essays on the Theory of Sexuality.* Standard Edition. Hogarth Press, London, 1953 (1905): 125–245; Hite, Shere. *The Hite Report: A Nationwide Study on Female Sexuality.* New York: Macmillan, 1976; Kinsey, Alfred, Wardell Pomeroy, Clyde Martin, and Paul Gebhard. *Sexual Behavior in the Human Female.* Philadelphia: W. B. Saunders; Bloomington: Indiana University Press, 1998 (1953); Laqueur, Thomas. *Making Sex: Body and Gender from the Greeks to Freud.* Cambridge, MA: Harvard University Press, 1990; Lloyd, Jillian, Naomi Crouch, Catherine Minto, Lih-Mei Liao, and Sarah Crieghton. "Female Genital Appearance: 'Normality' Unfolds." *British Journal of Obstetrics and Gynaecology* 112, 5 (2005): 643; *Men's Health.* "Sex Tricks from Skin Flicks." 15, 7 (2000): 54; Miller, Heather Lee. "Sexologists

Examine Lesbians and Prostitutes in the United States, 1840–1940." *NWSA Journal* 12, 3 (2000): 67–91; Mitchell, Marilyn Hall. "Sexist Art Criticism: Georgia O'Keeffe, A Case Study." *Signs* 3, 3 (1978): 681–687; Moore, Lisa Jean, and Adele E. Clarke. "Clitoral Conventions and Transgressions: Graphic Representations of Female Genital Anatomy, c. 1900–1991." *Feminist Studies* 21:2 (1995): 255–301; Moore, Lisa Jean, and Adele E. Clarke. "The Traffic in Cyberanatomies: Sex/Gender/Sexualities in Local and Global Formations." *Body and Society* 7:1 (2001): 57–96; Silverstein, Alvin. *Human Anatomy and Physiology.* New York: John Wiley and Sons, 1988; Webber, Sara. "Cutting History, Cutting Culture: Female Circumcision in the United States." *The American Journal of Bioethics* 3, 2 (2003): 65–66.

Lisa Jean Moore

Ear

Cultural History of the Ear

Of all the parts of the human body, the ear is perhaps the one that draws the least amount of attention, unless it looks unusual in some way. The story of the ear is one that needs to be told in reference to the eye. This may seem unfair to the ear, especially when the eye can largely be discussed in detail without mentioning the ear. The fact that both the ear and the eye are regarded as sensory organs is only a small part of this seemingly strange interdependence, which is as much physical as it is cultural and historical. When a person slowly turns her eyeballs sideways, she may sense very slight movements of her ears in the same directions. She will not hear anything more in the process, although she will see what is in front of her at different angles. Whatever makes the eye different from one person to another or from one time to another, it could be seen. Distinguishing features of a person's ear, on the other hand, can only be seen, but not heard.

Physiology

What is referred to as the ear includes the outer portion, the easily visible structure on each side of the head, as well as the middle and inner portions, which are inside the head. The outer ear is also known as pinna, auricle, and concha, and extends into the ear canal. The term "pinna" is derived from the Latin meaning feather, wing, or fin, while "concha," also from the Latin, is a reference to the mollusk-like shape of the ear. In some cultures and languages at least, the ear is named by the visual impressions it creates.

The shell formed by the soft tissue cartilage making up the outer ear is thought to have a role in guiding sound waves into the ear canal and further into the middle ear through the eardrum. Some people cup their palms and push the pinna from behind in order to hear better, albeit at the cost of hearing echoes. This gesture or those like it sometimes convey a request for repetition or increased volume in conversation. However, doing the opposite, or pushing the pinna back toward the head, usually does not make hearing more difficult. It is beyond the ear canal, where the essential mechanism for hearing is located. The middle and inner parts of the ear cannot be seen without the use of special equipment or surgery. In addition, whereas a diseased eye may look different, this is not the case with the ear. It is usually easier to notice a person who has lost sight by looking into their eyes compared to a person who has lost hearing by looking at their ears. Hearing loss becomes much more visible if a person is equipped with an external device such as a hearing aid. Hearing aids are most commonly worn in the ear canal or resting on the back of the pinna, which is also where the arms of eyeglasses are placed. Visible modifications to the ear form an important part of its cultural history.

Ear Modifications

Apart from the hearing aid, there are many kinds of modifications to the ear, most of which are directed at the outer portion. These are made either to be seen or to be invisible. For example, ear piercing is made to be seen, a sharp contrast to the hearing aid, which is often judged in relation to its discreetness. A contemporary urbanite may want to sport a tribal appearance with a large spool-shaped plug embedded in the earlobe. An elderly person may want a completely in-the-canal hearing aid to deal with hearing loss without appearing older than they are. Either way, the normally inconspicuous ear becomes a part of the body to which attention is deliberately drawn or from which focus is intentionally diverted. Further, the modified ear becomes an important part of identity, whether it is ascribed by the self, others, or both. Despite the often subtle and variable nuances surrounding modifications to the ear, there appears to be one common principle: the ear does not seem to mean much until it starts to look different. Conversely, to make the ear appear different is to make meaning, whether the meaning is welcomed or not. In this regard, it is interesting to consider how the latest fashions in headphones have varied so much in size over the last few decades, with earmuff-like models covering all of the pinna regaining popularity after a long phase dedicated to miniaturization. Part of the significance of the use of entertainment and telecommunications accessories lies in how much of the outer ear is visible. When in vogue, a pair of large headphones may attract attention and make sophistication attributable to the wearer. It is less certain what impact a pair of spectacles, which modify the eyes with the rims as well as the ears with the arms, would have from the point of view of the self or the observer. Intriguingly, a hearing aid is almost certain to encourage some to judge the wearer in negative ways, and this tendency increases with its size. Unlike headphones or certain styles of spectacles, large hearing aids have never been popular.

The acceptance of modifications to the ear is not well thought out, nor is the history of many of these modifications. Most accounts of hearing aid rejection are based on the concept of stigma, or the marking of wearer as being unacceptable in terms of functioning or age. Indeed, hearing aids are most commonly discussed in relation to the hearing impaired, while spectacles are not or are no longer linked to the visually impaired. Eyeglasses, in fact, have become a fashion item by a process that has not been well documented. Headphones, whether attached to a phone or a media player by a cord or connected by infrared signal transmission, resemble the now-disused body-worn hearing aids, but rarely stigmatize the wearer. Inspired by these trends and perhaps equating rejection with stigma, designers have attempted to make hearing aids stylish by embedding them in key rings or making them look like media players. These designs, while strictly conceptual as opposed to functional, highlight how much the ear could mean when the outer portion stands to be modified and when the invisible middle and inner portions are somehow damaged. Whether the hearing aid will gain greater acceptance in the same way as eyeglasses remains to be seen.

Otoplasty

Like other parts of the body, ears come in different shapes and sizes. A standard ear is hard to conceive of. Yet, it does make sense to most people to discuss big ears, small ears, strange-looking ears, and less commonly, beautiful ears. Some people are born with ears deemed to be abnormal in shape while others are born with no outer ear or ear canal. Some parents have their children undergo otoplasty or outer ear surgery to correct these abnormalities. Some adults elect to have otoplasty to improve the appearance of their ears based on the elusive "standard." Beyond conventional medical practice, a small number of people reshape their seemingly normal pinnas by surgical means to look distinct, for instance by creating an angle at the usually curved pole or top of the ear. Whatever meanings are generated by these surgical modifications, once again the eye plays a crucial part.

Human-Mouse Ears

The ear itself had also been unwittingly made a body modification. In 1997, surgeons published a scientific report of an experimental tissue-engineering procedure in which cartilage was grown in the shape of the human pinna on the back of specially bred mice. This was done by isolating, culturing, and transplanting a type of cells called chrondrocytes from calf forelimbs. The rationale behind the procedure was to find an alternative source of cartilage suitable for otoplasty apart from the human rib cage, which may prove unsatisfactory given the problems of procuring such cartilage. Media reports of this procedure began circulating with images of a human ear on the back of a mouse, causing an almost instant uproar from watchers of scientific developments. With these media events unfolding around the time of the birth of Dolly the sheep (the first animal to be cloned), confusion arose especially on the Internet, with some mistakenly linking the tissue-engineering procedure to genetic engineering. Panic over the dreaded possibility of human-animal hybrids spread for a period of time. Although the ear in this procedure is not human at all and devoid of the middle and inner portions, reports and reactions regard it as human. This attribution again shows how powerfully suggestive a strange-looking ear can be, even where it appears as part of a non-human body.

Punishment and Adornment

As a visual marker of cultural significance, the modified ear has had a history of at least thousands of years. At one extreme of its presence, the cutting off of the pinna had long been a form of punishment, especially in armed conflicts. A much milder form of disciplinary ear modification could be found in the twisting or pulling of a child's ear by his or her parent, often until it became red from the suddenly increased blood flow to vessels under the skin. Compared to punitive acts, of greater continuity with contemporary forms are different types of ear piercing. The location and style of ear piercing and the material making up ear piercings had been variously linked to social status, entry into adulthood, beauty, and other personal attributes. The variations were often geographically based and tied to membership in ethnic and linguistic groups, often those seen as exotic by a group that regarded itself as dominant. The dominant group tended to celebrate a more impoverished set of ear-piercing practices. Around the age of ten, boys of the Canela, and their neighbors, the Apanyekra in the Amazonian forest in Brazil, had both of their ears pierced. Eventually spools would be embedded in their earlobes. It is reported that to avoid being identified as "primitives," the Canela, but not the Apanyekra, had largely abandoned this practice. Ear-piercing procedures of the past and present may actually be closer to each other than initially apparent. Consider again the contemporary urbanite wanting to look "tribal" by wearing a spool plug embedded in his or her earlobe. Although the "tribal" label may have a limited historical basis, and be stereotypical of tribal peoples in all their diversity, ear piercing now can be just as much a matter of status, membership in a certain group, and fashion as in seemingly distant ethnic and linguistic cultures. Even the avoidance or choice of technologically sophisticated hearing aids can be seen in terms of the management of group membership and relations. Something would be amiss if the significance of the ear piercing of a tribal male at the age of ten is read as a sacred rite of passage while the multiple piercings of an urban teenage girl at the same age is thought of as merely a rebellious fad.

Symbolic Representations of Ears

Among physical modifications, the ear is judged largely by the eye. This principle extends to a limited degree to literary treatments of the ear, wherein it could serve as a metaphor for other parts of the body, such as the vulva, the labia, and the vagina. These metaphors are based on superficial similarities between the folded cartilage of the pinna and the folded fat and flesh forming the labia. The ear canal is similarly compared to the vaginal cavity and, by implication, the birth canal. In mythology, births are known to occur from ears as well as from shells. Recall that *concha*, Latin for a mollusk, is another term for the pinna. The Hindu personage Karma, son of Surya, was born through the ear of his mother Pritha. Venus, the Roman goddess of love, was born in the sea and depicted in a fifteenth-century painting by Italian artist Sandro Botticelli (ca. 1444–1510) as being transported in a shell, which probably shared the same metaphorical relationship to the vulva as the ear. More direct interpretations of the ear can also be found, for example in describing handles placed on the sides of cups and pitchers, or implements such as pile drivers.

Visual metaphors aside, the unmodified ear can also be a metonymic reference to qualities such as attention, empathy, comprehension, and even receptivity and retention. Expressions such as "being all ears," "having someone's ear," "pricking up one's ears," "turning a deaf ear," and "keeping one's ears open" are familiar to English speakers. Moving to the more abstract end of metonyms, in the Hindu epic poem *Mahabharata*, the five sensory organs are individually listed and collectively described as the doors of knowledge and desire. Metonymic meanings of the ear are also associated with ear piercing, for example among both genders of the Masai in Keyna, boys in Oman, and infant girls in Uzbekistan. Across these groups, the common purpose of ear piercing was to ward off harmful spirits from entering the body through the ear. Although the inner ear is also responsible for the sense of balance, there are probably no metonyms referring to this function and related qualities. Visual metaphors, self-evident metonyms, and biology interact to produce meanings attributed to elongated ears, especially earlobes. Over the life span, ears grow longer, and this occurs to a greater extent among men than women. In Asian portraiture and sculpture, it is not uncommon to find venerated figures and elderly subjects depicted with long ears. In China, for example, it is a popular belief that long ears signal longevity. In religious art, the long ears of the Buddha have been associated with ear piercing and wisdom.

There are many other ways by which the physical, cultural, and historical are bound up in story of the ear. Consider the range of emotions that can be aroused by hearing. In social environments where clarity and volume of sounds are emphasized, silence provides much welcome relief. Hearing a loud shout from behind can bring shock, while a spontaneous whisper near the ear may engender intimacy. The emotional impact of music is a combination of these and other aspects of hearing. This wealth of emotion parallels the complexity of the hearing process. Together with the brain, the ear is capable of analyzing, recognizing, and remembering hundreds of thousands of sounds. The ear is highly sensitive to differences in the location, loudness, and pitch of these sounds. Even when these factors are held constant, varying sounds from different sources such as musical instruments can be distinguished with ease and probably pleasure. Rather than being combined in impact, as would be the case when light rays of different colors reach the eye from similar directions, sounds make separable contributions to the sensory experience. Again, whereas objects in the same line of sight will be hidden from view, sounds do not block out each other so easily. In this regard, the ear has been labeled an analytic organ, and the eye a synthetic organ. The analytic prowess of the ear is also a key factor in the well-developed ability of the blind to avoid obstacles while in movement. This is done partly by detecting small changes in air pressure where obstacles are present. Sounds, after all, are the result of variations in air pressure. For the same reason, the deaf enjoy music by tactile perception of vibrations produced by instruments.

There does not appear to be a definitive ending to the story of the ear. In trying to make sense of the rich patterns of responses to sound, be it speech or music, writers have recently referred to "hearing cultures" or "auditory cultures." How these cultures relate to language, identity, place of residence, religion, technology, and lifestyle at different points in time is not well understood. Together with the abundance of meanings associated with the pinna, whether modified or not, there is more to the ear than meets the eye, even more so than first appears.

Further Reading: Adams-Spink, Geoff. "Call for 'Designer' Hearing Aids." http://news.bbc.co.uk/1/hi/technology/4706923.stm; Crocker, William H. *The Canela (Eastern Timbira), I: An Ethnographic Introduction*, Washington, D.C.: Smithsonian Institution Press, 1990; Cutsem, Anne van. *A World of Earrings: Africa, Asia, America from the Ghysels Collection.* Translated by Judith Landry. Edited by Eric Ghysels. 1st ed. Milan: Skira Editore, 2001; Erlmann, Veit, ed. *Hearing Cultures: Essays on Sound, Listening, and Modernity.* Oxford: Berg, 2004; Goldstein, E. Bruce. *Sensation and Perception.* Belmont, CA: Wadsworth, 2001; Hogle, Linda F. "Enhancement Technologies and the Body." *Annual Review of Anthropology* 34 (2005): 695–716; Pitts, Victoria. *In the Flesh: The Cultural Politics of Body Modification.* New York: Palgrave Macmillan, 2003; Sims, Michael. *Adam's Navel: A Natural and Cultural History of the Human Body.* London: Allen Lane, 2003.

Paul Cheung

Ear Cropping and Shaping

While various forms of ear piercing and lobe stretching have been widely practiced across a range of cultures for a large period of human history, the elective cropping or reshaping of the outer ear, or pinna, has no known historical ethnographic precedent. With the rise in the subcultural interest for more extreme, pseudosurgical forms of body modification, however, a number of practitioners began to develop techniques that enabled individuals to electively alter the appearance and shape of their ears.

Once piercings, brandings, scarification, and other minor modification procedures emerged from California's gay community in the late 1980s and early 1990s, individuals around the world began to increase the audacity of the modifications they were attempting, so much so that by the late 1990s they had became fairly invasive—see, for example, tongue splitting or subdermal implants. Ear-shaping methods are just another step along this same path: a step in complexity and aesthetic effect beyond stretched ear piercings, these techniques remove tissue from the ear or cut and suture the existing tissue to create a variety of novel configurations. Ear shaping of all forms is a relatively narrowly performed procedure, and remains fairly rare even within subcultural circles.

Broadly, subcultural ear shaping may be divided into three types: pointing, cropping, and lobe removal. Of these, the most popular form is ear pointing, which aims to change the shape of the outer ear so that it becomes somewhat elfin or cat-like in appearance. Phoenix-based modification artist Steve Haworth is widely acknowledged to have been the pioneer of this particular modification. The principal method is relatively simple to perform: it involves removing a small triangular notch of tissue from the upper portion of the outer fold of the ear, known as the helix, and then suturing the two sides together, permanently folding the ear into a defined point. The larger the section of removed tissue, the greater the pointing effect. Other methods of achieving a pointed ear appropriate procedural techniques from mainstream plastic surgery and entail a far more painstaking and complex set of procedures: in one method, the practitioner elevates the ear's skin from its cartilage, and, once the cartilage is exposed, trims it into a point with a scalpel or surgical scissors, leaving the helix intact. The skin of the ear is then sewn up, and the resulting scar lies behind the outer ear. This method is much trickier to perform than the previously described one and is inherently more prone to complications; thus, it is rarely used.

Pointing procedures are sometimes paired with total removal of the lobe, as this accentuates the newly created shape. Furthermore, following the body-modification subculture's appropriation of the stretching of earlobe piercings, there has also been an inevitable rise in the use of pseudosurgical procedures to remove the stretched lobe tissue if the wearer subsequently wishes to return his or her ears to a more natural-looking appearance. The lobe tissue that previously formed the opening of the stretched piercing is removed with a scalpel and sutured to facilitate healing. This procedure can render the existence of any previous stretching virtually invisible.

Aside from pointing, body-modification artists have found that it is also possible to cut the outer ear into any desired shape and suture or cauterize the resulting wound. Sections have been removed from the ear fold or main upper section of cartilage to change the shape of the ear itself, and shaped holes have been cut within the ear to a number of aesthetic ends. Nevertheless, although it is possible, for example, to cut away a section of the ear so that it looks as if it has been bitten, as some body-modification artists have discovered, the structural anatomy of the outer ear somewhat limits these types of procedures, and it is apparently difficult to preserve defined shapes due to the way in which the ear heals around excised cartilage.

While the healing and aftercare in all these procedures is relatively straightforward compared to many body modifications, ear reshaping is not to be undertaken lightly. The procedures are difficult if not impossible to reverse, and if an infection arises, the complications can be fairly severe due to the anatomical specificities of ear cartilage. If left untreated, an infection can result in permanent disfigurement of the elastic cartilage tissue and cause what body piercers have come to term "ear collapse"—the death of the cartilage tissue.

It should be noted that the legality of ear-cropping procedures in many jurisdictions is uncertain. Most, if not all, of these procedures are carried out by body-modification practitioners beyond the aegis of the medical community, and as such could possibly be seen to breach laws preventing the practicing of medicine without a license. While no one has, to date, been prosecuted for performing modifications of this particular type, several individuals have been successfully charged, fined, and imprisoned for performing other types of heavy modification; the fact remains that should the authorities wish to bring a prosecution, a case could probably be made. As such, as these types of procedures have become more widespread, a certain degree of controversy has arisen within the body-modification community itself as to whether to condone those willing to use self-taught, pseudosurgical techniques on paying clients. Nevertheless, while doctors and surgeons remain reticent to perform procedures they deem aesthetically deviant and ethically problematic, subcultural practitioners are currently the only feasible source should one want to change one's body in this way.

Further Reading: Favazza, Armando. *Bodies Under Siege: Self-Mutilation and Body Modification in Culture and Psychiatry.* Baltimore, MD: Johns Hopkins University Press, 1992; Larrat, Shannon. Body Modification E-Zine. http://www.bmezine.com; Larrat, Shannon. *ModCon: The Secret World of Extreme Body Modification.* Toronto: BMEBooks, 2002.

Matthew Lodder

Ear Piercing

Piercing the ears and wearing earrings are cross-cultural practices that have continued from prehistoric times to the present. Much of the existing information about prehistoric and ancient ear-piercing practices comes from a small number of mummified corpses, from burial sites, and from sculptures, reliefs, and other artist renderings. In recent times, anthropological studies have disclosed the ear-piercing practices of traditional societies. Contemporary body-modification enthusiasts have recently contributed to the rise in interest in ear piercing, including its tribal history and its possibilities for contemporary adornment and aesthetic experimentation.

There are various purposes behind ear piercing, ranging from rites of passage to beautification. Meaning and purpose often vary, depending on both the cultural context and culture and the gender of the individual pierced. In many cultures, both males and females practice ear piercing. Ear piercing takes many forms, as there are several parts of the ear that may be pierced, but earlobe piercing is the most common. It is also common for ear piercings to be stretched to accommodate larger ornamentations.

Ancient, Indigenous, and Tribal Ear Piercing

Some of the most ancient earrings are from prehistoric China. In both northeast and southwest China, earrings and pendants have been found and attributed to the Hongshan and Majabang cultures dating back to 5000 BCE. In the oldest sites, there were jade earrings, while a late-period Hongshan site contained a single copper earring with a raw jade pendant. With some evidence of crucibles, or containers used for melting materials, it is possible that the late-period Hongshan were manufacturing copper and other metal earrings. The Dawenkou made earrings of jade and other types of stone and bone dating to approximately

Ear piercings and earlobe stretching on a Tanzanian man. Courtesy of Corbis.

4250 BCE. Trumpet-shaped earrings made of metal were found in graves of the early Xiajidian culture dating to approximately 2200 BCE.

In the islands and mainland areas bordering the South China Sea, two types of stone earrings were popular from 550 BCE to 450 CE: a knobbed earring (*ling-lingo*) and a bicephalous earring (sometimes made of glass) that depicted two deer heads attached at the neck. Similar knobbed earrings have been found in Taiwan, southern China, and Indonesia.

Ear piercing has an ancient history on the Alaskan peninsula and in the Aleutian archipelago as well. Amber and lignite beads used for ear ornamentation and relating to the Aleutian tribes have been found that date to approximately 4000 BCE. Crescent earrings from the Kodiak tradition (2000 BCE to 1250 CE) also have been found.

Ear piercing was practiced in ancient times in the Middle East and across the African continent. Earrings dating to 2500 BCE have been found in the graves of royal women in the Sumerian city of Ur in present-day southern Iraq. They were made of gold in the shapes of single- and double-lobed crescents. Later in this period, with the rise of Assyria, men wore earrings as a symbol of rank. Pear-shaped drops or cone shapes were attached to a heavy ring. Later designs included a cross form and a group of balls.

There is a depiction of Ashurnasirpal II, King of Assyria (884–859 BCE) wearing thick hoop earrings with a large dangling ornament; this depiction is rendered on a section of a bas-relief from a palace in the ancient city of Nimrud, located in present-day northern Iraq. In neighboring modern-day Iran in the Zanjan province, a mummified man was found in a salt quarry in 1994. The Salt Man is thought to date to approximately 300 CE and had a gold earring in his left ear.

Early forms of Nubian jewelry crafted from stone, ivory, bone, and shell include earrings. Although items are scant, evidence of earrings precedes the Neolithic period. During the ancient Kerma period (2500–2050 BCE) in present-day Egypt and Sudan, Nubian gravesites show that the dead were adorned with earrings made of hard stone or wood. From 2050 to 1500 BCE, excavated sites of the Nubian Pan Grave culture include silver and copper earrings for pierced lobes. Designs include twisted forms and spirals. Other materials used various stones and ostrich eggshells.

Earrings were introduced in ancient Egypt during the latter part of the Intermediate period from 1600 to 1500 BCE by the Nubian Pan Grave culture. The Nubian practice of wearing earrings was common among members of both sexes and was readily accepted in Egyptian culture. Leech shapes and open hoops were common during this time. Later styles included stud-mounted ornaments.

Artwork from tomb paintings shows the pharaohs with ear piercings. Later in Egyptian history, the Fayum mummy portraits from Hawara dating from the first to the third centuries CE depict several females with various styles of earrings. In most cases, the portraits are thought to represent Greek colonists living in Egypt. Some early Greeks wore earrings for purposes of fashion as well as protection against evil.

The popularity of earrings is evident in the major cultures of the ancient world. In the middle Minoan period (2000–1600 BCE), gold, silver, and bronze hoop earrings with tapered ends were popular. In the late Minoan and early Mycenaean periods, the hoop evolved with a conical pendant. By the end of the second millennium BCE, the tapered hoop was common throughout the Aegean culture, western Asia, Cyprus, and Syria, as evidenced in several modern excavations.

Earrings became fashionable in Greece in the seventh century BCE due to increased contact with the East. Some earring styles included tapered hoops, crescent-shaped earrings, and spirals. Some of these earrings were elaborately decorated with embossing, filigree, granulation, and inlaid with stones, amber, and glass. Various finials were added that were in the shapes of griffin, ram heads, or pomegranates. By the fourth century BCE, designs became more complex and new styles were used. One such style was the disc-shaped stud earring with three dangling pendants and a boat-shaped design.

The Etruscans and the Romans on the Italian peninsula wore earrings. Some of the earliest Etruscan earrings date back to 625 BCE. Although many of the styles were similar to the Greek designs, the Etruscans created two unique styles of earring. One was the *baule* (Italian for "bag") and the other was a disc-shaped earring. Both were richly decorated.

Earrings had a spotty history in the Roman culture. Early Roman earrings were essentially Etruscan in design. In large part, the early Roman Republic frowned upon personal ornamentation. Not until the period of expansion of the Roman Empire did earrings become fashionable. In the third and fourth centuries CE, Syrian styles, including earrings made of three or four beads, became popular among Romans. Like the Greeks, young Roman males adopted the style of wearing earrings. The famous Roman medical writer Aulus Cornelius Celsus even described reconstructive earlobe surgery in the early first century CE. Yet, earrings would again be frowned upon. Earrings became very popular among Roman males, but Emperor Alexander Severus officially opposed the practice in 222 CE.

Long before the Etruscans, earrings were common in other parts of Europe. Earrings were worn during the Caucasian Bronze Age, which dates back to 3600 BCE. Bronze earrings have also been found in burial sites in Western Europe that date to approximately 1350 BCE.

In the area in and around present-day Kazakhstan, women of the Andronovo tradition wore earrings. Evidence of earrings, along with other personal ornaments, has been found in women's burial sites dating to approximately 2000 BCE. From roughly 800 to 400 BCE, earrings in west-central Europe were worn to express social messages such as age, gender, and status. The Avar people (Hungary and Ukraine, 500–600 CE) wore gold loops from which they hung ornate jewelry. These have been found among the graves of royal males. There are accounts of male and female peasants wearing earrings in northern Europe during the Middle Ages (476–1453 CE), but overall earrings were largely absent in fashion during this time throughout Europe. This in part may be due to hair coverings for women and hairstyles that covered the ears. It is less clear why male earrings fell out of favor.

Earrings regained popularity among men and women (with new ear-exposing hairstyles) in Europe from the 1500s to 1800s CE. It should also be kept in mind that some of the earrings popular during this time were clasp earrings, rather than earrings for pierced ears. Popular styles included pear-shaped ornaments that were usually worn in one ear by males. Throughout Europe, mariners wore gold rings, while soldiers threaded a black silk cord through the lobe. Mariners thought that pierced ears cured and prevented sore eyes.

Earrings were uncommon in colonial American culture. From the 1600s to the 1800s in America, pierced ears were most common among seafaring males. By the late 1800s, however, American newspapers were advertising earrings. These earrings were exclusively for women and were often clasp earrings. However, there were advertisements for earrings for pierced ears as well.

Ear piercing fared much better in Southeast Asia and India throughout the ages, as is evident among several reliefs and sculptures that depict the Hindu pantheon and the Buddha. The famous Indian physician, Sushutra, described a procedure for piercing the earlobes of children around the fifth century BCE. Piercing the ears was thought not only to be aesthetically pleasing, but also to keep evil spirits away. Earlobes were pierced with an awl or a needle. After the piercing, cotton-lint plugs were inserted into the holes.

In many cultures indigenous to North America, males and females frequently wore ear ornaments. Ear ornaments from burial sites dating from 250 BCE to 550 CE have been found in the Ohio River Valley and the present-day southeastern United States. By 1000 CE, people of the Ohio River Valley made earrings from animal teeth, bone, shells (freshwater and marine), and cannel coal. Scraps of metal from European-manufactured copper and brass kettles were also used to make earrings by the early 1700s.

In one account of a southern California tribe, the earlobes of girls were pierced as a rite of passage, which included feasting and singing throughout the night. This was an expensive rite of passage—so expensive that if the girl's piercings closed, they were not pierced a second time. In some tribes, earrings were a symbol of wealth. It cost one horse per piercing for the Omaha of the northeastern United States.

The Chiricahuas pierced the ears of male and female infants around two months old. The ears were pierced using a sharp, heated object, after which a bone sliver or a thorn was inserted into the hole. Later in life, turquoise or white bead earrings were inserted. Both the Chiricahuas and some Paiutes believed that piercing the ears of children made them more obedient. The practice was also related to health, growth, and the afterlife.

Some Native American tribes pierced more than just the earlobe. Many of the Plains Indians depicted by George Catlin in the 1830s, both male and female, wore multiple earrings from the lobe to the helix. Native Americans also used several materials for ear ornamentation, including bird claws, shells, pearls, dried and inflated fish bladders, wood, stones, silver, and gold.

Early European settlers in North America actually manufactured shell earrings for trade with Native Americans. Colonial silversmiths made dangling triangle earrings. Meriwether Lewis and William Clark, on expedition in

1804, brought earrings and nose trinkets with them for trading purposes. By the early twentieth century, however, the wearing of earrings among Native American males was declining. Part of this was due to the U. S. Bureau of Indian Affairs, which prohibited earrings among male youth.

Ear piercing was common in Mexico, Mesoamerica, the Caribbean, and South America. Ear piercing in present-day Mexico dates from 200 BCE to 1500 CE. Ear ornamentation often denoted a specific rank or office among the cultural elite. Some of the materials used were fired clay, obsidian, greenstone, jade, quartz, and onyx.

Ear piercing was common in the late Caribbean period from approximately 950 to 1450 CE. Materials used for ornamentation were metal, shell, and stone. It was recorded in Christopher Columbus' log in 1492 that people indigenous to the Caribbean Islands wore earrings made of gold.

Ear ornaments made from jade and later gold or *tumbaga* (gold-copper alloy) were used by the Chibcha tradition from roughly 1500 BCE to 1500 CE in what is now Honduras and Columbia. Mayan figurines (usually male) depict figures with large earrings in both ears. These date from 200 to 600 CE. In the classic Mayan period, ear ornamentation was made from shell, coral, bone, teeth, claws, jasper, greenstone, and jade.

In present-day Peru, ear ornamentation has been found that dates back to 1050 BCE. Some of the materials used were stone, bone, shell, gold, and silver. Males from the Inca tradition, which inhabited Peru from approximately 1150 to 1500 CE, also practiced ear piercing; among the Inca, the ear ornamentation worn indicated status.

Until the early twentieth century, Kuna (also Cuna) males of Panama wore earrings in pierced lobes. The practice died out due to coercion from the government to don Western modes of dress. The women, however, still pierce their earlobes and wear earrings in keeping with tradition.

The males and females of the Suya tribe in Brazil still pierce their ears in accordance with tradition and rites of passage. They believe that this helps enable better listening skills, which are linked to understanding and knowledge. So strong is this belief that children are not expected to listen until their ears are pierced.

The Ga'anda of Nigeria also pierce the ears of girls as part of a rite of passage. Traditionally, blades of grass were worn daily and were replaced with brass rings for ceremonial occasions. However, by the early 1980s, only imported and manufactured jewelry was used. The Turkana of northwestern Kenya pierce their ears from the helix to the lobe along the ridge of the ear.

Men and women from traditional societies in Australia, New Zealand, and Papua New Guinea practice ear piercing, often in accordance with rites of passage. In Borneo, Kayan boys and girls have their earlobes pierced while they are still infants. Up until the 1970s, all Kayan men also had a hole punched in the conch of the ear, in which they wore the canines of clouded leopards. As this practice was related to headhunting, it has greatly diminished.

The Wogeo of Papua New Guinea pierce the ears of male children around the age of three. The ear-piercing ceremony is usually done with a group of boys. After being allowed to fight each other, the boys are brought into a room and blindfolded. Loud, jarring sounds are made in the background. A sharpened bone is pushed through the lobe and through the top of the ear. Then a twisted cordyline leaf is pushed through the piercing. The boys are told that the *nibek* monsters, or spirits, have bitten them and that although they are gone for now, they will return.

Contemporary and Western Ear Piercing

In the early to mid-twentieth century, ear piercing was uncommon in Western culture. From the late 1800s to the 1950s, earrings for women were often screw-fitting or clasp earrings. Ear piercing was almost nonexistent for males. Women's attitudes about ear piercing changed in the 1950s and 1960s. By the 1970s, it was very common for women to have pierced ears. Ear piercing for men came about much more slowly and with great controversy in terms of gender and sexual norms throughout the 1970s and 1980s.

Males began experimenting with ear piercing from the 1950s to the early 1970s in the beatnik and hippie cultures. In the late 1960s and throughout the 1970s, ear piercing gained in popularity in the gay community, including in gay sadomasochism culture. The combination of female and gay male ear-piercing practices complicated ear piercing for heterosexual men in the 1980s. Depending on the region, a right or left ear piercing in males was thought to indicate sexual preference. Both ears often implied one might be bisexual. This stigma was relatively short lived and largely dissipated in the 1990s. This may be due to the fact that ear piercing became a sign of rebellion. In mainstream culture, ear piercing was rebellious in its relation to male and female punk ear piercing in the late 1970s and early 1980s. This practice of rebellion became widespread among all manner of popular-music bands and stars in the 1980s. Some school and work dress codes in the 1980s prohibited earrings for males. It was also throughout the 1980s that multiple ear piercings in each ear gained popularity, first among females, later for males.

In the late 1980s and throughout the 1990s, the modern-primitive movement and body-modification subculture played a large role in pushing the boundaries of ear piercing among males and females. They also challenged the standard practices of conventional ear piercers. Although ear-piercing guns helped usher in the popularity of ear piercing because they are quick, critics claim that the instrument is difficult to sterilize, that it is dull in comparison to a piercing needle, and may prolong healing. Piercing guns also can shatter the cartilage when used for ear-cartilage piercings.

The preferred method among professional body piercers is the piercing needle, which is hollow with a beveled edge. These are used once and then discarded. Proponents of this method claim that it is gentler on the part of the body being pierced, safer in terms of being likely to be sterile and minimizing trauma to the skin being pierced, and typically more precise in placement when used by a competent piercer.

The Variety of Contemporary Ear Piercings

Earlobe piercing is the most common form of ear piercing. The lobe may be pierced only once or multiple times. Two contemporary and less common forms of earlobe piercing are vertical and transverse earlobe piercings. The former involves piercing the lobe along a vertical axis from the antitragus to the bottom of the lobe. The latter travels sagittally through the earlobe.

Other than piercing the earlobe, piercing the helix is very common in both traditional and contemporary cultures. This piercing passes through the cartilage of the outer ear rim. The inner helix of the upper ear may also be pierced.

The tragus piercing is growing in popularity. The tragus is the projection of skin-covered cartilage in front of the ear canal. A variation on the tragus piercing is the vertical tragus. Using a curved barbell or other jewelry, the tragus is pierced vertically. There is also antitragus piercing, which is done below the tragus and above the earlobe through the cartilage. The conch can be pierced, too. The inner-conch piercing, sometimes referred to as the ear-bowl piercing, passes through the shell of cartilage immediately before and around the ear canal. There is also the outer-conch piercing; this piercing is often done with a dermal punch.

One of the more well-known pioneers of new types of ear piercing is body piercer Erik Dakota. He pioneered three new ear piercings popular among the body-modification community: the industrial piercing, the daith, and the rook. The industrial piercing is usually a single barbell running through two piercings. Often, the two piercings are helix piercings, although there are variations. The daith is a piercing through the cartilage fold of the conch above the external auditory canal. The rook piercing passes through the fold of cartilage between the inner and outer conch.

Another type of piercing related to the industrial is the orbital piercing. This connects two piercings with a single ring. Usually, the two piercings are done separately until fully healed; then a captive bead ring (a circular ball), circular barbell, or a D-ring can be inserted. The UFO piercing, which originated in Australia, is a specific type of orbital that connects the rook to the helix.

Further Reading: Bianchi, Robert Steven. *Daily Life of the Nubians.* Westport, CT: Greenwood Press, 2004; *Body Modification E-zine Encyclopedia.* http://wiki.bmezine. com/index.php (accessed May 3, 2007); Brain, Robert. *Decorated Body.* New York: Harper & Row, 1979; Favazza, Armando R. *Bodies under Siege.* Baltimore, MD: The Johns Hopkins University Press, 1996; Hogbin, Ian. *The Island of Menstruating Men.* London: Chandler, 1970; Mascetti, Daniela, and Amanda Triossi. *Earrings: From Antiquity to the Present.* London: Thames & Hudson, 1990; Peregrine, Peter N., and Melvin Ember, eds. *Encyclopedia of Prehistory.* Vols. 1, 2, 3, 4, and 6. New York: Plenum, 2001, 2002; Rousseau, Jérôme. *Kayan Religion.* Leiden, Netherlands: KITLV Press, 1998; Rubin, Arnold, ed. *Marks of Civilization.* Los Angeles: Museum of Cultural History, UCLA, 1988; Steinbach, Ronald D. *The Fashionable Ear.* New York: Vantage Press, 1995.

Jaime D. Wright

Earlobe Stretching

Earlobe stretching is the practice of piercing the ears and then using progressively larger insertions to stretch the hole in the earlobe gradually. When the piercing reaches a certain point, it begins to elongate the earlobe. Standard piercings range from 20 to 16 gauge (.81 to 1.29 mm). The ear piercing can be stretched to several inches from this point. Much contemporary literature on safety tips for earlobe stretching states that the initial piercing should be fully healed before the stretching begins.

There are methods of stretching the initial ear piercing that do not require starting with a small gauge. These methods involve the use of a larger-gauge needle, a scalpel, or a dermal punch for the initial piercing. Perhaps the most common method of stretching a piercing is to use progressively larger insertions. One contemporary method is to wrap non-adhesive tape, usually PTFE (polytetrafluoroethylene) tape, around an object (for example, a plug) before inserting it into the piercing. This process is repeated until the desired size is reached.

Although heavy pendants and weights can be used to stretch piercings, this approach tends to cause thinning in the tissue, which makes for an uneven-looking stretched earlobe. Other problems such as blowouts and tearing can occur, especially when the earlobe is stretched too rapidly. The most common types of jewelry worn in stretched earlobes are ear flares, ear spools, earplugs, ear disks, ear cylinders, and other forms of thick jewelry.

Indigenous Earlobe Stretching

Much of the information about prehistoric and ancient ear piercing and earlobe-stretching practices comes from artifacts recovered from archeological sites, from Egyptian mummies, and from artwork (for example, figurines, bas-reliefs, and murals). Anthropological studies have also described the practices of traditional societies. In the contemporary West, modern primitives and the body-modification subculture have experimented with traditional and non-Western forms of body modification.

In ancient Egypt, it was during the New Kingdom (1559–1085 BCE) that stretched earlobes became fashionable. Pierced earlobes were stretched using a series of progressively larger insertions. King Tutankhamen's mummy and his famous gold death mask from the fourteenth century BCE have stretched lobes. Other ancient cultures for which there is evidence of stretched ear piercings include the Phoenicians, Etruscans, and Greeks.

Large copper ear spools that date back to 250 BCE have been found in burial sites in the present-day United States. There is evidence from 200 BCE showing that the elite classes wore ear flares in present-day Mexico. Such ornaments often carried specific ranks or offices. Ear spools were manufactured using fired clay, obsidian, greenstone, jade, quartz, onyx, and gold. Sixteenth-century accounts from Spaniards record Aztec emperors with earplugs of green stone set in gold. Dating back to 200 CE, Mayan males wore large ear ornaments made from shell, coral, bone, teeth, claws, jasper, greenstone, and jade.

The Chibcha tradition, which dates from approximately 1500 BCE to 1500 CE in parts of present-day Honduras and Colombia, made ear spools from jade, gold, and gold-copper alloy. The Andes region from present-day Ecuador to northern Chile was occupied from 250 BCE to 650 CE by a civilization that used ear spools to communicate status, occupation, and ethnic origin. Religious and secular images were also inscribed on ear spools.

In what is now Peru, pre-Incan civilizations dating to 1050 BCE wore earplugs made of wood, stone, bone, shell, gold, and silver. Later, in the Incan tradition, elite males wore large, cylindrical earplugs. The Spanish conquistadors referred to the Incan aristocracy who stretched their earlobes as *orejones*, meaning "big ears."

Some traditional societies in Brazil still practice earlobe stretching. The Tchikrin pierce the ears of both males and females a few days after birth. Over time, the ears are stretched with cylindrically shaped ear cylinders of reddened wood. The Kayapo and the Suya also practice earlobe stretching. Suya men and women wear ear disks of wood or palm-leaf spirals. They believe that ear disks facilitate hearing, which is linked with concepts of understanding and knowing. Wearing ear disks is not a mere marker for when one reaches adulthood; the practice is thought to help one become an adult. This belief is so strong that before children get their ears pierced, they are not expected to listen or comprehend.

Earlobe stretching has long been practiced by cultures in India and Southeast Asia as well. One widespread practice of stretching the earlobe involves stretching the skin in ribbon-like sections, sometimes to the shoulder. Sushruta was a famous physician around 400 BCE in India. He described a procedure for piercing and stretching the earlobes of children. Piercing the ears was thought not only to be aesthetically pleasing, but also to keep evil spirits away. Earlobes were pierced with an awl or a needle. After the piercing, cotton-lint plugs were inserted into the holes. Every three days, the lint plugs were removed, the piercing was lubricated with oil, and the hole was stretched with a new and larger cotton-lint plug. After the healing process was completed, the piercing was stretched with rods of wood or reed weights. Sushruta also had a method for repairing lobes that had become overstretched or split.

Cultures in Polynesia, Australia, New Zealand, and Papua New Guinea have practiced earlobe stretching for the centuries. High-ranking individuals in the Marquesas, an archipelago of eastern Polynesia, wore whale-ivory earplugs from 300 to 1775 CE. When Captain James Cook arrived in New Zealand in 1769, he recorded that Maori males wore thick earrings of a tapered design.

Boys and girls in Borneo have their earlobes pierced during infancy. Girls wear heavy rings that stretch out their lobes. Men do not wear earrings as often, and their earrings are lighter so that the lobe does not become as stretched. The women of the Orang Ulu of Borneo stretch their lobes with heavy weights. Their earlobes may hang past their shoulders.

Some traditional societies in present-day Africa stretch their earlobes. The Maasai of Kenya and the United Republic of Tanzania, for example, have stretched earlobes. Some ornaments worn include wooden earplugs, beads wrapped around stretched lobes, strings of beads with pendants, brass or copper rings or U-shaped jewelry with flared ends, and copper or brass weights. There are several styles and combinations of this jewelry; it is not uncommon to see it combined with modern elements such as plastic buttons, large beads, small chains, or trinkets. The practice of stretching the lobes is shared by both males and females. For example, among the Maasai of Matapato (a region in Kenya), the father cuts the lobes of his daughters and his sons once they are old enough to heard cattle—an integral activity tied to Maasai identity. The father will cut the right earlobe during the wet season and then wait until the next wet season to cut the left earlobe. Although this is done to both daughters and sons and usually in the order of birth, the father may use the ritual strategically within the confines of other social norms. A father may opt to perform the earlobe cutting for a daughter when she begins to show signs of puberty, so that from that point on he can avoid physical contact with her, as according to traditional gender norms. When the girls marry, they can wear beaded leather flaps through their stretched lobes to indicate marriage; when they have a circumcised son, they will attach brass spirals to the ends of these leather earflaps.

For Maasai sons, earlobe cutting has an additional layer of meaning as it relates to the central Maasai ritual for males: circumcision. This ritual marks entry into manhood, and the male passes from a boy to a warrior; it is a test of bravery as the initiate should show no signs of pain or discomfort during the circumcision. Sometimes a father might wait to cut his son's earlobes until the boy is older in order to test how he handles pain. Because of the significance of the ritual, sons often plead to have their earlobes cut. Fathers sometimes postpone the earlobe cutting in order to sustain their command over the boys for a longer period of time.

Some traditional societies known as Dorobo who live Kenya and the United Republic of Tanzania also pierce and stretch their lobes. Some of the Dorobo are subtribes of the Maasai or of similar Nilotic ancestry. Men and women of the Surma peoples of Ethiopia also stretch their earlobes and wear large clay ear disks.

Further Reading: *Body Modification E-zine Encyclopedia*, http://wiki.bmezine.com/index.php (accessed May 3, 2007); Brain, Robert. *Decorated Body*. New York: Harper & Row, 1979; Rubin, Arnold, ed. *Marks of Civilization*. Los Angeles: Museum of Cultural History, UCLA, 1988; Spencer, Paul. *The Maasai of Matapato*. New York: Routledge, 2004.

Jaime Wright

Otoplasty

Otoplasty, or ear surgery, is a procedure used to set the ears closer to the head and to reduce the size of ears that appear overly large. Increasingly commonplace since the early twentieth century, otoplasty is frequently employed in children as young as five, in hopes that the operation will allow them to avoid the teasing often brought on by prominent ears. Historically, ear surgery has also been used to eliminate the physical characteristics associated with disparaged ethnic, religious, and immigrant groups such as Jews and the Irish.

Sushruta, a physician who practiced in India circa fifth century BCE, has been credited with early otoplastic techniques. Often regarded as the father of surgery, Sushruta and his students used otoplastic procedures to reconstruct ears that were partially or totally amputated as a punishment for crime. More recently in the West, the Prussian surgeon Johann Dieffenbach (1792–1847) described the first post-traumatic correction of the auricle (or pinna, the protruding part of the ear) in 1845. However, it was not until 1881 that the American physician Edward Talbot Ely (1850–1885) recorded the first cosmetic otoplasty in the medical literature.

While Ely's original technique involved excising a large wedge of skin from behind the ear to reduce its prominence, alternative methods for removing both skin and cartilage were developed throughout the twentieth century. In one of the more common approaches, the surgeon makes a small incision in the back of the ear, thereby exposing the ear cartilage. He or she then reshapes the cartilage and bends it back toward the head. Dissolvable stitches help maintain the new ear shape. A second technique involves making a similar incision in the back of the ear, removing skin and using permanent stitches to fold the cartilage back on itself, thus avoiding the need to excise cartilage. During the early twenty-first century, an incisionless otoplasty was also developed. The procedure enables the surgeon to remodel the ear cartilage and create an antihelical fold (the crease between the ear and head) via microincision, often using an endoscope. Incisionless otoplasty represents an advance over earlier approaches in that it both reduces the risk of scarring and infection and avoids the need for the postoperative compression bandages and retention headbands that are required by incision-based procedures. These techniques are most commonly intended to "correct" two conditions: in the first and most frequent, the antihelical fold is absent or underdeveloped; in the second, the depth of the concha (the dome-shaped part of the outer ear) makes the ear appear to stand away from the head. Whatever their form, protruding ears are usually inherited, with males and females equally affected.

According to the American Society for Aesthetic Plastic Surgery, otoplasty is the only aesthetic operation performed more often on children than adults. In fact, in 2005, 51 percent of otoplasty procedures were carried out on people under age 18, while the figures for those ages 19–34, 35–50, and 51+ were 30.9 percent percent, 13.3 percent, and 4.8 percent, respectively. The prevalence of otoplasty in young people derives from several factors. First, the cartilage in the ears becomes progressively more rigid over time, making it is easier to sculpt in youth. Second, because major ear growth is completed by age five, even children of this age can undergo treatment without the risk that their ears will enlarge significantly in subsequent years. And finally, performing otoplasty earlier in life is thought to reduce the derision and embarrassment often associated with large ears, and therefore to limit social trauma and encourage positive self-image. In fact, one of the earliest surgeons to employ the procedure reported that his young patients suffered constant harassment by classmates, which caused great distress and psychological problems in both the child and the parents. Such effects are well documented in contemporary medical literature as well. For instance, a recent British study of the psychological consequences of prominent ears and subsequent surgery showed that 10 percent of children awaiting otoplasty from the United Kingdom's National Health Service had seen a psychiatrist in the preceding twelve months.

Since the inner ear develops independently from the auricle, individuals with prominent ears generally have normal hearing. Thus, like many of the procedures covered in this encyclopedia, otoplasty is normally performed for aesthetic rather than functional reasons. Yet the importance of aesthetics should not be underestimated, given that they are tightly bound up with broader cultural constructions pertaining to well-being, honesty, intelligence, and morality. These are in turn linked to (or disassociated from) the physical markers of race/ethnicity, age, religion, and nationality, albeit in different ways in various times and places. In the Far East, protruding ears are taken as a sign of good fortune; in the West, they have less positive connotations and, therefore, negative implications for the bearer.

Historically, prominent ears (and especially those characterized by large conchal domes) have been associated with particular ethnic and immigrant groups. For example, anti-Semitic English-language texts published at the turn of the twentieth century refer to Jews, and especially Jewish males, as having fleshy earlobes, large red ears, and prominent ears that stick out. Furthermore, during the same period, Austrians used the term "Moritz ears" to refer to elongated ears and "ill-shapen ears of great size like those of a bat"; Moritz was a common Jewish name of the time. In the American context, caricatures of Irish immigrants represented them as having large, jug-shaped ears not unlike those of Jews. Such physical features represent a visible sign of difference and, in the context of racial, ethnic, and religious inequality, are taken as signs of both bodily weakness and moral failing.

Further Reading: Gilman, Sander. *Making the Body Beautiful: A Cultural History of Cosmetic Surgery.* Princeton, NJ: Princeton University Press, 1999; Lam, Samuel. "Edward Talbot Ely: Father of Aesthetic Otoplasty." *Archives of Facial Plastic Surgery* 6, 1 (2004): 64; Luckett, William. "A New Operation for Prominent Ears Based on the Anatomy of the Deformity." *Surgical Gynecology & Obstetrics* 10 (1910): 635–37. Reprinted in *Plastic and Reconstructive Surgery* 43, 1 (1969): 83–86.

Debra Gimlin

Eyes

Blepharoplasty

Blepharoplasty—or "eyelift"—is a type of functional or aesthetic surgery performed on the eyelids in order to remove or reposition fat and excess skin or muscle. It can be performed on either the upper or lower eyelids, and is designed to make vision clearer and/or to reduce the appearance of drooping, sagging, or puffy eyes. While some who seek blepharoplasty have an excessive amount of skin or fat protruding around their eyes and thus need the operation to enhance their vision, many seek the surgery for either cosmetic reasons associated with aging or to add a "superior palpebral fold" or "pretarsal crease" between the eyelid and eyebrow where it is not naturally occurring. In cases where this fold or crease is sought, the surgery is known alternately as "Asian blepharoplasty," "anchor blepharoplasty," or "double-eyelid surgery." As blepharoplasty is the most common cosmetic surgery procedure in Asia and the most common procedure performed on Asian Americans in the United States, it has been critiqued in recent years as reinforcing hegemonic Western beauty standards. By allowing Asians, particularly young Asian women, to "Westernize" or "Occidentalize" their eyes—which are traditionally considered one of the most obvious markers of Asian ethnic identity—blepharoplasty is considered by some to be a cosmetic surgery practice that is unnecessary and inherently racist.

The Rise of Blepharoplasty

Blepharoplasty is documented in the medical texts of first-century Rome, although its specific purpose during this time is unknown. The modern procedure was developed in the early 1800s by the German surgeon Karl Ferdinand von Gräfe (1787–1840). Von Gräfe, who specialized in reconstructive surgeries such as rhinoplasty and the treatment of wounds, originally used the procedure to repair the eyelids of patients who had been damaged by cancer.

One of the first surgeons to practice surgery on the eyes for purely aesthetic purposes was Charles C. Miller, a surgeon who has alternately been referred to as "the father of cosmetic surgery" and "an unabashed quack."

Between 1907 and 1927, Miller operated on many Americans—specifically women, whom he saw as being more susceptible to the physical symptoms of aging than men—and one of the most common procedures he performed was a rudimentary type of eyelift. In his popular journal *Dr. Charles Conrad Miller's Review of Plastic and Esthetic Surgery*, Miller discussed his operations to correct "crow's feet," or wrinkles around the eyes, and drooping, saggy eyelids, among many other facial cosmetic procedures. He referred to the conditions he "corrected" via surgery as "defects," "deformities," or "featural imperfections." Although his practice was not universally accepted at the time, his penchant for performing surgeries for purely aesthetic reasons, especially those related to aging, was highly prophetic of the acceptance many would eventually feel for cosmetic surgery and, ultimately, of the rise in cosmetic surgery as a legitimate specialty in medicine.

The American Academy of Facial Plastic and Reconstructive Surgery (AAFPRS) estimates that 100,000 men and women in the United States get blepharoplasty ever year. Though blepharoplasty is often sought as a single procedure, patients frequently have other procedures done simultaneously, including browlifts, facelifts, and/or skin resurfacing, in addition to having "their eyes done." According to the AAFPRS, the American Academy of Cosmetic Surgery (AACS), and the American Society of Plastic Surgeons (ASPS), blepharoplasty is designed to exact a younger, fresher, more awake appearance among patients, which should ultimately lead to enhanced self-esteem and self-confidence. These organizations specifically state that although many of those who seek surgery are thirty-five or older, it is not limited to older patients, as some people inherit a tendency for the appearance of these pouches when they are young. The best candidates for this type of surgery are those who are physically and psychologically healthy and stable, and who have realistic expectations regarding the procedure. Some organizations that endorse blepharoplasty explicitly state that it should not be sought as a means to "Westernize" the appearance of Asians. Thus, the surgery is marketed primarily to older Caucasian women (and increasingly to men) and others with excess eye skin, and is not endorsed as a method of changing specific features that are viewed as markers of ethnicity.

Blepharoplasty is generally performed on an outpatient basis under local anesthesia. The average cost for the procedure was about $3,000 in 2005. The operation takes between forty-five minutes and three hours to complete, depending on whether the upper eyelid, lower eyelid, or both eyelids are being surgically altered. If the procedure is being performed only to remove excess fat from the lower eyelids, a slightly different procedure, transconjunctival blepharoplasty, may be performed. In this procedure, the incision is made inside the lower eyelid, leaving no visible scar. Younger patients are better candidates for this version of the surgery, as they have thicker, more elastic skin. The procedure is generally not covered by insurance, unless—as in the case of severe ptosis of the eyelids—it can be demonstrated that it is specifically for vision enhancement and thus for functional, health-related purposes.

In 2005, blepharoplasty was performed by more members of the AACS than any other cosmetic surgery besides liposuction. In the United States, among men, it is the third most popular cosmetic surgery, behind hair transplant/restoration and liposuction; among women, it is the third most popular procedure, behind liposuction and nearly tied with breast augmentation. The majority of both men and women who request and receive blepharoplasty are between the ages of fifty and fifty-nine. The popularity and prevalence of blepharoplasty may be due in part to the quick length of time the surgery takes to complete and the short recovery period involved. Most patients who seek blepharoplasty describe feeling that their droopy or puffy eyelids make them feel that they look "tired" or "sleepy."

Asian Blepharoplasty

Blepharoplasty for Asians and Asian Americans is marketed quite differently from how eyelifts are marketed to Caucasians. Asian blepharoplasty is performed specifically to create a supratarsal fold or crease in the upper eyelid, and is often referred to as "double-eyelid" surgery. About half of the people of Asian descent are born without this crease. Cosmetic surgeons who perform Asian or "anchor" blepharoplasty often utilize the rhetoric of ameliorating the problem of eyes that look "tired" or "sleepy" in the same way they do with Caucasian patients, but the surgery itself is different when performed on Asian eyelids. For Asian patients, the procedure is specifically upper-lid blepharoplasty, and the typical patient is on average much younger. The "problem" or "condition" that is being altered is not due to aging, but to a naturally occurring phenomenon in half of the Asian population; therefore, the procedure is controversial, and has been referred to as "Westernizing," "Occidentalizing," "Caucanizing," or "Europeanizing" Asian eyes. Thus, when cosmetic surgery Web sites discuss how "genetic inheritance" of excess fat or skin on the eyelids may be a reason to seek blepharoplasty, it seems that this discourse might be pointing to the inheritance of so-called Asian racial/ethnic physical markers or identifying characteristics. Further reinforcing the notion that the procedure is "Westernizing," Asian blepharoplasty historically involved the restructuring or removal of the epicanthal fold—another physical identifier associated with those of Asian ancestry, and not found among most Caucasians. Although many cosmetic surgeons dispute that they are "Westernizing" their patients' eyes when performing these procedures, it is on this basis that Asian blepharoplasty has been widely criticized.

The first Asian blepharoplasty was performed in Japan in 1896 by K. Mikamo. This procedure was performed on a woman who had been born with one "double" and one "single" eyelid. She underwent surgery to "correct" her asymmetry—or to add a pretarsal crease to the eyelid that did not have one. This procedure was thus framed as functional or "reconstructive" in purpose. This first surgery was performed after the Meiji Restoration of 1868 and the Medical Act of 1874, under which it was mandated that all doctors in Japan be trained in Western medicine. Since the time of this first "double-eyelid" surgery, approximately thirty-two different alterations of the procedure have been designed and performed in Japan. Many of these first Asian blepharoplasties were performed on men, based on the belief that cosmetic surgery had the potential to enhance a man's masculinity and make him a better soldier. Upon hearing of the popularity of the surgery in Japan, some American doctors interpreted it as a method of improving the eyesight of Japanese soldiers who they believed to be inherently poor marksmen. Thus, the procedure was posited by American surgeons to improve the eyesight and thus the marksmanship of Japanese male soldiers and the beauty of Japanese women.

Khoo Boo-Chai, a cosmetic surgeon from Singapore who practiced in the late 1950s and early 1960s, developed the modern type of Asian blepharoplasty—an incarnation of which is most often used today. In order to create the appearance of a double eyelid or superior palpebral fold, he sewed a fine line of stitches along his patients' upper eyelids. Once healed, the scar tissue then created a permanent fold in the eyelid.

In the 1960s, Tokyo became a mecca for aesthetic surgery, and Fumio Umezawa's Jujin Hospital of Cosmetic Surgery was especially popular. It is reported that the hospital's record for the most surgeries performed in one day is 1,380, although the daily average was about forty procedures. One of the most popular surgeries performed at the clinic was blepharoplasty, which cost $8.33 in 1957 and $56 by 1965. Currently in Japan, China, and Thailand, cosmetic surgery in general, and blepharoplasty specifically, is targeted to women, and legal and illegal "aesthetic salons" offering quick and inexpensive cosmetic procedures proliferate.

Asian blepharoplasty, among other cosmetic surgeries, became exceedingly popular in Vietnam and other parts of Southeast Asia during and after the Vietnam War. This rise in instances of surgery, especially those procedures that are said to "Westernize" Asian facial features, such as rhinoplasty and blepharoplasty, is often attributed to the importation of Western beauty ideals by American GIs stationed in Vietnam during the war. Operations on the nose and eyes remain the most popular among Vietnamese women today, and upper-eyelid blepharoplasty can currently be obtained in certain areas of Hanoi for as little as $40.

One of the first Asian blepharoplasties performed in the United States was on a man named Shima Kito. In 1926, Kito had facial surgery—including a rudimentary blepharoplasty—to "Westernize" his Asian features. He did this is in order to marry a white woman whose parents would not permit her to marry a man who was "visibly Asian." The surgery was deemed a success by his fiancée's parents, who permitted Kito to marry their daughter after he changed his name to William White. Although this remarkable story took place early in the twentieth century, racialized plastic surgeries such as rhinoplasty and blepharoplasty were not sought by large numbers of Asian Americans until after World War II.

In 1955, D. Ralph Millard, a surgeon stationed for a time in Korea, published his report, "Plastic and Reconstructive Surgery," which outlined the process of transforming Asian-looking eyes to those of a Western appearance via surgery. While Millard was practicing cosmetic surgery in Korea, he stated that many of his patients had requested "Westernization" of their eyes, and that in performing blepharoplasty, he was simply meeting his patients' needs. Surgeons such as Millard have been critiqued as reifying medicine as an institution that seeks only to meet the challenges of science, rather than as an institution that must consciously interrogate the racism and sexism inherent in certain procedures. Many modern-day surgeons who perform Asian blepharoplasty also have been critiqued as lacking introspection on this basis.

Currently in the United States (and particularly in California), Asian blepharoplasty is the most popular aesthetic surgery performed on Asian Americans. The procedure is most frequently performed on young women, some as young as fifteen and sixteen, and is reportedly often offered to girls as birthday, high school, or college graduation gifts. Some young women go back to their countries of origin to have the surgery performed, but many go to one of the many cosmetic surgeons in the United States who specialize in the procedure. Most specialists state that blepharoplasty should not be performed on those patients who seek to change their "racial or ethnic appearance," and that rather than "Westernizing" Asian facial features, the procedure only enhances Asian features and allows patients to look more like their double-eyelided Asian counterparts. The benefits of Asian blepharoplasty cited by many specialists include that the eyelid opening appears to be wider, it gives a refreshed and more awake and alert appearance, and for women, enables easier application of eyeliner and other eye makeup.

Blepharoplasty is both quite common and generally accepted, yet at the same time, it is highly controversial when performed on certain patients. Its popularity is due to its widely held perception as a "gentle" and quick surgery, the fact that it is relatively inexpensive, and that in its current form, it tends to have permanent effects and leave little scarring. Among older, generally Caucasian men and women, the ethics of the procedure are generally not questioned; among younger, generally Asian women, the surgery has been interpreted as racist and as reifying and disseminating homogenizing and hegemonic Western standards of beauty, in which large, round, "Caucasoidal" eyes are idealized, especially for women. On the other hand, the idea that Asian blepharoplasty patients have simply internalized racist beauty ideals and the desire to look like white women has recently been challenged as essentializing and degrading. Poststructuralist, postcolonial, and multicultural feminist theory has instead put forth the notion that Asian women who seek blepharoplasty must not be seen as dupes of cultural imperialism, but as rational actors involved in cultural negotiations that consciously navigate racist scripts and form their own identities in light of constraints.

Further Reading: American Academy of Cosmetic Surgery official Web site, http://www.cosmeticsurgery.org (accessed June 1, 2007); American Academy of Facial Plastic and Reconstructive Surgery official Web site, http://www.aafprs.org (accessed June 1, 2007); American Society of Plastic Surgeons official Web site, http://www.plasticsurgery.org (accessed June 1, 2007); Copeland, Michelle. *Change Your Looks, Change Your Life: Quick Fixes and Cosmetic Surgery Solutions for Looking Younger, Feeling Healthier, and Living Better.* New York: HarperCollins, 2003; Davis, Kathy. *Dubious Equalities & Embodied Differences: Cultural Studies on Cosmetic Surgery.* Lanham, MD: Rowman & Littlefield, 2003; Gilman, Sander L. *Making the Body Beautiful: A Cultural History of Aesthetic Surgery.* Princeton, NJ: Princeton University Press, 1999; Haiken, Elizabeth. *Venus Envy: A History of Cosmetic Surgery.* Baltimore, MD: The Johns Hopkins

University Press, 1997; Kaw, Eugenia. "'Opening Faces:' The Politics of Cosmetic Surgery and Asian American Women." In Nicole Sault, ed. *Many Mirrors: Body Image and Social Relations*. New Brunswick, NJ: Rutgers University Press, 1994, pp. 241–265; Kobrin, Sandy. "There's Nothing Wrong With My Eyes," http://www.alternet.org (accessed June 1, 2007); Lin, Shirley. "In the Eye of the Beholder?: Eyelid Surgery and Young Asian-American Women," http://www.wiretapmag.org (accessed June 1, 2007); Zane, Kathleen. "Reflections on a Yellow Eye: Asian I(/Eye\)Cons and Cosmetic Surgery." In Ella Shohat, ed. *Talking Visions: Multicultural Feminism in a Transnational Age*. Cambridge, MA: MIT Press, 1998; WebMD. http://www.emedicine.com/plastic/topic425.htm; Center for Facial and Airway Reconstructive Surgery. http://www.sleepsurgery.com/eyelid.html.

Alyson Spurgas

Cultural History of the Eyes

The eyes are both instruments for and objects of vision. As such, the eyes have accumulated a wealth of metaphorical and religious significance. In Islamic cultures, the spiritual core of the absolute intellect is called "the eye of the heart." In Judeo-Christian cultures, the eyes are the windows to the soul. The eyes have excited and frustrated many a portrait artist—how to capture something as ethereal as a personality, spirit, or soul within an image or a sculpture? Eye metaphors populate the English language and are especially useful to describe social interactions. Humans make "eye contact," see "eye to eye" with others, "keep an eye" on people and things, and fear the power of the "evil eye." One can lose oneself in the eyes of a lover, yet if looks could kill, all would be dead. The eyes of the dead are ritualistically closed before they are buried, giving the sense that death is in fact a very long sleep.

The eyes are also visible objects, and have been studied in multiple ways and to as many ends. The face is the most photographed part of the human body. In Western medicine, ophthalmologists study the anatomy, function, and diseases of the eyes. Biometric scanning technology registers the patterns of the iris, which are unique to every individual, and grants or refuses access to information and space. Facial recognition software recognizes faces, in part by analyzing the structure of the eyes. Facial imaging software is used to imagine new faces, as in the cosmetic surgeon's office. The eyes have long intrigue for aesthetic reasons. Throughout history, people in different cultures have decorated the eyes with cosmetics as dark as black velvet and resplendent as tropical fish.

Mythology and Religion

The eyes have been the focus of a wealth of mythology in Western and non-Western cultures alike. One of the most common is that of the evil eye. The evil eye myth exists in different forms in the Middle East, South Asia, central Asia, and Europe. It is especially strong in the Mediterranean region. According to evil-eye mythology, those who possess the evil eye have the power to bestow a curse upon whomever they look at. Often, the evil eye is thought to result from envy. To be looked upon by the envious, even if they are not intentionally malevolent, is enough to become cursed by the evil eye. One similarity among cross-continental variations in evil-eye my-thology is that the evil eye is commonly attributed to those whose differen-ces, be they physical, mental, sexual, or otherwise, set them apart from the social order. Unmarried, widowed, and infertile women are frequently attributed the evil eye. By contrast, pregnant women, children, and crops are most likely to become victims of the evil eye because they attract the envy of outcasts. The Medusa myth is one example. In Greek mythology, Medusa was a monstrous female figure with a head of snakes for her hair. In some versions of the myth, Medusa's gaze can turn one to stone; in others, looking at her will turn one to stone. In the Philippines, people with physical and psychological ailments are sometimes thought to be victims of *usog*, which is the Filipino version of the evil-eye myth. In Greece and Turkey, where the evil-eye myth is strong, apotropaic talismans, or symbols that pro-tect by reflecting the evil eye, are commonplace. Medusa was beheaded by the heroic Perseus, who used a shiny shield to reflect her gaze. Perseus used her head as a weapon until he gave it to the goddess Athena, who placed it on her shield for protection against the evil eye. Drying, desiccation, wither-ing, and dehydration are thought to be symptoms of the evil eye. Conversely, the cure is related to moistness. In the Philippines, the way to cure a child afflicted with the evil eye is to boil the child's clothes in water. In many cul-tures, fish are thought to be immune from the evil eye because they are always wet. For this reason, protective talismans often portray fish.

Intriguingly, schizophrenics often exhibit delusional beliefs in the evil eye myth. Sigmund Freud's essay, "Das Medusenhaupt," German for "The Medusa," which was posthumously published in 1940, provides a psychoan-alytic account of the Medusa myth. Recalling this essay, psychiatrists explain the phenomenon of evil-eye delusions in schizophrenia as a manifestation of incestuous sexual desire and the fear of castration. Freud theorized that heterosexual male sexuality developed through the Oedipus complex, whereby the son desires to have sex with his mother but cannot do so because that is the father's privilege. The boy supposedly catches a glimpse of his mother's vagina and mistakes it for a castrated penis, then jumps to the conclusion that his father must have castrated his mother and that the father might also castrate him. The boy resolves this "castration anxiety" by fixating upon a fetish object, which he fantasies to be the mother's penis. According to Freud and his followers, Medusa's severed head is both an image of castration and a talisman against it. It is an image of castration because of the gaping wound at the neck, which the boy associates with the mother's vagina (in the boy's mind, the vagina is but a gaping hole where the mother's penis used to be). Medusa's snakes are fetish objects—multiple phalluses upon which the boy fixates in order to reassure himself that his mother has not been castrated, and thus he will not succumb to that terrible fate. The petrifaction, or turning to stone, that the Medusa's look causes, represents the boy's erection—another reassurance that he has not been castrated and is capable of heterosexual sexual relations with women, whom, according to Freud, are substitutes for the boy's mother.

The eye was important in ancient Egyptian religion, as in "the eye of Horus" and "the eye of Ra." Horus is the ancient Egyptian sky god. He also protected the Egyptian pharaoh and represented the pharaoh's divine authority. Horus was the son of Ra, the creator, and his wife Hathor, who was a representation of the Milky Way. Horus was often represented as a falcon-headed man. As the sky god, Horus was thought to contain both the sun and the moon. It was believed that the sun and the moon traversed the sky whenever a falcon, Horus, flew across it. One of Horus' eyes was the sun; the other the moon. The symbol known as the eye of Horus is a depiction of the right eye of the falcon god. The right eye also represents Ra, the sun god. The left eye, the mirror image of the right, represented the moon and the god Thoth. Thoth was the god of writing, magic, and learning. Thoth is depicted as an Ibis-headed man. Together, the eyes represent the entire universe as well as the combined power of Horus. Horus was such an important god that "the eye of Horus" eventually became an important Egyptian symbol of power and protection. The eye of Horus has manifested elsewhere as the all-seeing eye, or the eye of Providence.

The eye of Providence is usually depicted as an eye surrounded by rays of light, often enclosed in a triangle. The eye of Providence has a long history and exists within many cultures. It first appeared in a form other than the Egyptian eye of Horus in Buddhist scriptures, where it is known as "the eye of the world." Here, the eye of Providence took on its threefold significance. It represents "triratna," which Buddhists commit to. There are many versions of Buddhism, each with its own nuances. Generally speaking, triratna consists of Buddha, dharma, and sangha. Buddha was the founder of Buddhism, Siddhartha Guatama Buddha. Buddha can also refer to an ideal of perfection that exists in all things. Dharma is the teaching of Buddha, which pertains in particular to ethics, or the right way to live. Sangha is the Buddhist community.

In Christian contexts, the eye of Providence is always enclosed in a triangle because each side of the triangle refers to a different aspect of the Holy Trinity. A plethora of versions of Christianity exist, many of which believe in the Holy Trinity, or the threefold nature of God. The Holy Trinity consists of the Father, the Son, and the Holy Spirit, simultaneously. The eye in the center of the triangle represents the unity of the three aspects of God as well as God's omniscient (all-seeing) power.

The eye of Providence is included in the symbolism of the Freemasons. The Freemasons are a fraternal organization that excludes women from its ranks. They have existed since at least the mid-seventeenth century, but their origins are obscure. Today, the Freemasons have millions of members worldwide. Certain aspects of the Freemasons' beliefs and activities are private; however, it is known that they believe in the existence of a supreme being and that they profess to follow the principals of liberty, equality, and fraternity. The main Masonic symbol is the stone and compass, but the eye of Providence is also used to symbolize the supreme being's omniscience. Occasionally, the eye itself is replaced by a "G" for geometry and God.

Cultural Significance of Vision: The Gaze

Vision, in particular the gaze, is an important topic within feminism, film theory, and psychoanalysis. The gaze is a special form of sight, wherein a subject desires the object in view. The feminist film theorist Laura Mulvey was the first to integrate feminism, film theory, and psychoanalysis. In her landmark 1975 essay, "Visual Pleasure and Narrative Cinema," Mulvey analyzed classical Hollywood cinema and concluded that "men act, women appear." In other words, in classical Hollywood films, men are positioned as subjects (or "selves") whose prerogative is to desire women. Women are not subjects but "objects for the male gaze." Mulvey also noted that male characters drive the narrative forward whereas female characters halt it. Women, then, exist for man's pleasure in classic Hollywood cinema. Mulvey proposed a radical annihilation of man's pleasure, so that women may discover their own—through the creation of an avant-garde feminist cinema. Groundbreaking as Mulvey's work on the male gaze was, it was critiqued by feminists for reproducing the structures it claimed to reject because the position that Mulvey wrote from was heterosexist, thus denying the existence of lesbian and, following Mulvey's own logic, even heterosexual women. Nevertheless, Mulvey succeeded in drawing critical attention to the problem of the relationships of power that "the gaze" implies and creates. Her work has inspired a generation of film theorists, such as Richard Dyer, who examines the complex projections that many gay male viewers make onto female stars.

Cultural Impact of the Technological Enhancement of Vision

Not content with seeing the world with naked eyes, humans have invented a myriad of visual technologies to expose previously invisible surfaces to scrutiny. The enhancement of vision through technology has changed the way that humans understand their place on Earth and in the universe itself. It has allowed imaginations to run wild with seemingly insurmountable questions, which have consequences for the way people think about what it means to be human and about how human beings define a "good life."

Microscopes have enabled people to see objects as tiny as single-celled organisms. At the other end of the scale, telescopes seem to shrink vast distances so that one can see far beyond the natural limitations of vision. Telescopes have enabled people to see the galaxy, of which Earth is but a small part. Vision is also enhanced by producing images of objects that the eye cannot see. X-rays, a form of electromagnetic radiation, can be passed through dense structures to produce an image of aspects of the object, for example the skeletal system of the human body. In X-ray crystallography, X-rays are passed through the closely spaced atoms of a crystal to reveal its structure. English biophysicist Rosalind Franklin used X-ray crystallography when she discovered the double-helix structure of DNA. Ultrasound, the practice of using acoustic energy at a frequency that exceeds the upper limits of human hearing, is used to provide images of soft tissue in the human body. Ultrasound is not simply a medical technology. It has become a social technology, too. Ultrasounds are routinely used on pregnant women to check the health of the developing fetus. An expectant mother's first ultrasound has become a rite of passage, which is often attended by partners, family, and friends. Moreover, there is no politically neutral noun to describe what an ultrasound shows. This ultrasound image has become a highly contested representation, between "pro-choice" groups on the one hand and "pro-life" groups on the other. The pro-choice movement, which uses the noun "fetus" to describe what an ultrasound shows, argues that women have the right to fully control their reproductive health, including the right to safely terminate a pregnancy. In opposition, the pro-life movement, which is often associated with Christian churches, asserts that the ultrasound shows a human baby, which, they claim, has the "right to life." This contest over naming what an ultrasound shows illustrates that technologies that enhance the natural capabilities of the human eye necessitate new cultural and even religious paradigms. Vision and visual technologies are social technologies.

Anatomy and Physiology

The eyes are the instruments of vision, but vision is a process that involves the whole body as well as external conditions, such as the presence of light and objects. The eyes are lubricated via the process of blinking. Vision occurs when light enters the cornea, which is the colorless dome that shields the iris and the pupil. The iris is the colored part of the eye. It controls the amount of light that enters the eye. The pupil is the aperture through which light enters the eye, and is formed via the opening and closing of the iris. Fluctuations in the intensity of light modify the diameter of the pupil. When light is bright, the pupil constricts; when light is dim, the pupil dilates. Whenever light travels through a dense object, it is refracted, or bent. Light is first refracted by the cornea and then by the lens. The lens is a colorless structure with two convex surfaces, and sits immediately behind the iris and pupil. The lens inverts the image of the object and focuses it upon the retina. After passing through the lens but before landing on the retina, light travels through the vitreous humor, a colorless gel that composes about 80 percent of the eye. The vitreous humor plays the crucial role of maintaining the taunt, spherical shape of the eyeball. Within the layers of the retina, an image is converted into electrical signals. These signals travel through the optic nerve and into the occipital cortex, which is located at the back of the brain. In the occipital cortex, the image, which now takes the form of electrical signals, is registered the right way around rather than being inverted. Hence, humans do not see merely with the eyes but also with the brain and all the other aspects of the body, which nourish the visual system. Vision is a bodily process.

Ophthalmology

Ophthalmology is the speciality of medicine that treats disorders of the visual pathways, which include the eye and surrounding structures, as well as the brain. What Western medicine now calls "ophthalmology" has a long history. According to the earliest known records, this history begins in India in the fifth century. In his book *Sushruta Samhita*, Sushruta described about seventy-two disorders of the ocular system as well as a number of instruments and techniques for eye surgery. Arab scientists are the earliest known to have written about and diagrammed the anatomy of the eye. The pre-Hippocratics of ancient Greece speculated about the structure and function of the eye, but Aristotle cemented ancient Greek knowledge in empirical fact by dissecting the eyes of the dead. The Alexandrians are thought to have contributed to knowledge of the human eye, but most of the material written by them has been lost. Knowledge of the structure, function, and disorders of the human eye, as well as technologies and procedures for improving them, was greatly advanced by Islamic medicine. Iraqi physician Ammar ibn Ali invented a syringe that he used to extract soft cataracts. A cataract is a formation upon the surface of the eye that occludes vision. The father of modern ophthalmology, Ibn al-Haytham, was the first to correctly describe the physiology of vision in his groundbreaking 1020 text the *Book of Optics*. In the seventeenth and eighteenth centuries in Europe, the development of hand-held lenses and microscopes, as well as techniques for fixing the eyes of the dead for study, led to a more sophisticated knowledge of the visual system than ever before. But modern ophthalmology was born in London in 1805 with the establishment of the first ophthalmology hospital, Moorfield's Eye Hospital.

The Magnificent Eye: Evolution or Intelligent Design?

The problem of the origin and function of the human eye has become a zone of contest between two different systems of thinking: science and religion. Scientists propose that the human eye evolved over millions of years, whereas creationists claim that the beauty of the human eye is evidence of what they call "intelligent design." Scientists point to an abundance of evidence to support the hypothesis that the human eye evolved from a simple eyespot. An eyespot is a single, light-sensitive cell. Many very simple organisms have eyespots. Scientists think that that the eyespot evolved into both eyes and the plant cells responsible for photosynthesis. Scientists argue that, around the Cambrian period, there was an explosion of evolutionary activity, and the humble eyespot underwent numerous modifications. It became a curved eye, able to detect the direction of light and shapes. Later, this structure evolved to include a lens, which is responsible for focusing light upon the retina, the surface made from light-sensitive cells at the back of the eyeball. Later, the cornea, the clear, protective covering of the eye, developed—as did the iris. The iris is the colorful ring around the pupil. The iris blocks light from entering the eye, whereas the pupil is an aperture that allows light to enter the eye. The aqueous humor, the fluid inside the eyeball, also developed during the Cambrian period. Scientists think that as these features evolved, immense diversification emerged in eye structure among vertebrates. Humans have benefited greatly from the structure and capacities of the human eye across the processes of evolution, not only due to vision but also because the eyes are also socially important instruments. During the Jurassic period, the faces of mammals gradually become more mobile and expressive than those of their reptilian contemporaries. A mobile face, including the eyes and surrounding structures, made complex sociality possible. It was in the Jurassic period that mammals learned to express their emotions and, crucially, to read the emotions of others. Jurassic mammals began to base their interactions with each other upon more informed decisions about how others might be feeling; this led to greater reproductive success among them.

Creationists dispute the theory of evolution. Instead, creationists believe in the story of Genesis from the Christian bible. Genesis is the tale of how God created the world in seven days. According to creationists, the magnificence of the human eye is proof that it must have been created by an "intelligent designer," the Christian God, and not through the long process of evolution. Biologists retort that, over many generations, natural selection, which is the mechanism of evolution, gradually filtered out those eyes that were inadequate to keep an organism alive in its environment long enough to reproduce. In this way, the human eye evolved into the magnificent structure that it is. These debates about the origin of the human eye, and, by extension, of humanity and the world itself, are not simply about getting to the truth of how and why eyes look and work the way they do. The human eye has become the terrain upon which two different worldviews, the scientific and the religious, battle for the minds of Westerners, particularly in the United States.

Further Reading: Dawkins, Richard. *The God Delusion*. New York: Bantam Books, 2006; Dundes, Alan (ed). *The Evil Eye: A Case Book*. Madison, WI: University of Wisconsin Press, 1992; McNeill, Daniel. *The Face*. Boston: Little, Brown and Company, 1998; Mulvey, Laura. "Visual Pleasure and Narrative Cinema." *Screen* 16 (3) 1975: 6–18; Sims, Michael. *Adam's Navel: A Natural and Cultural History of the Human Form*. New York: Viking, 2003.

Gretchen Riordan

History of Eye Makeup

Throughout the history of makeup use, adorning the eyes has been a controversial cosmetic practice. While scorned in certain cultures and epochs, it has been the most important aspect of cosmetic routine in others. In many of the cultures of antiquity, enhancing the eyes with paints, powders, and even ground glass, gold, or metals was the most important aspect of ritual ceremonial and daily beauty regimens. In other cultures, the eye was left completely unadorned while other aspects of the face were emphasized. The controversial nature of eye makeup may be due to the fact that the eyes have alternately been considered mysterious, unabashedly expressive, and evocative of lust and sin in different cultures and times. In modern times, eye makeup was one of the last facial cosmetic products to become popularized and mass marketed. Now, eye makeup is crucial to many women's daily cosmetic routines, and has also been used in subcultural styles.

Adorning the Eyes in Antiquity

In many cultures throughout history, adorning the eyes with paints has been integral for use in religious and spiritual ceremonies, to distinguish rank and side in battles and warfare, and for the purposes of beautification and self-enhancement, particularly in courting rituals and to make one appear attractive to potential mates. Wearing eye makeup has also been utilized as camouflage and for medicinal purposes. In many societies, the removal of hair around the eyes has been a staple of cosmetic enhancement and has served a variety of purposes, including drawing attention to the eyes and providing a smooth foundation for the application of eye paints and makeup. The eyebrow tweezer has remained one of the most popular cosmetic devices across history and culture.

In ancient Egypt, eye makeup was the most important cosmetic implement, and was used for religious purposes, as protection from the glare of the sun, and to enhance the appearance of the face. The eye was accentuated over all other aspects of the face, and was associated with magic and superstition. The Egyptians used bright green paints made from ore of copper, malachite, and galena to accent their eyes, and black antimony powder made of galena to blacken their eyebrows. Antimony power was also used to create dark winged lines on the upper and lower eyelids to make the eye appear more almond-shaped, in the style that Cleopatra became renowned for. Both men and women, and even children, decorated their eyes in this manner, and other ointments were applied to the eyes to protect them from infection. Eye makeup was made by grinding metallic ingredients on a stone slab or schist palette. It was applied either as powder over a base of ointment, or mixed with animal fat or vegetable oil in preparation for application. Although Egypt is one of the first cultures associated with the prolific use of kohl, or eye makeup, the use of this cosmetic implement can be traced back to the Bronze Age and the Mesolithic period.

The ancient Greeks were much less interested in the use of eye makeup—and cosmetics in general—than were the Egyptians and other historic Middle Eastern cultures. In ancient Greece, respectable women were forbidden from using cosmetics, and eye makeup was considered particularly abhorrent. Eye makeup was associated with the lust and harlotry of the courtesans, or *hetarae*, who wore rouge and white lead powder, or *ceruse*, on their faces, in addition to rimming their eyes heavily with kohl. The Minoan peoples of Crete, both men and women, outlined their eyes with black paints and powders, although this was the exception to makeup standards in ancient Greece rather than the rule.

The Romans were significantly more liberal with their use of cosmetics than the Greeks; some of their eye makeup styles were borrowed directly from the Egyptians. Cosmetic usage was associated strictly with femininity, and Roman women used Egyptian kohl, ash, and saffron to outline their eyes in black and gold. They emphasized this feature by removing the hair from their eyebrows and darkening their lashes with burnt cork.

In ancient India, eye makeup was utilized by both men and women, and was associated with seduction and sensuality. Women in particular were expected to use cosmetics to attract men. The use of cosmetics and methods for appearing more attractive to potential sex partners are discussed at length in the *Kama Sutra*, the Sanskrit work on love and sexual pleasure by the philosopher Mallanaga Vatsyayana. Hindu men were expected to apply *collyrium*—the term for any eyewash or ointment—on their eyelids and below the eyes. A recipe for mascara is described in the *Kama Sutra* as well, and adorning the eyes with this black pigment was considered integral to making oneself attractive. The ancient Egyptians, Indians, and Romans were some of the last cultures of antiquity to sanction the wearing of eye makeup for women or men; eye makeup did not resurface as a staple of cosmetic wear until the twentieth century in the West.

Eye Makeup in the Middle Ages to Modernity

In early Britain in medieval times, bathing and the wearing of all cosmetics were deemed vain, evil, and ungodly. Although women were encouraged to care for their skin and hair with homeopathic creams and ointments to foster a youthful and unblemished appearance, eye makeup was considered anathema to the puritanical beauty ideals of the day. Female beauty was standardized, and pale skin, hair, and eyes were considered the height of attractiveness. Eyes should be small and demure, preferably a pale gray in color, unadorned and thus as unnoticeable as possible. The fact that women's eyes were often cast down in piety and reverence went hand-in-hand with the ideal that nothing should draw attention to the eyes. The white oval shape of the face was highlighted by removing all hair from the temples, forehead, and eyebrows, and if the eyelashes were too dark or unruly, they could be removed as well.

Although eye makeup conventions did not change drastically from early medieval times to the late fifteenth and sixteenth centuries, the symbolism and meaning associated with the eye itself did. Images of women in this era placed a newfound emphasis on the eyes, and the idea that darker eyes were more attractive, as they were more secretive, expressive, and mysterious, became widespread. Subsequent to the coronation of Queen Elizabeth I, the use of cosmetics and brighter and gaudier fashion became the norm. But even in Elizabethan England, eye makeup was not fashionable, although the trend of plucking the eyebrows remained popular. The fashion and makeup of Italian and French women, who darkened their eyebrows with black powder and tinted their eyelids, were significantly more elaborate than the styles of British women.

It wasn't until the Restoration in Europe in the seventeenth century that the eyes again became a focal point of facial beauty. The whiteness of the skin and rosy color of the lips still held precedence over the eyes during this period, but dark, luminous, or "heavy-lidded" eyes were described as beautiful. In the eighteenth century, eye makeup was still relatively unimportant in comparison to other cosmetics such as lip tint and white face powder, although a newfound attention to the eyebrows was instituted. The ideal eyebrows for the Georgians were jet-black, arched, and thick. A lead comb was used to darken and thicken the natural eyebrow, but frequently eyebrows were shaved off and replaced with false eyebrows made of mouse skin. Artificial eyebrows were deemed more elegant than natural ones, and thus false brows were associated with upper-class status. Fake eyebrows were adjusted publicly as a method of asserting one's class status, and they were often placed far away from the natural brow to further emphasize the fact that the eyebrows were artificial, and thus the wearer was wealthy.

In the Victorian era, roughly the second half of the nineteenth century, cosmetics were once again associated with debauchery and sinful vanity. Large, and particularly deep blue eyes, were considered beautiful, but they were not to be adorned or enhanced with cosmetics. The fashionable eyebrow was once again elegant, thin, and arched, rather than thick and black. In favor of an emphasis on pale skin and a pink mouth, the eyes were once again neglected. The ideal of natural, childlike, innocent beauty was reestablished, and if women pursued the enhancement of their appearances with cosmetics, they were forced to do so covertly, in fear of being associated with prostitutes. The only cosmetic products that were socially sanctioned were creams and ointments marked as medicinal.

Toward the end of the nineteenth century, subsequent to Polish-born Helena Rubenstein's (1870–1965) immigration to London and the opening of her salon there, some women began to experiment with eye-enhancement makeup once again. Bright color was virtually nonexistent in this market though, as it was associated with women of the theater and the stage, and most techniques were used to enhance the size and shape of the eye rather than to explicitly attract attention to it. As the moralizing of beauty in the Victoria era abated somewhat, kohl eye shadow, coconut oil as a method of thickening lashes, and "lampblack" mascara were used sparingly only by the most adventurous of women.

Changing Makeup Trends in the Modern Era

At the end of the nineteenth century and the beginning of the twentieth century, cosmetic adornment became disassociated from lasciviousness and lust, but the achievement of true beauty via the appropriate cosmetics was still attainable only by the wealthy. In the Edwardian beauty salons of London, rich women were primped with the utmost care and expertise. Makeup became more and more acceptable, and thus marketable, but poor women were left to make due with what they had at home to use for beautification. One practice that was common during this time was the use of burnt matchsticks to darken the eyelashes, while still keeping the appearance of naturalness.

The reappearance of color was gradual, and was also reserved for the wealthy woman. The beauty salons of the day began incorporating bright colors for rouge, lipstick, and eye makeup based on the styles of dancers in Russian ballets; Helena Rubenstein, the founder of some of the original salons and a successful line of cosmetics, was explicitly influenced by the stage in designing her makeup. Although not widespread until much later, the influence of the Russian ballet eventually created a market in gilded, glittering, and brightly colored eye shadows.

By 1910, cosmetics were becoming more acceptable and had started to become fundamental to status and beauty. *The Daily Mirror Beauty Booklet*, published in 1910, suggested ways to enhance the eyes, including through the use of pencils to make the eyes appear shapelier, devices to curl and lengthen lashes, and darkeners for the brows. For most women of the Edwardian era and prior to and during World War I, the emphasis was on skin quality, although eyebrow plucking was still a staple of cosmetic regimes, as thin and arched eyebrows were the epitome of style during this time. Although not widely popular yet, the wearing of eye makeup was considered sexy and sensual, but was no longer associated with debauchery and sin. This was due in large part to the advent of photography and the subsequent growth of the celebrity. The makeup-wearing celebrity soon became associated with ideal beauty, even if she wore eye makeup.

Until the 1920s, eye makeup such as mascara and eye shadow were considered the most questionable types of cosmetics for respectable women to use. During the flapper era, however, eye makeup began to be used more pervasively in the large metropolises, specifically New York City, followed by Chicago. By the end of World War I, mascara (known as such due to its derivation from *mascaro*, a type of hair dye) was used by many women, mainly the young, urban, and wealthy. This was due in part to the fact that mascara was now easier to apply, and came in a tube that could be easily transported. The first easy-to-apply "cake" mascara was created by Maybelline in 1917, and became widely available by the 1930s. This cosmetic staple replaced petroleum jelly as the primary method of lash beautification among women.

In 1923, the first eyelash curler was invented. Although it was expensive and required time and effort to use (sometimes up to ten minutes to curl the lashes of one eye), it became a favored item among upper-class women. Lining the eyes with kohl was popular during this time, although emphasis was indisputably on the red, cupid's bow-shaped mouth. During the flapper era, the eyebrow pencil, in addition to the tube of bright red lipstick, became the staple of many women's beauty regimens.

In the 1930s, "color harmony," or the notion that one's eye shadow should match one's lipstick, which should match one's apparel, became popular, allegedly influenced by makeup entrepreneur Elizabeth Arden (1878–1966). This principle led to the introduction of a variety of new shades of eye shadow. According to the *Vogue Beauty Book* of 1933, eye shadow should complement one's eye color, although shades of violet and silver may be appropriate for evening outings. Bright greens could also be worn in certain situations.

Blue and turquoise mascara became popular during this time; these shades were considered to look more natural than blacks and browns. Liquid mascara was made available after cream mascara was introduced, and came in a compact tube with a grooved metal device for easier application. Although it was becoming a staple of beautification, mascara was controversial in that it caused allergic reactions in certain women and had a foul odor (this early liquid mascara was approximately 50 percent turpentine). Lash dyes, popular for a short time during this era, were also criticized on the basis of health. One dye in particular, known as Lash Lure, was determined to be poisonous after it disfigured and blinded one young woman.

False eyelashes were marketed in the 1930s, although only the most daring women experimented with them at first. Eyeliner was also popularized in the later 1930s, mainly due to the popularity of enhancing the upper eyelid with a single dark line by actresses such as Greta Garbo (1905–1990). Although color was experimented with during this period, the 1930s were a time of elegance and simplicity, especially when it came to eye makeup.

In the 1940s and early 1950s, the use of eye makeup diminished considerably. The emphasis was again on the lips (in addition to the breasts and hips), and the look of a classic, stoic beauty associated with postwar patriotism became the ideal. In 1948, 80 to 90 percent of American women stated that they used lipstick, whereas only one quarter said that they wore eye makeup. The mascara wand used today was patented in the late 1930s, but wasn't marketed until the late 1950s, mainly due to the dismissal of the eyes as a focal point of beauty.

Around 1958, the emphasis on eyes began to make a comeback. Lipstick was light while eye makeup was increasingly dark and attention-attracting. Mascara in its current form—what Helena Rubenstein marketed as "mascaramatic"—became a seemingly permanent staple of beauty. Mascara was no longer made with turpentine, and the new liquid version was easy to apply, hypoallergenic, and frequently waterproof. Eyeliner was also made available in a liquid form, and became one of the most important cosmetics a woman could own. Eye shadows and brow pencils were reintroduced as essential, and quality was improved so that the products were less likely to run. Women could now pursue the large, dark, doe eyes—or the "Cleopatra look"—popularized by stars such as Audrey Hepburn without fear of being blinded, having allergic reactions, or having their makeup running down their faces.

The 1960s marked the dawn of a new era in cosmetics. The emphasis was firmly on the eyes, which were often adorned with false eyelashes, glitter, and a variety of brightly colored eye shadows, liners, and mascaras. Makeup became more and more experimental and creative. Large, dark eyes remained the ideal, and were frequently contrasted with pale or even white lips. This look was illustrated in the fashion of the well-known British model of the day, Twiggy Lawson (1949–). The trend in the use of wild and riotous colors for eye enhancement, in addition to nails and lips, continued into the 1970s.

The 1980s marked the return of the "natural look," which included wearing less eye makeup. Eyeliner became unfashionable for a time, and tanned skin with frosted lips and hair became the trend. In contrast to the manufactured "au natural" look, the punk scene of the 1980s appropriated the use of black and colored eyeliners and shadows, in addition to other makeup for the face and body. Eyeliner was also used for parody, camp, and drag, and by members of a variety of subversive and alternative communities and subcultures, including punk and Goth. In the 1990s and in the beginning of the twenty-first century, brightly colored eye makeup has made a comeback, and the use of makeup in general is associated with haute couture. Eye makeup is a fundamental aspect of self-adornment for many people from a diversity of backgrounds; for some it is so fundamental that they have eyeliner permanently tattooed on their eyelids.

Further Reading: Allen, Margaret. *Selling Dreams: Inside the Beauty Business.* New York: Simon & Schuster, 1981; Angeloglou, Maggie. *A History of Make-up.* London: The Macmillan Company, 1970; Corson, Richard. *Fashions in Makeup: From Ancient to Modern Times.* New York: Universe Books, 1972; Gunn, Fenja. *The Artificial Face: A History of Cosmetics.* New York: Hippocrene, 1983; Marwick, Arthur. *Beauty in History: Society, Politics and Personal Appearance c. 1500 to the Present.* London: Thames & Hudson, 1988; Mulvey, Kate, and Melissa Richards. *Decades of Beauty: The Changing Image of Women 1890s–1990s.* New York: Checkmark Books, 1998; Peiss, Kathy. *Hope in a Jar: The Making of America's Beauty Culture.* New York: Henry Holt and Company, 1998; Riordan, Theresa. *Inventing Beauty: A History of the Innovations That Have Made Us Beautiful.* New York: Broadway Books, 2004; Wykes-Joyce, Max. *Cosmetics and Adornment: Ancient and Contemporary Usage.* New York: Philosophical Library, 1961; http://www.fashion-era.com

Alyson Spurgas

History of Eyewear

Not only does eyewear significantly affect how its wearers view the world, but it also shapes the ways in which the world perceives its wearers. Today, corrective eyewear is assumed to remedy visual deficiencies in emmetropic, or normal, eyes. Corrective eyewear most commonly treats hyperopia (farsightedness), myopia (nearsightedness), blurring astigmatism, and presbyopia associated with the blurring of vision caused by aging. The invention of eyeglasses in the late thirteenth century correlates historically to the rise of literacy in Europe and was, thus, a response to socioeconomic changes as much as scientific and medical advances. The history of eyewear is not just a story about the correction of eyesight, but it is also an account of the body's changing public appearance. Soon after their invention,

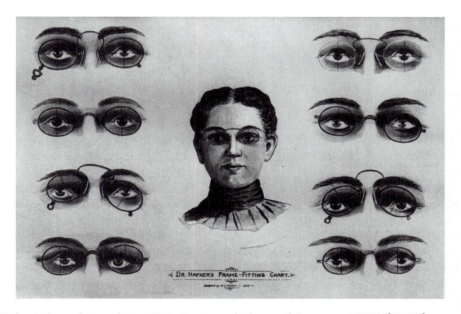

Hafner's frame-fitting chart, 1898. Courtesy of Library of Congress, LC-USZ62-71965.

eyeglasses were also used for purely cosmetic purposes. Undoubtedly, sunglasses, which ostensibly protect the eye from sun glare as well as harmful ultraviolet radiation, have become a common fashion accessory as well. Likewise, contact lenses, although initially developed to correct eyesight, also can serve the purely cosmetic purpose of altering eye color and appearance.

The earliest technologies for vision enhancement were, however, not used to correct vision. Both glass and crystals were molded into lenses in the ancient Mediterranean and Middle East. These handheld lenses, with convex refracting surfaces, could provide magnification or ignite the sun's rays into fire. Magnification was especially useful for artisans and scribes whose trades required exacting detail. Examples of such lenses have been found in Minoan Crete and were well known in ancient Egypt, Greece, and Rome. They were also used in China during the Sung dynasty (960–1280 CE) by judges to read legal documents. Such lenses were also known for their ability to modify vision. Roman emperor Nero observed gladiator contests through an emerald simply to enhance the pleasure of sight offered by the stone's color.

In the tenth century, the Arab scholar Ibn al-Haitham (ca. 965–1039 CE), or Alhazen, wrote that eyesight might be improved with a ground optical lens. Monks of the medieval period translated Alhazen's writings and developed crystal and quartz spheres to improve farsightedness. Such devices were not widely available, however. While farsightedness and nearsightedness are considered medical afflictions today, these differences polarized people socially before the invention of eyeglasses. Scholars have argued that those with nearsightedness found employment in trades requiring close-proximity vision, becoming artisans, scribes, and notaries. Those with farsightedness, however, likely worked in such professions as hunting and farming, which require long-distance vision. These divisions of labor were gradually eroded, however, with the invention and broader dissemination of eyeglasses in the late medieval period.

Italians first paired together two lenses to create corrective eyeglasses in the late thirteenth century. Historians debate whether they were first developed in Florence, Pisa, or Venice. Nevertheless, these early eyeglasses were created from translucent glass that was ground, polished, and smoothed into convex lenses to correct farsightedness. Concave lenses to correct nearsightedness, however, were not developed until the mid-fifteenth century. The correction of farsightedness became a pressing matter since literacy was a needed skill for the growing merchant class that required clerks to work at bookkeeping. There was also a need to ensure that those who developed farsightedness with age could continue working in this field. The technological advancement achieved by the first corrective lenses was, then, a response to specific social and economic forces at the time, and their invention was necessitated by increasing numbers of literate workers.

Because eyeglasses were associated with literacy, they soon became a prestigious item that suggested the intelligence and worldliness of their wearers. Soon after their invention, images of biblical saints and prophets were depicted wearing eyeglasses. This association soon created a fashion for spectacles. The Duke of Milan, Francesco Sforza, ordered a dozen pairs of eyeglasses without corrective lenses for his court in the mid-fifteenth century. Pope Leo X wore eyeglasses to improve his vision while hunting at the beginning of the sixteenth century, and Raphael painted his portraits wearing spectacles. These eyeglasses comprised two individual lenses with a horizontal handles riveted together, and, thus, were termed "rivets." Such eyeglasses were either handheld or were balanced upon the bridge of the nose. Devices to better keep spectacles in place were developed later for those with nearsightedness who needed to wear their glasses for longer periods of time. Early solutions to this problem included leather straps, as well as weighted cords that rested on the ears. Side arms, made from metal or horn, were introduced only in Spain and England during the eighteenth century.

The high-value and sophisticated fabrication of eyeglasses made their production an increasingly specialized trade. By 1320, Venetian eyeglass makers formed their own guild. Over the course of the fifteenth and sixteenth centuries, guilds for eyeglass making also arose in the German-speaking world, including Regensburg, Nuremberg, Augsburg, and Fürth. In Nuremberg, a decree of 1557 mandated that spectacles manufactured domestically be sold in shops, while imported spectacles, especially those from Venice, be sold on the street. French eyeglass makers and mirror makers joined together to create a single guild in 1525. Official associations of highly specialized and expertly trained opticians developed from these guilds and made further advances in eyeglass technology.

While the invention of bifocals is often attributed to Benjamin Franklin, he probably learned of them from British opticians who developed such eyeglasses in the late eighteenth century. First called "double spectacles," bifocals correct the vision of those with both nearsightedness and farsightedness with lenses that are divided into two parts to account for each affliction. Likewise, the correction of astigmatism causing blurred vision was accomplished in England with the development of a spherical lens first suggested by the astronomer Sir George Biddell Airy (1801–1892) in 1825.

Glassmakers traditionally produced the glass for lenses, and, therefore, long-established centers of glassmaking, such as Venice, cornered the lens-making market. These lenses, however, often contained such imperfections as bubbles and debris. At the end of the eighteenth century, Swiss craftsman Pierre-Louis Guinand (1748–1824) experimented with the production of optical glass and began stirring glass in its molten state with clay rods that brought bubbles to the surface and gave the material a uniform texture. Guinand brought his discoveries to the German-speaking world at the beginning of the nineteenth century, and they eventually became implemented by the Zeiss Optical Works in Jena. Lens production became regularized by the middle of the nineteenth century as the modes of producing eyeglasses became industrialized and factories opened for their mass production. Subsequent lens technology appeared in the twentieth century, when plastics were invented to provide lighter and less expensive eyewear.

Sequential lens inventions have modified how people see the world. Today, we assume that eyeglasses enhance vision. After their invention, however, many were skeptical about optical modification and believed that eyeglasses created a deceitful distortion of the world. Galileo Galilei (1564–1642) debunked these notions, and Johannes Kepler (1571–1630) reaffirmed Galileo's theories in his *Dioptrece* of 1611. While such studies made eyeglasses more acceptable within the scientific community, into the nineteenth century it was still thought that lenses could damage, or even distort, eyesight. The common use of spectacles among the farsighted elderly has also led to certain cultural beliefs. The wisdom associated with maturity has thus made eyeglasses a sign of intelligence. Yet, their use of eyeglasses has also fostered the negative assumption that all eyeglass wearers appear elderly.

The wearing of sunglasses, by contrast, has been associated with few of the negative connotations of corrective eyewear. Indeed, the practice of darkening eyeglass lenses has served different functions. Eyeglasses were worn with darkened lenses in China as early as 1430 by judges in the courtroom to hide the expression of their eyes. More common, however, has been the use of tinted lenses to obstruct the sun's rays from the eyes. While sunglasses have existed since the late eighteenth century, they gained broader popularity only in the twentieth century with the growth of outdoor activities such as sports and the automobile culture. As exposure to solar ultraviolet radiation has been shown to cause harmful effects, eyeglasses have been coated with protective treatments. Nevertheless, sunglasses have been traditionally associated with leisurely activity in the twentieth century and, therefore, developed into a major fashion accessory.

Attempts have been made to market corrective eyewear as a fashionable accoutrement, especially with the development of eyeglasses that do not rest on the face permanently, such as the monocle or lorgnettes. The monocle is comprised of a single lens held in place by the hand or by contracting the muscles around the eye. Because the monocle must be customized to fit the individual wearer, its costly price has typically made it an item associated with the upper class. Monocles probably developed from the quizzing glass, which was constructed of a single lens attached atop a handheld rod. While there are examples of monocles from the sixteenth century, they became more prevalent in the eighteenth and nineteenth centuries and gained a fashionable association with the English dandy. Viennese optician Johann Friedrich Voigtländer (1779–1859) imported the monocle to Austria from England at the beginning of the nineteenth century. By the time of the Congress of Vienna, the monocle became a key fashion article in the German-speaking world, and its popularity lasted through World War II. Along with tuxedos and the bob hairstyle, the monocle also became part of lesbian dress in Paris during the 1920s. Lorgnettes, however, have been more traditionally associated with women. Typically fastened to a cord, lorgnettes are comprised of two framed lenses held by an attached handle. Lorgnettes were developed from scissor glasses, which date back to the fifteenth century. Like their namesake, scissor glasses were formed from a V-shaped frame crowned by two lenses held above the nose.

Monocles and lorgnettes have attempted to correct vision while breaking down the parts of eyeglasses into more socially acceptable fashion accessories. The use of contact lenses has further reduced corrective eye-wear into a sheer layer of glass or plastic that rests precisely on the eyeball. English astronomer Sir John Herschel (1792–1871) suggested methods for grinding and molding glass lenses to be placed directly upon the cornea in the 1820s. Only by the late 1880s, however, were Herschel's theories put into practice individually by Adolf Eugen Fick and F. E. Müller. Glass contact lenses were costly, uncomfortable, and prevented the flow of oxygen to the eye. Plastic technologies in the twentieth century led to the modern con-tact lenses of today. Only in the 1970s were contact lenses developed from polymers that provided for a flexible or "soft" lens. Not only do contact lenses aid in the correction of nearsightedness and farsightedness, as well as astigmatism, but they may also be prescribed to assist colorblind patients to better differentiate color or to protect a damaged cornea or iris. Decora-tive, or non-corrective, contact lenses, first developed for theatrical pur-poses, are widely available today and are worn for cosmetic reasons. They are also useful for sports and other activities and can provide better periph-eral vision than glasses. These lenses can change eye color or even alter the appearance of the eye through a range of effects. Whether corrective or cosmetic, contact lenses also point to the passage of eye correction further into the body itself: a migration that LASIK, or Laser-Assisted In Situ Kerato-mileusis, eye surgery has achieved most fully for the treatment of myopia, hyperopia, and astigmatism. In this surgery, a hinged flap is sliced into the cornea either by a blade, called a microkeratome, or by a laser referred to as IntraLase. Having permeated the surface of the eye, the flap is raised and a laser reshapes the eye for vision adjustment. With this procedure, vision correction has truly become an embodied practice.

Further Reading: Andressen, B. Michael. *Spectacles: From Utility to Cult Object.* Stuttgart: Arnoldsche. 1998; Enoch, Jay M. "The Enigma of Early Lens Use." *Technology and Culture* 39, no. 2 (April 1998): 273–291; Iiardi, Vincent. "Eyeglasses and Concave Lenses in Fifteenth-century Florence and Milan: New Documents." *Renaissance Quar-terly* 29, no. 3 (Autumn 1976): 341–360; Levene, John R. "Sir George Biddell Airy, F. R. S. (1801–1892) and the Discovery and Correction of Astigmatism," *Notes and Records of the Royal Society of London* 21, no. 2 (December 1966): 180–199; Moldo-nado, Tomás. "Taking Eyeglasses Seriously." *Design Issues* 17, no. 4 (Autumn 2001): 32–43; Rosenthal, William J. *Spectacles and Other Vision Aids: A History and Guide to Collecting.* San Francisco: Norman Publishing, 1996; Vitols, Astrid. *Dictionnaire des lunettes, historique et symbolique d'un objet culturel.* Paris: Éditions Bonneton, 1994; Winkler, Wolf, ed. *A Spectacle of Spectacles.* Leipzig: Edition Leipzig, 1988.

Sean Weiss

Face

Cultural Ideals of Facial Beauty

Most cultures have a specific set of ideals about what constitutes a beautiful face. Western ideals of facial beauty include symmetry, proportion and harmony, clear skin, the appearance of youth, and a face that matches one's biological sex. The first three ideals arose in ancient Greece, although they were not applied directly to the face. Leonardo da Vinci applied these ideals to the human face during the Renaissance. Modern sociobiology has discovered the appeal of facial symmetry, proportion and harmony, clear skin, youth, and sexual specificity. Most cultures have developed beauty practices in order to make the face conform more closely to their particular set of beauty ideals. In Western nations, two of the most common beauty practices are the use of cosmetics and cosmetic surgery.

The question of whether beauty is innate or "in the eye of the beholder" is contested. The ancient Greeks thought beauty to be a mathematical property that some objects have. Sociobiological explanations claim that the attraction of the aforementioned ideals results from the evolutionary process. Both mathematical and sociobiological explanations locate beauty within the object itself. These also imply that the beauty ideals they identify are universal. Yet not all cultures find the same characteristics beautiful, and not everyone within Western cultures such as the United States, England, and Australia agrees that symmetry, proportion and harmony, clear skin, the appearance of youth, and a face that matches one's biological sex is necessarily beautiful.

Feminist scholars and antiracist scholars contest claims that beauty ideals of the face are innate and/or universal. Feminist scholars expose the gender politics behind, and the economic reasons for, the existence of ideals of facial beauty and the beauty industry. Antiracist scholars contest the assumption that beauty ideals are universal by exposing the racialized assumptions that tend to inform them.

Western Ideals: The Golden Ratio, Bilateral Symmetry, and Well-Being

There is a long history in Western nations of thinking that beauty is a universal and objective property, and that beauty and extremes are mutually exclusive. This tradition begins with the ancient Greeks.

The ancient Greeks believed that beauty consisted of three components: symmetry, proportion, and harmony. They considered these properties to be natural and intrinsic to all beautiful things. The pre-Socratic philosopher and mathematician Pythagoras (ca. 580–ca. 500 BCE) was the first to explicitly articulate this idea. Pythagoras led a school of elite mathematicians referred to as the Pythagoreans. The symbol of the Pythagoreans was the pentagram, a five-pointed star that conforms to what is now known as the ratio *phi*. For the Pythagoreans, to understand the properties of phi was to know beauty. Phi, also known as the golden ratio, is an irrational number almost equivalent to 1.618. Phi was named after the classical Greek sculptor Phidias (ca. 490–ca. 430 BCE), whose widely admired sculptures conformed to this ratio. The ancient Greek philosophers Socrates, Plato, and Aristotle also expressed the idea that proportion and harmony were essential to beauty in different ways.

During the Renaissance, Leonardo da Vinci applied phi to the human face in an illustration in his text *De Divina Proportione*. Art historians speculate that da Vinci used phi in the *Mona Lisa*.

Today, cosmetic surgeons and dentists use phi to a guide their work. Steven Marquardt, a California oral and maxillofacial surgeon, has invented a beauty analysis system called the Marquardt Beauty Analysis, or MBA. Marquardt lists the necessary qualities of a beautiful face as color (any shade of brown), a smooth texture, and proportion in relation to the rest of the body, specifically, a height of one-seventh to one-eighth of the rest of the body. Most important, however, is that a beautiful face must conform to phi. Marquardt has invented two Golden Decagon Masks, one male and one female, both of which are based on phi. The masks can be superimposed over an image of a person's face in order to judge how beautiful they are. According to Marquardt, the more beautiful a face is, the more closely the mask will fit. Marquardt claims that his masks will fit any beautiful face insofar as it is beautiful, regardless of a person's ethnic heritage. On his Web site, he applies the female mask to faces from a variety of different ethnic backgrounds and notes that the mask tends to fit each group differently. Marquardt suggests that his masks should be used in cosmetic makeup application, aesthetic surgery, and cosmetic dentistry.

Yosh Jefferson, an American dentist, has invented the Jefferson analysis and the Jefferson skeletal classification, which he combines in order to determine the beauty and health of a patient's teeth and surrounding structures. Like the MBA, the Jefferson analysis and the Jefferson skeletal classification are based upon phi. Further, Jefferson argues that bilateral symmetry is an important aspect of facial beauty. He claims that a beautiful face must conform to the golden ratio of phi, but such a face will not be beautiful unless it is also symmetrical. Jefferson advocates that his analysis be used to guide the work of dentists to improve their patient's physical beauty and health. According to Jefferson, not only are faces that conform to phi the most beautiful, the possession of these divine proportions signifies physical health, psychological health, and maximum fertility. Hence, for Jefferson, creating these proportions will improve a person's quality of life.

Ideals of Facial Beauty and the Theory of Evolution

In Jefferson's explanation of what facial beauty is and how it is beneficial, we see echoes of Charles Darwin's (1809–1882) theory of the evolution of species. In fact, contemporary explanations for the appeal of proportion, symmetry, clear skin, the appearance of youth, and a face that matches one's biological sex often rely upon the theory of evolution. Briefly, Darwin's theory holds that reproduction is the ultimate aim of all living organisms. Those that are best suited to their environment are the most likely to survive long enough to reproduce and pass on their genetic material to their offspring. Evolutionary explanations of why bilateral symmetry and certain facial proportions are seen as beautiful assert that these traits indicate (or at least, are perceived to indicate) good physical health and thus reproductive fitness.

Evolutionary explanations of beauty rely upon the theory of normalizing selection. Normalizing selection assumes that the offspring of two average parents are likely to fall within the average range. Normalizing selection increases the offspring's chance of survival by reducing the risk of disadvantageous genetic anomalies. Applying the theory of normalizing selection, faces with average proportions compared to the rest of the population indicate an individual's genetic normalcy, whereas extremes indicate a genetic predisposition to ill health. Hence, the appeal of average facial proportions is explained in evolutionary terms as an effect of each individual's desire to produce healthy offspring.

Bilateral symmetry is also thought to signify good health and reproductive fitness. The theory of evolution posits that an organism's ability to withstand stress is crucial to its chances of survival. Since asymmetries frequently make their first appearances when a human is in its embryonic form, some evolutionary theorists suggest that bilateral facial symmetry indicates the organism's ability to withstand stress. However, the fact that every human face exhibits a degree of natural asymmetry throws this particular explanation into question.

Making Beauty: Cosmetics

Historically, people in both Western and non-Western cultures have used cosmetics, clothing, accessories, and hairstyles to embody their cultures' particular ideals of beauty. Archaeological evidence suggests that the ancient Egyptians were the first to use cosmetics around 4000 BCE. In ancient Egypt, both women and men used kohl, a dark-colored powder, to line their eyes and eyebrows. Cosmetics were first used in Europe in the Middle Ages. During the reign of Queen Elizabeth I, a pale complexion was the beauty ideal. To achieve this look, both women and men applied toxic makeup that contained lead and arsenic to their faces. This caused many deaths by poisoning.

Today, the application of makeup is a routine aspect of the daily lives of many women worldwide. Although it is not considered masculine in Western cultures for males to wear makeup, men are increasingly joining women in skin-care regimes that require special facial scrubs for cleansing, toning liquid for "clarifying" the skin, and moisturizer to soften the skin and prevent it from drying out. In addition, some men make a rebellious statement against their prescribed gender role by wearing flamboyant makeup. The use of makeup among men is also common in subcultures where individuality and theatricality are prized over conformity to mainstream ideals of beauty, such as Goths and punks.

In these subcultures, makeup is often used by both sexes in ways that challenge, rather than reinforce, mainstream ideals of facial beauty. Although there are a wide variety of differences between individuals in any community, subcultural groups often distinguish themselves through particular ways of styling the face and body. Goths, for example, use pale foundation with very dark eye shadow and black eyeliner, often in combination with dark red, blue, purple, or black lipstick, to achieve a languid rather than a healthy complexion. Goths often challenge the ideal of bilateral symmetry by drawing patterns on the one side of the face with eyeliner, and by wearing different colored contact lenses simultaneously. Punks frequently use brightly colored eye shadow, like hot pink combined with fluorescent green, to challenge the ideal of "natural beauty."

Beauty Surgery

Surgery is defined loosely here as any practice that involves penetrating the skin. Cosmetic surgery is usually performed by a physician; however, "folk surgeons" often perform procedures such as facial piercing, cutting, and branding to produce aesthetic scarification and tongue splitting.

People in Western and non-Western cultures alike have long used cosmetic surgery to embody facial beauty ideals. Cosmetic surgery refers to a wide array of surgical procedures that share a common goal, to improve the patient's appearance. Cosmetic surgery is often distinguished from reconstructive surgery, the aim of which is to rebuild a damaged body part. However, this distinction is contested by the fact that, like cosmetic surgery, reconstructive procedures do normalize a patient's appearance.

India has been credited with the first cosmetic surgery procedure. Medical texts by Sushruta Samhita, who is believed to have taught surgery at the Banaras University in the fifth century BCE, described in detail the first rhinoplasty, or nose-reshaping surgery. Since early times, Indian surgeons have performed rhinoplasty and continue to refine the "Indian technique," which is still in use today.

The Romans were able to perform simple cosmetic procedures during the time of Aegineta (625–690 CE). However, cosmetic surgery developed slowly in the West, becoming routine only in the early twentieth century. World War I saw the development of many modern reconstructive and cosmetic techniques because many soldiers suffered horrific injuries. In response, pioneering surgeons like Hippolyte Morestin, a French army surgeon, and the New Zealand-born surgeon Sir Harold Delf Gillies, invented new procedures to reconstruct the faces of injured soldiers. The procedures that Morestin and Gillies pioneered are the basis of contemporary cosmetic surgery.

Cosmetic facial procedures include, but are not limited to: Botox injections, eyelid surgery, brow lifts, facelifts, chemical peels, dermabrasion, microdermabrasion, laser resurfacing, facial implants, rhinoplasty, mentoplasty (chin surgery), and more. What these procedures have in common is that they aim to make the patient's face conform more closely to beauty ideals, including better proportions, symmetry, smoothness of texture, and the appearance of youth.

Botox and Dysport are the commercial names for a neurotoxic protein, which is one of the most poisonous natural substances in the world. Botox causes muscle paralysis, the severity of which can be controlled in clinical settings. In cosmetic applications, Botox is injected into the face in order to reduce, and increasingly to prevent, the formation of frown lines between the eyebrows. It works by immobilizing the muscles responsible for this facial expression. It is also used in other areas such as to treat the lines outside the eyes referred to as crow's feet, although in the United States such uses are not officially approved by the Food and Drug Administration and are considered "off-label" applications.

Eyelid surgery is technically called blepharoplasty. Blepharoplasty is performed to remove fat, skin, and muscle tissue from the eyelids. Blepharoplasty is sometimes performed when a patient's eyelids are occluding their vision. Its cosmetic purpose is to reduce the sagging and tired appearance that aging is thought to give the eyes.

Asian blepharoplasty is a procedure to create an upper-eyelid crease in patients who were born with enough fatty tissue in their eyelids to fill them out, thereby creating the "single eyelid" appearance. Asian blepharoplasty is especially popular among women of Japanese and Korean heritage. Asian blepharoplasty is a controversial practice. Cosmetic surgeons claim that the procedure is designed to make the patient more beautiful, not to erase the visible signs of their ethnic heritage. However, those who oppose the procedure argue that the beauty ideal to which surgeons and their patients aspire is not universal, but a sign of Anglo-European anatomy.

A forehead lift is done to restore the appearance of youth to the area above the eyes by surgically lifting drooping brows and reducing the appearance of the horizontal wrinkles that form across the forehead as a person ages. The facelift is a more extensive procedure than the forehead lift, involving two thirds of the face. The facelift is done for the same reason as the forehead lift—to make the patient appear younger. A facelift involves removing sagging skin and tightening up the muscle tissue in the face and the neck. As facelifts do not remove all facial wrinkles, they are often performed in conjunction with other cosmetic procedures like Botox injections, blepharoplasty, chemical peels, and dermabrasion.

Skin treatments such as chemical peels, dermabrasion, microdermabrasion, laser resurfacing, and scar revision aim to enhance the facial skin, making it appear younger and smoother in accordance with contemporary ideals of facial beauty. There are many types of chemical peels, but they all involve the application of acidic chemicals of varying strengths to the surface of the skin. These chemicals penetrate the skin to various depths, depending upon the strength of the chemical involved, and cause the outer layers of the skin to blister and peel off. The closer a layer of skin is to the surface, the older it is. Hence, chemical peels expose younger, smoother skin.

Dermabrasion also exposes younger, smoother layers of skin using a high-speed rotary wheel instead of acidic chemicals. Dermabrasion was originally developed as a treatment for acne scars. It is now commonly used to reduce other scars, wrinkles, and irregular pigmentation of the skin, including some instances of rosacea—a skin condition characterized by facial redness, bumps and pimples, skin thickening, and eye irritation. Microdermabrasion is generally used to reduce fine wrinkles. The procedure involves blasting fine crystals across the patient's face and employs suction to remove the outer layers of skin. Laser resurfacing employs a carbon dioxide laser to vaporize the upper layers of damaged skin. Laser resurfacing is used to remove fine wrinkles, to treat facial scarring, and to even out inconsistent skin pigmentation.

Implants are most commonly placed in the cheeks, jaw, and chin. Implants are generally constructed from porus materials that emulate bone tissue, or from acrylate fill. They are used to normalize the faces of people who were born with congenital conditions, to rebuild the faces of accident victims and those who have had facial tumors removed, and to augment the bone structure of healthy people. Cheek augmentation is often done to balance a patient's cheeks with the rest of her or his face and help the patient look less gaunt. In other words, cheek augmentation, like most other cosmetic surgery procedures, is performed to make a person more attractive by making the face conform to the beauty ideals of correct proportion, symmetry, and health.

Facial beauty ideals are sex-specific. Some transsexual women (people who were born with a male body but who become, identify, as or live as women) use cosmetic facial surgery in conjunction with genital sex reassignment to help them fit into society as women. Biological women often undergo facial hair removal by electrolysis, but this is particularly important for transsexual women. There are also specific face feminization procedures of the hairline, forehead, nose, jaw, chin, and trachea to help transsexual women look more feminine. Some facial feminization procedures include, but are not limited to: hair transplantation to reverse a receding hairline; forehead recontouring, which involves the use of implants to round out a flat forehead; rhinoplasty to soften the visual impact of the nose; jaw reshaping procedures, sometimes accompanied by orthodontic work, to set the teeth to the new jaw structure; masseter muscle reduction; chin surgery to make the jaw appear more round; and chondrolaryngoplasty, or reduction of the Adam's apple. Of course, transsexual women also use conventional cosmetic surgery to curb the signs of aging.

The teeth and gums are vital aspects of the visage. Smiling is an important social signal, which often requires one to show one's teeth. Cosmetic dentistry consists of a group of procedures designed to improve the appearance of the teeth and to give patients "the perfect smile." The same beauty ideals of correct color, straightness, proportion, and symmetry inform the Western concept of the perfect smile, as the earlier discussion of Yosh

Jefferson's work indicates. In order for a smile to be considered beautiful, the teeth must be bright white and the gums pink. The teeth should be straight and there must not be too much gum showing during the smile. The teeth also must be symmetrical—corresponding teeth on either side of the mouth must be of the same size and all teeth should be present. It should be pointed out, however, that Western ideals of beauty are not universal. Following their concept of *wabi sabi*, which sees beauty in transience and imperfection, many Japanese people find crooked teeth attractive.

Teeth are susceptible to a number of processes that are not compatible with Western ideals of facial beauty. Cosmetic dentists modify the teeth and jaw to improve the function of the teeth and to make the patient fit these beauty ideals more closely. Naturally crooked teeth are often straightened with braces. Braces consist of a metal wire that is placed in front of the teeth in order to push them in line with one another, usually over a period of around two years.

The outermost layer of a tooth is hard enamel, which becomes yellowish due to disease, certain medications, coffee, tea, sugary soft drinks, and smoking. Cosmetic dentists offer chemical whitening, mild acid whitening, abrasive teeth whitening, and laser teeth whitening procedures to remove the yellowish stains from tooth enamel. Tooth veneers made from porcelain or plastic are often applied to cover stained teeth, and to change the size, shape, and surface appearance of the teeth. Dental bonding, which is commonly known as "filling," is used to fill gaps in the teeth, to rebuild chipped teeth and broken teeth, and to remold and recolor the teeth.

If a tooth is lost entirely, the gap may be filled in a number of ways. Dentists may install a bridge, which is a false tooth that is fused between two crowns that are applied to the teeth on either side of the gap. A crown is a covering made from various materials that are applied to a tooth to improve its strength and appearance. If the patient looks after his or her dental bridge properly, it may reduce the risk of gum disease, improve the bite (the alignment of the teeth when the mouth is closed in a natural position), and even change the patient's pattern of speech. Another option to replace missing teeth is a denture. A denture is a removable false tooth or a set of teeth that is crafted to fit the patient's mouth. Dentures not only improve the patient's appearance, they also help with speech problems caused by missing teeth and aid mastication. If the patient prefers a permanent replacement, dental implants may be fixed. Dental implants require a titanium fixture to be surgically attached to the mandible (jawbone). Titanium is a strong and lightweight metal that integrates well with bone tissue. The titanium fixture has threaded holes and acts as an anchor for false teeth. Once the implant has healed, false teeth, which are designed to look as natural as possible, are screwed into the implant.

Alternative Faces: Folk Surgery

Folk-surgery procedures like facial piercing, scarification, and branding are popular practices among Goths, punks, modern primitives, and other loosely formed groups of individuals who would refuse any subcultural label. Although these practices are not always understood as motivated by concerns about beauty but rather politics, sexuality, or spirituality, they are sometimes done for purely aesthetic reasons. They are related to beauty practices insofar as they are often defined in opposition to beauty practices as strategies to resist homogenizing beauty ideals.

In the 1970s, punks pierced one another's faces as a way of resisting mainstream beauty ideals. Today, facial piercing is a very common practice—so much so that most major cities support piercing shops, where facial piercing procedures are performed on a commercial basis. The face can be pierced in many areas, and a wide variety of jewellery can be inserted. A sterile medical needle is usually used to pierce the face. A cookie-cutter-like instrument called a dermal punch is used to create larger holes, especially though cartilage. For deep piercings, curved bars with beads on each end, or rings that do up with one bead are threaded through piercings in the ears, eyebrows, nasal bridge, nostrils, septum, labret, frenulum, and/or tongue. Piercings can be stretched by gradually inserting wider and wider jewellery. Surface piercing is a less common form of facial piercing than deep piercing. Surface piercing involves threading horizontal bars through the surface of the skin horizontally and vertically at various sites, like the forehead and cheeks. Often facial piercings are not symmetrical. For example, one eyebrow, one nostril, or one side of the lips may be pierced while the other side is not.

As the name suggests, cuttings involve incising a pattern into the skin with a scalpel. Sometimes ink is rubbed into the wound to create a colorful scar. In a rare mode of cutting called "packing," the wound is filled with an inert substance such as clay. This results in a special type of hypertrophic scarring called keloid scarring. Keloid scars are raised, red scars that grow beyond the boundaries of the original incision. During branding, a design is burned onto the skin using a variety of methods. The most common, strike branding, uses a very hot branding iron. Generally, a pattern is burned onto the skin in small sections rather than all in one go. Less common branding procedures include electrocautery and electrosurgical branding. These enable more detailed designs than strike branding. Like cutting, branding produces aesthetic scarring, usually keloid scarring. Piercings, cuttings, and brandings all disrupt the beauty ideal of smooth skin texture and color, replacing it with different visual and tactile qualities that some people find more interesting than plain, smooth skin.

Importantly, many folk-surgery practices have their origins in non-Western cultures. Nostril piercing, for example, is recoded in the both Christian Bible and the holy texts of the Vedas. The practice was brought to India by Nordic Aryan tribes, who invaded around 1500 BCE. Since then, nostril piercing has gone in and out of fashion in India. The practice has been sustained in part by Hindu women, who often have their left nostril pierced on the eve of marriage.

Although facial piercing is an acceptable alternative to mainstream beauty ideals, cuttings and brandings are rarely done on the face in Western cultures due to strong cultural taboos. Facial tattooing is a slightly different story. It is possible to have eyebrows, eyeliner, lip liner, and lipstick tattooed to the face. This form of facial tattooing is done to make the face conform to, rather than deviate from, normative ideals of facial beauty. This is the only form of facial tattooing that is socially acceptable in mainstream Western cultures. In Australia, for example, members of the New South Wales Association of Professional Tattooists agreed to a code of conduct that prohibits them from tattooing the face, head, neck, and hands.

Feminist Critiques

Beauty ideals in the West have been criticized by feminists since at least the eighteenth century. In her book *Unbearable Weight* (1993), Susan Bordo cites Mary Wollstonecraft's argument in 1792 that beauty ideals promoted the frailty of women's bodies and minds. And in 1914, the "right to ignore fashion" was listed at the first Feminist Mass Meeting in America as one of the rights women were demanding. Beauty became a significant issue for feminists in the 1970s as well. For many feminists of this era, beauty regimens were seen as practices of female oppression.

Of course, feminism is not one single and coherent way of thinking. Hence it is not surprising that considerable disagreement exists among feminists about whether or not Western beauty ideals and the practices they inspire are oppressive to women.

Radical feminists like Sheila Jeffreys argue that all beauty practices, from the use of removable cosmetics to cosmetic surgery and body piercing, are oppressive to women. Jeffreys points out that the beauty industry profits from products that can physically harm women. In May 2003, *The Economist* estimated the worth of the annual global beauty industry at $160 billion. Women doing their daily beauty routines will expose themselves to more than 2,000 synthetic chemicals before they have their morning coffee. Some of these chemicals are known to be dangerous to human health. One example is propylene glycol, which is widely used in cosmetics such as baby lotions and mascara, is an acknowledged neurotoxin, and has been linked to contact dermatitis, kidney damage, liver damage, and the inhibition of skin cell growth. In the United States, every year thousands of visits to hospital emergency rooms are the result of allergic reactions to cosmetics.

However, Jeffreys' central argument is not so much concerned with the effects that cosmetics have upon women's health as with the social structures that require women to use them. According to Jeffreys, in all patriarchal societies men use heterosexuality to create and maintain unequal relations of power between the sexes. Jeffreys views female beauty practices as avenues through which women become sexual objects for heterosexual men.

Not all feminists agree with radical feminist arguments such as Jeffreys'. Liberal feminists argue that the decision of whether or not to engage in beauty practices should be left to each individual woman. Many postmodern feminists, such as Susan Bordo, point out that distinctions between oppression and liberation, coercion and choice are far from clear-cut. Postmodern feminists therefore aim to articulate the complexities and (often) contradictions that characterize women's relationship to beauty ideals and practices.

Anti-Racist Critiques of Western Beauty Ideals

Anti-racist scholars argue that dominant ideals of facial beauty are products of their cultural and historical context. They argue that Anglo-European features are not intrinsically or objectively more attractive than, say, Asian or African features. Rather, Anglo-European ideals tend to be privileged in nations where there is a history of Anglo-European colonization. In the United States, Western Europe, and Australia, the dominant beauty ideal for women is an Anglo-European one. One important way that Anglo-European ideals of beauty are positioned as "universal" is via the constant repetition of these ideals in the public arena to the exclusion of others. For example, Eugenia Kaw points out that women of Asian heritage are radically underrepresented in American advertisements, especially advertisements for beauty products, on television programs, and in other public forums where physical beauty is an important qualification. In this way, specifically Anglo-European ideals of beauty become normalized. On these grounds, Kaw critiques the practice of so-called "Asian eyelid surgery" as a racist inscription of Anglo European beauty ideals upon the faces of Asian American women.

Anti-racist scholars have also critiqued Anglo-feminist arguments against beauty ideals and practices for failing to consider the different position of white women compared to women of color in relation to mainstream ideals of beauty. In her book, *Ain't I a Beauty Queen? Black Women, Beauty and the Politics of Race*, Maxine Leeds Craig traces the history of black American women's struggle to be seen as beautiful in a culture where ideals of beauty were specific to Anglo-European women. In September 1968 in the United States, the National Association for the Advancement of Colored People, or NAACP, staged a Miss Black America beauty contest to protest the exclusion of black women from the Miss America pageant. Meanwhile, feminists were protesting the objectification of white women in the Miss America contest. These events showcased the different positions of black and white American women in relation to dominant ideals of beauty—black women struggled to be perceived as beautiful whereas white women fought for liberation from their cultural position as "beautiful but unequal." This is not to imply that the women's liberation protesters were unaware of the racial politics involved in American beauty ideals and practices. Yet this example does suggest that ideals of beauty, including facial beauty, and the practices they inspire are inflected with culturally and historically specific notions of gender and race. *See also* Chin: Implants; Eyes: Blepharoplasty; Face: History of Antiaging Treatments; Face: Medical Antiaging Treatments; Nose: Nose Piercing; Skin: Body Piercing; Skin: Branding; Skin: Scarification; Skin: Tattooing; and Teeth: Cosmetic Dentistry

Further Reading: BME: Body Modification Ezine, http://www.bmezine.com; Bordo, Susan. *Unbearable Weight: Feminism, Western Culture, and the Body*. Berkeley: University of California Press, 1993; Cohen, Tony. *The Tattoo*. Mosman, NSW: Outback Print, 1994; Craig, Maxine Leeds. *Ain't I a Beauty Queen? Black Women, Beauty and the Politics of Race*. Oxford: Oxford University Press, 2002; Crawford M., and R. Under, eds. *In Our Own Words: Readings on the Psychology of Women and Gender*. New York: McGraw-Hill, 1997; *Encyclopedia of Surgery: A Guide for Patients and Caregivers*, http://www.surgeryencyclopedia.com; Jeffreys, Sheila. *Beauty and Misogyny Harmful*

Cultural Practices in the West. East Sussex: Routledge, 2005; Kaw, Eugenia. "Medicalization of Racial Features: Asian-American Women and Cosmetic Surgery." In Rose Weitz, ed. *The Politics of Women's Bodies*. Oxford: Oxford University Press, 2003, pp. 167–183; Marquardt, Steven. *Marquardt Beauty Analysis*, http://www.beautyanalysis.com/index2_mba.htm; *Phi, The Golden Number*, http://goldennumber.net/beauty.htm; Rhodes, Gillian, and Leslie A. Zebrowitz. (eds) *Facial Attractiveness: Evolutionary, Cognitive, and Social Perspectives*. Westport, CT: Ablex Publishing, 2002.

Gretchen Riordan

History of Antiaging Treatments

Antiaging is historically connected to the desire to be immortal, to prolonging or regaining youth, and to extending healthy, dynamic old age, or senescence. Broadly, antiaging consists of interventions into aging at any period in the life course for the purposes of lengthening life, maintaining or regaining health and virility, and appearing younger. Practices of antiaging have included myriad variations of scientific and medical endeavors, cultural ideas about diet, hygiene, and exercise, use of cosmetics and paint, and superstition and magic. Antiaging has deep cultural significance, and attitudes toward the aged and aging have always been connected to economic, religious, and scientific beliefs.

Myths, Stories, and Quests

There is a common belief that ancient and premodern cultures revered the elderly and that age discrimination is a modern phenomenon. But images of aging in art and literature rarely have been positive. There is only one elderly Greek god, Geras, and he is connected to darkness and described as loathsome. In *The Odyssey*, Homer disguises Odysseus as an old man and describes him thus as being "just a burden on the land." Many fairy tales include wicked older women who are desperately trying to regain their youths.

Myths about and quests for antiaging abound through history. *The Epic of Gilgamesh*, one of the earliest known works of literature (ca. 700 BCE), is partly about seeking immortality. An ancient Greek myth tells of how Medea restores the youth of her father-in-law, Aeson. Over nine days she built altars, begged the gods to intervene, sacrificed a black lamb, and boiled a concoction of plants, stones, sand, a wolf's entrails, and an owl's head. She cut Aeson's throat, drained him of his blood, replaced it with the potion, and he became youthful again. Chinese history tells of Emperor Qin Shi Huang (259 BCE–210 BCE), who died from eating mercury tablets that he believed would make him immortal. In the Old Testament of the Bible, the book of Kings suggests that ailing men will be rejuvenated if they lie with young virgins. In the fairy tale *Snow White and the Seven Dwarves*, an aging stepmother commands a hunter to kill her young stepdaughter so she can eat her heart and be rejuvenated. Spanish explorer Juan Ponce de León (1460–1521) searched in vain for a mythical rejuvenating water spring, the Fountain of Youth, in the Caribbean islands and Florida in the early 1500s. More recently, Oscar Wilde's gothic novel *The Picture of Dorian*

Gray (1890) tells the story of a beautiful young man who wishes that a portrait would age instead of him. His wish is fulfilled: he doesn't age, but over time his face in the portrait does and becomes utterly grotesque.

Cosmetics and Beauty Creams

Cosmetics have been closely linked to antiaging and, indeed, the distinction between beauty products and antiaging products remains blurred. Makeup and face paint can be used to adorn the self and to give the appearance of youth. Often, these two endeavors are connected: for example, rouging the cheeks is decorative but is also a way to mimic the rosiness of a youthful complexion, and dying the hair both ornaments the body and hides grayness. Nondecorative antiaging creams have existed for millennia: an Egyptian papyrus from about 1600 BCE gives instructions for a cream that will transform an old man into a twenty-year-old. Smooth skin is one of the most obvious indications of youth. Some 3000-year-old jars found in Tutankhamun's tomb contain skin cream made of animal fat and scented resin. An ancient Egyptian recipe for anti-wrinkle cream combines incense, wax, olive oil, and ground cypress, and a concoction to help hide gray hair includes the blood of a black cow, crushed tortoiseshell, and the neck of a gabgu bird cooked in oil. In ancient Rome, bathing included using abrasives made from clay, flour, crushed broad beans, ash, and crushed snail's shells. Pumice stones, also used to smooth the skin, have been found in Pompeii. After bathing, Roman skin care included using masks and poultices to soften and lighten the skin. These were made variously from plants, deer horn, kingfisher excrement, eggs, lead, and honey. Pliny the Elder's *Natural History* (circa 77 CE) recommends using ass's milk, honey, and swan's fat to smooth wrinkles. He describes a woman who spent her sixtieth birthday covered in a poultice of honey, wine lees, and ground narcissus bulbs in the hope of appearing more youthful. Roman poet Martial wrote in the first century AD of women using wigs and false teeth (which may have been made from wrought iron) to hide the changes brought about by age.

By 4 BCE, the ancient Greeks were using white lead with the hope of making their complexions lighter and younger-looking. Lead is a poison that can lead to neurological and gastrointestinal problems and even premature death. Despite lead poisoning being well documented, it was used to whiten faces and fill in wrinkles until as late as the mid-1800s. Queen Elizabeth I (1533–1603) was famous for having lead and rouge applied to her face in increasing quantities as she grew older. Elizabethan women also sometimes used egg whites as a glaze to tighten sagging skin. In the 1500s and 1600s, bear grease—the fat of the animal melted down—was used as a salve and a cream to prevent cracking and wrinkling of the skin. The recipe for Queen of Hungary water was first published in 1652, and remained immensely popular for two centuries. It was made by distilling rosemary flowers in alcoholic spirits and was said to be endorsed by Isabella, Queen of Hungary, as having "such a wondrous effect that I seemed to grow young and beautiful." French chemist Nicholas Lémery (1645–1715) wrote in 1685 of a method to remove wrinkles using river water, barley, and white balsam (the recipe took more than a day to make). A widely read French text, *Toilet of Flora* (1775), suggested that the juice of green pineapple "takes away wrinkles and gives the complexion an air of youth."

In the mid-seventeenth century in England, women began using an early version of the chemical skin peel. After brushing their faces with sulphuric acid (known as oil of vitriol), the skin would peel off to reveal new layers. Physician John Bulwer (1606–1656) described such women as looking like "peeld Ewes." In Victorian times, obvious cosmetics were frowned upon but people still worked to minimize wrinkles: brown paper soaked in cider vinegar was placed on the brows, and some who could afford it slept with their faces covered in thin slices of raw beef. A popular anti-wrinkle paste, caked on at night, was made of egg white, rose water, alum, and almonds.

Medicine and Science

From the sixteenth to the eighteenth centuries, the quest for longevity was largely about extending the healthy lives of elderly people. However, in the nineteenth through twenty-first centuries, the focus moved to avoiding old age entirely.

Luigi Cornaro (1468–1566) wrote *The Art of Living Long* in Italy in 1550. It was translated into many languages and went into its fiftieth edition in the 1800s. Cornaro argued that life could be extended by the simple strategy of moderation in all things and thus the maintenance of "vital energy." He did not advocate staving off old age but rather prolonging health and vigor throughout senescence, which he believed could be a cherished and healthy stage of life and a period of great happiness (he lived to ninety-eight). However, by the nineteenth century, the idea of senescence being a vital and meaningful phase of life had waned. Physicians began to believe that aging causes changes to pathology in much the same ways that disease does, and that aging and illness are utterly intertwined. By the twentieth century, aging was no longer seen as physiological but as pathological, and as always inevitably connected to loss of physical and mental capacities. Medical focus changed from how to make old age happy and healthy to how to halt or reverse it. Age is now commonly seen as a disease, and the elderly are believed (often falsely) to be economically burdensome because of illness and infirmity. These sorts of attitudes lead to the cultural worth of older people being diminished and perceptions of growing old being largely negative.

In the late 1800s and early 1900s, there was a surge of interest in Europe and the United States about how medicine might arrest or slow aging. Physicians at this time possessed advanced surgical skills, had access to antiseptic and anesthesia, and also had many opportunities to experiment on humans. In 1889, French professor Charles-Édouard Brown-Séquard (1817–1894) argued that aging was connected to a weakening of the sexual organs. He injected himself (and his colleagues injected more than 1,200 patients) with liquid extracts from guinea pigs and dog testicles, and declared he was restored to youth. In the late 1800s, "spermine" was widely used as an antiaging measure. This injectable product contained liquids from animal testes, prostrate glands, ovaries, pancreata, thyroid glands, and spleens. Some companies selling the compound were later charged with fraud. Chicago urologist Frank Lydston (1858–1923) upped the ante: he underwent a testes transplant himself and performed the same operation on several of his patients. He declared new vigor and said his hair had lost its grayness. In 1919, a physician at San Quentin prison, L. L. Stanley, removed the testicles of an executed prisoner and transplanted them onto a sixty-year-old senile prisoner. Despite medical organizations condemning his experiments, Stanley became internationally famous. By 1928, one writer guessed that the procedure had been performed on up to 50,000 people, all of whom had been "rejuvenated." Other surgeons conducted similar transplants and claimed similar success using the testes of chimpanzees or baboons. Vasoligation, a form of vasectomy, and ovary transplantation (using human or animal ovaries) were also practiced in the United States and Europe in the early twentieth century as ways to reverse aging. Modern medicine has totally discredited such procedures, but many scientists continue to search for ways to halt aging.

Elie Metchnikoff (1845–1916), winner of a Nobel Prize for Physiology or Medicine in 1908, was one of the first scientists to argue that cell degeneration caused old age. He advocated a diet high in lactic acid to halt the destruction of microbes that causes cells to decay. A 1908 reviewer of Metchnikoff's book *The Prolongation of Life* (1907) wrote, on contemplating living largely on curdled skim milk, "the prospect does not seem exhilarating." Aubrey de Grey (1963–) of Cambridge University, author of *Ending Aging* (2007) and head of the Strategies for Engineered Negligible Senescence (SENS) project, defines aging as "the set of accumulated side effects from metabolism that eventually kills us." He has identified seven causes of aging, all of which he argues will eventually be able to be cured. His work is internationally recognized but also highly controversial. It has been criticized as "pseudoscience" and was the subject of a widely read debate in MIT's *Technology Review* in 2005 and 2006.

Antiaging is now a multibillion-dollar industry. Scientists, doctors, and biogerontologists are employed in researching ways to extend both youth and life. Pharmacologists and plastic surgeons are continually looking for new chemical and surgical ways to make the human body look younger. Viagra and Botox, two of the most widely known contemporary medical brand names, are both designed with antiaging properties in mind.

It has been argued that societies that placed great value on physical beauty were less likely to value old age. This was the case in ancient Greece and in Europe during the Renaissance, and is perhaps applicable to many contemporary societies. Conversely, in Europe in the Middle Ages, when more emphasis was placed on spiritual goodness and internal beauty, wrinkled faces and frail bodies were not seen as so terrifying or characteristics that are always mediated by social and cultural beliefs.

Further Reading: Haber, C. "Life Extension and History: The Continual Search for the Fountain of Youth." *Journal of Gerontology* 59A, no. 6 (2004): 515–522; Minois, Georges. *History of Old Age: From Antiquity to the Renaissance*, trans. Sarah Hanbury

Tenison. Chicago: Chicago University Press, 1989; Post, Stephen G., and Robert H. Binstock. *The Fountain of Youth: Cultural, Scientific, and Ethical Perspectives on a Biomedical Goal*. Oxford: Oxford University Press, 2004.

Meredith Jones

History of Makeup Wearing

Makeup refers to a variety of cosmetic products—powders, paints, creams, and other potions—intended to change the wearer's appearance, generally but not exclusively on the face. Although makeup functions in varying ways for different people and groups, the wearing of cosmetics has been noted unequivocally in almost every recorded society. Both men and women wore makeup historically, although in recent times, particularly

Queen Elizabeth I. Courtesy of Library of Congress, LC-USZ62-120887.

in the West, women have worn it with much more frequency than men. The adornment that exists naturally in many animal species must be created artificially in humans, and people have used paints, oils, powders, and a variety of other technologies to mark group solidarity and belonging, status and rank differentiation, as attempts to achieve beauty ideals particular to their culture (or of a dominant culture), and for purposes of individuation and the physical attribution of uniqueness. According to biologically based theories of self-enhancement, the primary purpose for adornment and the use of cosmetics is to put forth an ideal self, and is often posited as a means of attracting mates or potential sex partners. This notion has been contested recently, primarily by those who believe the mass-marketing of makeup is used by cosmetics corporations to oppress women and coerce them into the relentless pursuit of beauty. In recent years, cosmetic use has also been appropriated for the purposes of camp and drag and among performance artists, members of punk and Goth communities, or those in other subversive communities who use makeup as as a means of parody or social critique.

Makeup Use in Antiquity

In many societies, wearing makeup was used as environmental camouflage, to evoke fear in enemies, and for a variety of social, spiritual, and medicinal reasons. Makeup was often worn in ceremonial rituals, and was applied to participants in order to signify class status, gender, age, and authority or position within the social hierarchy. As early as 100,000 BCE, there is evidence of humans using body paints and tattooing. Makeup was worn by both sexes in many cultures to mark men and women during courting rituals, and a variety of emollients and oils were applied to the bodies of the dead in burial ceremonies for both preservation and preparation for the afterlife.

Different-colored body paints have been used to signify diverse meanings; red was frequently used to symbolize blood and fertility, and thus women wore this color during ceremonies in some cultures, whereas it signified the reanimation of the dead or danger in other cultures. Black body paint has been associated with night and darkness—the netherworld in some cultures—whereas in others it signified virility and aggression, and was thus worn by men during certain ceremonial rituals. Cross-culturally, yellow paint has been used to signify life and peace, possibly due to its association with the powerful force of the sun, and white has been associated with nature and spirituality.

In ancient Egypt and in ancient cultures of the Middle East, makeup was worn in order to protect the skin and eyes from the sun, as well as for beautification during courting. Male and female Egyptians accentuated their facial and bodily features—especially their eyes—with brightly colored powders and paints made of malachite, copper, and galena, whereas people in other Middle Eastern cultures used flower petals and ochres to dye their skin and hair. Egyptian women frequently bronzed their skin and wore ebony wigs in order to fulfill a feminine ideal associated with sensuality and fertility. They also used kohl, or eye paint, to darken their eyes and make them appear more almond-shaped. This eye paint was used not only to enhance the appearance, but functioned medicinally as a method of protecting the eyes from the glare of the sun and from dust and particles that may have caused infection and disease. In other cultures of the Middle East, henna was used to dye the hair, and white lead was applied to make the skin appear paler. The use of scented oils and aromatics is documented in cultures throughout history and around the world, and served a variety of purposes, including religious and courting functions. The use of makeup in the ancient Middle East, Egypt, and India was associated with high class status—upper-class men and women spent hours each day adorning and perfuming their bodies and faces.

In ancient Greece, the use of cosmetics was a specifically male activity. Women were not permitted to wear makeup on their faces or bodies, but were encouraged to dye their hair. Beauty ideals were simple, and with the exception of the women of Crete, Greek women who wore makeup were condemned as harlots and seductresses. Ancient Greece is one of the first recorded societies in which the wearing of makeup was associated with morality—only courtesans were permitted to use cosmetics, and wearing makeup was used to signify their status as prostitutes. Greek men saw no reason for their wives to enhance their physical appearances, as their only purpose was to keep house and bear children. Thus, *not* wearing makeup was associated with purity for upper-class Greek women. Both Greeks and Romans did use perfumes, however, and bathing (and shaving, for men only) became essential cultural rituals.

In ancient Rome, the importance of class in relation to cosmetic usage was significant; bathing, hair and skin care, and the application of makeup were essential aspects of the daily activities of rich Roman women. The wealthy society lady even had a skilled attendant, called an *ornatrix*, to help her perform these duties. Both men and women in ancient Rome engaged in elaborate beautification and self-care rituals. The cultural aspects of the care of the body were solidified in this culture and epoch, as Roman men attended bathhouses and gymnasia both to bathe and to socialize with other men as part of their daily routines. The social and ritual aspects of self-care and adornment marked the beginning of a trend that would continue for centuries to come, particularly in the West.

The Middle Ages and Early Modern England

In early Britain during the middle ages, bathing and the use of cosmetics were associated with the debauchery of ancient Rome, and thus were rejected as vain and sinful. Female beauty was simplistic and representative of purity and piety; it was also standardized and lacked individual distinction. The ideal beauty was a woman with pale skin, small features, and light hair and eyes, which was exemplified in descriptions in the chivalric poetry of the day. Creams for the hands and face were permitted, but makeup was not. The most important aspects of the medieval woman's beauty regime were the application of cream to preserve the skin and make it as smooth as possible, and the subsequent application of *ceruse*, a face powder made of white lead (which was extremely toxic).

Feminine beauty ideals were also illustrated in the medieval practice of plucking all the hair from the forehead and temples by noble women during this time. It seems that this was to highlight the waxen whiteness and oval shape of the face and to emphasize the ornate headdresses and veils worn by women of the day. Another beauty ritual that was utilized during Tudor and Elizabethan times was the painting of veins on the plucked forehead with dark-colored dyes. The reasoning behind this practice is unclear, although it may have been intended to make the complexion appear more translucent and thus youthful. During the end of the medieval period, English women began to adorn their faces like the Italian and the French styles that had been in vogue for some time in other parts of Europe. Italian and French women during the Middle Ages were typically much more lavish with their makeup-wearing practices, often tinting their eyelashes and eyelids and sometimes even their lips and teeth. During the reign of Queen Elizabeth I (1533–1603), the wearing of white face powder, rouge, and lip color was permitted, and women's fashion became lighter, brighter, and more ornate.

During the Regency era in Britain in the late eighteenth and early nineteenth centuries, it became commonplace for young men of upper-class stature to engage in elaborate beautification regimes. These dandies or "painted men" took great care in dressing themselves, plucking their whiskers, arranging and pomading their hair, wearing cologne, and even applying blush or rouge. Although fashion was more ornate and sexier for women during this time, the wearing of any makeup other than white face powder and occasionally a very lightly tinted lip salve was scorned upon, even for upper-class ladies. During the rule of Queen Victoria, which began in 1837 and ended with her death in 1901, makeup was once again fully associated with impurity and lasciviousness.

Makeup from the Twentieth Century to the Present

Women in the twentieth century used the cosmetical framework of their English counterparts of the seventeenth, eighteenth, and nineteenth centuries. Cures for blemishes, skin rashes, sallow complexions, freckles, and dandruff were part of a quasi-medical body of knowledge that was passed down among women through generations and across cultures. This wisdom remained under the purview of women until skin and hair care recipes were co-opted by pharmacists, doctors, and eventually multinational cosmetics corporations. It is because this knowledge was under the jurisdiction of women for so long that the fields of makeup, cosmetics, and skin and hair care were some of the first and only lucrative business endeavors for female entrepreneurs in the early twentieth century.

During the mid-nineteenth century, self-care and adornment were associated explicitly with femininity. Masculine virtue was deemed inherent, and thus physical adornment was unnecessary (and artificial) for men. At the same time, the moralization of beauty, and thus the paradoxes of and contradictions inherent in cosmetic use, were solidified for women. In line with the pseudosciences of the day, such as physiognomy, craniology, and phrenology, a woman's virtue and goodness were purported to be visually evidenced by her physical beauty, specifically in the proportions of her face and in her skin, eye, hair, and lip color. Beauty was deemed a duty for women, and those who did not conform to the beauty ideals of the day were sometimes seen as immoral and impure. The wearing of makeup, however, was paradoxically posited as sinful. The biblical reference to Jezebel was invoked as evidence of the licentiousness of women who wore cosmetics, and the use of makeup was likened to witchcraft. Thus, a hierarchy based on the privileging of "natural" beauty was established, in which women of color were relegated to the bottom. The pursuit of beauty had to be covert and undetectable, and was often costly if the results were to appear natural. Women of lower socioeconomic statuses did not have a chance at achieving the ideal either, both because they could not always afford enhancement techniques and because the work they engaged in was often physically straining and taxing on their appearances. Prior to the twentieth century, therapeutic and herbal remedies for ailments and natural beautification were distinguished from commercial preparations, such as face paint. The fact that commercial enhancement techniques were often toxic (most face paint and skin lighteners still used ceruse, or white lead) further added to the aura of threat and danger associated with the use of cosmetics.

Throughout the nineteenth century, the beauty ideal remained defined by a smooth, unblemished (and unfreckled) white face with slightly rosy cheeks, but no color on the lips or around the eyes. A variety of skin-lightening products were sold to white women and also targeted to black women, but products such as eyeliner, lipstick, and rouge were still taboo. With the advent of photography and the rise of celebrity culture in the twentieth century, makeup started to make the transition from the stage to everyday life. Lipstick was the first product to become popular on a wide scale in the 1910s and 1920s. This process was gradual, but as a variety of different kinds of makeup eventually became more acceptable, the market for beautification products became increasingly diverse and lucrative.

The Beauty Industry: Makeup and Consumer Culture

As makeup usage became commonplace among women of all classes, races, and backgrounds, a market that women themselves could cash in on developed. Some of the first entrepreneurs in this area were working-class women and women of color. Florence Nightingale Graham (1878–1966), later known as Elizabeth Arden, and Helena Rubenstein (1871–1965), the daughters of Canadian tenant farmers and middle-class Polish Jews, respectively, established highly lucrative and successful businesses around makeup and feminine beautification. Annie Turnbo Malone (1869–1957) and Sarah Breedlove (1867–1919), later known as Madame C. J. Walker, African American women of modest means, each became wealthy selling hair treatment products to African American women. These women's businesses flourished through house-to-house canvassing, mail order, and a highly connected word-of-mouth system, in which women were the consumers, experts, designers, and salespeople of a variety of different beautification products.

Once it became apparent that the beauty industry was becoming highly profitable, a mass market developed, in which the intimate networks of woman-owned businesses were made largely superfluous, and beauty products and makeup were sold on a much larger scale, primarily by corporations. By the 1920s, corporations profited from the newfound interest in makeup. Although some independent female entrepreneurs, such as Rubenstein and Arden, were able to stay afloat in the burgeoning makeup business, most of the new cosmetics firms were run by men, and have been criticized as homogenizing beauty standards in the push for a so-called "democratization" of feminine beauty. The new advertisements for makeup argued that all women should seek to enhance their beauty through the use of products they could now buy at their local drugstores. This also marked the birth of skincare and makeup regimens, in which women were encouraged to buy not just a single product but a whole line of products. The new consumer culture reversed the moral stigma against makeup, emphasizing instead women's duty to enhance their physical appearance with cosmetics.

Changing Cosmetic Trends and Conventions

The initial period of widespread accessibility of makeup and other beautification products was accompanied by a new emphasis on women's individuality and freedom. During the flapper era of the 1920s, mascara, lipstick, and eyebrow pencils became staples of many women's beauty regimens, and the application of makeup was posited as something to be proud of. Many women applied their makeup publicly as a way of asserting their femininity and to draw attention to their physical appearances. Wearing makeup was no longer associated with harlotry or deceit, but rather with sensuality and eroticism. So-called "exotic" looks were also popularized during this era, and the emphasizing of certain "ethnic" features—such as almond-shaped or "Egyptian" eyes with eyeliner—was fashionable. Tanning was even acceptable for a time, and associated with upper-class status. Only women who were wealthy enough to vacation in exotic locales were purported to have the ability and leisure time to sunbathe.

Although makeup wearing was now acceptable for almost all women, standards dictated the appropriate time and place for certain styles. For instance, too much lipstick was still associated with sexual impurity and prurience, and in the early twentieth century, eye makeup was reserved specifically for evening wear, especially for younger women. By the 1930s, however, makeup was much more widely used. Even eye makeup, such as brightly colored eyeshadows and mascaras, was used by adventurous women during the daytime.

In the 1940s and 1950s, the ideal standard of beauty reverted back to youthful, white, and simplistic. The post-World War II look of femininity was highly regimented; the association of beauty with duty was stronger than ever and had become fundamentally linked to a sense of national identity in the United States. Lipstick was by far the most important element of every respectable woman's beauty regimen; in 1948, 80 to 90 percent of American women wore lipstick, with dark red the most popular color.

In the 1950s and 1960s, makeup styles became increasingly exotic and experimental. The sensual and erotic look was marketed just as pervasively as the clean and natural appearance. Differences of age and race were focused on by big corporations in terms of marketing, and many companies began to develop multiple lines of cosmetics to sell to different communities of women. Accentuating the eyes became increasingly popular, and heavy eye makeup combined with pale lipstick, worn by models like Twiggy (1949–), became the style for some time, particularly among younger women,. Older women during this era tended to use darker lipstick and lighter eye makeup, and, generally, just mascara.

The civil rights era marked a return to a "natural" look by women of myriad backgrounds. The feminist movement of this time shunned the dictates of Parisian haute couture and spurned makeup altogether. Many young African American women rejected the practice of straightening their hair, opting instead for natural hair or Afros. In the following decades, cosmetic fads fluctuated among women who continued to wear makeup; however, one of the most popular fads in the 1980s and 1990s was the "clean" or "no makeup" look. The idea was that makeup should be less visible, enhancing a woman's natural beauty. Along with this new angle was a focus on multiculturalism as a beauty aesthetic. Darker shades of skin and hair were said to be celebrated, but as late as 1991, Cover Girl offered seven shades of foundation, almost all of which were suitable only for light-skinned and white women.

Debates Over Makeup in the Twenty-first Century

During the women's rights movement of the 1960s and 1970s, often referred to as the "second wave" of the women's movement to distinguish it from the earlier women's suffrage movement, wearing makeup was heavily critiqued by feminists and other political activists. For many feminists, the mass marketing of cosmetics appeared as a method of homogenizing beauty ideals and oppressing women. The hierarchical construction of beauty inherent in the white, Anglicized beauty standards that had remained so prolific since the advent of the mass beauty market was publicly interrogated; corporations were criticized for the racism and ageism of their marketing tactics and product designs. Although many companies responded by increasing the diversity of shades of foundation and other skin-tinting products, many women saw these attempts as shortsighted and fabricated. The toxicity of some products was also exposed, and the environmental impact of creating makeup was recognized in the latter part of the twentieth century. Organic, nontoxic, and ecologically sound ingredients for cosmetics and skin and hair products are currently popular.

The use of cosmetics and makeup also was appropriated as camp and drag in the twentieth century, particularly among members of gay communities, punk and Goth communities, performance artists, and a variety of other political activists and social critics. Women and men of a variety of social backgrounds now use makeup for the purposes of physical enhancement, performance, and social commentary. A sense of choice has been reinstituted in beauty culture to combat the notion of oppression exposed in the last few decades, and some women have reappropriated makeup—its use, manufacture, and dispersal—for financial, social, and community-building ventures. In a return to its original use, makeup has come full circle—it is no longer something women must consciously avoid or at least evaluate due to its perceived oppressive nature, but is once again frequently used for the purposes of strategic power and play. *See Also* Hair: Hair Straightening

Further Reading: Allen, Margaret. *Selling Dreams: Inside the Beauty Business*. New York: Simon & Schuster, 1981; Angeloglou, Maggie. *A History of Make-up*. London: The Macmillan Company, 1970; Corson, Richard. *Fashions in Makeup: From Ancient to Modern Times*. New York: Universe Books, 1972; Gunn, Fenja. *The Artificial Face: A History of Cosmetics*. New York: Hippocrene, 1983; Marwick, Arthur. *Beauty in History: Society, Politics and Personal Appearance c. 1500 to the Present*. London: Thames & Hudson, 1988; Mulvey, Kate, and Melissa Richards. *Decades of Beauty: The Changing Image of Women 1890s–1990s*. New York: Reed Consumer Books Limited; Peiss, Kathy. *Hope in a Jar: The Making of America's Beauty Culture*. New York: Henry Holt and Company, 1998; Riordan, Theresa. *Inventing Beauty: A History of the Innovations That Have Made Us Beautiful*. New York: Broadway Books, 2004; Wykes-Joyce, Max. *Cosmetics and Adornment: Ancient and Contemporary Usage*. New York: Philosophical Library, 1961; http://www.fashion-era.com.

Alyson Spurgas

Medical Antiaging Procedures

Surgical operations designed to improve human appearance can be traced back to ancient Egypt. However, antiaging cosmetic surgery is a phenomenon that came to prominence only in the second half of the twentieth century. In most highly developed cultures, individuals enjoy healthier and longer lives than ever before—we cure many cancers, control heart disease, and benefit from advanced pharmaceuticals and hormone replacement therapies—and many people remain active and disease-free into old age. It might be supposed that in these circumstances, aging would be more palatable than ever, but this is not the case. In the contemporary world, youthful bodies are privileged, and youth is often associated, especially in the mass media, with sexuality, independence, beauty, and productivity. Aging, on the other hand, is commonly represented as an undesirable state of frailty, unattractiveness, and dependency. Aged bodies are often shown in mass media as unattractive and lacking in sexual and aesthetic appeal. This is especially the case for women: in cultures that glorify youthfulness, particularly youthful femininity, aging for women can be a traumatic event associated with loss of cultural value and social visibility.

Aging bodies are never simply organic structures subjected to decline over time; they are continually inscribed with cultural meanings and reflect societal influences and attitudes. In this way, the aging body is marked simultaneously by biological changes to its cellular and organic structure and by many cultural and social labels. Aging has come to be seen as so undesirable that the aged body has become pathological—aging is now considered by many as a condition that must be medically fought against and controlled rather than as a natural part of life. Many people experience a sense of disjuncture between their appearance and their internal selves as they age. Some seek antiaging cosmetic surgery to manage these feelings and some seek it to avoid being labelled with the negative stereotypes commonly attached to older people.

Antiaging

Antiaging cosmetic surgery is conducted on bodies that are generally accepted as undamaged except by time and everyday circumstances; it aims to minimize or eradicate surface signs of aging such as wrinkles, drooping, sagging, loss of skin lustre, and "middle-age spread" (the weight gain common to later life). Throughout the twentieth century, instances of cosmetic surgery in general rose while cultural and social perceptions of it changed dramatically, especially in the wealthy, developed world. In 2006, nearly 11 million surgically invasive cosmetic procedures

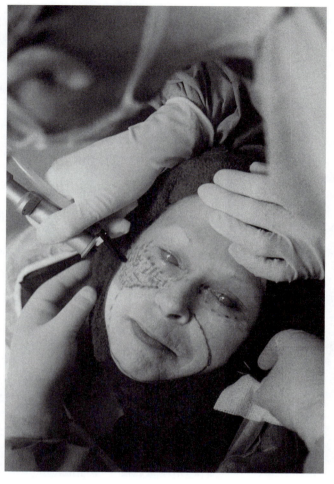

In the "laser face lift," the outer layer of skin is burned off with a laser, which vaporizes a mozaic grid of tiny squares one at a time. Opaque grey contact lenses shield the patient from any stray flash. (AP Photo/The Day, J. Ross Baughman)

were recorded by members of the American Society of Plastic Surgeons (ASPS). Blepharoplasty (eyelid lift) was the fourth most common cosmetic surgery in 2006 after breast augmentation, rhinoplasty (nose job), and liposuction. In addition to these surgical procedures, there were 9.1 million nonsurgical or "minimally invasive" procedures recorded in 2006 by ASPS, nearly all of which were intended to reduce signs of aging.

Most antiaging surgery works to remove or diminish skin wrinkles. Wrinkles are in no way detrimental to good health, nor do they indicate being unfit or without energy: they are merely often *associated* with these qualities. Some wrinkling is genetic, but up to 80 percent is caused by ultraviolet rays from sunlight, a process called "photo-aging." Smoking has also been found to increase wrinkles, although exactly why this happens is not yet known. Smokers are two to three times more likely than nonsmokers to have noticeably wrinkled skin (smoking is also sometimes blamed for complications in healing for facelift patients). Other minor causes of wrinkles are gravity—which slowly pulls down skin, muscle, and other tissue over time—facial expressions, squinting, and loss of teeth, which makes skin around the mouth appear concave and furrowed. Weight loss, especially significant weight loss later in life, can also cause wrinkles, as it may leave the skin stretched. Although many cosmetic companies promise that various creams and lotions will reduce wrinkles and lines, there is only one product, Tretinoin (best known under the brand name Retin-A), that appears to have a real effect on fine lines. A prescription drug, Tretinoin contains a vitamin A derivative and encourages collagen to grow by peeling off the outer layer of skin. It has been linked to birth deformities, and the effects of prolonged use are unknown.

Antiaging procedures are continually being adjusted and new techniques developed. Cosmetic surgery is a lucrative and growing area that is undergoing rapid change with different techniques being invented and marketed on an almost weekly basis. Generally, it can be divided into two broad categories: surgical (invasive) and nonsurgical (minimally invasive). Recently there has been a slight trend away from surgical procedures and a huge increase in the number of nonsurgical procedures. For example, demand for facelifts has decreased in recent years: ASPS reported a 20 percent drop for women and a 39 percent drop for men from 2000 to 2006. However, this has been more than replaced by a massive increase in minimally invasive procedures. The most dramatic of these is Botox injections, which rose by 449 percent for women from 2000 to 2006.

Surgical Antiaging Treatments

The Face

The first account of antiaging cosmetic surgery is from 1901, when German surgeon Eugen Hollander (1867–1932) performed a rhytidectomy (literally, excision of wrinkles), or facelift, on an aristocratic Polish woman. The average age for a facelift is about fifty; most facelifts are done on people between forty and sixty-five, and up to 85 percent of those seeking facelifts are women. Because the facelift is meant to allow its recipients to "pass" as younger than they are, the signs that surgery has been done are required to be minimal. One of the signs of a high-quality modern facelift is the near-invisibility of scars. To achieve this, the surgery must be meticulous: wound edges need to be parallel, and suturing must be very fine. However, some scarring is always unavoidable, and surgeons should always warn patients that scars can sometimes extend and grow (keloid scars). Complications of facelifts may include damage to the facial nerves resulting in paralysis of some muscles, infection, and hematoma (blood clot). The facelift is commonly thought of as a single operation but is in fact usually a selection of procedures that might include any of the facial operations discussed here. Often, multiple procedures are performed under one anesthetic.

Rhytidectomy usually refers to procedures done on the lower face and neck but can also include a browlift. The subcutaneous musculoaponeurotic system (SMAS) lift is a popular form of rhytidectomy. The SMAS is a layer of muscles and fibrous tissue that lies directly beneath the fat on the face. This layer sags with time, causing jowls. The SMAS can be surgically tightened. Incisions are generally made from the temple, just inside the hairline, down in front of the ear and then back into the hairline behind the ear. The skin covering the cheeks, chin, and neck is then separated (or "undermined") from muscle and deeper tissue using a scalpel or scissors. The SMAS tissues can then be tightened with stitches. Most SMAS operations last about three hours. They are performed under general anesthetic or local anesthetic plus sedation, in a hospital or in a surgical suite. Drains and firm dressings are used postoperatively to minimize risks of bleeding and hematoma. A similar procedure is the "S" lift rhytidectomy in which the skin and the muscles of the jaw and neck are lifted and tightened after cutting an "S" shape around the ear.

Browlift or forehead lift surgery aims to reduce wrinkles and lines on the brow. It was first described by Raymond Passot (1886–1933) in 1919 and is performed using traditional line incisions or endoscopic (keyhole) surgery. Browlifts often create a higher, more arched eyebrow as well as smoother forehead skin. Traditional browlift surgery is usually done under general anesthetic in a hospital or surgical suite. Incisions are made from the ears to the top of the forehead about two centimeters above the hairline. Sometimes the scalp is peeled down to just above the eyebrows. The underlying muscles (the frontalis and the corrugators) are then tightened or shortened and excess skin is sometimes removed before suturing. Recovery takes two to three weeks and infections are rare, as blood flow to the forehead is very strong. Complications can include severing of nerves, causing numbness.

Endoscopic browlift surgery is increasingly common. It sometimes requires a general anesthetic but is popular because it can also be performed using a combination of local anesthetic and intravenous sedation. This procedure is less invasive than the traditional method, although more skill is required and it takes longer. It is favored because the scars it leaves are less obvious and the healing period is quicker. Centimeter-wide incisions are made in about five places above the hairline. An endoscope (a tiny telescope and camera) is inserted and the surgeon is able to view images on a screen while lifting and tightening muscle and tissue using surgical instruments. Complications are rare although nerve damage may occur.

Blepharoplasty, or eyelid lift, aims to remove wrinkled or loose skin, and sometimes fat, from the upper and lower eyelids. Karl Ferdinand von Gräfe (1787–1840), a German surgeon, coined the phrase in 1818. He used the technique to repair deformities in the eyelids caused by cancer. On the upper lid, it aims to lift the lid so it becomes more visible and less "hooded." On the lower lid, it tries to minimize concave or convex "bags" from beneath the eye. Blepharoplasty operations usually make the eyes appear larger and more open. They require great skill as the skin around the eyes is very delicate. Blepharoplasties are sometimes performed under general anesthetic but are increasingly carried out using local anesthetic and intravenous sedation (sometimes called "twilight sedation"). For the upper lids, incisions of about 2.5 centimeters are made in the curved fold of the lid. Skin, muscle, and sometimes fat are removed before the incision is sutured closed. For the lower lids, an incision is made along the crease that runs underneath the lower eyelashes. Skin, muscle, and sometimes fat are removed and the closing sutures again follow the crease in order to hide scarring. Complications from blepharoplasty are rare. However, this procedure can cause blindness if there is excessive bleeding into the orbital cavity.

LASER is the acronym for Light Amplification by Stimulated Emission of Radiation. These light-based technologies were first used on skin in 1964 and gained widespread acceptance in the 1990s. They are used in cosmetic surgery to reduce wrinkles and discolorations and leave skin with a more even tone. Operations can be done in a hospital or clinic. After anesthesia (general, intravenous, or local), bursts of concentrated light are applied to the skin. They heat the water in the skin until it vaporizes, effectively destroying layers of skin. New skin grows and often looks younger and smoother. As with other skin resurfacing techniques, there is a risk of hyperpigmentation (dark spots) and hypopigmentation (light spots) with laser resurfacing; the procedure is rarely recommended for dark-skinned people. The recovery period after laser resurfacing is long (two to four weeks) and painful, with swollen red skin much like a severe sunburn. Final results take between three months and a year to become apparent. Lasers can also be used for "nonablative" facial treatments, and especially for removal of "spider veins." These treatments are minor, and do not result in skin that peels away—anesthetic is rarely needed. They usually need to be repeated between three and five times before a result is seen.

The Neck

Platysmaplasty, or neck lifting, aims to remove wrinkles and pouches of baggy or fatty tissue from the neck by retracting skin and muscles upward behind the ears. This operation is often done in conjunction with liposuction to reduce "double chins" for which an incision is made just below the lower jaw. Neck lifts can be performed under general anesthetic, intravenous sedation, and occasionally an oral sedative such as Valium combined with a local anesthetic. Incisions are made under the chin or behind the ear. Sections of skin, fat, and muscle are removed and the skin is sutured under or behind the ear. Complications can include hematoma, asymmetry, and postsurgical lumpiness.

The Body

While most medical antiaging procedures concentrate on the face, there are many cosmetic surgery procedures used to minimize the signs of age on the body. Breast surgeries such as reduction and augmentation (mammoplasties) or tightening (mastoplexy) are sometimes connected to aging as breasts change over time and may become bigger, smaller, or droopier. Vaginaplasty and labiaplasty may be used for antiaging purposes, as the labia majora sometimes become thin with age and the vagina less tight. Liposuction—also called lipectomy and lipoplasty—is used to remove fatty cells that tend to accumulate as people age. Abdominoplasty, or "tummy tuck"—also called abdominal aprondectomy—aims to tighten and remove adipose tissue (fat) while reshaping and firming the abdomen. Less common antiaging procedures for the body include arm lift (brachioplasty), which tightens the skin of the upper arms, buttock lift, which tightens the skin above the upper part of the buttocks and may also deploy fat injections or implants, and thigh lift or thighplasty, which removes sagging skin from the thighs.

Nonsurgical Antiaging Treatments

There are hundreds of techniques and products in the suite of "minimally invasive" cosmetic surgeries. These operations use no scalpel. "Injectables" may be deployed to minimize wrinkles, "plump up" the skin, and make lips fuller. Various dermabrasion procedures—which may be mechanical or chemical—aim to remove the outer layers of skin in order to promote new, younger-looking growth. Dermal fillers and some dermabrasion procedures can be performed by nonsurgeons, and licensing rules for technicians vary according to state and country. However, most of these procedures are still done by cosmetic surgeons, plastic surgeons, and dermatologists. In 2006, members of the ASPS performed 1.1 million chemical peels, 817,000 microdermabrasion procedures, and 778,000 hyaluronic acid filler (such as Restylane) treatments.

Injectable Dermal Fillers

A variety of synthetic and organic substances can be injected into the skin and lips. Organic substances include bovine collagen (made from cow skin), fat from the patient's own body, and a substance made from the combs of roosters (Hylaform®). Synthetic substances are made from hyaluronic acid (Restlylane and Dermalive), polyacrylamide (Aquamid), and lactic acid (New Fill). All, apart from polyacrylamide, are absorbed into the body in three to six months, so treatments must be regularly repeated in order to maintain results. Because polyacrylamide is not absorbed into the body, it is classified as an implant and requires a treatment of antibiotics to minimize infection. Some dermal fillers require local anesthetic because they are acidic but most do not. The use of hyaluronic acid fillers like Restylane increased by 59 percent from 2006 to 2007, according to the ASPS. The long-term effects of these substances are unknown.

Liquid silicone is still used as a dermal filler in some countries, often illegally, to minimize wrinkles and fill out thin lips. Liquid silicone is a highly dangerous substance that is not approved for injection into the body for cosmetic applications in the United States. It is banned in Australia. Liquid silicone never leaves the body—it can migrate, causing lumps, attracts scar formation, and may be rejected and cause infection.

Botox

Botox is one brand name for botulinum toxin type A, a purified form of the botulinum toxin (botulinum causes the food-poisoning condition botulism). In 1949, Arnold Burgen (1922–) and his colleagues discovered that the botulinum toxin blocks neuromuscular transmission and paralyzes or weakens the muscles into which it is injected. Through the 1950s and 1960s, the substance was experimented with as a treatment for muscular conditions of the eye, such as uncontrollable blinking and crossed eyes. It was first approved in the United States for therapeutic use for eye conditions in 1984. By 1987, doctors and patients had noticed that the wrinkles of those who had been treated for eye disorders were diminished or "softened" after injections of Botox. In 2002, the drug was approved in many countries for use in the treatment of facial lines, and has since been aggressively marketed as a wrinkle treatment. Botox is most often used to "soften" wrinkles around the eyes, horizontal forehead lines, and the vertical lines between the eyebrows (glabellar lines), but also can be injected into other facial muscles. It is also increasingly used as a wrinkle prevention treatment as it stops muscles from contracting and therefore wrinkles are less likely to form. Generally, no anesthetic is necessary for Botox. A microneedle is used to make between one and three injections into each muscle. Many patients report a burning sensation during the injections; many say there is no discomfort at all. The ASPS reported 4.1 million Botox treatments in 2006. Side effects can include temporary headaches, hematoma, bruising, eye ptosis (paralysis or droopiness of the eyelids), and diplopia, or double vision, wherein two images of a single object are seen because of unequal eye muscle action.

The effects of Botox last between three and six months, so treatments need to be ongoing to maintain results. Because Botox is a living substance, each vial—which holds enough for several injections—must be reconstituted and used within four hours of opening. Sometimes patients have to pay for an entire vial whether they require all of the contents or not. Botox parties, held in private homes and sometimes resorts and spas, are a way to share the cost and reduce each recipient's bill, but have also been associated with the glamorization and normalization of this procedure.

Skin Resurfacing

Skin resurfacing covers a wide-ranging set of techniques that aim to destroy old skin so that new (and younger-looking) skin grows in its place. Procedures fall into two main groups: chemical and mechanical.

Chemical face peeling aims to remove fine lines and minor skin blemishes. Chemical peels commonly involve carbolic acid (phenol), trichloroacetic acid (TCA), glycolic acid (AHA), or salicylic acid (BHA) as their active agent. They are classified as light, medium, or deep, depending on the strength of the solution and how long it is left to penetrate the skin. They burn the outer layers of the skin causing them to peel off. After being painted or dabbed directly onto the skin, they are left for between ten minutes and half an hour, after which the skin peels and flakes off for about a week. New skin that has formed beneath is revealed. Originally used by nonmedical practitioners, the medical profession has now standardized the chemical compositions of these products. Chemical peels can happen in salons, consulting rooms, or hospitals. Full-face deep peels require anesthetic and a hospital stay and have recovery periods of up to a month. After the procedure, a thin layer of lotion or antibacterial ointment is applied, under which the skin dries, cracks, and flakes. Burn dressing membranes are sometimes applied after deep peels. Complications can include accidental burning of the eyeballs and the upper respiratory tract from vapor, loss of sensation, scarring, hyperpigmentation, and hypopigmentation.

Dermabrasion is now being somewhat superseded by newer skin-resurfacing technologies using laser and pulsed light. Dermabrasion procedures can be traced back to World War II when doctors used fine sandpaper connected to an electric motor to remove ingrained dirt and shrapnel from soldiers' faces. Nowadays they are used to stimulate new growth by causing friction injuries to the skin. This is done with surgical sandpaper or motorized instruments such as wire brushes and diamond fraises, which leave a raw, weeping surface for some weeks, upon which new skin eventually grows. Most dermabrasion procedures are performed under intravenous sedation, although local anesthetics with oral sedation can be used, as can general anesthetic. Recovery time is about two weeks but complete healing can take months. Complications may include scarring, hyperpigmentation, and hypopigmentation.

Collagen induction therapy (CIT) consists of rolling a device that contains hundreds of fine surgical-grade steel needles over the skin. The concept for this treatment came from recognizing that tattooed skin often looked smooth and unwrinkled. The microneedles puncture the outer layer of skin and stimulate the deeper layers, which are responsible for collagen creation.

Hair

Replacement of hair is mainly sought to counteract male-pattern baldness, which affects more than 50 percent of men over fifty. Two drugs, Minoxidil and Finasteride, have been proved to be somewhat effective in treating hair loss, but surgery is still the most effective treatment for significant hair loss. Hair-transplant techniques have improved vastly in the past decade. Scalp reduction, which was popular in the 1970s and 1980s, is becoming less common. This method simply removed a section of bald scalp; then, skin with more hair coverage was pulled up or across to cover the gap. Another method currently being superseded is plugs, or punch grafts, a technique invented in 1959. Plugs of hair containing about twenty hairs each were removed and replanted into the bald area. Plugs had to be placed three to four millimeters apart to maintain blood flow to the scalp, so a somewhat comic "doll's hair" look was common. Recently improved hair-transplant techniques include the micrograft, or follicular unit graft, where only one to four hairs is transplanted with each plug—this procedure now accounts for most modern hair transplants and looks natural. Hair transplants require only local anesthetic and can be performed in surgical suites over a number of sessions. Complications are rare.

Representations of Antiaging Cosmetic Surgery

Cosmetic surgery was once widely seen as a luxury available only to the rich and famous, or as a strange activity undertaken by narcissists. Through the twentieth century it gained increasing acceptance as an everyday practice, especially in the United States. The idea that inner selves (which always seem to be young and beautiful) should match outer appearances is one strongly linked to the rise of antiaging cosmetic surgery. For many people, such as actors and professional entertainers, antiaging cosmetic surgery is now an aesthetic and cultural imperative. People are now less likely to be secretive about their antiaging surgeries, and some are pleased to share their experiences with the public. In the popular media, cosmetic surgery is increasingly represented as something ordinary people "deserve" and as a practice that will enable people's "true selves" to emerge. It is increasingly used as a subject for films, novels, reality television programs, and television dramas. However, the media can be very unpredictable in how they represent antiaging cosmetic surgery—it is often simultaneously glorified and condemned, advertised and ridiculed. Culturally, we have a complex love-hate relationship with this medical technology. People are both fascinated and appalled by it.

Before/After

The dominant way in which cosmetic surgery is represented visually—in advertising, in the popular media, and even in medical texts—is through the before/after trope. Before/after consists of a pair of photos, usually side by side. The photo on the left represents "before" and shows a presurgical image, while the photo on the right shows an "after" or postsurgical image. In Western visual literacy, we tend to "read" images from left to right, associating left with old and "real" and right with new and "ideal." The after photos are usually taken some months after the operation has been completed, so bruising and swelling has disappeared. Often, they are also better lit than the before photos. This mode of representation hides the serious labor and pain of surgery and recovery, obfuscating images that show process or "during." Before/after represents cosmetic surgery as pain-free, instantaneous, and almost magical—taken at face value, it implies that cosmetic surgery is as easy as putting on makeup or a new hat. This has been a source of consternation for feminists—and also for some surgeons—because major surgery happens within this hidden space between before and after. Feminists, artists, and journalists have tried to expose what happens between before/after by describing or demonstrating how operations are done and by refusing to accept the before/after model. One of the strongest anti-before/after statements was made by Orlan, a French performance artist. She enacted a "theater of becoming" through the 1990s, undergoing cosmetic surgeries in galleries and widely publicizing what happens in "the between." Part of Orlan's artistic purpose was to demonstrate how surgery is hazardous and gruesome.

Reality Television

Reality television has played a particularly powerful role in changing attitudes towards antiaging cosmetic surgery in the early twenty-first century.

The United States's *Extreme Makeover* and *The Swan* and the UK's *Ten Years Younger* presented "looking old" as an unfortunate and unacceptable, but an ultimately fixable physical condition. Participants on these programs received multiple major cosmetic surgery procedures worth many thousands of dollars. *Extreme Makeover*, a series produced from 2002 to 2006, often paralleled antiaging cosmetic procedures such as facelifts with reconstructive surgeries such as postmastectomy implants and harelip corrections, and even hearing and eyesight-improving operations. The program both reflected and helped to create dramatic cultural changes in attitudes toward cosmetic surgery evident in the early twenty-first century. It presented cosmetic surgery as an antidote equally applicable to all. By paralleling anxieties that once fell into the category of vanity with real physical deformities, each became as valid a treatment as the other. The suffering of the woman with droopy breasts was now commonly represented as equally deserving of intervention as the suffering of the cancer survivor with only one breast. The cosmetic surgery reality television genre is very much based around the before/after model, with continual references to transformation and "new selves." However, the programs also brought surgical and recovery images into the mainstream, introducing real blood and gore to primetime television. This helped to further normalize cosmetic surgery, making it seem more common.

Health and Illness

Although cosmetic surgery and especially cosmetic surgery for antiaging is now widely accepted and even commonplace, many people still believe that those who try to change healthy appearances need psychological rather than surgical help. Some physicians have deep reservations about antiaging cosmetic surgery, believing that healthy tissue should not be operated on, while supporters of antiaging procedures claim that because they complement personal growth and improve quality of life they can be justified as medically necessary. So connected has cosmetic surgery become to notions of mental well-being that some critics call it "scalpel psychiatry." It is therefore ironic that higher levels of anxiety and mental illness have been found to be associated with people who seek cosmetic surgery than those in the wider populace, and cosmetic surgery patients have a higher rate of suicide than the general population. Some recent studies funded by cosmetic surgery associations, however, dispute these claims. Body dysmorphic disorder (BDD) is a psychiatric condition that causes people to see some of their physical features as unacceptably ugly, even when those features seem normal to others. The condition is utterly disabling and prevents individuals from leading functional lives. Some BDD sufferers turn to cosmetic surgery for relief, which it cannot offer them, despite its advertised promises of creating a beautiful, youthful appearance. BDD sufferers who have cosmetic surgery are often highly dissatisfied with the results, and many of them return for further procedures. Some psychologists believe that cosmetic surgery may even exacerbate BDD, and advise surgeons to refer patients who may suffer from the condition to a mental health practitioner rather than encourage them to have surgery.

Feminist Views

Cosmetic surgery is mainly done by men upon women: this makes it of fundamental interest to anyone interested in gender relations. Nine out of ten cosmetic surgery patients are women while nine out of ten cosmetic surgeons are men. Feminists have been and remain deeply concerned with cosmetic surgery and are particularly troubled by antiaging cosmetic surgery. Many feminists are highly critical of it as an essentially commercial, repressive, demeaning, and hazardous practice. This fast-growing global industry, already worth billions of dollars, is based largely upon the belief that looking old, especially if you are female, is unacceptable. One of the side effects of a youth-obsessed culture is that older women become severely culturally and socially undervalued. Most feminists believe that antiaging cosmetic surgery exacerbates the situation by making looking old even more unacceptable.

Some feminists argue that women who have antiaging cosmetic surgery are victims of two increasingly repressive and interlocking cultures: one that glorifies youth, and one that sees women's bodies as raw material that can always be improved upon. This mode of feminist critique identifies cosmetic surgery as a destructive practice for individual patients and also for women as a whole, all of whom suffer from ageist scrutiny and discrimination. Another important feminist position argues that in deciding to have cosmetic surgery, women are taking some control of the aging process and the ways in which they are viewed. They are able, through cosmetic surgery, to initiate change and become "agents" in the transformation of their own bodies and lives. This analysis acknowledges and examines the fact that many cosmetic surgery recipients describe antiaging surgery as a form of liberation.

While most feminists see cosmetic surgery as inevitably opposed to values and goals that empower women, some consider the possibility of feminist cosmetic surgery. Their arguments suggest that, in itself, cosmetic surgery is not oppressive or demeaning to women; only the cultural ways in which it is used are problematic. These thinkers often examine experimental uses of the technology, such as using it with other body-modification techniques to explore possibilities of alternative physical identities. In these ways, antiaging cosmetic surgery could be inverted or reinvented for feminist means. For example, instead of eradicating wrinkles, they could be chosen and scored on, and instead of lifting the breasts, they could deliberately be made pendulous. In the context of a beauty system that glorifies youth, actions such as these would be revolutionary, destabilizing mainstream notions of what is beautiful and what types of bodies are valuable and desirable.

There are complex and fascinating issues around trust, identity, and authenticity when we consider antiaging cosmetic surgery. For example, how can one trust someone who is eighty but looks fifty? Is that person wearing some sort of mask, or have they simply taken control of their body's appearance using the most modern technologies available? Put simply, antiaging cosmetic surgery can be seen either as part of a "good grooming" regime or as "cheating"—a way to look like something you're not. Most media products and representations of it oscillate between these two views. Because of the rise of antiaging cosmetic surgery, the phrase "growing old gracefully" has taken on new meanings in the twenty-first century and is being questioned and continually reappraised.

Further Reading: American Society for Aesthetic Plastic Surgery, http://www.surgery. org/; American Society of Plastic Surgeons, http://www.plasticsurgery.org/; Balsamo, Anne. *Technologies of the Gendered Body: Reading Cyborg Women*. Durham, NC: Duke University Press, 1996; British Association of Aesthetic Plastic Surgeons, http:// www.baaps.org.uk/; Davis, Kathy. *Reshaping the Female Body: the Dilemma of Cosmetic Surgery*. New York: Routledge, 1995; Gilman, Sander. L. *Making the Body Beautiful: A Cultural History of Aesthetic Surgery*. Princeton, NJ: Princeton University Press, 1999; Gullette, Margaret. *Aged by Culture*. Chicago: University of Chicago Press, 2004; Haiken, Elizabeth. *Venus Envy: a History of Cosmetic Surgery*. Baltimore, MD: The Johns Hopkins University Press, 1997; Jones, Meredith. *Skintight: A Cultural Anatomy of Cosmetic Surgery*. Oxford: Berg Publishers, 2008; Morgan, Kathryn Pauly. "Women and the Knife: Cosmetic Surgery and the Colonization of Women's Bodies" *Hypatia* vol. 6, no. 3 (1991): 25–53; Wolf, Naomi. *The Beauty Myth*. New York: William Morrow, 1991.

Meredith Jones

Michael Jackson's Face

Michael Jackson was born in Indiana in 1958, the seventh of nine children. He began his musical career at the age of five as the lead singer of The Jackson 5, who later became known as The Jacksons. He made his debut album as a solo artist in 1979, and in 1982 released *Thriller*, the best-selling album of all time. Jackson's two marriages have caused much controversy, as have the birth and raising of his three children, Joseph Jackson Jr. (also known as Prince), Paris Katherine Jackson, and Prince Michael "Blanket" Jackson II, and the allegations of child molestation on which Jackson was tried and acquitted. But Jackson's notoriety also rests on the physical transformations he has undergone during his time in the media spotlight. Despite Jackson's objections, it has been claimed that he has lightened his skin, straightened his hair, and undergone numerous cosmetic procedures, including multiple rhinoplasties. Jackson attributes his changing skin color to vitiligo, a condition in which skin pigmentation is lost, and claims that he has had two operations to enhance his breathing and enable him to hit higher notes.

Michael Jackson, 2005. (AP Photo/Michael Mariant, file).

The promotional material for the British-made documentary, *Michael Jackson's Face*

(2003)—a television program which tellingly achieved BBC Channel 5's highest-ever documentary rating, and was nominated for Best New Program at the 2003 Broadcast Awards—states that, "Over the past twenty years, the world has watched amazed as Michael Jackson has undergone the most startling physical transformation of any celebrity ever ... drastically alter[ing] his appearance from that of a normal, happy-looking black kid to that of a bizarre-looking white woman." The question that drives the documentary, and which no doubt inspired a large number of viewers to watch it, is "What has driven this person to alter his appearance so radically?" Tied to this question is the assumption that Jackson's face and the transformations it has undergone can tell us important truths not only about the man himself, but also about aspects of life relevant to us all, in particular, race, gender, and sexuality. But despite such assumptions, Michael Jackson's face, like Lolo Ferrari's breasts, which were surgically enlarged to such a degree that they created controversy, seem to refuse to tell a single coherent story. As *New York* magazine journalist Simon Dumenco sees it, Jackson's face is "no longer technically a human face.... It's now, chiefly, a metaphor. It represents ... self-transformation gone horribly awry ... self-hatred, and self-destruction." Jackson's face, Dumenco claims, is an "American tragedy" in which all members of a celebrity-obsessed culture are implicated. UK journalist and cultural critic Ben Arogundade reads Jackson's face similarly, but for him the tragedy lies not so much in the cult of celebrity and the effects it produces, but rather in the globalization of an aesthetic ideal that excludes racial markers associated with all forms of nonwhiteness, and leads individuals to undergo what he regards as grotesque and alienating transformations. Interestingly, rather than perceiving Jackson's face as evidence of his traitorous desire to pass as white, author Virginia L. Blum argues that in fact his surgical transformation says something about the problematic ways in which in contemporary Western society (in which the body has become the commodity par excellence), race, like other aspects of identity, is becoming just another surgical outcome.

The comments made by various people who appear in *Michael Jackson's Face* rely on a similar logic, although, like those cited above, these commentators identify different factors as the cause of Jackson's alleged problems and increasingly "bizarre" behavior. Psychologist Elizabeth Bradbury, for example, whose appearance in the documentary is accompanied by the title "psychologist and face expert," and who has seemingly never met Jackson, describes his behavior as "that of somebody addicted to surgery." Bradbury invites the viewer to identify with her position by explaining that she is disturbed that Jackson continues to have surgery, whereas "rational" people would not continue. Further, as Bradbury sees it, not only does Jackson's visage—which she describes as "abnormal and appalling," much like that of "the bearded lady in the freak show"—function as a sort of fleshly confession of his inner turmoil, it also has the power to predict what is yet to come. Jackson's face and the desires that have led to its "deformation" do not augur well, this modern-day physiognomist tells us, for a happy, healthy, and successful future. Jackson's future, she says after scrutinizing his face, "looks pretty bleak really. With somebody on his trajectory there is always the fear that in the end there is nowhere to go apart from complete self-destruction."

Indeed, in many media accounts of Jackson's physical transformations so-called "specialists"–in particular medical practitioners of one sort or another–are called upon to authorize popular claims about the association between Jackson's face and his alleged problems. But, rather than simply being "true," the kinds of assertions made about Jackson's face (and thus his person) could be said to be symptomatic of historically and culturally specific ways of seeing, knowing, and being: in particular, of the problematic but nevertheless "recurring idea that is deeply rooted in Western scientific and popular thought that individuals identified as socially deviant are somatically different from 'normal' people" (Terry, J. & J. Urla. Eds. *Deviant Bodies: Critical Perspectives on Difference in Science and Popular Culture*, Indianapolis: Indiana University Press, 1995:1). Rather than discovering the truth about Jackson, then, in and through a process of what one might call "dermal diagnosis," critics inspired by the work of philosopher Michel Foucault (1926–1984) who criticized the processes by which bodies and selves come to be ruled by social norms, would no doubt argue that Jackson's interior self (allegedly projected onto the surface of his body) is less the source or origin of desires, actions, and selfhood, than the "truth effect" of specific inscriptive processes in and through which bodies come to matter. If this is the case, then the various accounts mentioned, all of which constitute Jackson's visage as pathological, and thus, in turn, his selfhood, as other, alienating, and alienated, could be said to be as violent in their effects as the surgical procedures he has allegedly undergone. *See also* Breasts: Lolo Ferrari.

Further Reading: Arogundade, Ben. *Black Beauty*. London: Pavilion Books, 2000; Blum, Virginia L. *Flesh Wounds: The Culture of Cosmetic Surgery*. Berkeley: University of California Press, 2005; Dumenco, Simon. www.nymag.com/mymetro/news/trends/n_9587/ (accessed June 20, 2007); Pitts-Taylor, Victoria. *Surgery Junkies: Wellness and Pathology in Cosmetic Culture*. New Brunswick, NJ: Rutgers University Press, 2007; Sullivan, Nikki. "'It's as Plain as the Nose on his Face:' Michael Jackson, Body Modification, and the Question of Ethics." *Scan: Journal of Media Arts Culture* 3:1 (2004); Terry, J., and J. Urla, eds. *Deviant Bodies: Critical Perspectives on Difference in Science and Popular Culture*. Indianapolis: Indiana University Press, 1995:1.

Nikki Sullivan

Performance Art of the Face: Orlan

Orlan is perhaps the most prominent contemporary artist who uses her own body, and in particular, her face, as a canvas. In her most famous project, cosmetic surgery was her tool.

Orlan was born on May 30, 1947, in the French town of Saint-Étienne. She adopted the name Orlan at seventeen, and says that with this act she gave birth to herself. Her work consists of art installations and performances, some of which have been highly controversial. She uses many forms of media, including the Internet, photography, film, live performance, sound, sculpture, cloth, video, and, most importantly, her own body, which she

Orlan in 2004. A bulging implant is visible above her left eye. (AP Photo/Joe Kohen)

says is "a site of public debate." Her work is heavily influenced by both the past (much of it refers to art history) and by an imagined future (she works with many of the latest technologies and biotechnologies).

Orlan's art is deeply feminist and comments strongly on representations of the female body in traditional art and the status of the woman artist. From 1964 to 1966, she took extremely long slow-motion walks along Saint-Étienne's rush-hour routes, inviting people to consider how space and the body intersect. She also used her body as a unit of measurement with which to calculate the size and shape of places and buildings. In 1974, in an elaborate commentary about women, art, and the institution of marriage, Orlan performed a controversial striptease as the Madonna. She wore trousseau sheets, some of which were stained with blood and semen.

Her work has many facets, but the project for which she is most famous consisted of nine cosmetic surgery "operation-performances" called *La Réincarnation de Sainte Orlan* (*The Reincarnation of St. Orlan*). Orlan first announced she would use plastic surgery as art in May 1990, in Newcastle, England, at the "Art and Life in the 1990s" event. She then set about making a computer-generated template borrowing features from female icons of Renaissance and post-Renaissance Western art: the chin of Sandro Botticelli's *Venus*, the forehead of Leonardo da Vinci's *Mona Lisa*, the lips of Francois Boucher's *Europa*, the nose of the School of Fountainbleau sculpture of Diana, and the eyes of Francois Gérard's *Psyche*. Then, using this template as a broad inspiration, she set about having her own face surgically altered. Each model in the template was chosen for her historical significance rather than for her beauty. Orlan did not seek to look classically beautiful, and certainly did not intend to resemble Venus or Mona Lisa, although these are commonly held misconceptions. Instead, she created a pastiche out of these many iconic figures.

The operations were broadcast live via satellite to audiences at the Centre Pompidou in Paris and the Sandra Gehring Gallery in New York. Orlan transformed the operating theaters into colorful artists' studios and created a carnivalesque atmosphere using dancing boys, electronic music, mimes, giant bowls of plastic tropical fruit, crucifixes, and flowers. She remained conscious throughout the surgeries, having only epidurals or local anesthetics, and would smile, laugh, direct the surgeons, and read philosophical and literary texts aloud. She and her medical team wore designer gowns made by famous French couturiers such as Paco Rabanne and Issey Miyake. After some of the operations, Orlan created "relics" out of her own liposuctioned fat and excised skin, which were exhibited inside small rounds of Perspex, an acrylic glass. She also produced "sacred shrouds" from pieces of gauze that had been bloodied during the operations. Like much of her work, these referents to the Shroud of Turin are playfully irreverent and can be interpreted as a mockery and critique of Christianity. Importantly, Orlan's own stance against traditional cosmetic surgery practices and aesthetics doesn't stem from a belief in a "natural" body that should be left alone. On the contrary, she declares that the body is a mere envelope, and that people should have the chance to remold it as they desire.

The Reincarnation of St. Orlan is Orlan's most controversial work so far. Psychologists have debated whether she is insane, and both critics and audiences have expressed moral outrage about the project. Some audience members were unable to watch the operation-performances because of nausea and disgust at the sight of the body opened and the skin peeled away from Orlan's face. One reason for this outrage is that cosmetic surgery is commonly represented in media and popular culture by a before/after schematic, where the actual processes behind the transformations are hidden. By seeing only "before" and "after" photos of cosmetic surgery recipients, the public is normally protected from images of blood and gore, and the processes of cosmetic surgery are somewhat sanitized. In contrast, Orlan's project focused spectacularly on what happens between the before and after. In this way, she challenged a strong cultural taboo.

The project also invited the public to reconsider and question mainstream beauty ideals, especially those that are commonly acquired through cosmetic surgery. Orlan has spoken forcefully against Western versions of beauty being literally inscribed upon the female body, and much of her work shows how beauty is not "natural," but can be manufactured, purchased, and designed. She maintains that she isn't against cosmetic surgery per se, but rather wishes to challenge the ways it is used to enforce an unrealistic standard of female beauty. Her surgical performances showed that cosmetic surgery can be used for alternative and artistic purposes, not just for reproducing traditional or narrow versions of beauty. In *Omnipresence*, the seventh surgery-performance, Orlan had two kidney-shaped implants, normally used to heighten cheekbones, inserted at her temples. Ironically, *The Reincarnation of St. Orlan* was a precursor to the U.S. reality television program *Extreme Makeover* (ABC, 2002–2006), in which operations were shown in graphic (although brief) detail, with the aim of creating utterly standard versions of beauty.

The Reincarnation of St. Orlan has been celebrated for the ways in which it reversed traditional surgeon-patient relationships. In her operation-performances, Orlan was the visionary and the architect of the action, while the doctors were more like technicians. In designing her own face, and by refusing general anesthetic, she invited audiences to consider power relations in cosmetic surgery, in which most surgeons are men, and most surgery recipients are women. The inversion of power in her performances has been much discussed by feminists and art scholars, and is often seen as a dramatic feminist statement about the ways in which patriarchal society molds women's bodies.

Since her surgery-performances, Orlan's work has developed in many different directions. *Self-Hybridizations*, begun in 1999, is another form of self-portraiture. It consists of large, striking photographs in which Orlan's face is transformed using digital morphing techniques. Inspired by ancient Olmec, Aztec, and Mayan artifacts, and African masks, she brings together ancient and modern versions of beauty, Western and non-Western images, and real and virtual worlds. In 2007, Orlan participated in the *Still, Living* exhibition in Perth, Australia, for which she grew ten-centimeter squares of human skin in petri dishes from her own skin cells and those of many other people from around the world. Displayed in the shape of a colorful "harlequin" coat, the skin prompts questions about human diversity, ethnicity, multiculturalism, and genetic engineering. The project is one more exmple of how Orlan uses her own body as "a site of public debate."

Further Reading: Blistene, Bernard. *Orlan: Carnal Art*. Paris: Editions Flammarion, 2004; Brand, Peg Z. "Bound to Beauty: An Interview with Orlan," in *Beauty Matters* (Ed. Brand, P. Z.). Bloomington: Indiana University Press, 2000; Ince, Kate. *Orlan: Millennial Female*. Oxford: Berg Publishers, 2000; O'Bryan, C. Jill. *Carnal Art: Orlan's Refacing*. Minneapolis: University of Minnesota Press, 2005; Orlan's Website. www.orlan.net

Meredith Jones

Fat

Cellulite Reduction

Cellulite is a type of subcutaneous fat that gives the skin a dimpled or uneven appearance (something colloquially referred to as "orange-peel skin" or "cottage cheese" for its visible texture); it is more commonly found in women than in men. The term "cellulite" was coined in France and became commonly used in the United States in the mid-twentieth century. Most physicians and scientists agree that cellulite is caused by fat pressing through a web of fibrous connective tissue beneath the skin. Cellulite can be found in many areas of the body, but tends to accumulate in the thighs, buttocks, and abdomen. Women of all body sizes and shapes have cellulite; it is not limited to the overweight.

Various methods have been developed to attempt to reduce or do away with the appearance of cellulite, including topical creams, massage, diet and exercise regimens, liposuction, electric therapy, herbal supplements, mesotherapy, injections of fillers or one's own fat, and endermologie ("vacuum therapy"), among others. The goal of these practices is to eliminate the bumpy appearance of cellulite in favor of a smooth, toned, or muscular appearance. This ideal of smooth, toned skin is supported by the media, which both advertise cellulite-reduction practices and publicly ridicule female celebrities who are seen in photographs to have cellulite. Cellulite-reducing creams, lotions, and gels have now become mainstream, with established cosmetics and skin-care companies such as Dove, Avon, and Estée Lauder offering products that claim to reduce the appearance of cellulite. A recent Dove advertising campaign featuring "real women," who are heavier than the models usually seen promoting beauty products, was created to sell a "firming" (anti-cellulite) cream. This paradox shows that while acceptance of larger body sizes may be achievable, cellulite is still taboo. It would seem that women of all ages and ethnic groups consume these products and cellulite-reduction services.

The most popular cellulite-reduction practice involves creams, gels, and topical treatments, which may be used as "body wraps." They are spread on the skin, and the body is then enveloped in cloth or another material. With or without wrapping, topical creams are the most common method used to try to reduce cellulite. The ingredients in such creams vary widely, but may include retinoids (also used to treat wrinkles), aminophylline (a vasodilator used in asthma medicines), seaweed extract, caffeine, or alpha-hydroxy acids (which exfoliate the skin). These treatments come in a wide variety of prices and forms, and there is generally no scientific evidence that supports these products' claims to reduce the appearance of cellulite. It has been suggested that any temporary effects that follow the application of these topical substances are more likely due to the stimulation of the tissue by massage than the ingredients in the product.

Endermologie, used in the United States and Europe, is the only cellulite treatment that has been approved by the U.S. Food and Drug Administration (FDA) for "temporarily improving the appearance of cellulite." This system, devised by Louis Paul Guitay in France in the 1980s to reduce the appearance of scars, is based on a motorized device that uses a vacuum to suck tissue through two rollers. Marketers and practitioners of endermologie (which first appeared in the United States in the mid-1990s) claim that it stimulates lymphatic and blood flow, which supposedly reduces the visibility of cellulite. This procedure is offered by spas and beauty salons and generally costs around $100 per session. Since providers of this service claim to offer only temporary results, they recommend a regular regimen of treatments.

Mesotherapy involves the injection of substances or drugs (including aminophylline), herbal remedies, and vitamins into the mesoderm, or middle layer of skin. This technique was developed by French physician Michael Pistor in the 1950s and became popular in the United States beginning in the 1990s. The American Society of Plastic Surgeons (ASPS) does not endorse mesotherapy, as it has not been proven effective in scientific studies and is not regulated by medical or legal bodies.

Other practices are touted as the solution to cellulite, which is increasingly seen as undesirable and unattractive. Massage is sometimes promoted with topical treatments. Promoters of cellulite reduction claim that massage breaks up fat deposits and promotes circulation, which are said to alter the appearance of cellulite. A healthy diet is thought to improve circulation and break up cellulite, and exercise is said to build muscle and reduce cellulite. Liposuction is not generally used to lessen cellulite, as its primary aim is to reduce girth. In fact, in liposuction, fat is often removed unevenly, resulting in residual cellulite. The injection of fat (to fill the dimples associated with cellulite) is often uneven and temporary. Electric therapy, of the type used by physical therapists to increase blood flow and stimulate muscles, has also been used to treat cellulite. Herbal supplements recommended for cellulite reduction include gingko biloba, clover extract, various natural oils, and diuretics.

Cellulite and attempts to reduce it are surrounded by controversy. Most scientific studies find that there is no highly effective way to remove or reduce cellulite's uneven appearance, although some treatments have limited temporary effects. The assertions of purveyors of products and services claiming to alter the appearance of cellulite are often challenged by the

FDA, consumer advocates, and/or media outlets. The marketers of such products and services are generally quick to provide examples of happy customers, but usually cannot point to scientific studies to back up their claims. A recent study publicized by the ASPS claims that weight loss has been shown to reduce cellulite, independent of other activities or treatments. According to the ASPS, 43,296 individuals underwent cellulite treatment by physicians in 2005.

Further Reading: Bordo, Susan. *Unbearable Weight: Feminism, Western Culture, and the Body.* Berkeley: University of California Press, 2004; Goldman, Mitchel P., Pier Antonio Bacci, Gustavo Leibaschoff, and Doris Hexsel, eds. *Cellulite: Pathophysiology and Treatment.* London: Informa Healthcare, 2006.

Erynn Masi de Casanova

Cultural History of Fat

As a noun, the term "fat" in relation to the human body refers to the deposits of adipose tissue that reside in layers between organs and tissues and supply energy reserves. The term is also used as an adjective to refer to the overall corpulence or largess of the human body. In relation to the latter, "fat" refers to excess weight or overweight bodies and generally has a negative connotation. Fat, however, can also imply richness and abundance. Since the standards for the size and shape of the human body change throughout history, what is considered a fat body is variable; moreover, the fat body has held various, and often contradictory, meanings. Currently, the control or reduction of human fat is a global public health issue.

Historical Attitudes Toward Body Weight

The standards for ideal body shape and size over different cultural contexts and historical epochs have varied widely over time. However, defining the bodily norm in various historical periods is difficult. There is a lack of demographic data on body weights prior to the mid-twentieth century. Only since the 1960s have national surveys detailing nutrition provided data about body weight.

Before the beginning of the twentieth century in Europe and the United States, in the wake of a number of infectious-disease epidemics, being plump was seen as a way to ward off consumption. There is strong evidence in paintings, literature, and sculpture from previous centuries to suggest that, historically, corpulence and fleshiness were not to be weighed and measured for treatment, but rather enjoyed and recorded as a celebration of beauty and fine bodily aesthetics.

The cultural appeal of the fat body stretches back to Paleolithic times. The small statuette of the Venus of Willendorf, discovered in Austria in 1908 and dating from 24,000 to 22,000 BCE, depicts a woman with pendulous breasts, a round belly, bulging wide hips, and a prominent vulva. This statuette confirms the ideal of feminine beauty in ancient civilizations as being characterized by voluptuousness and fertility. Representations such as the Venus of Willendorf have been uncovered from several ancient cultures

that demonstrate a reverence for a fleshy female form that is linked symbolically to nurturance and childbearing. The voluptuous ideal of female beauty
was also explored in the art of the Renaissance. Perhaps the best-known
proponent of voluptuous female bodies of this period was the sixteenth-
century Flemish artist Peter Paul Rubens (1577–1640), whose artistic muse
in paintings like *Venus at the Mirror* was Hélène Fourment, his sixteen-
year-old second wife, whose proportions would be regarded as fat and
unappealing today.

Historically, in many cultures, corpulence was a symbol of high social
standing and of wealth. One could eat enough food to fatten one's body
only if one had the financial means to afford it; a fat body also spoke of leisure rather than toil. In classical and Renaissance societies, the fat body in
both men and women was a sign of membership of the upper classes, financial security, and, in the context of public concerns over disease epidemics, robust good health. But while plumpness was often linked with the
positive attributes of wealth and status, there were also medical concerns
about fat. The term "obesity" comes from the Latin word *obesus*, which
tellingly has a dual meaning: overweight or coarse or vulgar. The term "obesity" in a medical context may have been first used in the seventeenth century in Thomas Venner's 1620 work *Via Recta*. Venner argued that obesity
was generally found in the elite, and that a return to a balanced diet and
exercise regimen could cure individuals of their acquired "fleshiness." In the
subsequent eighteenth and nineteenth centuries, writings on health preferred the term "corpulence," and regarded this condition as a result of
overindulgence, and thus, as self-inflicted. Consequently, as the "fat" body
became resituated not as a marker of wealth and status, but as a symbol of
abhorrent excess and the pathology of obesity, the onus was placed upon
individuals to cure themselves.

Regardless of the uncertainty regarding body weight in populations, it is
generally accepted that the rates of the overweight have been steadily
increasing since the middle of the nineteenth century. Concurrently,
weight-loss regimes have increased in popularity. The 1863 publication of
William Banting's pamphlet entitled *A Letter on Corpulence Addressed to
the Public* detailed how he "cured" himself of his own excesses. Banting's
pamphlet sold thousands, and the active participation in weight-loss
regimes became a populist pastime. The real turning point in attitudes toward weight loss appears to have emerged at the beginning of the twentieth century, however, when weight loss-strategies became more available
and widely practiced, and attitudes toward corpulence as a marker of
wealth and status begin to decline. At the turn of the twentieth century,
slenderness became prized and popular among the upper classes, which
had the capital to devote time and effort to the various regimes for the
maintenance of one's body.

Height-Weight Tables and Body Mass Index

In a number of Western countries (with research particularly focused on
nations such as the United States, the United Kingdom, and Australia), data

has been released that confirms that more than half of the population of these countries are considered to be morbidly obese. The current medical preoccupation with measuring and quantifying weight follows standards set by the Metropolitan Life Insurance Company, which developed well-known height-weight scales to determine whether one falls within an "ideal" weight range, is overweight, or obese. Based on an analysis of demographic information about the company's policy holders which linked body size and mortality, Louis Dublin, an executive for the Metropolitan Life Insurance Company, developed the height-weight tables in 1943. The tables attempt to establish a standard for body size. The height-weight tables demanded unattainably low weights for men and women taller or shorter than average height, and the original 1943 tables were revised to take into account the increase in weight and height of the general populace over time. However, they have remained unchanged since 1983, and are still used widely by medical professionals today, although the use of a measurement system known as the BMI (or Body Mass Index) has largely replaced the height-weight tables. The height-weight chart prescribes five weight ranges: very underweight, underweight, healthy weight, overweight, and obese. One is deemed overweight at a height of 5 feet 5 inches and weighing 155 pounds, and as obese when one weighs more than 200 pounds at the same height. The BMI calculator requires dividing one's body weight by one's height squared. Doctors accept that a BMI of between 20 and 25 is within a healthy range. Between 25 and 30, an individual is regarded as being overweight, and a BMI higher than 30 means the patient is considered obese.

Obesity as a Global Epidemic

Obesity looms large on the agenda of global health crises. Despite evidence of the medical usage of the term "obesity" in the nineteenth century, it was not until the final decade of the twentieth century that the World Health Organization (WHO) officially recognized obesity as a physiological disease. Since this pronouncement, WHO has developed a *Global Strategy on Diet, Physical Activity and Health*, which focuses on macro-actions to promote healthy behaviors and healthier food options for the entire population. WHO advocates public-health policies concerned with making healthy lifestyles more accessible, and in doing so, constitutes obesity as both a disease and as a condition that is the moral and the civic responsibility of the individual. In designating obesity as a global epidemic, WHO has underscored views that obesity is a crisis requiring state intervention and urgent imperatives for citizens to lose weight.

The Causes of and Treatments for Obesity

Although obesity is identified as a medical pathology, attempts made to uncover the causes for fatness have proven slippery and difficult. Genetics, environmental factors, lifestyle, compulsive overeating, personal irresponsibility, poor food choices, and inadequate exercise have been cited as the causes of obesity. Clear changes are evident in medical literature over the twentieth century regarding obesity's cause. The initial clinical attitudes toward fatness in medical narratives conceptualized being overweight as a result of individual moral failing and deficient self-control in the early years of the twentieth century. By the middle of the twentieth century, greater emphasis came to be placed on environmental factors. These include patterns of overeating set up by parents during childhood, changes in consumer culture such as mass processing and production advances in the food industry (for example, the affordability of mass-produced food with low nutritional value), and increasingly sedentary lifestyles due to changes in work patterns. In these accounts, responsibility for obesity lies in social institutions and broad cultural changes. But toward the end of the twentieth century, medical narratives began to conceptualize obesity as a disease that might be genetically influenced. At the same time, negative aspersions about the "fat" subject are increasingly linked to understandings of obesity as a result of addiction, with particular reference to the category of the so-called "compulsive overeater."

Treatments for obesity are as difficult and controversial as its causes. Since studies have regularly shown that dieting is not reliable as a permanent method of weight loss, high-tech solutions have been deployed. But pharmaceutical drugs have thus far proven to be costly and sometimes unsafe. For example, a number of recent weight-loss drugs initially approved by the Food and Drug Administration (FDA) in the United States have been pulled from the market after cases of cardiac stress and even death. Surgical procedures such as gastric bypass surgery are now being promoted for morbid obesity, but they are highly controversial.

Gender and Fat

Feminist critics have noted that gender differences are significant in men and women's respective motivations to lose weight. Women's motivations to lose weight are often linked to becoming normative, "healthy," and aesthetically beautiful, and, in heteronormative frameworks, therefore desirable to men. In contrast, men's desire to lose weight often reveals a relationship to their bodies that is premised on the privileging of masculine bodily strength, power, and the ability to protect. For men, "fatness" can be a feminizing characteristic that has significant implications for their gender identity. Other differences include that men's motivations are often described in terms of action about what they will be able, or unable, to do, whereas women's motivations tend to be centred on their appearance.

Fatness is now regarded as being particularly socially offensive in women, and feminist scholars have argued that Western societies expect women to more rigorously manage and maintain their bodies than men. Feminist literature critiquing beauty ideals has argued that thinness is an unhealthy ideal, and links expectations for women's thinness with anorexia and bulimia. In addition to questioning the standards by which we measure ideal body weight, feminist writers have also considered the various ways in which heavier women are discriminated against. "Fat" women are sometimes regarded as sexually unattractive, unclean, unhealthy, unintelligent, or unwilling to change.

In public-health discourses, fat women are sometimes perceived as being "out of control," as having appetites that have gone unmanaged, and as having eating disorders. Health professionals often suggest that fat women must be addicted to food, or at the very least, have a disordered relationship with it. Helen Keane, in *What's Wrong with Addiction?*, notes that the bodies associated with eating disorders such as compulsive overeating, anorexia, and bulimia have been positioned as pathological. However, overeaters are conceptualized differently than anorexics or people with other eating disorders. Keane notes that even though public-health discourse sees constantly changing claims about what constitutes a "healthy" diet, "compulsive eaters" are depicted as recalcitrant subjects in need of education as to how to control themselves around food and as addicts that lack the capacity for self-control.

Overeaters Anonymous

The notion of regulated food consumption as the means by which one can master oneself, or shape oneself as a moral success and as a model of health, underpins programs such as Overeaters Anonymous (OA). OA is a self-help program modeled on the twelve-step program developed by Alcoholics Anonymous. The first OA group was founded in Hollywood, California, in 1960, and the organization now consists of over 6,500 groups in more than sixty-five countries.

Interestingly, the fat body and its visibility are not of primary importance in OA programs. Certainly, physical transformation is vital, but more important is an internal, even spiritual cleansing of the self through surrender to a higher power. The cornerstone of the OA program is abstinence from overeating, and thus the first step must be an admission of fat as a disease caused by overeating and compulsion. Strict food plans are generally implemented for members, who are diagnosed as having addictions to white flour and sugar. These should then be eliminated from the diet. Like the problem of alcoholism, fat is medicalized, and fat bodies are explained as the products of the disease of addiction to food.

At the heart of the OA program is the framing of control as opposed to "addiction." Thus OA draws on and reaffirms the causal relation posited by health professionals between obesity and overeating. However, a paradox emerges in the OA philosophy, insofar as members are asked to exert their agency in taking control of their eating, and yet simultaneously, they are asked to surrender themselves to the complete powerlessness they have over their "disease." Indeed, one of the most controversial aspects of OA is its insistence on surrender. This reinforces obesity's status as a "disease" for which the individual is responsible.

Fat Pride

In contrast to the medicalization and pathologization of "fatness", fat activists, some of whom are influenced by the feminist movement and its critique of beauty ideals, have launched radical political responses to "fat phobia." The "size acceptance" or fat-activist movement in the United

States, Britain, and elsewhere has urged a new vision of fatness. In the United States in 1969, William Fabrey, a husband tired of seeing the distress caused to his wife by a society who reviled her "fat" body, founded the National Association to Aid Fat Americans, or NAAFA. In 1970, Llewellyn Louderback published a groundbreaking book, *Fat Power*. Louderback's primary concern was to assert the novel notion that "the fat person's major problem is not his obesity but the view that society takes of it." This way of thinking is reflected in the decision to later rename NAAFA the National Association to Advance Fat Acceptance.

NAAFA is the largest size-acceptance organization in the world, and it aims to stop discrimination against fat people and to combat "fat phobia" through political action. This has included lobbying airlines that charge two airfares for a fat passenger to travel, movie theatres that do not accommodate the expansive hips of fat patrons, and fighting employer prejudice against fat interviewees. Fat activists also have criticized the multibillion dollar weight-loss industry. They have pointed out its gendered focus and its privileging of thin beauty ideals. They have argued that fat women have been objectified and dehumanized by the industry. The fat-pride movement have said that fat oppression in Western society is akin to the oppression of other groups. They have underscored the moral imperatives implied in social anxiety about fat bodies, and have challenged dominant conceptions of the fat body as a moral failure. It should be noted however, that fat pride and size-acceptance activism is not a unified or singular political movement. *See also* Fat: Dieting Practices; and Fat: Surgical Fat Reduction and Weight-Loss Surgeries.

Further Reading: Barnett, R. "Historical Keywords: Obesity." *The Lancet* 365, 1843 (2005); Cooper, Charlotte. *Fat and Proud: The Politics of Size*. London: The Women's Press, 1998; Gard, Michael, and Jan Wright. *The Obesity Epidemic: Science, Morality and Ideology*. New York: Routledge, 2005; Keane, Helen. *What's Wrong with Addiction?* Carlton South: Melbourne University Press, 2002; Louderback, Lewellyn. *Fat Power: Whatever you Weigh Is Right*. New York: Hawthorn Books, 1970; National Association to Advance Fat Acceptance (NAAFA), 1969–2006, http://www.naafa.org (accessed March 21, 2006); Overeaters Anonymous, 1998–2006, http://www.overeatersanonymous.org (accessed March 21, 2006); Schwartz, Hillel. *Never Satisfied: A Cultural History of Diets, Fantasies and Fat*. New York: The Free Press, 1986; Sobal, J. "Social and Cultural Influences on Obesity." Per Bjorntorp, ed., *International Textbook of Obesity*. Chichester: John Wiley & Sons, 2001; Spitzack, Carole. *Confessing Excess: Women and the Politics of Body Reduction*. Albany: State University of New York Press, 1990; World Health Organization. *Obesity: Preventing and Managing the Global Epidemic*. Geneva: World Health Organization, 2000.

Samantha Murray

Dieting Practices

Dieting practices include various regimens and products that aim to reduce the amount of fat in the human body, specifically those that involve modifying one's intake of various types of food and calories. Since antiquity, physicians have recommended various kinds of diets for maintaining ideal body weight, but not until the twentieth century did dieting become widespread and popular for all classes. Some of the most high-tech practices related to dieting and weight loss currently include medical surgeries and pharmaceutical supplements.

Origins of Modern Dieting

Thomas Venner's 1620 work *Via Recta* first used the term obesity and described it as a hazard of the genteel classes. He argued that a return to a balanced diet and an exercise regimen could cure individuals of their acquired "fleshiness." In the eighteenth and nineteenth centuries, "corpulence" was the preferred term in writings on health, regarding it as a self-inflicted condition that resulted from overindulgence. Once a marker of wealth and status, by the late nineteenth and early twentieth centuries, the fat body became considered a symbol of excess and pathology. Dieting regimens placed the onus upon individuals to cure themselves.

One of the early mass diets was generated by the 1863 publication of William Banting's pamphlet *A Letter on Corpulence Addressed to the Public*, which sold thousands. In it, Banting describes obesity as the most distressing of all the "parasites that affect humanity," and argues that obesity and a proper diet are widely misunderstood. Banting detailed how he "cured" himself of his own excesses after trying, in vain, to reduce his weight through various forms of exercise, trying sea air and Turkish bathing, eating only light food, and consuming gallons of "psychic and liver potassae." The only tactic that worked, he argued, was to reduce his consumption of starch and sugar. After Banting, the active participation in weight-loss regimes became a populist pastime. It was not until the beginning of the twentieth century, however, that weight-loss strategies became widely available and practiced.

Currently in the West, the diet industry is enjoying a time of massive popularity given the current public-health warnings about obesity and its various co-morbidities (heart disease, diabetes, cancer, and many others). Weight-loss services, gyms, and preprepared diet food companies are advertising in every available Western media format.

The Rise of the Fad Diet

Following the popularity of William Banting's diet regimen in the mid-nineteenth century, a slew of radical diets promising quick weight loss appeared in the early twentieth century. These new "fad diets" drew millions of adherents in Western societies in the wake of the shift in bodily aesthetics from corpulence to slimness in the late nineteenth century.

In 1917, Lulu Hunt Peters published *Diet and Health, With Key to the Calories*, which advocated a diet plan that limited one's intake to 1,200 calories per day. The influence of Peters' thesis has endured for nearly a century, with nutritionists continuing to prescribe diet plans between 1,200 and 1,500 calories per day for weight loss in obese patients. Calorie counting also continues to be the cornerstone of many popular diet regimens.

In the 1920s, cigarette companies began to address the increasing public concern with slenderness by promoting cigarettes as a means of suppressing the appetite and maintaining a "good" figure. The 1930s saw the emergence of the first marketed diet pills. These drugs contained dinitrophenol, a central ingredient in insecticides, dyes, and explosives. However, research conducted by doctors at the time also found that the chemical had the ability to raise one's metabolism, thus enabling one to burn calories more easily. By the mid-1930s, thousands of U.S. dieters had tried dinitrophenol. However, following numerous cases of blindness and some deaths, the drug was banned.

As well as diet aids such as tobacco and pills, food combinations became the focus of diet fads into the 1930s. The Hay Diet, developed by William Hay, encouraged dieters to separate foods at mealtimes, suggesting that's one's body could not cope with numerous combinations of foods simultaneously. The Hay Diet encourages followers to eat meat, dairy, bread, potatoes, and fruit at separate meals, in combination with the administering of enemas several times weekly.

Food fads and diet aids/supplements came together in the 1960s with a diet plan devised by Herman Taller. Taller rejected the importance of counting calories, and instead insisted that a high-protein diet could be enjoyed without consequence, provided dieters supplemented their food intake with a pill (invented by Taller) that contained polyunsaturated vegetable oil. Taller published his diet plan in the book *Calories Don't Count*, which sold more than 2 million copies.

In the 1970s, food fads continued, with the grapefruit Diet (also known as the Hollywood Diet) enjoying widespread appeal among women seeking rapid weight loss. The diet promised a loss of ten pounds in two weeks, and involved variants from eating half a grapefruit prior to each meal (with no more than a mere 800 calories consumed daily), to simply drinking grapefruit juice and eating the fruit for eighteen days. The diet was condemned as dangerous and hazardous to the health of dieters, and yet it continued to be popular, and is still promoted as an effective crash diet.

Beginning in the 1970s, anti-carbohydrate fad diets promised to be the new and ultimate weight-loss solution. The best known and most enduring of these diets was the Atkins Diet (known formally as the Atkins Nutritional Approach), developed by Robert Atkins (1930–2003) in 1972. Atkins devised the diet to address his own weight problem; it is based on a commitment to a high protein, low carbohydrate daily food intake. Thousands of patients sought treatment from Atkins, and in the early years of the twenty-first century, the Atkins diet continued to be one of the most popular fad diets, with celebrity adherents endorsing its effectiveness and ensuring its ongoing influence.

Numerous other fad diets emerged in the latter part of the twentieth century, many concerned with finding a fine balance or ratio for food intake. One such popular diet is the Zone Diet, devised by Barry Sears (1947–), which is concerned primarily with achieving optimal hormone balance, particularly insulin levels. Sears suggests that a particular intake ratio of protein to carbohydrate effects a harmony in one's hormone levels, thus triggering weight loss.

One of the more recent fad diets developed in Miami, Florida, by Arthur Agatson is the South Beach Diet. This plan designates "good carbs" and "good fats," and positions these as the cornerstones of the diet plan for weight loss and cardiac health. Agatson draws on evidence that suggests that refined carbohydrates ("bad carbs") are absorbed by the body too rapidly, affecting insulin's ability to metabolize fats and sugars. Similarly, he insists on the link between "bad fats" and cardiovascular disease.

In the last few decades, diet fads have been propelled by the endorsements of celebrities who have allegedly had weight-loss successes with particular fad diets. In light of this, the term "fad diet" has come to be replaced more commonly with "celebrity diet"—a variety of which are routinely offered in women's magazines.

Weight-Loss Companies

Jenny Craig, an American woman, cofounded her highly successful weight-loss company of the same name in 1983 following weight gain after pregnancy. Craig pioneered a prepackaged food diet program that became one of the most well-known weight-loss solutions in the West. The Jenny Craig plan consists of more than 500 weight-loss centers as well as an extensive line of packaged foods. The core of the Jenny Craig diet program (and of many other similar organizations) is the "diet plan:" usually a menu grid of seven days, prescribing foods to be eaten at breakfast, lunch, and dinner (with snacks) that is limited to between 1,200 and 1,500 calories daily, depending on one's "starting weight." Many weight-loss companies provide services including weekly consultations or meetings in order for the client to be "weighed in" and to provide social support for weight loss. Between weekly meetings, many plans insist that one record one's daily eating and activity patterns, as well as any difficulties or food challenges one may face. This is often known as a "food diary," in which one must detail precisely what is eaten at each meal, at each snack time, the size of portions, the times at which one eats, and so on.

What marks the diet strategy of Jenny Craig and similar weight-loss organizations, like Weight Watchers, is total vigilance. Weight-loss organizations generally advocate highly regulated food intake. Ironically, food does not become a secondary concern for the fat body, but instead eating is brought to the fore and is scrutinized more intensely than ever before. Weighing out portions of meat, learning what constitutes a fat or bread exchange, and careful negotiation of dining out with friends makes eating a matter of constant surveillance.

Criticisms of Dieting

Gender and Dieting

Although both men and women are overweight, overwhelmingly, the target audience for modern advertising about diets and food intake regulation is female. Some feminists have argued that dieting amounts to a form of disciplining women's bodies to conform to the pressures of normative beauty ideals that are highly gendered. Others have linked the Western obsession with dieting to eating disorders.

Feminist theorist Susan Bordo looks at the phenomenon of dieting and the endlessly fraught relationship women have with food in her best-selling book *Unbearable Weight*. She argues that society insists this relationship must be stringently managed; that the image of a woman surrendering herself to delicious food with abandon is "taboo." Bordo argues that there is a moral panic about excessive desire in contemporary Western societies. To allow desires to run unchecked connotes a modern understanding of addiction. All women are supposed to have a desire for food, beset by a number of anxieties about her intake, and as Bordo highlights, many advertising campaigns generate food anxieties. Analyzing advertisers' manipulation of the problem of "weight-watching" for the contemporary woman, Bordo argues that diet food advertising targets women's anxieties by proposing guilt-free solutions to their desire for food and hunger for satisfaction. Bordo explores the current trope of control used in food advertisements, which suggests that women are constantly battling their desire for food. Words such as "mastery" and "control" feature prominently now in advertisements targeting women.

Dieting, Control, and Loss of Pleasure

Dale Atrens has argued that food has replaced sex as the leading source of guilt in our society. His work *The Power of Pleasure* is a rebuttal of the ascetic restraint and self-denial of the dieting culture. Atrens argues that in following constant and massive trends such as low-fat, low-salt, high-protein, and low-carbohydrate diets, we are endangering our health rather than improving it. Atrens exposes a "New Puritanism" in dieting culture which suggests that ill health results from unbridled passions, and is therefore a symptom of moral weakness. In this logic, fat people are victims of their own "sins." Atrens notes that the eating practices of our everyday lives have taken on an almost religious significance. One's status as a "believer" or an "infidel" is to be found in the condition of one's body.

Many alternative modes of eating have been posited in order to redress the problems with dieting, particularly where they affect women's sense of self and lived experiences. One such model is proposed by psychotherapist Susie Orbach in her landmark text, *Fat Is a Feminist Issue*. Orbach's central theory is that fat women eat compulsively to stay fat, in order to create a sexual buffer between themselves and a repressive patriarchal society. The conception that fat surrounds a female body as a kind of armor to protect against one's sexuality, or the exploitation of it, is central. Orbach posits that women are taught from a very young age that our female bodies are coveted as sexual commodities, that they must be aesthetically pleasing in order to fulfill feminine roles (Orbach 1984, 20). The role of women is a sexualized one, and female participation in society is regulated by the attractiveness of their bodies and what they can offer. Fat emerges as a barrier to a fulfillment of traditional female sexual roles that are upheld by a continuing maintenance of the body (43). In response to diet practices and a weight-loss culture, Orbach urges women to be more accepting of their bodies. Rather than promoting diets as a response to excess weight, Orbach suggest the need to reconnect to one's body and appetite, to eat only when hungry, and to reject the notion of dieting.

Critics of Orbach have argued that her thesis automatically links fatness to compulsive overeating. Some women argue that their weight is caused by genetic or physiological issues or that it resulted from pregnancy and childbearing.

Obesity as a Global Epidemic

Despite the long history of diet regimens and the immense expansion of the weight-loss industry in Western countries (and its opponents such as Orbach), the World Health Organization has declared that the world (but with particular emphasis on the West) is in the grip of an obesity epidemic. Studies have confirmed that the number of people now medically considered to be clinically (and often morbidly) obese has risen steadily, and accounts for the dramatic increases in rates of heart disease, diabetes, and other obesity-related illnesses. Given this, obesity has begun to be reconceptualized within medical discourses as a "disease," rather than as an effect of the absence of individual moral fortitude and self-control. However, the moral aspersions cast on people deemed as "fat" persist in the popular imagination. Morality and medicine are thus irrevocably intertwined in discourses about obesity, and a panic has emerged about the "disease" of obesity and how best to treat it, given the relative failure of a range of dieting practices. In response to the moral panic engendered in and through medical discourses and Western public-health directives, drastic (and mainly irreversible) surgical techniques and interventions into the obese body have been developed, and have grown in popularity as "last-resort" options for those deemed obese. These procedures are known as bariatric or weight-loss surgeries, and while they vary in specific surgical techniques, all share a common premise: that is, to alter the shape, size, or function of a patient's stomach to force a regulation and reduction of one's food intake.

Bariatric Surgeries

In the past decade, surgery has become a significant weight-loss practice for people who have been determined to be obese, especially for those deemed morbidly obese (or have a BMI of 40 or greater). Various bariatric procedures involve creating malabsorption, interfering with the body's ability to absorb nutrients that are ingested, or restriction, severely limiting the amount of food a person eats to the point of feeling full. Gastric bypass involves dividing the patient's stomach into two sections, consisting of a smaller upper pouch and a larger lower section. A section of the patient's intestine is rerouted to the smaller upper pouch, thereby bypassing the larger stomach section (and the volume of food it can potentially hold). While this is clearly major surgery, what is appealing about bariatric surgeries is the fact that they are most often undertaken via laparoscopy, or "key-hole surgery." This means that rather than one long incision, a series of very small incisions are made, and tools are inserted (one of these a camera) to conduct the procedure, and minimize invasiveness and patient-recovery times.

Bariatric surgery has a number of variant procedures, including laparo-scopic gastric band, which is reversible. The gastric band (of which there are a number of types) is a silicone structure that encircles the stomach, creating a small upper pouch and larger lower pouch. The band has on its inner surface an adjustable balloon that can be filled with saline to increase a patient's restriction, or deflated to allow greater food intake (for example, during pregnancy). Gastric banding has become increasingly popular, given that it has fewer risks than radical bypass surgery, and a patient's food intake can be adjusted after surgery simply via local anesthetic.

The result of bariatric surgery is to radically limit the amount of food a patient can ingest, thereby reducing the calories absorbed by the body, or to decrease the amount of nutrients absorbed by food that is ingested, or both. The result is rapid and dramatic weight loss. It should be noted that patients are routinely screened for eligibility for this procedure prior to undergoing surgery, but the baseline BMI varies according to whether a patient is clinically diagnosed as being morbidly obese, or whether a patient is obese with associated comorbidities (having a BMI between 35 and 40).

The increased popularity of bariatric surgeries over the last decade demon-strates the fact that these procedures have come to be regarded as another option for those wishing to lose weight. Weight loss is popularly understood as a task that is defined by deprivation, hardship, and work: rigidly monitor-ing one's food intake and exercise is required in any diet, and is often not a pleasurable or enjoyable experience. Because of this dominant way of imagin-ing the project of weight loss, bariatric surgical interventions are simultane-ously appealing to those who have undertaken numerous diets previously, and regarded by others as radical procedures deployed by those who have failed in their attempts to lose weight "naturally." Weight-loss surgeries have been conceptualized by many as a "quick-fix" option and a way out of living in a fat body in a culture that abhors excess flesh. These processes are linked to cultural understandings about morality. *See also* Fat: Cultural History.

Further Reading: Atrens, Dale. *The Power of Pleasure*. Sydney: Duffy and Snell-grove, 2000; Bordo, Susan. *Unbearable Weight: Feminism, Western Culture, and the Body*. Berkeley: University of California Press, 1993; Chernin, Kim. *The Obsession: Reflections on the Tyranny of Slenderness*. New York: Harper Perennial, 1994; Orbach, Susie. *Fat Is a Feminist Issue*. London: Arrow Books, 1978.

Samantha Murray

Eating Disorders

An eating disorder is a type of mental disorder that involves a marked alteration of what is considered to be normal food intake. Perhaps the best-known eating disorders in the United States are anorexia nervosa and buli-mia nervosa, with binge-eating disorder recently gaining increased preva-lence. While each of these can be present in a variety of ways, each disorder is generally marked by one main symptom. The hallmark symptom of anorexia nervosa, for example, is the severe restriction of food intake, of-ten to dangerously low levels. The hallmark symptom for bulimia nervosa, on the other hand, is the rapid intake of food (up to thousands of calories in one sitting)—called a binge—followed by a purge of some sort (usually self-induced vomiting, but for some can include the abuse of laxatives). Binge-eating disorder is marked by frequent binge eating, usually without a purge.

While most laypersons would tentatively recognize an eating disorder by the presence of its hallmark symptom, the American Psychiatric Association has set forth rather rigid guidelines that medical professionals must use in the diagnosis of eating disorders. These guidelines are collected in a volume called the Diagnostic and Statistical Manual for Mental Disorders, currently in its fourth revision (DSM-IV).

Eating disorders in general are thought to be most prevalent among young, upper- and upper-middle-class white females. However, emerging research suggests that more women of color are suffering from body-image issues and developing eating disorders than was previously thought—both in the United States and abroad.

"Normal" versus "Disordered" Eating

Generally speaking, in the West it is generally expected that eating when one experiences the sensation of hunger is normal. However, there are times when acting outside of this norm is embraced. For instance, it is perfectly acceptable (and perhaps expected) that we overeat during certain holidays, festivities, and celebrations. Similarly, it is expected and accepted that we refrain from eating (or at least refrain from eating in large quantities) when medically required (such as before a surgery or medical procedure), when advised by a physician in order to maintain a "healthy" weight, or on religious fasting days, to name but a few examples. It is also understood that there are those for whom eating in socially acceptable quantities at appointed times or when one experiences hunger is not possible, such as for economic reasons. Although the latter example may be a cause for civic unrest, none of the aforementioned behaviors would cause us to question our mental state or overall mental wellness. There are, however, situations in which eating behaviors can deviate so far and so compulsively from the norm that they fall under the province of mental illness or mental disorder.

For some, the desire to exert control over one's eating habits, or to maintain a particular body type/body weight, becomes such a compulsion that they are (arguably) willing to subject themselves to extreme food deprivation and malnourishment even in the face of resultant major health problems. Two of the most prevalent, medically recognized eating disorders are anorexia nervosa (AN) and bulimia nervosa (BN), with binge-eating disorder becoming more prevalent as of late.

Anorexia Nervosa

Anorexia nervosa, according to current DSM-IV criteria, is an eating disorder in which the sufferer engages in compulsive restriction of food and/or inappropriate behaviors to compensate for food consumption. An official diagnosis of AN is given to one who has sustained a marked weight loss and generally refuses to maintain a "healthy, normal" weight, has a distorted experience and significance of body weight and appearance, has an extreme fear of becoming fat (that does not disappear as they lose weight), and suffers from amenorrhea (or the cessation of menstrual periods for three or more consecutive months). Most anorexics present a marked denial of the existence of a problem. Medical professionals estimate that roughly 0.5 percent of women will suffer from AN at some point. However, medical professionals readily admit that if the criteria for cessation of periods, or weight loss within a normal range are altered even slightly, that the percentage of sufferers becomes much higher.

Bulimia Nervosa

Bulimia nervosa, according to current DSM-IV criteria, is an eating disorder in which the sufferer engages in binges (the rapid consumption of extremely large quantities of food in a relatively short time), which are generally followed by a purge or some type of inappropriate compensatory behavior. The most notable compensatory behaviors are induced vomiting and the abuse of laxatives, diuretics, or enemas. The bulimic generally purges to avoid gaining weight as a result of the binge. This cycle, however, is not necessarily triggered by body-image issues. Medical professionals agree that BN can arise as a pathological response to stressful life situations, as well as in response to negative feelings about the body. However, when bulimics seek treatment in clinics, most place a high importance on body image. Professionals estimate that 1 to 3 percent of women will suffer from BN at some point.

Binge-Eating Disorder

Binge-eating disorder (sometimes referred to as compulsive overeating) is markedly similar to bulimia nervosa. A binge eater will engage in a binge, sometimes consuming thousands of calories in a single sitting, several times per week. The binge eater will often stop only when food stores are exhausted, or when a feeling of sickness has been reached. Unlike the bulimic, however, the binge eater generally does not purge. As such, binge-eating disorder is frequently marked by obesity or rapid weight gain. Binge eating, for both the bulimic and the binge eater, often triggers great feelings of shame, and as such is generally done in secret.

Etiology

Psychologists and psychiatrists commonly believe that the behaviors associated with both AN and BN serve not only to alter the physical shape of the body, but also to give the sufferer (usually a woman) a sense of control over her immediate (internal) environment. In fact, to many mental health professionals, the need to assert control of one's life takes precedence over one's body-image issues in predicting the development of eating disorders. There is also a strong correlation between the presence of AN/BN and other mental or emotional affects, such as depression or anxiety. Also of note, many anorexics will occasionally binge and/or purge, and bulimics or binge eaters will frequently severely restrict food intake. As such, eating disorders are complex syndromes encompassing a variety of behaviors (including hallmark behaviors of other disorders), in spite of their respective "classifications" in the DSM-IV.

Demographics

The DSM-IV states that eating disorders such as AN and BN are by and large found only in industrialized societies, such as the United States, Canada, Australia, Europe, Japan, New Zealand, and South Africa. The DSM-IV also states that the vast majority of diagnosed eating-disorder sufferers are white, and that well over 90 percent of them are females between the ages of fourteen and twenty-four. However, these statistics come from clinical samples in the aforementioned nations. Countless other sources also suggest that the vast majority of eating-disorder sufferers are young, white, female, and upper- (or upper-middle) class with backgrounds indicating high achievement and high levels of external control.

Historically and globally, women of color are thought to be less affected by disordered eating (as conceptualized by the DSM-IV) for a number of reasons. The majority of women of color, generally speaking, still live in nonindustrialized nations or in lower-class areas of industrialized nations. As such, many researchers suggest that they are more preoccupied with issues of basic survival and sustenance than are their white, more affluent counterparts. Purportedly, then, women of color (particularly those of lower economic classes) have fewer mental resources to dedicate to social expectations around issues of weight and body image. Also, until relatively recently, the majority of mainstream actresses, models, and beauty icons have been Caucasian, which leads some researchers to believe that women of color will not identify with or base their own self images on prevalent beauty standards and therefore will not feel the same general social pressure to be thin. However, relatively little is currently known about the true beauty standards and practices of women of color in cross-cultural contexts. It is largely assumed that women of color hold themselves (and are held by society as a whole) to different standards of beauty than the white female in industrialized nations. These assumptions are reinforced by the fact that relatively few women of color seek treatment or help from medical professionals for eating issues. Among those who do, many don't fall under the rather strict and subjective criteria for diagnosing an eating disorder. As such, women of color are not present in significant quantities in medical studies of eating disorders and disordered eating behaviors, and are not considered a group in which eating disorders are thought to flourish.

Emerging Research

Most studies that address issues of diversity among eating-disorder sufferers still suggest that race and ethnicity are significant factors; they indicate that white women are more prone to having negative body images, being dissatisfied with their bodies, and showing disordered eating symptoms than their nonwhite counterparts. However, an increasing number of researchers suggest that this effect may not be due to race itself, but to the fact that clinical samples used to carry out research on eating disorders generally reflect race and class bias, systematically excluding people of color and those for whom access to medical care may be restricted.

It is a well known that clinical populations are not representative. Historically, access to medical care has been limited to those with means. In addition, different cultural groups place varying importance on a variety of health issues, and as such are less likely to seek professional care for certain illnesses. By and large, the poor and people of color have been underrepresented in many clinical settings, both in terms of physical and mental health. At the same time, they have been overrepresented among those who are confined involuntarily to public mental health hospitals, incarcerated, or forced into psychiatric care for psychotic disorders. Historically, people of color are highly underrepresented in studies of certain disorders and vastly overrepresented in others.

Community-level studies (and studies that do not restrict their focus to those with a clinical diagnosis) of disordered eating behaviors and negative body image suggest that women of color in general are more strongly affected by eating disorders and increased body dissatisfaction than was once suspected. In spite of fewer social pressures for black women to be thin, several studies suggest that there are far fewer differences in eating and dieting behaviors between racial groups than there are similarities, and, in some cases, no statistically significant differences in behaviors between groups.

One must also consider that beauty ideals on a global level are changing rapidly. With the advent of the information age, images and ideas can be seen around the globe simultaneously. Whereas many people were once limited to consuming beauty images of people who looked quite similar to themselves, those in far-flung regions of the globe are now able to see and internalize homogenous images of feminine beauty. Thus, some research suggests that the current white and Western ideal of beauty, which includes thinness, is gaining increased acceptance among even those in largely nonindustrialized nations and/or countries with high proportions of people of color. This is supported by changes in the beauty industries in nations around the world, including those in many African nations and parts of the Indian subcontinent.

Further Reading: American Psychiatric Association. *DSM-IV: Diagnostic and Statistical Manual of Mental Disorders*. American Psychiatric Publishing, 1994; Brodey, Denise. "Blacks join the eating-disorder mainstream." *New York Times*, September 20, 2005, F5; Bulik, Cynthia, Patrick Sullivan, and Kenneth Kendler. "An empirical study of the classification of eating disorders." *American Journal of Psychiatry* 157 (2000): 886–895; Hay, P. J., C. G. Fairburn, and H. A. Doll. "The classification of bulimic eating disorders: A community-based cluster analysis study." *Psychological Medicine* 26 (1996): 801–812; Lijmer, Jeroen, Ben Willem Mol, Siem Heisterkamp, Gouke Bonsel, Martin Prins, Jan van der Meulen, and Patrick Bossuyt. "Emprical evidence of design-related bias in studies of diagnostic tests." *Journal of the American Medical Association* 282 (1999): 1,061–1,066; Milkie, Melissa. "Social comparisons, reflected appraisals, and mass media: The impact of pervasive beauty images on black and white girls' self-concepts." *Social Psychology Quarterly* 62 (1999): 190–210; National Eating Disorders Association Web site, http://www.edap.org (accessed July 2007); Swartz, Marvin, H. Ryan Wagner, Jeffrey

Swanson, Barbara Burns, Linda George, and Deborah Padgett. "Comparing use of public and private mental health services: The enduring barriers of race and age." *Community Mental Health Journal* 34 (1998): 133–144.

Alena J. Singleton

Fat Activism

Fat activists generally assert that fat people are an oppressed group and face systematic discrimination on personal, cultural, and social levels. Fat activists hold this to be unjust and challenge the stereotypes and prejudice that keep fat people from fully participating in society. The fat-activist movement largely disputes both the notion that fatness is fundamentally related to ill health, and the belief that fat is the simple result of a greater intake than expenditure of calories. Many in the movement argue that, regardless of the connections between size and health, health status should be divorced from moral value. The assertion that bodies come in a variety of shapes and sizes and therefore a diversity of forms should be celebrated is a fundamental principle of fat activism.

History of U.S. Fat Activism

Although there were earlier moments of fat-activist action, as a social movement, fat activism can be said to have begun in 1969 with William Fabrey's founding of the National Association to Advance Fat Acceptance (NAAFA), then the National Association to Aid Fat Americans. The group was organized around the idea of "fat pride," and though it was guided by a belief in fat civil

Women pose for a photo in 1997 in Philadelphia after a rally sponsored by the National Association to Advance Fat Acceptance (NAAFA). The rally was held to draw attention to size discrimination and prejudice. (AP Photo/H. Rumph, Jr.).

rights, NAAFA initially operated as more of a social club than a rights-based organization. It later became a nonprofit organization dedicated to challenging anti-fat discrimination and to improving the lives of fat people though the social component of NAAFA gatherings. Today, NAAFA stands as the foremost group in the fat-activist movement. Throughout the 1970s, NAAFA chapters worked to gain social acceptance for fat people spread throughout the United States. The Los Angeles chapter, founded by Sara Golda Bracha Fishman and Judy Freespirit, took a direct-action-oriented approach to this work; their tactics eventually caused tension with the larger parent organization. The group eventually split from NAAFA to form the Fat Underground.

Influenced by the philosophy of Radical Therapy, which located psychological problems in larger social conditions of oppression, the Fat Underground aligned itself with the radical left and saw fat liberation as fundamentally connected to a larger movement for social justice. In 1973, Freespirit and another fat activist, Aldebaran (born Vivian Mayer), released the "Fat Liberation Manifesto" in which they argued that the diet industry, based on unsound science, promoted fat hatred for financial gain. Throughout the 1970s, the group used direct-action tactics, often by disrupting weight-loss lecturers in public forums and protesting negative portrayals of fat people in the media. The Fat Underground issued a number of position papers drawing connections between feminism and fat liberation and highlighting the common origins of the oppression of fat people and other marginalized groups. The Fat Underground argued that patriarchal values placed too great an emphasis on appearance, promoted homogeneous bodies, and denigrated those who did not meet a narrow set of beauty ideals. The group disbanded in the mid-1970s.

In 1977, New Haven, Connecticut, NAAFA members Karen W. Stimson and Daryl Scott-Jones and former Fat Underground members Sharon Bas Hannah and Fishman founded the New Haven Fat Liberation Front. The group held workshops on the connections between fat and feminism, and in 1980, along with the Boston Fat Liberation group, held the first forum on the topic. In 1983, Hannah, Lisa Schoenfielder, and Barb Wieser released the first anthology of writing by fat women entitled *Shadow on a Tightrope*. A year later, the fat-activist feminist magazine *Radiance* was launched.

Important fat-activist movement events during the early 1990s included the resolution by the National Organization of Women to oppose size discrimination, and the founding of No Diet Day by Mary Evans Young, director of the group Diet Breakers in England. Other important British fat activism includes The Fat Women's Group, which was founded in the late 1980s to address fat phobia. In addition to local meetings, the group organized the National Fat Women's Conference in 1989. The Fat Women's Group disbanded shortly after the conference; however, it was later restarted by fat activist and author Charlotte Cooper.

Current Key Organizations and Leaders

The 1990s also saw a proliferation of fat-activist organizations, leaders, and publications, and while they differ in many respects, they share a common goal of fighting size discrimination. The majority of organizations described herein are based in the United States, but fat activism is also strong in Canada and England and can be found in other countries throughout the world.

NAAFA remains the largest fat-activist organization. It works to achieve its goals of ending size discrimination through education, advocacy, and support of other fat people. NAAFA also utilizes protest as a means of social change, and in 1998 sponsored the Million Pound March, a fat-activist coalition effort, which drew more than 200 supporters. The organization has shifted in recent years to allow for a stronger feminist focus through their feminist caucus and to better support the participation of gay, lesbian, and bisexual members through the Lavender Caucus and the Lesbian Fat Activist Network.

The International Size Acceptance Association was founded in 1997 and is dedicated to fighting size discrimination and promoting size acceptance worldwide. The organization has branches in the United States, Canada, Brazil, the Philippines, New Zealand, France, Russia, Norway, and England. The Association for Size Diversity and Health is a professional organization that promotes research and services that are health enhancing and free of weight-based discrimination. The organization specifically challenges the linkages between obesity and illness (and the association of thinness with health), arguing that health and well-being are multidimensional phenomena. The Council on Size and Weight Discrimination acts as a consumer advocate for fat people, challenges fat-phobic stereotypes, and promotes a world in which individuals—regardless of size—receive proper and respectful medical care. NOLOSE, originally the National Organization of Lesbians of Size, is an organization of fat lesbian, bisexual, and queer women, transgender individuals, and their allies. It seeks to challenge fat oppression and create fat, queer culture. Finally, Fat Girl Speaks is an annual daylong celebration founded on principles of feminism, sexual diversity, and size diversity. Other performance-based fat-activist groups of note include Toronto's Pretty, Porky and Pissed Off, and San Francisco's Big Burlesque/Original Fat-Bottom Review, founded by the late fat activist, performance artist, and artistic director Heather MacAllister, who performed under the name "RevaLucian."

Influential fat-activist texts published during the 1990s and early 2000s include, but are not limited to, Marilyn Wann's *Fat?So!*, Charlotte Cooper's *Fat and Proud*, and Paul Campos' *Obesity Myth*. Wann, an influential fat activist and NAAFA board member, began *Fat?So!* as a zine in 1993 and later adapted her work into a book-length format. While addressing the seriousness of fat phobia, the harmful nature of the diet industry, and the need for the reclamation and celebration of the fat body, Wann takes a lighthearted and humorous approach to her work. The premise of *Fat?So!* is that fat people should not have to apologize to the world for their size, and that a fear of fat inhibits fat people from fully participating in their own lives. Published the same year as Wann's work, Cooper's *Fat and Proud* came from her graduate research at the University of East London on the emerging fat-activist movement in England and the United States. Cooper details the lived experience of fat phobia and the medicalization of obesity, reviews the history of fat activism, and advocates for fat liberation. Campos, a professor of law and a columnist, critically reviews contemporary medical, social, cultural, and political meanings of fatness. He argues that contemporary measures of obesity, such as the BMI, or the Body Mass Index, offer little meaningful information about health, and that fatness, as such, does not necessarily indicate ill health. He further examines the moral panic that surrounds discourse on the obesity "epidemic" and argues that social hysteria about obesity, rather than fatness per se, is a social problem.

Terminology

Most fat activists challenge the use of the terms "overweight" and "obesity." The former is considered to reinforce a normative standard of weight, which fat activists challenge. The latter is increasingly tied to a framing of fatness as disease, a notion contested by many in the fat-activist movement. Instead, the term "fat" is generally preferred as it is a descriptor of size that, in and of itself, does not refer to a normative ideal of size or health. Others use the term "people of size" to refer to the same idea. Discrimination against fat people is commonly referred to as "fat phobia," "fat hatred," or "fat oppression."

The fat-activist movement has at times been referred to as the Fat Pride Movement, the Fat Liberation Movement, and the Fat Acceptance Movement. Different terms reflect varied ways of framing the issue of size discrimination. Some organizations, such as NAAFA, have taken a more reformist approach to challenging fat bias by seeking to fully include fat people in mainstream society; for example, its members have campaigned to add height and weight to the list of characteristics protected against discrimination at the state level. Other groups, such as the Fat Underground, have taken a radical stance, locating fat hatred in a larger system of hierarchy, oppression, domination, and capitalism, and advocating for broad-based revolutionary change.

Fat activists often use the terms "midsize" and "supersize" to designate different sizes and experiences of being fat. While there is no commonly accepted definition of where the boundary between the two lies, generally speaking, those who can purchase clothes in mainstream plus-size stores and can somewhat comfortably fit into theater, airplane, and other public seating are considered "midsize," whereas those who cannot are considered "supersize." Some fat activists who dislike its association with the fast-food industry have contested the term "supersize."

Health and Fat

Fat activists generally challenge the ideas that fatness is the result of eating more calories than one expends, that dieting is an effective weight-loss strategy, and that fatness is an effective predictor of poor health. Instead, they argue that inactivity, poor nutrition, and often poverty and lack of access to medical treatment are more efficient predictors of morbidity and mortality. Elucidating the causes of fatness is not a central concern for much of fat activism, as activists prefer to focus on addressing fat phobia and discrimination. However, it is generally held that many pathways can lead to fatness, and genetic predisposition, inactivity, side effects from medication, and consumption of energy-dense, low-nutrient foods are sometimes cited as explanations. As early as 1970, *Fat Power: Whatever You Weigh Is Right* author Llewellyn Louderback argued that the claims of the medical and diet industries surrounding fatness and health were largely unfounded. NAAFA argues that the health risks that are generally associated with fatness are better attributed to the effects of yo-yo dieting, an avoidance of health services by fat people because of systemic anti-fat bias in the medical profession, and reluctance to exercise because of the widespread stigmatization of fat individuals. They further maintain that up to 98 percent of diets fail to achieve long-term weight-loss results, with fat individuals often regaining all of the lost weight and more within a few years. Other fat-activist groups commonly share these sentiments.

Fat activists often subscribe to the Health At Every Size Movement, which is an association of health professionals and laypeople dedicated to a harm-reduction approach and the belief that, for those considered to be "overweight," exercise and proper nutrition have better long-term health effects than does weight loss. While some fat activists and fat-activist organizations are avowedly anti-diet, others believe that some weight loss can have healthful effects, especially for who are supersized. Weight loss within the fat-activist community is a contentious issue, and the use of weight-loss surgeries to achieve weight reduction is particularly controversial.

Some fat-activist groups, such as NOLOSE, challenge normative ideas of health and the associations between health status and morality. The group locates its understanding of health firmly in disability politics, arguing that health is a complex and multifaceted phenomenon and asserting that all individuals, regardless of health status, deserve bodily self determination and human rights.

Connections to Other Social Movements

Although NAAFA's feminist stance was a later development for the organization, fat-activist groups tend to see fat liberation through a feminist lens, noting that fat-hatred impacts women more strongly than it does men. Feminists and queer women have been at the forefront of fat activism since its inception. Feminist critiques of the diet industry frequently maintain that the images put forth by weight-loss businesses, which collectively bring an annual return of more than $40 billion, reinforce oppressive beauty standards that are not only fat-phobic but also sexist and racist.

A somewhat common assertion within fat activism is that fat-phobia is the "last socially acceptable oppression." Those who make such claims often point to the unparalleled ease with which fat people are ridiculed and stigmatized by the media, by the medical profession, in the workplace, and in other sectors. While advocates of this position acknowledge that other forms of oppression continue to exist, the focus here is on the socially acceptable nature of anti-fat sentiment and practice. Other fat activists take issue with this claim, arguing that myriad forms of oppression continue to exist in systemic ways within society, and eschew comparisons between fat-hatred and other oppressions. Fat liberation, these activists maintain, must see itself as fundamentally tied to a larger movement for social change that challenges all forms and manifestations of oppression and domination.

Social Organizations

While generally not considered fat activism per se, groups organized around dating and socializing do challenge the notion that larger people are unworthy of romantic and sexual attraction. Big Beautiful Women's (BBW) groups are generally forums for heterosexual fat women and thin men to meet. In the gay male community, Bears clubs exist internationally and are made up of men who are hairy and often, but not necessarily, fat. Girth and Mirth is a gay fat men's group with chapters in cities throughout North America and Europe.

Criticism

Fat activism is not uncontroversial, and critics have challenged its basic tenets. In an era where news of the "obesity epidemic" is constant, fatness is increasingly tied to ill health; as such, fat activism has been accused of reinforcing health-harming behaviors. Some critics have denigrated fat activists by asserting that their platform is the result of a refusal to take responsibility for losing weight and getting in shape. Others have seen fat activism as the epitome of the ridiculousness of political correctness. Finally, some have argued that the fat-activist movement is dominated by the white and middle class, and therefore does not fully reflect or include the experiences of fat people of color and the poor and working class.

Further Reading: Blank, Hanne. *Big, Big Love: A Sourcebook on Sex for People of Size and Those Who Love Them.* Oakland, CA: Greenery Press, 2000; Braziel, Jana Evans, and Kathleen LeBesco. *Bodies Out of Bounds: Fatness and Transgression.* Berkeley: University of California Press, 2001; Frater, Lara. *Fat Chicks Rule!: How To Survive In A Thin-centric World.* New York: Gamble Guides, 2005; Gaesser, Glenn. *Big Fat Lies: The Truth about Your Weight and Your Health.* Carlsbad, CA: Gurze Books, 2002; Kulick, Don. *Fat: The Anthropology of an Obsession.* New York: Tarcher, 2005; LeBesco, Kathleen. *Revolting Bodies? The Struggle to Redefine Fat Identity.* Amherst: University of Massachusetts Press, 2004; Shankar, Wendy. *The Fat Girl's Guide to Life.* New York: Bloomsbury, 2004; Solovay, Sondra. *Tipping the Scales of Justice: Fighting Weight-Based Discrimination.* Amherst, NY: Prometheus Books, 2000; Stinson, Susan. *Venus of Chalk.* Ann Arbor, MI: Firebrand Books, 2004; Thomas, Pattie. *Taking Up Space: How Eating Well and Exercising Regularly Changed My Life.* Nashville, TN: Pearlsong Press, 2005; Big Fat Blog. http://www.bigfatblog.com/; Council on Size and Weight Discrimination. http://www.cswd.org/; FatGirl Speaks. http://www.fatgirlspeaks.com/; Junkfood Science. http://junkfoodscience.blogspot.com/; Largesse. http://www.largesse.net/; HAES. http://www.lindabacon.org/LindaBaconHAES.html; National Association to Advance Fat Acceptance. http://www.naafa.org/; Nomylamm. http://www.nomylamm.com/; International Size Acceptance Association. http://www.size-acceptance.org/.

Zoë C. Meleo-Erwin

Fat Injections

Fat injection (also known as fat transfer, dermal filling, or autologous fat transplantation) refers to an elective cosmetic surgery procedure wherein fatty tissue is voluntarily harvested from a site on a patient's body and injected into another body part such as the face or hands, most commonly to restore a youthful plumpness to wrinkled or aged skin.

Procedures involving injections of fatty tissue to reconstruct the faces of patients who suffered injury or illness are reported to have begun in Europe in the late nineteenth century. The first documented fat injection procedure is said to have taken place in 1893 in Germany; Franz Neuber transferred fat taken from a patient's upper arm to the face in order to "fill out" a sunken cheek caused by a tubercular illness. Two years later, in 1895, another German doctor, Karl Czerny, performed the first known breast-enhancement surgery, in which a fatty mass was relocated from a patient's lower back to correct a breast anomaly. However, it was not until the 1980s, when procedures such as liposuction became more widespread and popular in Western cultures, that techniques of harvesting fat from patients and injecting it into other bodily sites became refined.

The increased interest in the practice of fat injection in the late twentieth century was no longer for the sole purpose of reconstructing sunken cheeks or other body sites that had been damaged through illness or injury. Rather, the new technique was embraced as an option to retain a youthful, smooth complexion and to regain the appearance of unwrinkled skin in a culture that inarguably privileges youth and beauty (particularly in women).

While cosmetic plastic surgery dates back to before the common era, it was not until the introduction of anesthesia, proper sterilization of instruments, and the development of antibiotics that cosmetic surgeries became more accessible as elective procedures. The twentieth century in the United States marked an acceleration in the specialty of cosmetic plastic surgery, with the establishment of the American Association of Plastic Surgeons in 1921. With the advent of elective surgeries, plastic surgery moved from reconstructive techniques to offering possibilities for cosmetic enhancement. Reconstructive surgeons wished to distinguish themselves from cosmetic surgeons who they perceived as simply improving one's appearance through a variety of popular techniques such as breast augmentation, face lifts, and tummy tucks. Following rapid developments in cosmetic surgery in the second half of the twentieth century, fat injections became favored among patients seeking cosmetic plastic surgery, as the procedure uses the patient's own fat as a dermal filler. Because of this, patients are not subjected to the possibility of complications related to tissue rejection by the body. The procedure, while simple, is not without risks, despite its popularity. Apart from expected complications such as possible infection and bleeding, other risks can include nerve damage or the reopening of the wound site. However, cosmetic plastic surgeons emphasise that these complications can be easily treated.

The procedure of fat-tissue harvesting is performed using a cannula or bore needle. Most fat tissue is harvested from the lower stomach, inner thighs, and inner knees. When the tissue has been extracted, the fat is cleared of blood and other possible pollutants that could precipitate infection or other complications. After the tissue has been prepared, the fat is injected into the site chosen for filling. Some doctors prefer to excise small areas of fat and relocate them—a procedure called fat transfer—rather than redistributing the fat tissue via injection. Fat transfer is predominantly used to plump wrinkled skin on aged hands and faces (as well as being used to augment the shape of breasts and buttocks). Fat-transfer procedure is expanding to include implants in the chin and cheeks, penile-girth enhancement, and the repair of inverted nipples.

The dermal "filling" offered by fat injections is not a permanent measure, and each fat transplant lasts between three to nine months, necessitating ongoing injections to maintain dermal fullness. Thus, fat injections become an ongoing form of maintenance within an increasingly consumerist cosmetic surgery culture that markets the possibility of attaining, regaining, and maintaining the appearance of youth.

Cosmetic surgeons promote their procedures as options for women (and increasingly men as well) to choose in order to feel better about their appearance, to feel more confident, and to eradicate the signs of aging. Critics of cosmetic surgery argue that the procedures simultaneously constitute and reproduce a variety of women's body neuroses in order to legitimize the "treatment" of female insecurities with cosmetic surgery. For example, it has been argued that women who desire cosmetic surgery are destined to become cosmetic-surgery addicts, because cosmetic surgery renders women's bodies in need of constant improvement. Yet cosmetic surgeons themselves argue that the ideal surgery candidate is psychologically stable and has realistic expectations about the risks and benefits of cosmetic surgical intervention.

In presenting cosmetic treatments and procedures in and through a discourse of female choice and autonomy, the procedures are transformed from superficial, trivial, or vain into legitimate courses of action that restore and promote psychological and physiological well-being. This is important because cosmetic surgery has long been criticized as a morally dubious practice. Additionally, cosmetic surgeons describe procedures such as fat-transfer injections as correcting flaws and creating a "natural" look. The paradox of this kind of "naturalness" is that it can be achieved only in and through invasive surgical intervention and ongoing maintenance. Cosmetic surgery advertisements make liberal use of "before" and "after" photographs in promoting procedures such as fat injections, in which the viewer (and potential patient) is invited to bear witness to the aesthetic "miracle" of sorts offered by surgeons, reflecting the cultural values placed on youth and normative beauty in Western culture.

The phenomenon of fat injection as a cosmetic remedy involves the positioning of "fat" as a positive, rejuvenating, and desirable substance that enhances beauty and connotes youth. In the context of current Western moral panic about obesity and the cultural anxiety over the apparent aesthetic affront that fat flesh poses to society as a whole, the treatment of fatty tissue as a tool in aesthetic perfection is ironic. In this instance, cosmetic surgery has managed to transform the cultural significance of fat. In most cases, socially marked as an indicator of poor health and socially devalued, here fat is linked to beautification and desirability, and to health, youth, and beauty.

Further Reading: Blum, Virginia L. *Flesh Wounds: The Culture of Cosmetic Surgery.* Berkeley: University of California Press, 2003; Fraser, Suzanne. *Cosmetic Surgery, Gender and Culture.* London: Palgrave Macmillan, 2003; Pitts-Taylor, Victoria. *Surgery Junkies: Wellness and Pathology in Cosmetic Culture.* New Brunswick, NJ: Rutgers University Press, 2007.

Samantha Murray

Surgical Fat Reduction and Weight-Loss Surgeries

Fat is surgically removed in a group of procedures in cosmetic plastic surgery that alter the shape of the body, including after pregnancy or massive weight loss. Fat and tissue removal and sculpture are used in abdominoplasty, liposuction, abdominal etching, and body-lift surgeries, among other

Cutting your hunger

Gastric bypass surgery is effective for helping appropriate patients achieve significant weight loss. The Roux-en-Y procedure is one of several variations of the surgery, which is raising concerns about serious risks.

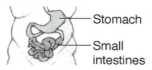
Stomach
Small intestines

An estimated 110,000 people will have gastric bypass surgery this year, 85 percent will be women.

20% may have complications

0.5% to 2% may be fatal

Step one

Procedure Reduce stomach size

Step two

Curtail calorie absorption

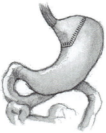

The stomach is divided with staples into a small, upper part (through which food will pass) and a large, lower part.

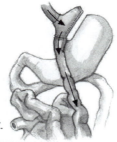

A portion of the small intestines is attached to the small, upper part of the stomach so that food bypasses the large, lower part.

Intended result

Person feels full faster because there is less room for food.

Less calories are absorbed because parts of stomach and small intestines are bypassed.

SOURCE: National Institutes of Health   AP

Illustrated description of one version of gastric bypass surgery and its risks. (AP Graphic).

procedures. In addition, surgery is also used to reduce fat indirectly, in so-called "weight-loss" medical procedures such as gastric bypass surgery, in which it is intended to reduce caloric intake and promote weight loss.

Surgical Fat Removal

Abdominoplasty (also popularly known as a "tummy tuck") refers to a cosmetic surgical procedure designed to restore firmness to the patient's lower abdomen. Abdominoplasty removes excess fatty tissue from one's abdomen and tightens the muscles and skin to give the appearance of a taut and firm torso. The first documented abdominoplasty was performed in 1899; the procedure was improved upon with the removal and replacement of the navel, first performed in the mid-1920s. Since the 1990s, abdominoplasties have often included suction-assisted lipectomy (SAL) as a means of fat removal. Abdominoplasty rates grew continuously throughout the twentieth century, becoming the fifth most popular cosmetic surgery procedure in 2005 in the United States. The vast majority of abdominoplasty patients are women. The procedure has become popular in particular with women seeking to restore their bodies to a prepregancy shape, or following significant weight loss where abdominal skin has become loose and sagged.

Another key procedure in this branch of cosmetic plastic surgery is liposuction (also referred to as suction lipectomy). This procedure seeks to remove excess from fat from a range of bodily sites through suction. It was first used in 1977 by French plastic surgeon Yves-Gerard Illouz. Most commonly, liposuction is applied to body sites such as the lower abdomen, thighs, buttocks, and upper arms. Fat is removed from these areas using a hollow needle known as a cannula and a suction device (aspirator), under either a localized or general anesthesia. While liposuction was originally thought to offer the possibility of sucking fatty tissue from overweight patients, in reality the total amount of fat that can be removed in this procedure is generally only a maximum of five kilograms. Patients who have more fat removed (or are "over-suctioned") are at a significantly higher risk of postoperative complications, such as the appearance of lumpy or dented skin. Given this, the technique has evolved toward liposculpture, which suggests the possibility of body contouring rather than mass fat removal. Tumescent liposculpture, developed in the United States in 1987, improved upon previous liposuction procedures because it refined fat removal, partly by using smaller cannulas and resulting in less bleeding.

These procedures were developed to answer patient frustration over excess fat deposits not easily reduced or eradicated through conventional methods of weight loss, such as diet and exercise regimens. However, patients who have not previously made considerable attempts to lose excess weight through diet and exercise plans will not be considered by cosmetic surgeons as eligible candidates for these procedures. Initially, cosmetic surgeries such as the tummy tuck and liposuction were understood as offering "quick-fix" options for women wishing to lose weight and to contour their bodies to attain a normative, youthful, and slender shape. What has become evident as these procedures have become more popular and widespread (especially in Western nations) is that they carry considerable risks to the patient (particularly those undergoing liposuction), and cannot be regarded as a simple, easy methods to lose weight and eliminate body fat.

Popular cultural representations of fat-related cosmetic surgery in film and television have contributed to widespread misunderstandings about the possibilities of some procedures, especially liposuction, to be a "quick fix" for excess fat. In these representations, liposuction and those who elect to undergo it are mocked and depicted as sources of humor. Liposuction itself is often portrayed in graphic and comically repulsive ways, with copious amounts of thick, oleaginous liquid fat being sucked out of "fat" characters. This comic response is coupled with the dominant popular understanding of the fat person as lazy, unintelligent, unclean, and aberrant.

Another form of cosmetic fat-reduction surgery is a procedure known as abdominal etching (a trademarked cosmetic surgery procedure developed in the late 1990s). Abdominal etching is a specialized form of liposuction, using a specific cannula needle to selectively remove fat from the patient's abdomen. However, beyond simple fat removal, this procedure involves actually "etching" into a patient's abdominal fat along one's natural muscular contours in order to give the appearance of "six-pack" sculpted abdomen, a bodily aesthetic that has seen increasing cultural popularity and value. Cosmetic surgeons who are trained in this patented surgical procedure first mark the patient's skin along his or her specific lines of abdominal muscularity prior to commencing the fat "etching." Fat is then selectively removed along the lines of the patient's abdominal muscles to achieve more pronounced muscle shape and definition, as well as flattening the stomach. This surgical technique has become increasingly popular among those in industries that require a specific body ideal, such as modelling, acting, and body building.

Weight-Loss Surgeries

The procedures described above fall into dominant understandings of cosmetic plastic surgeries which involve surface or similarly superficial interventions into the body of the patient who is seeking to achieve a particular bodily aesthetic, usually that which meets normative ideals of beauty and youth. However, in recent years, the range of procedures concerned with the alteration of body shape has expanded beyond conventional understandings of cosmetic surgeries. Cosmetic surgery techniques for fat removal have been joined by other medical interventions to rid the body of excess fat, especially bariatric surgeries (also known as "weight-loss" and "obesity" surgeries). Beyond cosmetic aims, these procedures usually are undertaken with the medical rationale of improving the patient's health by reducing health risks, such as Type II diabetes, hypertension, cardiovascular disease, and fatty-liver disease, related to morbid obesity.

Weight-loss surgery was first developed in the 1960s after doctors noted the dramatic weight loss of patients who had received surgeries to remove parts of the stomach in order to treat ulcers. Today, weight-loss surgeries, also called bariatric surgeries, are generally performed by specialist bariatric surgeons on patients who have been clinically diagnosed as morbidly obese: that is, as having a BMI greater than 40 (the accepted normal BMI range is between 20 and 25). Bariatric surgeries include surgeries that are malabsorptive, which means that they aim to reduce the body's absorption of nutrients, as well as those that are restrictive, which significantly reduces the amount of food a patient can eat at any given time. The result is usually rapid, dramatic, and long-term weight loss.

The most popular bariatric surgeries are gastric bypass surgery and its variants, and the implantation of an adjustable laparoscopic gastric band. Gastric bypass surgery involves dividing the patient's stomach into two sections, consisting of a smaller upper pouch, and a larger lower section. A section of the patient's intestine is then rerouted to the smaller upper pouch, thereby bypassing the larger stomach section (and the volume of food it can potentially hold). There are a number of surgical variations on gastric bypass surgery, depending on the method of intestinal reconnection. The division of the stomach into a smaller upper pouch and larger lower pouch is also central to the implanting of the adjustable gastric band. In this procedure, the band is placed around the upper part of the patient's stomach, thereby limiting his or her food intake. However, with the gastric band procedure, the patient's intestines are not rerouted, and the band is fully adjustable and reversible. This surgery radically limits the amount of food a patient can ingest. The Roux-en-Y gastric bypass surgery, a popular procedure, combines both malabsorptive and restrictive aims.

The increased popularity of bariatric surgeries in the last decade has led to a greater public awareness of surgery as a major tool in losing weight. Just as cosmetic surgery has been regarded as offering procedures to eradicate fat in a society that privileges a slender and youthful bodily aesthetic, so too have bariatric surgeries come to be accepted as another option for those wishing to lose weight. However, the practices are controversial. Weight loss is popularly understood as an arduous and difficult task involving monitoring one's food intake rigidly and avidly exercising. Surgical interventions that can seemingly "bypass" the hard work of diet and exercise are appealing to some, appearing to draw on the same principles as cosmetic surgery used for bodily alteration. Weight-loss surgeries have been conceptualized by some observers as a "quick-fix" option and a way out of living in a fat body is a culture that abhors excess flesh. But in contemporary Western culture, body weight is linked with discourses of morality. Thus, some regard weight-loss surgeries as radical procedures deployed by those who have failed in their attempts to lose weight "naturally"—that is, those who (allegedly) do not possess the strength, willpower, commitment, or personal fortitude to engage in the rigorous processes of dieting and exercise.

The surgeries are also controversial because they have significant side effects and risks that can endanger or make life difficult for some patients who have undergone the procedures. According to the American Society for Metabolic and Bariatric Surgery, the possible major early complications from surgery include pulmonary embolism, gastrointestinal leak and bleeding, heart complications, and other problems. Long-terms complications can include diarrhea, nausea, stomach and bowel obstructions, abdominal pain, and blood clots. Some patients need follow-up surgeries.

Further, bariatric surgeries are not the simple "end point" for patients seeking significant weight loss. Increasingly, cosmetic surgery is more becoming a supplement to, and final destination for, weight-loss surgery patients. Given the rapid weight loss bariatric surgeries effect, many patients experience sagging skin folds as they get close to their medically determined ideal weight. The most radical of cosmetic surgical techniques to remedy excess skin following massive weight loss is total body-lift surgery.

Body Lift

Body-lift surgery circumferentially "lifts" sagging skin specifically around the torso and hips of the patient, but can also include a number of procedures to tighten loose skin on the upper arms, breasts, and the upper body. The main procedure in body lift is the lower body-lift procedure, comprised of a combination of abdominoplasty ("tummy tuck"), thigh, and buttock lifts, as well as a major circumferential body-sculpting procedure around the patient's waist, known as a "belt lipectomy." The collection of procedures performed in lower body-lift surgery primarily involves the removal of excess skin and fat tissue as well as the tightening of the abdominal wall muscles. Liposuction removes localized pockets of fat, while the connective tissue between the abdominal skin and muscle is resuspended.

This surgery has become more popular with the rise of bariatric surgeries as an option for major weight loss, particularly in Western countries. However, body-lift surgery is a major surgical procedure with significant and multiple attendant risks. These can include severe infection, healing problems, and bleeding complications. Additionally, while the patient may emerge from the procedure with more taut skin, he or she must also contend with extensive scarring.

Despite these risks and problems, advertisements of surgeons who offer body-lift surgery emphasize the culturally unappealing aesthetic appearance of "loose, sagging skin," and the surgery is thus marketed as an appropriate, and in fact necessary, final procedure for those who have undergone massive weight loss. However, patients who have experienced a loss of tissue elasticity due to pregnancies, aging processes, and specific skin conditions are also targeted. The presence of loose excess skin is explained on many cosmetic surgery advertisements as being an obstacle to normal daily activities such as sitting and walking, and even compromising personal hygiene through bacterial infection under sagging skin flaps. Marketing strategies for body-lift surgery also use the discourse of youth; skin that is not slim and taut is associated with the devalued aging body. However, surgeons who perform these procedures are at pains to point out that body-lift surgery should not be imagined as a weight-loss tool, but as a measure to "complete" one's body project following weight loss or other physical changes. It is decribed as a "refinement tool," to be mobilized following the "coarse tool" of weight loss. Sagging flesh, then, emerges as being only marginally more socially acceptable than "fat" flesh. *See also* Abdomen: Abdomino-plasty; Fat: Cultural History of Fat; and Fat: Dieting Practices.

Further Reading: Fraser, Suzanne. *Cosmetic Surgery, Gender and Culture*. London: Palgrave Macmillan, 2003; Gimlin, Debra. L. *Body Work: Beauty and Self-Image in American Culture*. Berkeley: University of California Press, 2002; Pitts-Taylor, Victoria. *Surgery Junkies: Wellness and Pathology in Cosmetic Culture*. New Brunswick, NJ: Rutgers, 2007.

Samantha Murray

Feet

Feet: Cultural History of the Feet

The human foot has two basic uses: to create a solid balance for humans and to facilitate movement of the legs for walking. The foot has gone through a few stages of evolution in order to function and look as it does today: it evolved from the pronograde prehensile foot, the hylobatian or small orthograde foot, and the troglodytian or massive orthograde foot, to finally the plantigrade foot. Feet have been the subject of literature, medical advancements, sexual fantasies, and cultural rituals throughout history.

The foot also has a role in alternative medicine and is subject to various forms of modification. While acupuncture and reflexology have offered relief from pain for many people, others regularly go for pedicures and foot massages. The human foot has thiry-eight bones, but it also holds what reflexologists call "pressure points" that can eliviate pain in a holistic approach to the whole body. Reflexologists hold that, when certian areas of the foot are massaged with the proper amount of pressure, organs and muscles throughout the body are directly affected, including the sinuses, kidney, colon, heart, stomach, and bladder.

There are many common medical problems associated with the foot. According to a report by the American Academy of Orthopaedic Surgeons, approximately 4 million patients with foot or ankle problems make office visits each year. While some afflictions are more common than others, they are all painful and can lead to more serious health problems. Due to footwear designed to enhance a woman's sexuality, women have the most problems with their feet. In fact, according to the American Podiatric Medical Association, more than sixty percent of American women suffer from foot problems. A few of the most commonly reported are blisters, bunions, heel spurs, calluses, corns, neuromas, and ingrown toenails.

Military and Athletics

Dancers, soldiers, and many athletes often have unique foot injuries. They also have the opportunity to defy gravity, physical boundaries, and become models of endurance, courage, strength, and grace. While the protection of the foot has spawned literally thousands of designs for athletic and dance shoes, military boots and sandals, the aesthetics of footwear are as significant as function. This has been a problem primarily for the feet of "foot soldiers" who trudged miles in combat, since proper footwear or the lack of it meant survival or demise on the battlefield. One particular problem for soldiers was a condition called "trench foot," which usually led to gangrene and the amputation of the foot or portion of the leg. This was particulary an issue for World War I and World War II soldiers fighting in the winter because of cold and wet conditions. Covering the foot with whale oil as well as consistently changing their socks were the only defenses against the horrible trench foot; thousands of men were treated for it.

In ballet dancers, the foot is put under constant strain. When ballet, or "toe shoes" are worn, they can cause serious problems that can become permanent. Ballet dancers have rituals to help with the pain, such as wrapping the foot with lamb's wool, taping the toes, and cramming chamois leather or soft, old pairs of tights into their satin pointe shoes.

Almost every athlete needs the use of the foot to compete, but certain athletes have proven themselves in their sport swithout the use of their legs or feet. A common problem called "athlete's foot" is a fungus, referred to in medical terms as "tinea pedis." Although it implies a problem unique to athletes, many people are affected by it, and it can be easily treated. Males tend to have the fugus more often than females, usually between the toes.

Unusual and Famous Feet

One unusual condition of the feet is called polydactilism, or having more than the usual number of digits on the feet. It can also affect the hands. This is extremely rare in humans. However, numerous people have in fact been born with more than five toes on each foot. Historians have claimed that King Charles VIII of France had six toes and needed special shoes because of the abnormally large toes. The Dominican baseball player Antonio Alfonseca has an extra digit on each hand and foot. His nicknames include "Six Fingers." Alfonseca has pitched for the Chicago Cubs, the Atlanta Braves, and the Philadelphia Phillies; his condition is of little handicap. An English dart player also has polydactilism. Eric Bristow, also known as "the Crafty Cockney," is a world dart champion and has six toes on his right foot.

One condition known as "flat feet" has affected people throughout the centuries. This condition, also called "pes planus" or "fallen arches," is common in children and pregnant women. However, during the European Middle Ages, people with flat feet were considered unattractive and were often isolated from society. There are numerous odd tales and superstitions about this condition being a bad omen. In some cultures, seeing people who had flat feet immediately before a journey could bring bad luck to the traveller. Another condition, called syndactylism, evinces toes or fingers that are fused, giving them a slightly webbed appearance.

Abnormalities of the feet and legs are often experienced as disabilities, but some athletes have demonstrated impressive athleticism even without feet or legs. Oscar Pistorius, who hails from South Africa, was born with lower legs but no feet. After playing rugby in school and becoming injured, he tried running track. After using a number of kinds of prosthetic feet, he found most success with sickle-shaped feet, and went on to become the first so-called amputee to break the 200-meter record in 2004 at the Athens Paralympics. Companies such as Germany's Otto Bock and Iceland's Ossur make it possible for Pistorius and many others to continue reaching their goals in athletics despite their physical differences.

Art and Literature

Centuries of paintings, tapestries, and sculptures have represented the foot in various ways, whether shod with shoes of the latest royal fashions, in military attire, or religious garb. In Eastern art, the foot has almost always referenced the erotic; in Japanese paintings, the bare foot often suggests eroticism. If the toes are curled, this often suggests an aroused mood. In Western paintings of the sixteenth through eighteenth centuries, women of high social status are rarely shown without shoes. Revealing the bare foot of a woman who was a prostitute or had a lower social status was more acceptable. Men with bare feet in art have been interpreted as indicating infidelity or marital estrangement.

Kissing or bowing to another's feet is highly suggestive of servitude or loyalty. In *Titus Andronicus*, one of William Shakespeare's first tragedies, the character Lavinia expresses her loyalty through paying homage to the feet of her father. She says, "In peace and honor live Lord Titus long; My noble lord and father, live in fame! Lo, at this tomb my tributary tears I render, for my brethren's obsequies; And at thy feet I kneel, with tears of joy, shed on the earth, for thy return to Rome." The feet can also suggest femininity, purity, and propriety, in contrast to the ground upon which the feet stand. English poet John Gay's *Trivia: Or, the Art of Walking the Streets of London*, written in 1716, described the feet of a beautiful woman: "... since in braided Gold her Foot is bound / And a long trailing Manteau sweeps the Ground / Her Shoe disdains the Street."

Sexual and Fetishized Feet

While many psychologists, such as Sigmund Freud and Vilayanur S. Ramachandran, have suggested reasons for the foot's eroticism, the human foot remains unattractive and grotesque to some even as it is fascinating and pornographic to others. Foot fetishism varies within cultures, influenced by personal preferences, literature, fashion, and psychosocial behaviors. High-heeled shoes, including stilletos, have tight spaces to fit the toes, and are responsible for certain conditions and deformities such as hammertoes and Haglund's deformity, a growth on the back of the heel due to the back or straps of high heels. Another condition is metatarsalgia, which causes severe pain in the ball of the foot. While the high heel was initially worn by both men and women, its specificity as women's attire in the contemporary era has drawn the ire of feminists, who see it as an instance of female suffering for the sake of beauty.

The practice of breaking and binding the foot to make it smaller has been associated primarily with Eastern countries, China in particular. Footbinding, while having obvious painful physical drawbacks, was considered a privilege and duty for Chinese women over the centuries. While legend and folklore suggests numerous origins of the practice, this custom began around the time of the tenth century, and rose to popularity during the Song (Sung) dynasty. One of the most popular and widespread explanations for the custom is the story of a Song dynasty prince, Li Yu. He had a particular sexual interest in small feet, and required his concubine to dance on her tiny toes for him. His concubine was named Yao Niang, and the story reports her as such a delicate woman of grace that when she danced, she resembled a person floating on "golden lilies." Nevertheless, after this custom became popular, throughout the Yuan and Ming dynasties in twelfth- and thireenth-century China, women of all social classes began to practice footbinding in order to marry and retain social acceptance. However, by 1644 and the rise of the Manchu Qing dynasty, footbinding began to slowly diminish. It was first outlawed in the seventeenth century, and in 1895, the first society was started in Shanghai to abolish the practice. It was again declared illegal in 1911. The legal history of this custom shows how long the femininity of women was concentrated on the foot. Some feminists argue that footbinding is echoed in the fashion of women's high-heeled and pointed footwear of today.

While uncomfortable and deforming shoes have been the focus of feminist criticism, many contemporary women support the fashion industry by wearing and coveting shoes with high heels, such as stilettos. Certain subcultures exist for women who feel their image is improved by wearing four- , five- , or six-inch heels, mules, and platform shoes created by fashion icons such as Manolo Blahnik and Jimmy Choo. These shoes put tremendous pressure on the toes in a very tight space, often crushing the smaller toes and requiring the wearer to walk slowly and with the hips moving from side to side. This accentuates the swinging gate of the woman's hips and buttocks, thus catching the attention of others. Such shoes are worn by a variety of women all over the world, from businesswomen to prostitutes, erotic dancers, pornographic actors, dominatrices, and even young girls trying to look older than they are. The pain and long-term effects on the foot, ankle, spine, and legs appear to be outweighed by the aesthetic and symbolic effects of such shoes. However, the Society of Chiropidists and Podiatrists warns against wearing these shoes for more than six months in a row, due to the possibility of shortening the calf muscle, lowering the arch of the foot, and seriously affecting the spine, knee, and hip joints.

Cultural and Religious Customs

Many rites and rituals involve the feet. In the time of Tutankhamen, the Egyptian Pharoah of the Eighteenth dynasty (1341–1323 BCE), the care and dressing of the foot was important. One Egyptian custom was to perfume and bathe the feet before eating. In Yorubaland, West Africa, a widespread ceremonial custom for a bride before the twentieth century was to paint the soles of the feet with "osun," or camwood lotion. The groom would also do this in order to differentiate him from the other men of the tribe on his wedding day. The Hindu religion has a similar custom in marriage ceremonies. One part of a traditional Hindu wedding, known as the "Aashirvad" or "parental blessing," is when the parents acknowledge the new couple and bless their union. Immediately thereafter, the newly married couple touches their parents' feet as a gesture of respect. Jewish weddings often include the ritual of stomping on a glass with the foot, usually by the groom with his right foot after the vows and blessings and drinking from a cup. His act is a symbolic reminder of the Jewish people's hearts breaking when the Holy Temple in Jerusalem was destroyed.

In societies with warm climates where people primarily wore sandals and thus often had dirty feet, the washing of feet was often seen as a duty for a host to perform for guests. The act of washing the feet also has religious significance. In John 13:1-17, Jesus washes the disciples' feet as an act of purity and lesson of equality. This scene was painted by many artists, and one famous painting called *Christ Washing the Feet of the Apostles* was completed in 1475 by the German painter Meister des Hausbuches. The religious significance of washing the feet varies; in some countries, feet have been washed during baptism.

The feet are especially significant in Indian religious life and culture. The Theemidhi is a Hindu ceremony that is part of a festival held in the late fall season in India, Singapore, South Africa, and Malaysia. A priest will initiate the Theemidhi by first walking on hot coals while holding on his head the Karagam, which is a sacred vessel full of water. He is then followed by others wishing to prove their devotion and faith.

The largest South African ethnic group, the Zulu nation, had a painful induction to the military that involves the feet. Each African Zulu tribal warrior, called "ibutho," went through a unique training exercise of crushing thorns into the earth with their bare feet.

One of the most breathtaking practices is the art of fire walking. This is done for many reasons worldwide, including purification, rites of passage to adulthood, and religious healing. In Japan, Taoist and Buddhist monks continue this practice.

Further Reading: Clarke, G. W. "Cyprian's Epistle 64 and the Kissing of Feet in Baptism." *The Harvard Theological Review* vol. 66, no. 1. (January 1973); Danforth, Loring. *Firewalking and Religious Healing.* Princeton, NJ: Princeton University Press, 1989; Erickson R. J., and B. Edwards. "Medically unresponsive foot pain treated successfully with acupuncture." *Acupuncture in Medicine* (November 1996); Gay, John. *Court Poems.* Toronto: Fisher Rare Book Library, 1716; Hood, Marlowe. "Running Against the Wind." *IEEE Spectrum* (June 2005); Wharton, Greg. *Love Under Foot: An Erotic Celebration of Feet.* Phildelphia, PA: Haworth Press: May 2004.

Margaret Howard

Footbinding

Footbinding is a practice of wrapping the foot in cloth to form its shape and size into that which is socially deemed beautiful or fashionable. The practice involves forcing all the toes but the big toe under the sole of the

Chinese woman with lotus feet, ca. 1900. Courtesy of Library of Congress, LC-USZ62-80206.

foot with cloth bandages, stunting the foot's growth and increasing the arch. In practice for more than 1,000 years, it was predominantly used in imperial China by the Hans until the early twentieth century.

The bound foot remains a well-known icon of China's history, often conjuring images of China's barbarous past and of the subordination of women. However, this understanding of footbinding is overly simplified, leaving the complexities of this practice unexplored. Footbinding was undoubtedly painful for the women and girls who underwent this two-year process, which involves breaking the bones to deform the foot into the desired "three-inch golden lotus" shape. However, reducing footbinding to misogyny neglects the way that class, ethnic identity, and sexuality intertwined with gender roles to shape the cultural significance of footbinding.

Origins

It is unknown precisely when this practice emerged, though scholars have put forth several possible roots. The earliest records trace back as far as the twenty-first century BCE, where a founder of the Xia dynasty, Da Yu, married a woman rumored to have tiny fox feet. A similar record of Da Ji, a concubine to the last ruler of the Shang dynasty in the sixteenth through the eleventh centuries BCE, was also said to have the feet of a fox, which she wrapped in cloth to hide. When she became the king's favorite concubine, other women began mimicking her bindings and this tradition took root. The founder of the first feudal dynasty in 221 BCE, Qin Shihuang, further fueled footbinding, as he only picked small-footed concubines and maids. Similarly, in the Han dynasty, Emperor Chengdi (32–6 CE) was rumored to be aroused only by rubbing his concubines' bound feet. However, the type of binding and the symbolic meaning in these early examples is unknown.

Later, during Xiao Baojuan's reign of 498–501, footbinding's association with "the golden lotus" emerged. Modeled after an Indian tale of a deer lady who left lotus flowers with her every step, the emperor created a structure of gold, made to look like lotus petals, where palace dancers walked and danced. The last emperor of the later Tang dynasty, Li Yu (reigned 961–75), maintained this performance style and structure, but also ordered his concubine to bind her feet before this dance to enhance the effect, which was soon replicated by many other upper-class women.

Despite these ancient roots, footbinding was still infrequent until the end of the eleventh century. In a period of social change, resulting in the rise of Neo-Confucian doctrine, footbinding started to spread throughout China such that by the end of the Song dynasty in 1125, footbinding extended from the north to the south and from the rich to the poor. During the Yuan dynasty (1271–1368), Mongol rulers encouraged footbinding's spread through poetry and song, putting forth the idea that bound feet determined a woman's beauty on the national scale.

Footbinding expanded from a tool for assessing beauty to a measurement of social status and proper womanhood during the Ming dynasty (1368–1644), when footbinding continued to spread throughout China, but was forbidden for beggar women. Throughout this development, the desired shape of footbinding changed, culminating in this period with the ultimate ideal of the "three-inch golden lotus." By the end of the Ming dynasty, both the practice and the specific shape of footbinding had become widespread. Footbinding peaked in late imperial China during the Qing dynasty (1644–1911), even though the Manchu emperors attempted to forbid this practice as an attempt to assimilate Han women, the predominant footbinders and the largest ethnic minority, into Manchu culture. With increasing Western influence and the dispersal of anti-footbinding propaganda, the Qing period also marked the decline of footbinding.

Footbinders

Footbinding was first developed by courtesans, then copied by upper-class women, and further imitated by the poor. By the Ming dynasty, it had spread to women of all ages and classes such that any woman, ugly or beautiful, could be made desirable through her feet. Footbinding was mostly practiced by Han Chinese women, serving as a marker to distinguish Han Chinese and "other," but some Manchu women and even upper-class Korean women used some form of footbinding.

Women in regions where their labor was needed for producing wet rice, especially in the southern coastal provinces, were less likely to bind because they could not remove their shoes to go into the mud. However, it is a common misconception that only upper-class women could afford the privilege of footbinding. Lower-class women also bound their feet while still performing physical labor and chores, and even most upper-class women with bound feet worked as well in caretaking or reproductive labor. As late imperial China shifted to petty capitalism, footbinding offered a means of social climbing, justifying the motivation for women of all classes to bind their feet as it made them more valuable for marriage, despite the difficulty this posed for labor. Still, footbinding did play a role in the gendered division of labor, as it limited women's ability to walk and thus constrained their work in or around the house. Still, there was sufficient labor for China's silk trade by having women weave in the home.

Complicating the common use of footbinding as a patriarchal practice is the fact that footbinding was not always limited to women. When a male child was predicted to have an ominous future, families often raised the boy as a girl and bound his feet to circumvent this fate. Male footbinding was also practiced for financial means, either by male prostitutes or convicts, who bound their feet to get engaged and then escaped with the dowry on the wedding night. Male footbinding was even adopted by some men for fashion, narrowing their feet to fit the upper-class shoes stylish for males.

Binding Process

Most females began footbinding when they were five to seven years old to ensure that the bones would still be flexible. This age was additionally chosen because the Chinese believed this was when children become mindful of their bodies. While boys developed new responsibilities at this age, such as learning the written word, footbinding pushed girls to mature rapidly, teaching them to endure the pain that they would later have to face during childbirth.

Varying with astronomy and the Chinese calendar, footbinding traditionally began on the twenty-fourth day of the eighth moon in August, when the cooler weather was most suitable for binding. The mother made her daughter's first pair of "lotus shoes" and gave them to her on the morning when the binding would begin, incorporating her daughter into the process of constructing the shoes from then on. Using a bandage of cotton or silk, two inches wide and ten feet long, the feet were wrapped in a meticulous way so that it pulled the small toes back in toward the sole, leaving the big toe unbound to form the point of the foot. After the initial binding, mothers then forced their daughters to walk around on their bound feet to facilitate the deforming of the foot, often breaking the bones into this new position. For the next two years, this process was continued. Girls often had to hold onto walls to move about, bandaging and washing their feet, and putting them into new pairs of lotus shoes, slightly smaller than the week before. When the bandages were removed, the flesh and even toes fell off.

The goal of this process was to completely reshape the foot, bringing the sole and heel as close together as possible to form an arch and reduce the foot to three inches long and one-half inch wide in front. If done correctly, the foot looked more like a hoof, elongating the leg. To assess the perfect golden lotus, seven characteristics were used, which dictated that the foot should be small, slim, pointed, arched, fragrant, soft, and straight. In addition, the ideal bound foot resembled both a penis in its shape and a vagina through the appearance of the foot inside the lotus shoes. These aesthetic connections make sense given the belief that footbinding was connected to reproduction, as it concentrated the blood in the upper parts of the legs and groin instead of the feet.

Throughout this time, women also learned how to sew and embroider lotus shoes. As their mothers inducted them into footbinding, it connected the mother to the daughter, teaching girls their domestic and symbolic roles in Neo-Confucian society. Lotus shoes were ideally red or green; white was worn only for funerals. In order to maintain the effect of the bound foot at all times, women also made special sleeping shoes that emphasized the erotic appeal more so than their daytime shoes. The style of shoes varied within each region, but the desired effect of these shoes was similar.

Symbolism

In the late imperial period, when footbinding peaked, China was facing many threats, from foreign invaders abroad to economic and social changes at home. Footbinding arose as a way to deal with many of these tensions through the symbolism it invoked of proper womanhood. However, the various symbolic uses of footbinding were full of dualisms, used to represent reason, morality, and logic, while simultaneously evoking extravagance, eroticism, and transgression.

One example of this was the role of footbinding as a cultural symbol for the relationship between nature and culture. Because the foot is the only part of the body that must touch the ground, it was seen as polluted and impure, even used as a symbol for death. In binding the foot, women overcame their degraded humanness, connecting them to the immortals. At the same time, however, the bound foot was made to resemble the hoof of an animal, specifically a fox or deer. Mediating between the celestial and the bestial then became central to the erotic appeal of footbinding, as chimeras have symbolized in many cultures. Footbinding represented the making and remaking of nature. The natural foot was made into artifice as it was transformed into the culturally valued foot shape, but was then remade to signify nature as an indicator of womanhood and femininity that served the same purpose as the genitals for determining one's sex, despite the rare male footbinding.

The symbolism of the bound foot was additionally inseparable from cultural metaphors for food. Euphemisms for footbinding included bamboo shoots, water chestnuts, dumplings, red beans, and, most commonly, the lotus, an especially meaningful sacred symbol of transcendence to purity. The ties between food and footbinding also add up given the sexual value of both; the bound foot, like food, was meant to be smelled, tasted, and viewed, turning the female body into something that can be consumed for pleasure like a meal.

Footbinding as a Neo-Confucian symbol of pure womanhood was also fraught, as it simultaneously evoked sexuality. This tension was mediated by containing women within the home, so footbinding was able to represent a chaste but erotic wife. In symbolizing femininity, footbinding also enabled Chinese men to become more genteel in late imperial China without threatening their masculinity. As a practice passed down from woman to woman, footbinding exempted men from the responsibility of dominating women, though they reaped the benefits of it as husbands and sole consumers of their wives' feet.

Sexual Rituals

The bound foot became a highly sexualized object for "lotus lovers" who had this fetish. Sex play with the feet was numerous, from caressing the toes with the lips and tongue to nibbling at the heels. Touching any part of the body with the bound foot was highly arousing, especially when in direct contact with the penis, and many lotus lovers even enjoyed the distinct smell of the feet. In addition to the foot's role in foreplay, many special sexual positions were used by lotus lovers to place bound feet in a highly visible place during intercourse.

Many theories exist as to why the bound foot was so appealing. Some records suggest that men enjoyed the way it made women walk, tensing up their lower bodies and incidentally making the posterior larger while tightening the vagina. However, this cannot fully account for the centrality of the bound feet in eroticism. The Freudian explanation for the fetish suggests that men desired the lotus foot because of its phallic shape, comforting their castration anxieties. A further explanation looks to the symbolic dualisms explored above, where the lotus foot was desired precisely because it traversed so many boundaries, nature/culture, celestial/bestial, and chaste/erotic. For all these reasons, the removal of the shoe was strictly taboo, and seen as the end of eroticism.

Although there were definitely cases of men whose desire for lotus feet was sadistic, aroused by the violence visible in the bound foot, the eroticism cannot be entirely explained by this, especially because several historic accounts suggest that some women were equally stimulated by having their bound foot rubbed or touched. In addition, bound feet may have allowed for homoeroticism, as they enabled women to turn their gaze to other women and express amorous feelings through their shared experiences of binding. Bound feet also played a role in validating male prostitutes as feminine.

Cultural Practices

The interest in the bound foot did not end in the bedroom, but extended to wider cultural practices as well. Many women could expect to confront this on their wedding night, as it was the custom of "*nao fang*" to taunt a bride on the size of her feet. Games like "crossing the bridge" judged the bride's feet by laying out glasses, connecting them with chopsticks, and challenging the bride to step between them without knocking any "bridges" over. Many drinking games developed around lotus shoes as well. Some regions even had annual foot contests, exemplifying how successful lotus feet could trump other factors in defining beauty, as women of all classes and ages, ugly or beautiful, had a shot at winning.

The cultural interaction with footbinding also extended to literature and poetry during footbinding's heyday. This dates back to the ninth century, when a Chinese story, closely paralleling the later Brothers Grimm's Cinderella, became popular, praising the Cinderella character's tiny foot as a symbol of beauty and as a route for social climbing. Other representations of footbinding in literature and poetry helped construct this as a symbol for femininity that is pitiable and weak. These images entered folk art, proverbs, and erotica. However, almost all of these representations were produced by men. Women were predominantly excluded from a written voice.

In the rare women's writings available, bound feet were more than a symbol of eroticism and beauty, as in male literature, but also an expression for women's networks, binding women together in support. Embroidering the lotus shoes also provided a medium for women's voices to be heard. Giving shoes as gifts to female friends and relatives was a means of communication and expression.

Decline

Though the first royal decree to ban footbinding was in 1642, it was not until the end of the nineteenth century that these efforts began to make advances. Leading up to this, eighteenth-century liberal scholars, writers, and poets began demonizing footbinding, but with minimal impact. After another royal decree to end footbinding in 1882, the Unbound Foot Association was founded in 1894, eventually attracting more than 10,000 supporters. This began the natural foot movement of the 1890s, which used poetry, songs, and even X-rays of bound feet to promote anti-footbinding propaganda that could resonate with the uneducated poor. Through their efforts as well as that of Christian missionaries, the cultural perception toward bound feet dramatically changed; footbinding transformed from a sign of beauty and status to a mark of national shame and backwardness.

Anti-footbinding government propaganda emphasized China's hope for modernization to resist Western colonialism, situating footbinding as an outdated practice impeding national progress. As China shifted from a feudal to an agricultural economy with increasing capitalist ideology, the government had strong motivation for ending this practice in order to make women more efficient workers. The government even offered rewards for people who turned in someone's bindings, humiliating these women for their once-precious trait.

Just as this practice had spread from courtesans to the rich and then down to the masses, it declined in this order as well. However, the practice still lingered in rural areas of the country until the Great Leap Forward in 1958 increased pressure for total mobilization of women into the labor force. Still, given the long duration of this tradition, the anti-footbinding propaganda of schools, missions, natural-foot societies, and the government was clearly effective, relegating this practice to a thing of the past.

Though footbinding has been more or less abolished, interest in this topic has continued by Western scholars. Feminist scholars have identified footbinding as a prime example of women's subordination that physically disables women to ensure male dominance. Sheila Jeffreys, for example, writes, "Footbinding, if it continued today, is likely to be recognized by most as a harmful cultural practice. It fulfills all the criteria: it creates stereotyped roles for men and women, it emerges from the subordination of women and is for the benefit of men, it is justified by tradition, and it clearly harms the health of women and girl children" (2005: 147–148). Marking footbinding as an antecedent to the current Western practice of wearing high heels, Jeffreys urges Western feminists to see the comparison, suggesting, "Women are immediately recognizable as they walk with difficulty on their toes in public places. Thus high heels enable women to complement the male sex role of masculinity, in which men look sturdy and have both feet on the ground, with clear evidence of female fragility" (2005: 130). However, others have criticized the reductionism of this view and much other Western scholarship on footbinding that looks upon this practice with a curious Western gaze. These debates continue today, as research into this custom further complicates footbinding's cultural significance.

Further Reading: Blake, C. Fred. "Foot-Binding in Neo-Confucian China and the Appropriation of Female Labor." In Londa Schiebinger, ed. *Feminism and the Body.* New York: Oxford University Press, 2000, pp. 429–464; Ebrey, Patricia Buckley. "Women, Marriage, and the Family in Chinese History." In Paul S. Ropp, ed. *Heritage of China: Contemporary Perspectives on Chinese Civilization.* Berkeley: University of California Press, 1990, pp. 197–223; Jackson, Beverley. *Splendid Slippers: A Thousand Years of an Erotic Tradition.* Berkeley: Ten Speed Press, 2000; Jeffreys, Sheila. *Beauty and Misogyny: Harmful Cultural Practices in the West.* New York: Routledge, 2005; Ko, Dorothy. *Cinderella's Sisters: A Revisionist History of Footbinding.* Berkeley: University of California Press, 2005; Ko, Dorothy. *Every Step a Lotus: Shoes for Bound Feet.* Berkeley: University of California Press, 2001; Levy, Howard S. *The Lotus Lovers: The Complete History of the Curious Erotic Custom of Footbinding in China.* Buffalo, NY: Prometheus Books, 1991; Ping, Wang. *Aching for Beauty: Footbinding in China.* Minneapolis: University of Minnesota Press, 2000; Yung, Judy. *Unbound Voices: A Documentary History of Chinese Women in San Francisco.* Berkeley: University of California Press, 1999.

Emily Laurel Smith

History of Shoes

The history of shoes suggests the depth and variety of the human foot's symbolic significance. Shoes have been widely linked to both class status and gender relations. Shoe customs have been ritually significant: removing one's shoes, for example, can mark a space as sacred; tying shoelaces can represent marriage and status transition. Shoes have been identified with warfare and labor, as well as with domesticity and eroticism. Shoe customs have troubled dynasties and monarchs and have inspired fashion and fetishism.

Varieties of Shoes

Many materials have been used over the centuries to make and adorn shoes for spiritual, functional, or social reasons. Some materials are still used today, but some have been outlawed or are no longer in fashion. Materials used to create shoes include bamboo bark, felt, cork, wicker, fish skin, sealskin, snake, lizard, alligator, papyrus/palm leaves, canvas, satin, velvet, silk, and straw. Leather made from various animal skins has also been used, including antelope, reindeer, moose, ox, cow, deer, buffalo, kangaroo, goat, wild boar, and monkey. Decorations for shoes worldwide have included animal horns, tiny silver bells, beads, iron spikes, buckles, lacings, and sequins, to name only a few. Shoes are widely varied, as some examples will show.

The sealskin slippers worn by the Caribou Inuit have traditional and cultural importance sewn into their linings. Their slippers and boots range

Contemporary platforms, and a modern twist on the clog. Courtesy of Corbis.

in size from shin to thigh high, some are even as high as the chest for wading and fishing. These boots can convey through beaded designs or tribe-specific use of pelts seasonal changes, gender, and generational bonds. Often, a young woman will give her grandparents her first sewn pair of boots to symbolize her bond to the Inuit culture.

In Japan, shoes with thongs were constructed of a simple piece of cord, cotton, silk, or velvet. A few parts of the shoe can be translated today using terms associated with parts of the human body. The thong between the toes, or "nose" cord, is the "hana-o"; the wooden platforms that the "geta" stand on are "teeth" or "ha"; and the part of the bottom that sticks out past the "teeth" is the "chin," or "ago".

In Yorubaland, Africa, the population did not wear shoes as Westerners did until the fifteenth century. This was due to trans-Saharan trade and commercial distribution by European and North African traders. Beginning about this time and in select areas still today, a particular clog, the "bata epogi," was made from hard bark, which is removed and bent to create the shoe. Another flat pod shoe, the "panseke," is about three inches wide, and when converted into a thong, it is called "bata panseke."

Early Shoe History

As far back as 14,000 BCE, during the Upper Paleolithic period, there is evidence that Magdalenians wore fur boots. By 3300 BCE, basic footwear had also been filled with grasses. The Louvre museum holds an ancient pair of sandals taken from the embalmed feet of an Egyptian mummy. The soles are multiple layers of leather, using oxen, buffalo, or cow. On tomb walls dating to the fifteenth century BCE, Theban frescoes depict Egyptian cobblers and the craft of shoemaking.

Shoes have held a spiritual significance since antiquity. In ancient Egypt, when a pharaoh or any of his subjects would enter a temple, all shoes were left at the entrance. In symbolic terms, the shoe often suggests traveling or transition, and shoe removal is widely symbolic of entering a sacred area. It is customary in the Far East to remove one's shoes if entering a temple, worshipping a divine statue, or making a sacrifice. The Old Testament of the Bible, in Exodus (3:5), commands that one should "put off thy shoes from thy feet for the place where on thou standest is holy ground." This custom was also adopted by those of the Muslim faith, whose followers remove their shoes when entering a mosque. Shoes that are made of cow leather are forbidden to the Hindu, because the cow is sacred. Footwear in India has consistently been influenced by religion, affecting the Moslems, Sikhs, and Parsis.

Evidence in hieroglyphic texts written in the tombs during the decades of the pyramids suggests that the dead wanted to proceed along the blessed paths to the heavens in white sandals. As in Egypt, Japanese spirits were also believed to travel, so large "waraji" were often hung at the borders of villages to deflect evil spirits and prevent infectious diseases from entering. In China, it is believed that when a dead person's shoe is banged about on the door, the soul would recognize the home. In late Qing China, it was also customary to use shoes for medicinal purposes. If a person had an unhealthy addiction to tea, it was thought that buying a new pair of shoes and filling them with tea made with the leaves inside the shoe and drinking the tea would cure the addiction.

In many countries around the world, footwear customs still exist today that began in antiquity. For example, in ancient Greece, when a bride would travel to her new husband's home, she used new sandals known as "nymphides." This tradition still exists in some weddings, but other shoe traditions have died out. For example, the practice of shoe tying in ancient Greek wedding ceremonies symbolized a woman's life transitioning through marriage, integrating both sexual and social meanings. In the Temple of Zeus at Olympia, built around 460 BCE, the east pediment had a sculpture that has since been destroyed showing laced shoes. The Etruscans also wore shoes with turned up toes and high laces until the fifth century, when the Greek influence became more intrusive. In the Athenian acropolis, Nike, the goddess of victory, is portrayed in a sculpture bending down to untie her shoe. This act often suggests the end of a long journey. Farther to the east, there is also ancient evidence of shoes.

Tales of the Roman senator Lucius Vitellus are told by Suetonius who lived until about 128 CE. According to Suetonius, Vitellus carried the red slipper of his mistress's right foot under his clothes, and would kiss it in public. The color red has been used to signify not only this kind of secret love, but many emotions in shoe fashion, making statements of power, wealth, and social status. An early example of this shows Emperor Aurelius (121–180) wearing red shoes, which subsequently became a symbol of importance. The color red has been a fashion choice of Catholic popes since about the thirteenth century CE. Also, King Henry VIII and Edward IV were reportedly buried wearing red shoes as symbols of their imperial status.

Two Roman shoemaker brothers, St. Crispin and St. Crispinian, were sent by Pope Caius to convert Gaul; they settled there to give Christian sermons and make shoes. However, when Roman General Maximianus Herculeus demanded they begin to worship pagan gods and they refused, he had them killed in 287 CE. In 1379, when the shoemaker's guild was established in the Paris Cathedral, the brothers were named the patron saints of shoemakers. St. Crispin and St. Crispinian are celebrated each year on October 25 in France.

Footbinding and Shoelessness in Asia

Although there is earlier precedent as far back as the Shang dynasty (sixteenth to eleventh centuries BCE), the Chinese tradition of foot binding developed in the tenth century CE, sometime between the end of the Tang dynasty and the beginning of the Song dynasty. There are many legends of how this began. One narrative describes how one ruler, Li Yu (reign 961–75), had his favored attendant Yao-niang dance for him, and she supposedly did so with bound feet to suggest a new moon, or to represent lotus petals. Footbinding was infrequent until the Song dynasty, and by 1125, the practice was widespread. Mongol rulers of China also encouraged footbinding in the Yuan dynasty (1271–1368). The practice was initially undertaken by courtesans and the upper classes, but eventually expanded to the poor. The practice was associated with upward mobility and status; while in the Ming period, beggar women were banned from footbinding, poor women as well as elite women aspired to bind their feet. The practice was believed to improve a woman's beauty and emphasize her delicate nature; it dually reflected her sexual allure and her chaste character.

Footbinding was accomplished through wrapping the feet of children beginning at around the age of five; over years of foot wrapping, the soles and toes of girls' feet would be permanently reshaped. Sometimes the bones would break, and the toes would grow inward; eventually the foot would resemble a small hoof. Girls and women whose feet were bound would sew and wear lotus shoes, as well as special shoes for sleeping which would maintain the foot's new shape. Attempts to ban the practice began in the seventeenth century; however, footbinding remained popular until the late nineteenth century. In some rural areas, it was practiced until the mid-twentieth century.

It was common in China for a girl to make anywhere from four to sixteen pairs of shoes as part of her dowry. This was to show off her needlework skills as well as her small feet. White shoes were worn only at funerals; red and green were common colors for shoes. Men who held the rank of Mandarin, or wealthy men, wore black satin boots. Working-class men and women also wore black shoes, usually made of cloth. The beaded slipper was most commonly worn by Chinese women from the 1920s until the World War II. For centuries, much of the working class did not wear shoes at all, and today many field laborers still go barefoot. In parts of Korea, footwear customs have endured since the fourteenth century, with a warm weather wicker shoe or a thong with a white felt sole, as well as the Mongolian boot made of black leather.

Until 1901, in Tokyo, Japan, it was legal and not uncommon to go barefoot, without shoes of any kind. Japan developed many different variations of "geta" and "zori" shoes, which were worn for centuries in some areas beginning in 200 BCE. One example that is particularly unique is the geta that had a section of the sole that held a heated coal for warming the foot. Architecture was a large influence for why the thong has been incorporated in many shoe designs, including the zori and geta. One reason for this is the cultural and architectural choice to use reed and straw mats called "tatami" in the home. This began around the mid-fourteenth century CE, and from that time forward, outdoor footwear was not allowed to be worn indoors, even if the floor was dirt or other materials. This is a major reason why Japanese shoes are designed to be effortlessly removed.

Artifacts found in Japanese tombs from the Kofun (Tumulus period, AD 250–552), bronze reproductions of leather shoes, suggest that these were socially valuable in some way. The word "kutsu" means shoe in today's jargon, but it also refers to a particular kind of shoe made of woven straw and cloth that was primarily allowed to be worn by the aristocracy. Beginning in the thirteenth century, zori were often worn with a sock with a split toe for the thong, called the "tabi."

Shoes in Medieval and Renaissance Europe

When anyone goes to buy new shoes, they can either try on all the shoes in the store or simply give their size to the salesperson, simplifying the process. That is made possible largely because King Edward I decreed in 1305 that one inch (92.5cm), which was the same length of three dried barleycorns, would be the measure for shoes in England. A few years later, in 1324, King Edward II made the shoe size vary to the English inch, which was one-twelfth of the length of a normal-size foot, the longest being the length of thirty-nine barleycorns, and so forth.

One particular type of shoe, the "poulaine," was often made of velvet, brocade, or leather, and was worn across Europe for many years. There was the military poulaine, as well, which had such long points on the toes that the knights who fought in the battle of Sempach in 1386 had to cut off the long points of their shoes as they were interfering in battle. The flamboyance of shoes, whether in high courts, common villages, or on the battlefield, became a standard for the next four centuries, varying in extremes from country to country. Evidence seems to suggest that this development of the Western fashion world began in the fourteenth century, with men being much more fabulously dressed than women, and the monarchy influencing the trends of each decade. These trends often became law, punishable by prison or death. In fact, in 1431, Joan of Arc was charged with, among other things, wearing a type of poulaine boot, which was apparently only for men.

While the shoes of the fourteenth and fifteenth centuries were longer and the toes more pointed, King Edward III decreed that the points of shoes should not exceed the length of two inches. King Richard II (reigned 1377–99) allowed the toes of a type of shoes called "crakows" to reach eighteen inches, which then became rounded in the end of the fifteenth century.

Another type of shoe, the "*valois*," was worn during the reign of Louis XII (1462–1515). It was common for this shoe to have the end be stuffed and adorned with animal horns, and resembled a cow's head, leading to the epithet "*muffle de vache*," meaning cow muzzle, "*pied d'ours*," or bear foot and "*bec de cane*," meaning duck bill. Venetians of this era wore shoes called "chopines," also known as "mules echasses" or "mules on stilts."

The wearing of chopines was outlawed in Spain by the archbishop of Talavera, who labeled women who wore them as immoral and degenerate. William Shakespeare even referred to these shoes in his play *Hamlet* in Act 2: "your ladyship is nearer to heaven then when I saw you last by the altitude of a chopine." During the reigns of Francis I (1494–1547) and Henry the III (1551–1589), shoes known as "*eschappins*" or "*escarfignons*" were common. These were satin or velvet fat slippers, sometimes with slashes to allow the expensive stockings underneath to show through. Apparently this decorative element had its origin in the soldiers who had cuts on the tops of their shoes from battle or extensive bandages from injuries or marching on wounded feet.

During the Middle Ages, shoes with mid-thigh straps were often worn by the Franks, and only their rulers wore shoes with pointed ends. In the later Middle Ages, clogs were common, usually those made of wood or cork. Charlemagne's grandson, Bernard I, the Frankish King of Italy (reign 810–818), was reportedly buried wearing clogs. The "pianelle" became common in many medieval cities, due to the mud and dirt. Men and women wore these very high shoes, with the soles being from a few inches high to twenty inches. Laws in Sicily, enforced in Florence in 1464, outlawed a particular kind of clogs called "tappini." The Italian slang word "tappinaire" originated from this shoe, and means a sexual act done by a prostitute.

Wooden clogs, including the sabot, were worn by members of all classes through the eighteenth and nineteenth centuries, although they began to be associated with the lower classes, especially in France. Clog dancing was popular in nineteenth-century Europe. The Dutch version of the clog is well known as the "klompen," often hollowed out of a single piece of wood; another version has a wooden sole with a strong leather form for the foot. The sabot, or clog, is similar to the sabotine made of leather and wood, and was used during World War I.

Renaissance Shoes and Modern High Heels

Footwear over the centuries has indicated both class status and gender assignments. The high heel common today can be traced back to King Louis XIV of France, whose red shoes and similar ones worn in the courts became symbolic of exclusivity and privilege for the fancy high heel well into the seventeenth century. However, by the early eighteenth century, the high heel's class symbolism was replaced by a gender significance, and eventually became a symbol for eroticism and femininity. By the start of the eighteenth century, Western shoes for men and women started to look very different. Gender became a factor in the design of shoes and began to filter into production and sales. Men's footwear eventually became associated with function and durability, while women's shoes continued to express a social statement of class and domesticity. The design of boots also became superior by the early twentieth century. The boot became associated with masculinity, power, and domination.

The high-heel shoe has changed throughout the decades of the twentieth century. Designers in the 1930s and 1940s, such as Salvatore Ferragamo, helped the platform shoe transform into the stiletto of the 1950s. Ferragamo made casts for custom-fit shoes for many famous Hollywood women of the last century. From the silent-film era until the end of his career, Ferragamo was the sole shoemaker to Greta Garbo, Sophia Loren, Lauren Bacall, Audrey Hepburn, Mae West, and many others. Ferragamo is known for his use of bizarre types of materials for his expensive couture shoes, including lizard, crocodile, kangaroo, and antelope, as well as fish skin. He is arguably one of the most influential shoemakers of the last century, creating most of the styles worn today by merging high fashion with affordability and originality. Beginning in the late 1960s, the women's liberation movement has consistently challenged this type of shoe as a symbol of the oppression of women by highlighting the patriarchal roots and objectification of women related to the high heel, especially the tiny stiletto.

Fantasy and Fetish

Many characters, both real and fictitious, have been famous for their shoes. Imelda Marcos with her reported 1,060 pairs of shoes, Puss 'n' Boots, Cinderella, and Dorothy of Oz are all known for their unique shoes. Hans Christian Andersen's *The Red Shoes* and Dorothy's ruby slippers both spotlighted the hue of the shoe. Records indicate that King Charles VIII had six toes on each foot, and large shoes had to be custom-made for him. Passionate Romans used to place messages inside their lover's shoes, turning the sandal into a "mailbox of love."

While the ultimate love story and fairy tale of Cinderella has many versions, the author most credited with the original story is the French writer Charles Perrault (1628–1703). However, an Egyptian tale of Psammetichus, a pharaoh, and the beautiful slave Rhopodis, whose tiny sandal is taken by an eagle and dropped into his lap, bears a strong resemblance to Perrault's story. *See also* Feet: Footbinding.

Further Reading: Bossan, Marie-Josephe. *The Art of the Shoe*. New York: Parkstone Press, 2004; Cardona, Melissa. *The Sneaker Book: 50 Years of Sports Shoe Design*. Philadelphia, PA: Schiffer Publishing, 2005; Garrett, Valery M. *Traditional Chinese Clothing in Hong Kong and South China, 1840–1980*. New York: Oxford University Press, 1987; McNeil, Peter, and Giorgio Riello. *Shoes: A History from Sandals to Sneakers*. New York: Berg Publishers, 2006; Oakes, Jill, and Rick Riewe. *Our Boots: An Inuit Women's Art*. London: Thames & Hudson, 1995; Onassis, Jacqueline, ed. *In the Russian Style*. New York: Viking Penguin, 1976; Scott, Margaret. *A Visual History of Costume: The Fourteenth & Fifteenth Centuries*. London: Great Britain: B. T. Batsford, 1986; Weir, Shelagh. *Palestinian Costume*. Austin, Texas: University of Texas Press, 1989; Wilcox, R. Turner. *The Mode in Footwear*. New York: Charles Scribner's Sons, 1948.

Margaret Howard

Genitals

Cultural History of Intersexuality

Intersexuality is the term for a physical variation in sex chromosomes and/or reproductive organs that renders an individual neither strictly male nor female. Until the mid-twentieth century, people born with ambiguous external genitalia or other conditions of sexual variance were referred to as hermaphrodites rather than intersexuals. The term "hermaphrodite" is derived from combining the name Hermes—the Greek god of livestock, music, or dreams, and the son of Zeus—with the name Aphrodite—the Greek goddess of love and beauty. The intersexual was generally tolerated rather than stigmatized in ancient Greece. In ancient Rome, treatment of intersexuals varied and depended on the current ruler. For instance, in the time of Romulus, the birth of intersex infants was understood to prophesize a calamity at the level of the state and they were regularly killed, whereas in the time of Pliny, intersex individuals were afforded the right to marry. Some cultures assimilate sex and gender diversity into their societies, while others stigmatize those who do not conform to binary sex and gender categories. Currently, intersexuality is treated medically, although this approach to intersexuality is highly controversial.

Cross-Cultural Treatment of Intersexuality

Prior to medicalization, intersexuality was treated in a variety of different ways depending on the cultural context in which the variance occurred. In many cultures, both historically and today, intersex and transgender individuals were held in high regard; some were perceived as having special cultural knowledge or insight. Certain non-Western cultures afford a special social status to those born with variant genitals or to those whose social genders do not cohere with their sexed embodiment, and create spaces for these liminal or "third-gender" individuals in the societal structure. In particular, the existence of the Native American *nadles* and *berdaches*, the *hijras* and *sadhins* of India, the *kathoeys* (or "ladyboys") of Thailand, and the *xaniths* of Oman remind us that there is nothing necessary, normal, or natural about contemporary Western treatment of intersexuality or gender variability.

Eunuchs dance during the inauguration of a Eunuch's conference in Bhopal, India, 2006. (AP Photo/Prakash Hatvalne)

Many Native American cultures are significantly more tolerant of sex and gender variance than contemporary Western cultures. The Navajos, for example, believe that intersex babies are augurs of future wealth and success, and their families celebrate the births of intersex individuals with special ceremonies. Navajo intersexuals, or *nadles*, are afforded favored social and economic positions because of their perceived supernatural and divine ordination as protectors of society. Intersexuals act as the heads of their families and thus have complete control of finances. They are given the freedom to choose what gender role they want to conform to and are afforded more sexual freedom than conventionally sexed members of society.

As in native North America, Hindu society provides specific roles for those who do not fit easily into the distinct biological/cultural classifications of "male" and "female." Gender diversity and androgyny are embraced in Hindu India, although this society may still be characterized as binary and patriarchal. The most culturally prominent and accepted role for a gender variant is the *hijra*—one who is "neither man nor woman." Hijras are born either with ambiguous sex organs or as biological males, and are ritually and surgically transformed into a third sex after experiencing a divine calling to take on this role. They are associated with male impotence and adopt a feminine appearance and cultural, occupational, and behavioral role, but are viewed as distinct from either men or women (specifically because they cannot reproduce). They may engage in sex with men (exclusively as the receptive partners), but are defined by their social function as "sexual ascetics" (that is, nonreproducers) rather than by their sexual orientation.

Hijras are frequently members of the lowest castes in hierarchical Indian society, but are generally revered and seen as vital members of society, performing blessings of fertility and ceremonial rituals at births and weddings. Though hijras are not necessarily born with ambiguous genitalia or sex organs, their social role is distinct from both traditional masculine and feminine roles, and they are considered powerful and necessary in a culture structured around sexual reproduction and difference.

Intersexuality may be better tolerated in societies where it occurs more frequently. In certain areas of the Dominican Republic and Papua New Guinea, an intersex condition known as 5-alpha reductase deficiency (5-ARD) arises with more regularity than in most other parts of the world. In these societies, individuals with 5-ARD are alternately known as *guevedoche* or *guevedoces* ("testes at twelve" or "penis at twelve"), *machihembras* ("first woman, then man"), and *kwolu-aatmwol* ("female thing transforming into male thing"), depending on the society in which they live. Although these people are generally raised as girls, they are not chastised or considered deviant when their bodies begin to change at puberty, and they are often afforded the freedom to alter their social role when this physical change occurs.

Western Treatment of Intersex before Medicalization

In the West, prior to the period of medicalization, treatment of intersexuality was relegated mainly to the state and church. In 1629, one of the first recorded cases of an intersex individual being persecuted in a court of law in America was documented. The case was that of Thomas/Thomasine Hall, an adult living as a man who was investigated for dressing in women's apparel. Hall had been baptized a girl, but claimed to have both male and female genitalia (which was corroborated upon inspection by court authorities), and had lived as both a man and a woman at various times throughout his/her life. The common treatment of intersexuals at this time in colonial America involved forcing the individual to choose a gender based on the sex that reportedly "dominated" the person's personality, and then to remain within the conventions of that sex for the rest of his/her life—or face dire consequences. Because court authorities could not come to a consensus regarding which sex "dominated" Hall's personality, it was decided that he/she should be forced to wear men's clothing along with feminine headwear and an apron. This interesting anecdote alludes to the discomfort with which early American society regarded sex, and hence gender, ambiguity.

Similar to the conception of intersex individuals as bad omens during Romulus's rule in Rome, early American Puritans saw the births of intersex babies as portents of evil, and attributed this misfortune to the sins of the children's mothers. Even though the mother was perceived to be at fault in these cases, intersex infants, if they did not die or were killed during infancy, were chastised for the wrongdoings of their mothers for the rest of their lives. Intersexuals were equated with animals, monsters, and demons, and were thought to have been born without souls (which was considered truly catastrophic for early Puritans). The stigmatization of the intersex individual as a freak or monstrosity has endured in contemporary Western cultural depictions. It was this religious conception that formed the basis of the "scientific" field of teratology, which was established in the early nineteenth century and laid the groundwork for the medicalization of sex as a scientific endeavor.

Medicalization of Intersexuality

During the Victorian era, intersexuality fell under the purview of medicine. This was the logical outgrowth of post-enlightenment philosophy, which signified the move from traditionalism and the moral categorization of individuals based on religious dogma to scientific and medical categorizations. A variety of important social distinctions were medicalized, and individuals inflicted with diseases were pathologized—their physical afflictions were purported to be indicators of their social ills, of their moral depravity, or conversely, for those in "good" health, of their worth and moral superiority. During the period of medicalization, or the use of medical perspectives to define physical and social problems, morality, decency, intelligence, and human worth were linked to physical health and the perceived condition of the body under the newly authoritative gaze of the physician.

One of the first fields to develop was the study of physical anomalies, or teratology. The founder of this field was French anatomist Isidore Geoffroy Saint-Hilaire (1805–1861). This field generated conceptions of the healthy or normal human body, and also medicalized and naturalized sexual differences. Whereas previous to the Enlightenment, tradition, superstition, and religious notions deemed so-called monstrous births supernatural auguries of doom, teratologists dictated that hermaphrodites and other "freaks of nature" were actually just part of the natural order of things. Saint-Hilaire and his followers sought to explain all anatomical anomalies through the natural sciences, and eventually concluded that intersexuality was due to abnormal fetal development. Ultimately, intersexuals were simply underdeveloped males or overdeveloped females—not monsters at all. Although analysis under this model removed the intersexual from the realm of superstitiously sinful or unnatural freakery, by medicalizing intersexuality in opposition to "true" and "natural" malehood or femalehood, teratology nonetheless pathologized intersexual embodiment. Not only should doctors seek to study intersexuality in order to understand what is normal, but they also had an ethical commitment to prevent and ultimately cure intersexuality.

By the end of the nineteenth century, cases of intersexuality or "hermaphroditism" were well documented. The story of Alexina/Abel Barbin (born Adélaïde Herculine Barbin) is a telling example of the treatment of intersexuals during the initial period of medicalization and of physicians' and scientists' struggles to understand sex. Barbin was an intersexual brought up as a woman who spent most of her early years and adolescence in an all-girl Catholic boarding school. In her memoirs, Alexina recounts being attracted to women, and developed a sexually intimate relationship with one of her fellow classmates. Although she was a good student, Alexina's relationship with her female classmate was excoriated by the nuns, who eventually drove her to confess her physical ambiguity to both priests and doctors. It was ultimately decided—based on rigorous examination of her genitalia—that Alexina was and had always been a man, and that she (now he) should change his name to Abel and live within the conventions of his "true" sex. Before the age of thirty, Alexina/Abel, who was never reunited with his/her lost love from the convent, committed suicide.

The intersex individual was an important analytical subject during the period of medicalization, namely because of the importance of sexual categorization in maintaining the social and—according to physicians of the time—also the *natural* order of society. Not only was the maintenance of sexual difference between men and women crucial to the ordering of society, but equally important was the maintenance of its logical outgrowth, the heterosexual imperative. The intersexual poses a threat to the heterosexual ordering of society in his/her very liminal embodiment—she/he raises the "specter of homosexuality." During this time, doctors were also sought to "identify, classify, and characterize the different types of perversions" (Foucault 1980). Thus, intersexuality was classified not only as a sexual or anatomical anomaly, but as a perversion, along with bisexuality and homosexuality. In fact, homosexuals and bisexuals were frequently referred to as "behavioral hermaphrodites" or "psychic hermaphrodites."

Once intersexuality fell under the purview of medicine, doctors were quick to assign intersex individuals to the sex that would most likely put them within the realm of traditional heterosexuality. If an intersex individual had a history of sexual relations with men, the best choice would be to assign him/her to the female sex; if an intersexual appeared to be attracted to women, this person should be made into a man. Often, the heterosexual imperative trumped any prominence apparent in the external (and/or internal) genitalia, other secondary sex characteristics, or "masculine" or "feminine" personality traits, disposition, or demeanor. Even today, the "specter of homosexuality" inherent in intersexual embodiment is considered treated only when the intersex individual is surgically "corrected" to conform to his/her true sex; treatment is often only considered complete if that person then functions within a strictly heterosexual role.

The period of early medicalization established a system of social classification that was inscribed on the body. The field of teratology in particular ushered in a new naturalization and simultaneous pathologization of intersexuality, and laid the groundwork for the distinction between "true" and "false" hermaphrodites, which became the basis for current systems of medical categorization by sex. By stating that "true" hermaphrodites could not be found among humans, individuals born with ambiguous genitalia were believed to be malformed or incomplete males or females. This classification system relegated intersexuality—the state of being between, lacking, or of both sexes—to the realm of the invisible, improbable, or impossible. This ethos paved the way for seeking cures for intersexuality, and if no cure or means of prevention could be found, for correcting the body.

As the power of medicine grew during the twentieth century, sexuality became increasingly regulated by physicians and scientists. Sexual classification systems were delineated, and the question of how to categorize intersexuals was highly debated. Embryological theories of sexual difference mutated during the "Age of Gonads" (Dreger, 1998), and doctors decided that an individual's true sex resided within his/her ovarian or testicular tissue, and thus the potential for reproduction. True hermaphroditism was eradicated under this classification system, and almost all people with intersexed conditions were classified as male or female "pseudohermaphrodites." Although classification was significantly expanded in the twentieth century, the gonadal classification system informs current medical discourse. By the mid-twentieth century, the birth of an intersexed infant was viewed as a psychosocial trauma or medical emergency.

The work of John Money (1921–2006), a Johns Hopkins psychologist pre-eminent in the 1970s, and his team of colleagues concluded that psychosocial development was the most crucial aspect in determining successful gender identity. Money and his team conjectured that as long as the external genitalia of an intersex individual were surgically "corrected" and the surgically assigned sex was reinforced through upbringing, then an individual's gender identity would be congruous with his/her assigned sex regardless of what that person's gonads, chromosomes, or hormones indicated at birth. Although Money and other medical practitioners aligned with this "constructionist" view believed in the malleability of psychosocial gender, they paradoxically believed in the fixity of biological sex. They saw intersexuality as pathological, and studied it first and foremost to elicit a better understanding of *normal* human sexual development. They found sexual ambiguity to be particularly problematic later in life, especially during adolescence and adulthood.

Money's constructionist theory regarding the malleability of gender soon became popular and his suggested surgical sex assignment practices widespread. In the early 1960s, Money counseled the parents of a seven-month-old boy named David, whose penis had been cut off in a circumcision accident, to have the rest of the boy's external male genitalia removed and to have female genitalia constructed in its place. Based on his constructionist views of gender development, Money believed that David was young enough to be successfully raised as a girl (who would now be called "Brenda"). The parents agreed to the surgical assignment and raised the child according to strict feminine gender roles, and, until her early teens, the child's female assignment seemed a success. In 1976, however, a team of researchers led by Milton Diamond who were publicly opposed to Money's constructionist views located Brenda and discovered that she had not adjusted to her feminine gender role as well as Money would have liked the public to believe.

Based on his interviews with Brenda and the discovery in 1980 that she had had her breasts removed, a penis reconstructed, and was now living as a man (again as David), Diamond publicly challenged Money, arguing that infants were in no way sexually neutral at birth. Their brains instead were organized dimorphically in utero via hormones, and that this male or female organization was reactivated by hormones during puberty, resulting in sex-specific behaviors. Diamond suggested that the human brain was, in fact, gendered prenatally. After this seemingly evidenced refutation of Money's constructionist view, many doctors, scholars (including some feminist scholars), and laypeople found Diamond's biologically deterministic theory convincing, and believed that the experience of David/Brenda amounted to a cautionary tale.

Contemporary Treatment of Intersexuality

The frequency with which intersex occurs is extremely difficult to gauge, primarily due to cross-cultural disparities in occurrence, the existence of myriad conditions which may or may not be classified as intersex within disparate scientific, medical, and cultural circles, and the broad taxonomy with which Western physicians classify sex. It is estimated that between one and three of every 2,000 individuals are born with anatomies that do not conform to either a typical male or typical female form. Definitively sexing these questionable infants is further problematized by the fact that, currently, determinations regarding sex classification must take into account genetics, chromosomes, gonads, internal phenotype, external phenotype, sex of rearing, childhood gender, and gender at adulthood. It is important to note that in the case of intersex individuals (and even among individuals *not* categorized as "intersex"), there may be conflict between or among these different levels or classification categories, making a definitive sex determination impossible. It is in these cases that the socioculturally constructed nature of the sexed body becomes apparent; doctors and other "medical experts" ultimately make the decision regarding which sex—out of only two legitimate choices—these intersex infants will become.

Currently, most physicians tend to make their judgments regarding sex assignment of intersex infants based first on external appearance (specifically the size of the phallus, if one is present), and then in conjunction with the karyotype, or chromosomal status, of the infant. Thus, if an infant's genitalia is ambiguous, but it has a penis that could potentially allow it to urinate standing up and to penetrate a vagina, along with the presence of a Y chromosome (but not necessarily XY status), the infant will almost invariably be made male. If the size of the penis is questionable in terms of the aforementioned functions, and a Y chromosome is not present in the infant's karyotype, the infant will most likely be made female (especially if there is any possibility of the infant reproducing as a female). Once a sex is assigned based on these criteria, hormonal treatments, aesthetic surgeries, psychological/behavioral modification therapy, and gender-role ascription via the child's parents are typically encouraged throughout childhood (and often continuously throughout life) to help the individual "adjust to" and ultimately to feel "at home" within the ascribed gender role based on this initial sex assignment.

Some critics of this process argue that it is phallocentric and heteronormative in nature. The most important aspect of a male sex assignment is that the newly created boy's penis be "large enough" for him to function socially and to participate (that is, penetrate) in heterosexual intercourse;

the most important aspect of a female sex assignment is that the newly created girl's vagina be "deep enough" to be penetrated during heterosexual intercourse (and more rarely, but if at all possible, to bear children). The criteria for boys are thus normative social and sexual functioning, and for girls reproduction and reception. Orgasm and sexual pleasure are not factors when it comes to female assignment; in fact, the clitoris is often reduced or removed completely in tandem with vaginoplasty.

Recently, scholars and activists within intersex, feminist, and queer communities, among others, have taken up intersexuality and the protection of intersexed individuals as a human rights or a children's rights issue. Most in these communities who fight for intersex rights argue that current standards for the medical management of intersexuality must be improved upon significantly within a human rights framework. The Intersex Society of North America and many others have argued that no surgery should be performed on intersexed infants unless it is necessary to save the child's life or significantly improve his/her health. Instead, physicians should assign a "provisional sex" to the infant so that he/she does not have to bear the hostility of growing up in a world that abhors ambiguity, but should not surgically normalize their genitalia. Both the parents and the child should be informed and educated about intersexuality, counseled by a qualified medical care team, and linked to a support network so they can connect with those who have had similar experiences. Intersex activists argue that only when an intersex person is old enough to consent to more invasive procedures should the individual decide what type of body, and what type of gender, he/she feels most comfortable with. It is also becoming more accepted that some intersex children (just like children in general) may never develop binary or traditional notions of their own sex, gender, and sexuality, nor will all children's notions of these three categories necessarily cohere in terms of the logic of heteronormativity. One of the pillars of the intersex movement is the importance of choice and consent at every level of the process.

Further Reading: Butler, Judith. *Undoing Gender.* New York: Routledge, 2004; Chase, Cheryl. "Hermaphrodites with Attitude: Mapping the Emergence of Intersex Political Activism." *GLQ: A Journal of Lesbian and Gay Studies* 4 (1998): 189–211; Dreger, Alice Domurat. *Hermaphrodites and the Medical Invention of Sex.* Cambridge, MA: Harvard University Press, 1998; Dreger, Alice Domurat, ed. *Intersex in the Age of Ethics.* Hagerstown, MD: University Publishing Group, 1999; Fausto-Sterling, Anne. *Sexing the Body: Gender Politics and the Construction of Sexuality.* New York: Basic Books, 2000; Foucault, Michel. *Herculine Barbin: Being the Recently Discovered Memoirs of a Nineteenth-Century French Hermaphrodite.* New York: Pantheon, 1980; Kessler, Suzanne J. *Lessons from the Intersexed.* New Brunswick, NJ: Rutgers University Press, 1998; Money, John, and Anke A. Ehrhardt. *Man & Woman, Boy & Girl: The Differentiation and Dimorphism of Gender Identity from Conception to Maturity.* Baltimore, MD: The Johns Hopkins University Press, 1972; Preves, Sharon. *Intersex and Identity: The Contested Self.* New Brunswick, NJ: Rutgers University Press, 2003; Reis, Elizabeth. "Impossible Hermaphrodites: Intersex in America, 1620–1960." *The Journal of American History* (September 2005): 411–441; Warnke, Georgia. "Intersexuality and the Categories of Sex." *Hypatia* 16 (2001): 126–137; Intersex Society of North America official Web site, http://www.isna.org.

Alyson Spurgas

Female Genital Cutting

The practice of female genital cutting, which involves removing some or all of the external female genitalia, including the labia minora and majora and clitoris, is hotly contested and stirs strong feelings among many. The variety of terms used to describe or classify the practice speaks directly to this fact. While some sources prefer to use expressions such as "female circumcision," "clitoridectomy," "excision," or "female genital cutting," others are adamant in their use of the term "female genital mutilation." Perhaps because of the variety of valences and considerations that pertain to the subject, there are no universally accepted or agreed-upon terms or definitions for the practices referred to herein. For the sake of clarity, "female genital cutting" will be used throughout this entry unless source documents specifically dictate otherwise. The term "female genital mutilation" will be used to refer to the same practices when discussing them from the perspectives of various health and human rights organizations and other critics, who prefer this term.

Overview

Female genital cutting is used to describe the practice of removing all or part of the external female genitalia. The United Nations (UN), the World Health Organization (WHO), and several other organizations use the term "female genital mutilation" to describe this and various other injurious procedures inflicted on the vagina, external genitalia, or vulva for cultural or non-medical reasons. Current estimates suggest that anywhere from

Circumciser washes her hands after the circumcision of a 6-year-old girl in Hargeisa, Somalia, 1996. At left is the girl's grandmother, who assisted in the operation. (AP Photo/Jean-Marc Bouju)

Egyptian girls carry posters showing Badour Shaker, who died while being circumcised in an illegal clinic in the southern city of Maghagha, Egypt, during a rally against circumcision in Assiut, Egypt, in 2007. The death sparked a public outcry, prompting health and religious authorities to issue a ban on the practice. (AP Photo/Mamdouh Thabet)

100 million to 140 million girls and women have already undergone some form of female genital cutting, with an additional 3 million undergoing the procedure each year. Female genital cutting as it is currently defined is broadly practiced in twenty-eight countries, most of which are in Africa or Asia, even though it has been outlawed in fifteen African nations. There have also been recent increases in the incidence of female genital cutting in the West among immigrant populations from these countries. The practice of female genital cutting has been shown to have numerous negative health outcomes—both immediate and long term—and no known health benefits. For this reason, many condemn the practice as barbaric and work to eradicate it entirely. However, there are those who caution against using Western norms and values to condemn the practice outright, stressing that female genital cutting must be evaluated in a cultural context. Further, studies show that these cultural functions and contexts must be taken into consideration in order for eradication efforts to be successful.

Types of Female Genital Cutting

Many international health and human rights organizations (such as WHO, UNICEF, and the UN) use the term "mutilation" to describe these practices. They define female genital mutilation (FGM) as the partial or total removal of the female external genitalia, or other injury to the female genital organs for cultural or other non-therapeutic reasons. More specifically, the UN and WHO classify female genital mutilation into four distinct categories. Type I female genital mutilation consists of the removal of the clitoral prepuce (hood), with or without excision of all or part of the clitoris. Type II female genital mutilation consists of the total excision of the clitoris and the partial or total removal of the labia minora (inner vaginal lips). Type III female genital mutilation, also known as infibulation, involves the total removal of all external female genitalia, including the clitoris, prepuce (hood), labia majora (outer vaginal lips), and labia minora (inner vaginal lips). The remaining flesh is then tightly stitched together, leaving only a slight opening for the passage of menstrual blood and urine. The woman or girl is then bound tightly from the hip down until the incision heals—generally several weeks. In this type of female genital cutting, the woman must generally be cut open along her scar in order to permit intercourse and childbirth. After childbirth, most women who have undergone type III female genital mutilation are reinfibulated to re-narrow the vaginal opening. Type IV female genital mutilation involves any number of procedures that involve pricking, piercing, or cutting the clitoris or labia, burning, scraping, or cauterization of the vagina or external genitals, or the introduction of corrosive substances into the vagina to cause bleeding or to narrow and tighten the vaginal canal. Infibulation (Type III FGM), the most extensive form of the practice, is also called pharaonic circumcision because, among practitioners, it is thought to have been first practiced among ancient Egyptians. Type II FGM is the most commonly observed form of female genital cutting, affecting roughly 80 percent of known cases. Infibulation counts for approximately 15 percent of all known cases. Virtually all of the female genital cuttings done in traditional settings are done without anesthesia, and most new procedures are performed on girls under the age of fifteen.

History of Female Genital Cutting in Western Medicine

Many people in the West believe that the practice of female genital cutting has been relegated to African and Muslim subpopulations for the duration of its history. However, clitoridectomy (the removal of the clitoris) was once a commonly accepted and practiced element of Western medicine. In the West, clitoridectomy was first formally reported as a viable medical treatment in an 1825 edition of the British medical journal *The Lancet*. The procedure in question had been performed by a German surgeon to treat a patient suffering from what was then described as "excessive masturbation and nymphomania." After its initial appearance in the medical community, the procedure became a popular treatment for a variety of what were considered to be "female ills," including hysteria, epilepsy, melancholy, insanity, and their associated troubles—including what was considered excessive masturbation and nymphomania. Clitoridectomy reached the height of its popularity during the mid-nineteenth century, especially in France, Germany, England, and the United States. Although it is no longer an accepted treatment in Western medicine, some sources report that the last clitoridectomy performed on medical grounds occurred in 1927. Other reports suggest that it continued in the United States as late as 1953. Now that clitoridectomy is universally frowned upon in the West and has been discredited as a legitimate medical practice, current Western medical scholarship has instead focused on addressing the health and safety of women and girls who have undergone female genital cutting in traditional contexts.

History of Female Genital Cutting in Africa and the Islamic World

Many who currently practice female genital cutting say they do so because they believe it is mandated by Islamic law. However, the roots of contemporary female genital cutting practices and procedures predate Islam by more than 1,500 years. Also of note, the practice did not originate among Muslim populations. The historical record shows that female genital cutting first achieved widespread popularity among the Phoenicians, Hittites, and Ethiopians as early as the fifth century BCE. It is believed that female genital cutting was somehow incorporated into the practice and spread of Islam once it reached Africa, although the exact mechanism through which this occurred is unknown. The fact that female genital cutting is not practiced in Saudi Arabia (known as the cradle of Islam) supports this hypothesis. Interestingly, some Islamic scholars suggest that Islamic legal discourse actually discourages and frowns upon any sort of female genital cutting, as it "alters Allah's creation." This interpretation draws upon the same portions of Islamic scripture that are interpreted as discouraging tattoos, castration, or disfiguration of any sort.

At present, some form of female genital cutting is known to be practiced in approximately twenty-eight countries around the world. Many of these are in northern or central Africa, but it is also practiced in Oman, Yemen, the United Arab Emirates, and Muslim populations in Indonesia, Malaysia, India, and Pakistan, among others. Female genital cutting also has increasingly been seen among migrants from these countries in Europe and North America. It is important to note that even in countries where female genital cutting practices are widespread, it is almost never ubiquitous. The type, extent, and circumstances under which female genital cutting occurs varies from ethnic group to ethnic group both within and between countries. For example, in the Republic of Gambia, young girls are circumcised in large groups. In other places, such as in Egypt, circumcision is considered a private family matter, and girls are circumcised individually. In the vast majority of circumstances, specially trained women are responsible for performing the procedure. There are, however, a few examples wherein the cuttings are performed by men. Quite often, midwives or traditional healers perform circumcisions, although certain cultural groups specially select and train women alone to perform this function. In Somalia, such a woman is traditionally called a "gedda." Her Sudanese counterpart is called a "daya." In Egypt, the procedure was traditionally carried out by male barbers; however, at present, it has been largely medicalized, with the vast majority (90 percent) of cuttings now performed by medical professionals.

Among the countries where female genital cutting is a known and popular practice, it is estimated that anywhere from 5 percent to 97 percent of women have undergone the procedure. Egypt and Ethiopia have the highest prevalence rates, and nearly half of all women who have undergone female genital cuttings live in these two countries.

Critiques of Female Genital Cutting

The practice of female genital cutting is critiqued—even condemned—by many the world over. The basis generally is medical in nature, with the remainder focusing on human rights abuses. In addition to the immediate pain and suffering girls experience when undergoing an unanesthetized procedure, numerous studies suggest that the practice of female genital cutting entails a wide variety of severe, immediate health risks including hemorrhage, shock, infection, abscesses, septicemia, anemia (from unchecked bleeding), broken bones (from struggling against restraints while being cut), tetanus, gangrene, and pelvic inflammatory infection. These hazards are particularly acute for cuttings that are done in traditional (that is, non-medical) settings with unsterile tools and/or by those with little or no medical training. Studies have also shown that women who have undergone female genital cuttings are significantly more likely than those who have not to have negative obstetric outcomes. In 2006, WHO published a landmark study documenting these various adverse outcomes, including severe fetal injury, fetal brain damage, hemorrhage, shock, and fetal and/or maternal death. The likelihood and extent of harm, injury, or damage increase with more extensive forms of female genital cutting. Female genital cutting can have a number of adverse health outcomes for men as well. In addition to various psychological and psychosexual problems experienced by both women who have undergone female genital cutting and the men who partner with them, researchers have found that men are more likely to report difficulty with penetration, pain, and wounds or infections on the penis.

Many medical professionals believe the practice of female genital cutting may present an increased risk for HIV infection via a number of channels. Genital injury (in both women and men) sustained during normal intercourse after infibulation increases one's susceptibility to infection from or passing on of HIV and other sexually transmitted diseases. Given the higher likelihood of injury or blood loss during childbirth among those who have undergone female genital cutting, such women are more likely to need blood transfusions. Unfortunately, in many countries where female genital cutting is prevalent, governments and hospitals lack adequate blood-screening procedures and technologies, making these women more likely to contract bloodborne diseases such as HIV. Also, in cultures where many girls are cut at once using the same tools, transmission via direct blood-to-blood contact is possible.

Proponents of Cutting

Despite the negative health outcomes and the pain and suffering associated with female genital cutting, studies suggest that there are some positive cultural aspects and functions of the practice. Even among those who disagree with the practice or actively work to eradicate it, many think that female genital cutting should be viewed through a lens of cultural relativity, lack of moral judgment, and the right to agency and self-determination.

The two viewpoints most frequently adopted when speaking in defense of cutting are those of cultural relativism, or the need to maintain a culturally relative, morally neutral stance on international relations, and those emphasizing the positive cultural functions associated with the practice. Among cultures where female genital cutting has been studied, the procedure appears to have several common functions. Chiefly, in many societies, it is associated with a rite of passage or an initiation into womanhood wherein girls receive information and training on how to become fully functional adult women. Not only does this rite of passage afford a girl a sense of pride and accomplishment, the young woman is celebrated, welcomed, and showered with gifts and public recognition. Conversely, failure to undergo the procedure may brand a girl as an outcast and bar her from marriage or even being recognized as a functional adult. Also, the presence of a tightly infibulated vulva serves much the same purpose as an intact hymen in other cultures—signifying chastity, morality, and virginity. Many ethnic groups that practice some sort of female genital cutting also hold that circumcision scars—much like other markings from scarifications, tattoos, piercings, or other body modifications—set them apart from the surrounding tribes or ethnic groups in their area, making them a distinct, cohesive unit.

In spite of these positive cultural functions, many would still argue that female genital cutting is barbaric, and that the socialization it serves could best be realized in other ways. However, some argue that these judgments stem from an ethnocentric manner of thinking that privileges Western values, viewpoints, and interpretations over the values, viewpoints, and interpretations of those who themselves engage in this practice. As mentioned, the very terms used to describe the practice speaks volumes about who is doing the speaking and the lens through which it is interpreted (that is, referring to "mutilation" as opposed to "cutting"). Muslim and African critics who have written about the practice question why what is done in these societies is called "mutilation," whereas various procedures in the West (including plastic surgeries, genital piercings, and sex reassignment surgeries) are considered to be medically legitimate or simply cosmetic. They argue that these procedures could fall under the same definitions used to condemn traditional or ritualized female genital cuttings. Others have questioned why male circumcision is not considered mutilation, or why female circumcision is not thought of as a legitimate ritualized surgery.

Some also suggest that female genital cutting is sensationalized in the West. Much of what is said about female genital mutilation pertains specifically to infibulation, the most extensive form of female genital cutting. These negative aspects are often generalized to all women who have undergone any form of female genital cutting, making problems and concerns seem more widespread than they are in actuality. Few studies document the health consequences and concerns associated with less severe forms of female genital cutting. Also, much Western literature and thought on the practice of female genital cutting paints all women who undergo the procedure as passive victims in need of rescue from African and/or Muslim patriarchal structures. This may ignore the agency of women who undergo the procedure, and may overlook the fact that many women cling to it willingly, even enthusiastically. Those in the West who object to the practice, particularly those of a feminist bent, view these women as subservient beings whose bodies and sexuality are entirely controlled by men. Ironically, studies suggest that in many cases, women are more likely to support and ensure the tradition's continuance than men.

Eradication Efforts, Past and Present

The first formally recorded Western attempt to end the practice of female genital cutting began in Kenya in 1906. In this and many other instances of early eradication efforts, the crusade against female genital cutting was coupled with the Christianizing and "civilizing" missions of European colonial projects. Perhaps because of this connection, many natives came to feel that efforts to stop female genital cutting were not about the health and safety of women at all (as Europeans suggested), but were instead racist, anti-Muslim, or otherwise Eurocentric attempts to stymie or undermine "traditional" African or Islamic cultures and governments. As such, many historical Western attempts to end the practice have incited tribes to increase female genital cutting in protest of oppression, occupation, and colonization. Many modern-day attempts to eradicate female genital cutting are met with the same animosity and skepticism, making eradication efforts difficult and often resulting in bitter political and cultural struggles.

Despite these problems, organizations such as UNICEF and WHO have taken zero-tolerance stances on the subject and continue to work for an immediate end to all forms of female genital cutting. Many country and state governments have joined WHO in its zero-tolerance stance, making the practice of any sort of female genital cutting a crime. However, such laws can be difficult to enforce. In addition, the institution of harsh legislation often forces those who are adamant about keeping the tradition alive to push its practice further underground, effectively making it harder to detect and eradicate.

While top-down eradication efforts (such as imposing harsh fines or imprisonment) have had only minimal success, there are several eradication approaches that appear to have made modest gains. Some governments have created programs to retrain or offer alternative sources of funding to career circumcisers, thereby providing an incentive for them to abandon the practice without fear of losing their livelihoods. Other governments and nongovernmental organizations have instituted various public health education campaigns to inform both men and women about the negative health outcomes associated with female genital cutting in its various forms. One particularly well-accepted strategy has been the creation of alternate rite-of-passage ceremonies, such as the "Ntanira Na Mugambo (Circumcision Through Words)" program in Kenya. Such programs generally provide safe spaces in which young women can receive counseling and training that would usually take place during the isolated healing period immediately following a ritual circumcision.

Further Reading: Abusharaf, Rogaia Mustafa. "Virtuous Cuts: Female Genital Circumcision in an African Ontology." *Differences: A Journal of Feminist Cultural Studies* 12 (2001): 112–140; Almroth, Lars, Vanja Almroth-Berggren, Osman Mahmoud Hassanein, Said Salak Eldin Al-Said, Sharis Siddiq Alamin Hasan, Ulla-Britt Lithell, and Staffan Bergstrom. "Male Complications of Female Genital Mutilation." *Social Science and Medicine* 53 (2001): 1,455–1,460; Chelala, C. "An Alternative Way to Stop Female Genital Mutilation." *The Lancet* 352 (1998): 122–126; Elachalal, Uriel, Barbara Ben-Ami, Rebecca Gillis, and Ammon Brzezinski. "Ritualistic Female Genital Mutilation: Current Status and Future Outlook." *Obstetrical and Gynecological Survey* 52 (1997): 643–651; Winkel, Eric. "A Muslim Perspective on Female Circumcision." *Women and Health* 23 (1995): 1–7; WHO study group on female genital mutilation and obstetric outcome. "Female genital mutilation and obstetric outcome: WHO collaborative prospective study in six African countries." *The Lancet* 367 (2006): 1,835–1,841; World Health Organization. Female Genital Mutilation. World Health Organization Web Site, http://www.who.int/reproductive-health/fgm/ (accessed July 2007).

Alena J. Singleton

Genital Piercing

Contemporary genital piercing is practiced by both males and females. Until the late twentieth century, both the variety of genital piercings that occur today and female genital piercings were virtually nonexistent. There appear to be only a few instances of genital piercing throughout history and in traditional societies. These include male genital piercings known as "apadravya," "ampallang," and "foreskin piercing."

The apadravya is described in the *Kama Sutra*, the Sanskrit text of aphorisms on love. The *Kama Sutra* of Vatsyayana, thought to have been written sometime around the fourth century CE in India, explicitly describes the art of lovemaking. The sage Vatsyayana mentions the use of the apadravya piercing, which is a piercing through the glans of the penis. The apadravya is mentioned in the section of the *Kama Sutra* that deals with the enlargement of the penis for sexual intercourse. In the *Kama Sutra*, the apadravya includes cock rings as well as objects inserted into the pierced glans. Vatsyayana also explains how one should perforate the penis, and the herbs and processes one should use to promote healing. He describes the materials one should insert into the piercing: small pieces of cane to help increase the size of the hole. Once the desired size is achieved, the author suggests various objects, or apadravyas, that one can wear for sexual intercourse; these include armlets or objects made of bone or wood.

Contemporary apadravyas are piercings that pass from the top to the bottom of the glans. Variations include the shaft apadravya and the halfadravya. The shaft apadravya is the same kind of piercing, but is placed through the shaft rather than the glans. The halfadravya requires a subincision or meatotomy of the penis. A meatotomy is a splitting of the underside of the glans at the meatus, and a subincision is a splitting of the urethra from the underside of the glans at the meatus and along the shaft. In this sense, the halfadravya is a piercing only through the top of the glans, as the bottom is split—hence the name.

Another piercing that has a history in traditional societies is the ampallang. It was common among some indigenous tribes of Borneo including the Dayaks and the Kayan. It is claimed in some secondary literature that the Dayaks have a ceremony that accompanies this piercing. However, an anthropological study of the Kayan claims that the piercing is given without a ritual and is used solely for the purpose of enhancing sex when a rod is inserted into the piercing. As there is a general belief that the rod may prevent conception, it is used more rarely after marriage.

The contemporary ampallang, like the traditional ampallang, is a piercing through the glans of the penis. Today, the standard orientation is a horizontal piercing, either above or through the urethra. Piercing through the urethra is often thought to be superior, as it heals more quickly and is less likely to migrate (or gradually move over time and perhaps be rejected or pushed out of the skin). One of the variations is the shaft ampallang, which is a horizontal piercing through the shaft rather than the glans. This is usually done directly behind the glans to avoid complications.

One of the most common genital piercings, the Prince Albert, carries with it a widespread fictional story about English royalty. The Prince Albert piercing (PA) is a piercing that passes through or near the frenulum (or frenulum remnant in those who are circumcised) directly behind the glans and exits from the urethra. According to legend, Prince Albert, the husband of Queen Victoria of England (1837–1901), pierced the lower part of his glans and inserted a dressing ring. The ring supposedly had two purposes: one was to secure the genitals to the leg in order to hide the bulging genitalia in the tight-fitting pants of the day, and the other was to push the foreskin back in order to keep the glans "sweet smelling"—or perhaps smegma-free. However, there appears to be no evidence to support this story. With the popularity of the PA, variations have emerged. One is the reverse Prince Albert, which is identical to the PA except that it exits from the top of the glans rather than the bottom. The other is the deep PA. This differs from the regular PA only in the size of the ring, which necessitates placement farther down the shaft on the underside of the penis.

The most common piercing in Western history is the piercing of the foreskin. The purpose of this piercing—known as male infibulation—was not to enhance sex, but to prevent sex altogether. Infibulation is the act of putting a clasp, string, or ring through the male foreskin. In ancient Rome, infibulation was used to induce men to refrain from sex and to improve male performance. It made a comeback in the early modern period as a tool against not intercourse as much as masturbation and nocturnal emissions.

In the first century CE, the famous Roman medical writer Aulus Cornelius Celsus (ca. 25–50 BCE) described the practice of infibulation. A needle and thread were used to make holes in the foreskin. Once the holes healed, the string was removed and a fibula (a clasp or safety pin of sorts, usually used for togas) was attached. Once in place, the fibula made erections difficult or impossible. People such as singers, actors, athletes, and gladiators were infibulated, because it was thought that sexual activity would weaken their performance. Oddly enough, infibulation was thought to keep the voice of actors and singers sounding more feminine, and it was believed to endow more masculine strength for athletes and gladiators.

In 1827, a German physician and scientist, Karl August Weinhold (1782–1829), advocated mandatory infibulation for all those deemed unfit to reproduce. He thought that the practice would create a more productive and better world. Throughout the eighteenth and early twentieth centuries, there was major concern about the ills of masturbation. Masturbation and nocturnal emissions were thought to cause everything from headaches to insanity and even epileptic seizures. During this period, infibulation became a panacea—even circumcision was advocated, as it was thought to make masturbation less pleasurable. John Harvey Kellogg (1852–1943), a health reformer and cofounder of Kellogg's cereal, published a best-selling book praising infibulation as a cure for masturbation, which he considered one of the worst plagues upon mankind. Glasgow physician David Yellowlees (1837–1921) also promoted infibulation in the *Dictionary of Psychological Medicine* in 1892. Contemporary infibulation in the West is now mostly practiced in BDSM (bondage/domination/sadomasochism) subcultures and is eroticized.

Genital piercing was popularized in the late twentieth century in Western cultures as an erotic and aesthetic practice, which is remarkable, considering the history of male infibulation. Not only have the variations on male genital piercing multiplied, but female genital piercing has also gained momentum.

One of the most common piercings among women is the clitoral hood piercing. Although this is usually termed a "clit piercing" (referring to the clitoral glans), actual clitoral glans piercing is rare. The hood piercing is said to heal quickly and to provide physical pleasure for the woman. It also has a reputation for being aesthetically pleasing for both females and males. The two most common types of hood piercing are horizontal and vertical, with the choice of configuration depending upon a woman's taste and possibly her anatomy.

Other variations on the hood piercing are the deep hood piercing and the Nefertiti piercing. These are rare. The deep hood piercing is a deep horizontal hood piercing, while the Nefertiti piercing is a deep vertical hood piercing. A deep hood piercing is a piercing done under the clitoral shaft. When the right-sized ring is worn through the healed piercing, it can hug and hence stimulate the entire clitoral glans. The Nefertiti piercing is a vertical hood piercing that exits at the top of the hood or in the pubic area.

Other types that involve piercing around or near the clitoral glans are the triangle piercing and the Isabella piercing. The triangle piercing requires a specific type of anatomy. This piercing passes underneath the clitoral shaft where the inner labia and hood meet. It is called a triangle piercing because that area feels like a triangle when pinched. The Isabella piercing passes through the clitoral shaft. The piercing starts between the clitoral glans and the urethra and exits at the top of the clitoral hood. This piercing is extremely rare and is thought to be highly risky in terms of intersecting nerves.

A common type of female genital piercing is the labia piercing. Inner labia piercings heal faster than outer labia piercings, which pass through more tissue. These piercings may be stretched to accommodate larger jewelry or may allow for weights to be hung in order to stretch the labia.

Although extremely rare, there is also the Princess Albertina. Intended to be the female equivalent of the Prince Albert, this piercing starts at the urethra and exits at the top of the vagina. There is also the Christina piercing. Depending on anatomy, for some women this may be just a surface piercing, as it enters and exits along a flat area of skin. The piercing starts at the top of the clitoral hood and exits in the pubic area. Because of the nature of surface piercings, in some women this piercing rejects jewelry (that is, it pushes jewelry out of the skin).

There are also several new male genital piercings. A quick-healing and relatively painless piercing for males is the frenum piercing. The frenum or frenulum is the membrane attaching the foreskin to the glans of the shaft on the underside of the penis. There is often a remnant for males who are circumcised. It is usually pierced transversely. However, the term "frenum" is often used to refer to other piercings on the underside of the penis along the perineal raphe, or the seam from the bottom of the meatus to the anus. One of these piercings is the frenum ladder, which is a series of multiple piercings in a row. The other is the lorum piercing (that is, "low-frenum"), which is a piercing on the perineal raphe close to the base of the penis or scrotum.

The scrotum may also be pierced. There are several possibilities; two scrotal piercings worth noting are the hafada and the scrotal ladder. The hafada is a piercing on one of the upper sides of the scrotum. Although some believe that the hafada was once used as a rite of passage among Middle Eastern boys, it is difficult to find supporting evidence. The scrotal ladder, like any other ladder piercing, is a series of multiple piercings in a row. Sometimes, the scrotal ladder is part of a larger ladder piercing from the glans to the perineum.

Another option is to pierce the corona or ridge of the glans. This piercing is called a dydoe. It is usually done on men who are circumcised, but it can be done on an uncircumcised male if he has a loose foreskin. Another version of this piercing is the deep dydoe. This piercing enters the corona and exits near the urethral opening. Body piercer Erik Dakota pioneered a male genital piercing that connects the dydoe and the apadravya: the apadydoe. After these piercings heal, one takes an orbital ring and runs it through the coronal ridge, then through the vertical piercing through the glans. This can be done with one orbital ring on each side of the glans, creating a symmetrical look. There are other types of piercings that combine multiple piercings, including the dolphin (a combination of a PA and a deep PA) and the magic cross (a combination of an ampallang and an apadravya).

One genital piercing that can be done on both males and females, although it is rare for females, is the guiche piercing. This is the piercing of the perineum. One can customize the guiche piercing by choosing to stretch the piercings with jewelry or weights. This also is true for many of the piercings described above.

Genital piercing has been largely underground in the West until recently; with the popularization of body art at the end of the twentieth century, genital and other forms of body piercing have become more widespread. Genital piercing remains controversial and even illegal in some places. One of the most notable legal cases was that of Alan Oversby (1933–1996) in Britain. In 1987, he and fifteen other men were arrested for gay BDSM activities in what came to be known as Operation Spanner. Oversby and the others had taken part in consensual genital piercing, and were charged with assault and bodily harm. *See also* Penis: Infibulation.

Further Reading: *Body Modification E-zine Encyclopedia.* http://wiki.bmezine.com/index.php (accessed May 2007); Body Modification Ezine Web Site, http://www.bmezine.com; Brain, Robert. *Decorated Body.* New York: Harper & Row, 1979; Favazza, Armando R. *Bodies Under Siege.* Baltimore, MD: The Johns Hopkins University Press, 1996; Rousseau, Jérôme. *Kayan Religion.* Leiden, Netherlands: KITLV Press, 1998; Schultheiss, D., J. J. Mattelaer, and F. M. Hodges. "Preputial Infibulation: From Ancient Medicine to Modern Genital Piercing." *BJU International* 92, no. 7 (2003): 758–763; Vale, V., and Andrea Juno, eds. *Modern Primitives.* San Francisco: Re/Search, 1989; Ward, Jim. "Who Was Doug Malloy?" *Body Modification E-zine.* March 15, 2004. http://www.bmezine.com/news/jimward/20040315.html (accessed May 21, 2007).

Jaime Wright

Sex Reassignment Surgery

Sex reassignment surgery refers to a range of surgical procedures that modify the form and function of the human body's sexual characteristics from one gender to another. It is associated with transsexuality, a complex state of being in which an individual expresses the deep-seated and permanent desire to embody, and be recognized as, a gender other than the one assigned at birth. These are sometimes called cross-gender desires. Sex reassignment surgery is sometimes known euphemistically as a "sex change"; this term is now considered to be archaic. Sex reassignment surgery is usually different for transmen (female-to-male) and transwomen (male-to-female). While the term "sex reassignment surgery" is generally used to denote genital reconstruction, non-genital surgeries that transform the appearance of a body's sex are also prevalent and are seen as important to the overall transformation of an individual from one sex to another.

The terminology of this set of practices is controversial. Some prefer to use terms such as "gender reassignment surgery," "sex reconstruction surgery," or "genital reconstruction surgery." Another school of thought speaks of these procedures as affirming, rather than reassigning, a person's sex, hence the emergence of phrases such as "sex affirmation surgery." Many schools of thought exist about what is the most accurate terminology, both in medical circles and transsexual and gender-variant communities. Specific procedures for transwomen include castration, the construction of a neovagina, breast augmentation, and facial feminization surgery. Female-to-male surgeries might involve breast removal and the construction of a masculine chest, the removal of the uterus and ovaries, the release of the clitoris from the labia to construct a microphallus, or the creation of a penis and testicles.

While the physiology of sex reassignment surgery is a complex body of knowledge in itself, debates about, and cultural representations of, sex reassignment proliferate. Sex reassignment is most often understood as a part of transsexuality, a Euro-American concept denoting the desire to embody, and to be seen as, a gender other than that assigned at birth. Culturally and in academic research, transsexuality is often treated as part of a larger body of gender-variant practices: gender variant here simply means to be outside the common understanding of male or female.

Transsexuality and Sex Reassignment Surgery

In modern Western culture, sex is thought to be self-evident and binary: one is classified as either male or female, depending on the appearance of one's genitals, or on one's chromosomal markers (XX for females and XY for males). Sex is also understood to be static. Once a person has been identified as male or female, Western culture dictates that they must continue to live as a member of that gender throughout their life. While intersexuality presents a biological exception to the rule that everyone is either male or female, transsexuality presents another kind of exception, in which a person's psychic experience of embodying a sex differs from the apparent biological or anatomical reality. Many cultural practices involve resisting culturally gendered expectations, from men wearing eyeliner to forms of cross-dressing and drag, to passing as a different sex throughout one's life, to surgical alteration. "Transgender" is the most common term used to describe any and all cross-gender practices. Transsexuality, however, is distinguished from other cross-gender practices by a person's desire to not only live as another gender, but to surgically modify their body in concordance with their internal self-perception. Thus, a transwoman may desire to have, and may feel the phantom presence of, a vagina. Conversely, a transman may desire, and feel the phantom presence of, a flat, masculine chest and a penis and testicles.

In Western psychiatry, gender variance is considered to be a mental disorder. The *Diagnostic and Statistical Manual of Mental Disorders* lists transsexuality under gender identity disorder (GID). Sex reassignment surgery is suggested as one form of treatment for gender identity disorder. Other medical treatment includes hormone therapy, using testosterone or estrogen/progesterone supplements, to masculinize or feminize the body. Along with changing the name, pronouns, and the gender one is administratively recognized to be, hormonal and surgical transformation are usually referred to as the process of "transition," or, more recently, "sex affirmation." Because sex reassignment surgery is still considered controversial, transpeople are often required to undergo stringent psychiatric assessment before being approved for surgical intervention. The World Professional Association for Transgender Health (WPATH) Standards of Care outlines what doctors should ascertain in making a diagnosis of gender identity disorder, and how transition should proceed. Many debates have taken place in medical circles and elsewhere about the wisdom of permitting individuals to undergo sex reassignment surgery.

There are no verifiable statistics on the prevalence of transsexuality within the general population, or how many people seek sex reassignment surgery per year. However, a recent study, based on four decades of records from the Amsterdam Gender Clinic, claims that the incidence of transsexuality is one in 4,500 for people assigned male at birth, and one in 8,000 for those assigned female at birth. Not all transpeople desire sex reassignment surgery or hormonal transformation, and the availability and functionality of sex reassignment procedures is different for transmen and transwomen. Access also often depends on the candidate being able to individually finance the cost of the operation(s).

Many theories exist about what causes transsexuality, but none so far has been proven. One theory suggests that humans' sense of what sex they are is just as biologically determined as genital or chromosomal sex: this sense is referred to as "brain sex." According to this theory, transsexuality occurs when a person's brain sex does not match up with their other markers of biological sex. Proponents of this idea point to two studies comparing the size of a small part of the brain, the bed nucleus of the stria terminalis (BSTc) in men, women, and transwomen who had undergone hormone therapy. Both nontrans women and transwomen in the study had smaller BSTcs, on average, than did men in the study. Thus far, no research has indicated what the size of the BSTc might determine in terms of a person's sex and gender identity. Many contemporary health professionals seem less interested in explaining the cause of transsexuality than in assisting individuals who transition sex to do so safely and with appropriate support.

History of Sex Reassignment Surgery

The idea of sex reassignment surgery has circulated for centuries. Roman Emperor Nero is said to have killed one of his favorite wives by accident, and when he realized his mistake, he commanded a male slave to impersonate the dead wife, requiring surgeons to transform the slave into a female. No accounts exist of what this surgery involved. Castration has been practiced in numerous societies to prevent males from undergoing the masculinizing effects of puberty. Documentation of sex reassignment surgery as a scientific practice began with the emergence of sexology as a popular science in Europe in the late nineteenth century. Sexologists studied sexual differences, what they thought to be "perversions," and took detailed case histories. Sometimes, open-minded doctors would assist individuals with cross-gender desires to obtain surgeries. These early precursors of sex reassignment surgery usually involved castration for male-bodied people, and hysterectomy or breast removal for female-bodied people. German sexology archives refer to the 1882 "genital masculinization" of a woman, although the exact procedure is unknown.

By the early twentieth century, biologists had begun to successfully change the sexes of rats and guinea pigs. Scientists had also isolated the "male" and "female" hormones, testosterone and estrogen, respectively. In medical circles, the theory of "human bisexuality" was becoming popular. Unrelated to sexual orientation, this theory of bisexuality used the new discovery that men and women normally produced a combination of both "male" and "female" hormones to theorize that sex was determined not only by the gonads but also by the hormones. Consequently, changing sex was no longer thought to be such a fantastic leap of the imagination.

At this time, cross-gender desires were considered to be a marker of homosexuality, and a common name for both conditions was "psychosexual inversion." German sexologist Magnus Hirschfeld (1868–1935) studied and was sympathetic to the needs of both homosexuals and gender-variant people. In 1919, Hirschfeld opened the Institute for Sexual Research in Berlin. It housed a large library and offered medical consultations to inverts, transvestites, homosexuals, and other people considered sexual "deviants." Hirschfeld coined the term "*transsexualismus*" to describe those who, distinct from homosexuals or those who merely wanted to dress as a different sex, desired to *be* a different sex. These individuals requested surgical transformation. Hirschfeld was sympathetic and arranged for some patients to consult surgeons. Berlin became known as the destination to obtain sex reassignment surgery. At the same time, "sex reversal" was becoming more common, although the press perceived it as sensational and freakish. In Europe, at least three athletes gained notoriety for having transitioned from female to male, obtaining from doctors breast removal, hysterectomies, and testosterone therapy. The first "complete genital transformation" of an MTF (male-to-female transsexual) is said to have occurred in Berlin in 1931, and the first scientific study of sex reassignment surgery appeared the same year, with photographs. The Nazis destroyed Hirschfeld's institute in 1933, and he fled to the United States, thus ending Berlin's period as a location of sexual permissiveness and the only source of sex reassignment surgery in Europe.

In 1952, George Jorgensen, a former U.S. soldier, gained international celebrity when she returned from two years in Denmark transformed into a woman, Christine. Jorgensen was the first transsexual person in the United States to achieve widespread public attention. Raised in New York, Jorgensen began self-medicating with estrogen she obtained from a drugstore pharmacist. She traveled to Denmark in 1950, finding doctors who were prepared to transform her into a woman. Before returning to the United States in 1952, Jorgensen is said to have engineered a leak to the press of her correspondence with her parents about her transformation. The U.S. media went wild, publishing a number of stories on Jorgensen, the most famous headline of which is "Ex-GI Becomes Blonde Beauty." This pushed sex change into the public eye and encouraged those who also desired to undergo surgical transformation to write to Jorgensen and other experts.

Jorgensen's fame, and media coverage of other "sex-change" cases, initiated a debate in American medical circles about whether surgical intervention was an acceptable form of treatment. This coincided with the entry of the word "transsexualism" into mainstream medical discourse. Sexologist David O. Cauldwell had begun using the term "transsexualism" in his advice columns in *Sexology* magazine in the late 1940s. But it was Harry Benjamin (1885–1986), an endocrinologist and old associate of Magnus Hirschfeld, who would "father" transsexuality in the United States. Benjamin was an advocate of hormonal and surgical transformation, and set out to study and categorize those with gender-identity issues. With the appearance of Benjamin's book *The Transsexual Phenomenon* in 1966, transsexuality emerged as a subject: a documented way of being, with particular childhood histories, adult symptoms, and treatment regimes.

But in the 1950s and 1960s, few surgeons in Europe or North America would publicly admit to performing sex reassignment surgery. Most transwomen traveled to Casablanca, where French surgeon Georges Burou (1917–1987) performed a new vaginoplasty technique. Some obtained surgery in Mexico from a surgeon named Barbosa. By the late 1960s, sex reassignment surgery was becoming accepted as a viable treatment strategy for transsexualism in U.S. and European medical circles. In the United Kingdom, a change in law allowed the Charing Cross Hospital Gender Identity Clinic to offer sex reassignment surgery to a limited number of patients. In the United States, it became possible to obtain sex reassignment surgeries in gender clinics set up at universities, including the Johns Hopkins University Medical Center, Stanford, UCLA, and Northwestern. However, by the late 1970s, these gender clinics were almost all closed, due to debates about the efficacy of reassignment surgery. With increased privatization of the United States health care system in the 1980s, and the growth of the cosmetic surgery industry, surgeons began offering sex reassignment surgery techniques privately, circumventing the provision of care by researchers. In the twenty-first century, sex reassignment surgery is available in many countries across the globe.

Physiology

Sex reassignment surgery is usually different for transmen (female-to-male) and transwomen (male-to-female). The range of procedures grouped together under sex reassignment surgeries includes both genital reconstruction and non-genital procedures.

Transwomen might obtain the following surgeries. Genital procedures include orchiectomy, penectomy, and vaginoplasty. Orchiectomy, or castration, refers to the removal of the testicles. A penectomy is the removal of the penis and reconstruction of a shortened urethral opening, allowing for urination. Vaginoplasty refers to the surgical construction of a vagina. Contemporary vaginoplasty techniques use the skin of the penis, the scrotal skin, or, less often, a length of the small intestine to construct vaginal walls and inner and outer labia. The urethra is relocated just above the vaginal opening, where it would be placed on a non-transsexual woman. Flesh from the glans, or tip, of the penis is relocated to form a clitoris, enabling erotic sensation and often orgasm. A cylindrical dressing is inserted into the neo-vagina to help the skin graft to heal; after the initial period of healing, cylindrical plugs must be inserted daily to retain the depth of the vaginal canal.

Non-genital procedures for transwomen include breast augmentation, which means reshaping the breasts to be larger; they are usually somewhat developed after estrogen therapy. Facial feminization may involve lowering a receding hairline, recontouring the brow, chin, and cheekbones, and other cosmetic surgery techniques to give a more feminine appearance.

Sex reassignment surgery techniques for transmen are quite different. The most common form of sex reassignment surgery for transmen is chest reconstruction, or top surgery. This refers to the removal of breast tissue and the reconstruction of a masculine chest and nipples. Many transmen are advised to undergo hysterectomy, removing the uterus and ovaries, as this permanently removes the body's source of estrogen production.

Hysterectomy is also advised as a preventive measure against ovarian or cervical cancer, although its necessity is not universally agreed on.

Genital surgeries include hysterectomy, phalloplasty, and metoidioplasty. Phalloplasty is the surgical construction of a penis and testes. It is a complex and difficult procedure, and often takes more than one operation to accomplish. The most common contemporary phalloplasty technique is radial forearm phalloplasty, which utilizes the soft skin on the forearm to create the skin of the new penis. A vertical tube of skin is grafted into the forearm, creating a urethra with which to urinate. Simultaneously, the surgeon closes the patient's vaginal opening. The outer labia are often reformed as a scrotum, and silicon implants form testes. Finally, a rectangular piece of forearm skin (including the urethra) is removed, shaped into a phallus, and grafted onto the genital area to form the flesh of the penis, while clitoral tissue forms a glans. Insertable rods are sometimes used to aid erection after the penis has healed. Because of its complexity, phalloplasty often risks complications, such as urine leakage, skin graft failure, and loss of erotic sensation. Since construction of a penis is a less developed and more expensive a procedure than vaginoplasty, around 80 percent of transmen never obtain phalloplasty.

An alternative is metoidioplasty. Metoidioplasty refers to detaching a testosterone-enlarged clitoris from the labial folds, so that it forms a small penis, or microphallus. Sometimes the urethra will be lengthened and relocated through the microphallus, enabling a transman to urinate standing up. As with phalloplasty, the outer labia may be refashioned as a scrotal sac with silicon testicular implants. The point of metoidioplasty is to retain tissue that yields erotic sensation, but to reform it so that penetration and standing urination become possibilities. Finally, some transmen who prefer not to undergo genital surgery have been known to stretch the labia and clitoris using piercings with weights attached.

Medical Developments

The development of sex reassignment techniques mirrors the development and refinement of plastic surgery procedures across the twentieth century. Compared with contemporary plastic surgery, the earliest documented vaginoplasties were crude. Published photographs of vaginoplasty were included in a 1931 German journal article by Felix Abraham, a doctor at Hirschfeld's Institute for Sexual Science. The article, "Genital Reassignment on Two Male Transvestites," describes the procedure surgeons followed. Penectomy and castration were performed in advance, leaving a penis stump. An opening was made in the perineal area to a depth of 11 or 12 centimeters (4.5 to 5 inches). Skin grafts from the upper leg were used to form the vaginal walls, and a cylindrical sponge was inserted to aid healing and encourage dilation. This technique was plagued with problems: the neovagina often healed badly, and the skin grafts taken from the thighs were disfiguring. The article does not mention erotic sensation.

Georges Burou is said to have been the first to adapt a vaginoplasty technique including the construction of a clitoris, enabling the recipient to experience erotic sensation and orgasm. By this time, surgeons were no longer automatically amputating the penis and testicles before constructing a vagina, and had begun to utilize the penile and scrotal skin to form vaginal walls. Burou gave the first public presentation of vaginoplasty in 1973 at a conference on sex reassignment surgery, and surgeons worldwide used his technique. More recent innovations in vaginoplasty include variations on Burou's procedure, with refinements aimed at reproducing the precise anatomy of a non-transsexual female. A surgeon working in Thailand, Suporn Watanyusakul, not only constructs a sensate clitoris, but places the remainder of the glans penis at the opening of the vagina to encourage clitoral and vaginal orgasm. Contemporary vaginoplasty is also generally expected to yield a deeper vaginal depth, sometimes up to eight inches.

Phalloplasty has a more recent history. The first phalloplasties were performed during and after World War II on wounded soldiers whose genitals has been damaged or amputated. The pioneer of phalloplasty was Harold Gillies (1882–1960), a British surgeon who treated war casualties. He experimented with creating a tubular flap on the abdomen, made by lifting a flap of skin and making a tube, enclosing another tube of skin within the outer tube to fashion a urethra, and grafting the tube to a different location, end over end, until it was placed in the groin. Other surgeons in Europe were performing early genital procedures on transsexual men. One account of an early phalloplasty notes that a section of rib was inserted into the neophallus to make it erect, while other surgeons used muscles to "flesh out" the new organ. These experiments did not often meet with success. The tubular flap technique remained standard until the development of microsurgery techniques in the 1980s. In 1984, the first radial forearm phalloplasty took place. By this stage, surgeons had begun to regraft the enlarged clitoris onto the neophallus to construct a glans. Phalloplasty is still experimental: ejaculation is impossible, and the results rarely capture the exact appearance of a non-transsexual man's penis. Some transmen hold out hope that bioengineering techniques may result in scientists "growing" transplantable, fully functional penises and testes.

Debates and Controversies

The effectiveness of sex reassignment surgery in affirming and treating gender-identity issues is hotly debated. Sex reassignment surgery is sometimes thought of as a form of self-mutilation. Some psychiatric opponents of sex reassignment surgery regard transsexuality as a delusional mental illness. According to this perspective, experiences of gender dysphoria can be treated with long-term therapy.

Beyond psychiatry, the politics of sex reassignment have been hotly debated within feminist circles. The most extreme feminist opponents of sex reassignment, such as Janice Raymond, author of the 1979 book *The Transsexual Empire*, regard transsexuality as a form of masculine imperialism in which men appropriate the "trappings" of femaleness in order to replace women. In Raymond's analysis, transwomen universally desire to embody conservative, or normative, femininity, something that the women's movement sought to reject. Therefore, transsexuals are not only colonialist, but also politically conservative by default. A more contemporary, though uncommon, radical feminist analysis of female-to-male transsexuality regards female-to-male surgery as a form of abject self-mutilation, expressing hatred of femaleness. According to Sheila Jeffreys, for example, transmen react to the oppression of women in society by rejecting their female bodies, and joining the oppressors as men. Other debates have taken place over whether transpeople are welcome within gender-segregated spaces. The Michigan Womyn's Music Festival, an annual female-only festival, has held a policy inviting only "womyn-born-womyn" since its inception in 1975. It has been picketed annually by trans activists since 1991, when a trans-woman was ejected from the campsite. However, many feminist writers are not opposed to sex reassignment. Dialogues about the role of transsexual and transgendered people within feminist politics are complex. Perspectives seeking to join together trans and feminist theory and politics include Emi Koyama's *The Transfeminist Manifesto*, and many other works.

Many debates have taken place within transsexual and transgender communities about the medicalization of transsexuality. This process has continued with the growth of academic theory about transsexuality into its own field, trans studies. Regarding the psychiatric categorization of transsexuality as a mental disorder, many advocates see this as evidence of Western culture's refusal to accept gender diversity. They argue that gender-identity disorder should be dropped from the DSM-IV. However, others argue that the label is necessary; they see a direct correlation between transsexuality's status as a medical condition and the continued battle to gain publicly funded treatment, including sex reassignment surgery. Other debates turn on whether adult individuals should need to be psychiatrically assessed before accessing sex reassignment surgery. Still other debates have taken place about the provision of surgery only to those people who fit the traditional category of transsexuals, those who want to live exclusively as men or as women. Advocates argue that many transpeople who feel themselves to be in-between genders desire surgery as genuinely as those who feel themselves to be masculine men and feminine women. They ask that the WPATH Standards of Care be altered to reflect the diversity of expression of sexes and genders, or that restrictions on who can access sex reassignment surgery be removed altogether.

Sex Reassignment Globally

Sex reassignment has probably been documented most comprehensively in Europe and North America, perhaps because of the Western obsession with detailing and categorizing those who are deemed to be sexually abnormal. However, they are common in many different places across the globe. Sex reassignment surgery is also practiced in different forms outside of the medicalized framework of Western society. For instance, Indian gender-variant people, known as *hijras*, sometimes undergo castration and penectomy while in a form of spiritual trance. Plastic surgery, however, is a global industry, and similar sex reassignment surgical techniques are used the world over.

In fact, sex reassignment surgery has often been easier for transpeople to obtain outside the English-speaking world. Sometimes this is because legal or medical regulation may be less stringent, or may be bypassed more easily, in less economically developed regions. Georges Burou's clinic in Casablanca did not require his patients to meet the psychiatric guidelines so carefully adapted in the United States and Europe. Just as often, however, particular surgeons have worked in places "off the beaten track." Stanley Biber operated on many transwomen in his hometown of Trinidad, Colorado, causing the town to be described as the "sex-change capital of the world." Belgrade has become a popular destination to for transmen to obtain metoidioplasty, due to the work of Sava Perovic, a Serbian reconstructive surgeon renowned for his innovative phalloplasty and metoidioplasty techniques.

Some popular sex reassignment surgery destinations become so precisely because of their geocultural specificity. Many transpeople from North America, Asia-Pacific, and Europe travel annually to Thailand, where a relatively large number of surgeons specialize in sex reassignment surgery. Thailand has a large and visible population of male-to-female gender-variant people, providing the impetus for surgeons to begin specializing in this area. In recent years, the most popular surgeons performing sex reassignment in Thailand have shifted from operating mainly on Thai citizens to a foreign client base. The booming Thai medical-tourism industry, a lack of legal restrictions on which procedures are performed, and the relatively low cost of surgery compared to elsewhere have facilitated the growth of a niche market. Iran, too, is said to have recently become a popular destination to obtain sex reassignment surgery. While homosexuality is considered a serious crime in Iran, transsexuality is legally recognized, and transpeople are assessed for access to hormones and surgery as in the medical model used by many Western doctors.

Cultural Representations of Sex Reassignment and Transsexuality

Representations of people undergoing sex reassignment began in the first half of the twentieth century with some mass-media coverage of "sex conversion." Early accounts of sex reassignment often narrated these stories as cases of hermaphroditism, as in the story of Lili Elbe, a Danish painter who occasionally cross-dressed, but traveled to Berlin to seek sex reassignment surgery. A book about Elbe's life, *Man Into Woman* (1933), presented her as intersexed. In these depictions, sex reassignment candidates were often portrayed as unnatural oddities whose secrets were being solved by the wonders of modern science. One headline in a 1939 edition of *True* magazine reads, "Sex Repeal! Science Solves the Riddle of Man-Women Wonders." And yet mass-media coverage also provided an opportunity for readers who identified with the stories and desired sex reassignment to collect information about the subject and find doctors to consult. The pinnacle of early mass-media coverage was Christine Jorgensen's debut onto the international stage in 1952.

In the second half of the twentieth century, three modes of representation of sex reassignment dominated the cultural field: film, autobiography, and contemporary art (particularly photography).

Cinematic representations of transsexual and gender-variant people began only in the 1950s, starting with the 1953 Hollywood B-movie *Glen or Glenda* (*I Changed My Sex*), directed by Ed Wood. *Glen or Glenda* tells a version of the Christine Jorgensen story, as well as the tale of a transvestite (or cross-dresser). While Wood himself was a cross-dresser, the movie inaugurated the Hollywood tendency to present transsexual people as freaks or comedy figures, a trend continued in *Myra Breckinridge* (1970), in which a sex-crazed transsexual woman played by Raquel Welch avenges herself on men by taking over a Hollywood acting academy. The director John Waters presents an avant-garde taste of "freak" life in *Desperate Living* (1979), in which a transman, Mole McHenry, undergoes sex reassignment. Thai *kathoey* are commonly depicted in dramas depicting transpeople in a more serious light, beginning with the Sidney Lumet film *Dog Day Afternoon* (1975). The main character, played by Al Pacino, arranges a bank robbery to pay for his partner's sex reassignment surgery. Other feature films of note include *The Crying Game* (1992), *Boys Don't Cry* (1999), *Normal* (2003), and, of course, *Transamerica* (2005), for which Felicity Huffman was nominated for an Academy Award. Documentary film has been one of the richest genres used to tell transsexual and gender-variant stories, and the number of movies featuring transsexual experiences has proliferated since the late 1990s, giving rise to transgender-themed film festivals in the Netherlands, San Francisco, and Seattle.

Autobiography and contemporary photography constitute the area of cultural representations in which transpeople have most often told their own stories and produced their own images. Christine Jorgensen published a heavily edited account of her life in 1967; this was followed by the travel writer Jan Morris' memoir *Conundrum* in 1974, showgirl April Ashley's autobiography *April Ashley's Odyssey* in 1982, and tennis player Renee Richards' *Second Serve* (1986), among others. Most of the early transsexual memoirs were written by transwomen, with some exceptions: *Emergence: An Autobiography* by Mario Martino (1977) and *Dear Sir or Madam: The Autobiography of Mark Rees* (1996). In the area of photography, Loren Cameron's *Body Alchemy: Transsexual Portraits* (1996) presents photographs of a number of transmen, including the author. Other photographers of note include Del La Grace Volcano, who began producing queer and avant-garde works that focused on gender play. Mariette Pathy Allen, author of *The Gender Frontier* (2003), is considered to be one of the best nontranssexual photographers whose subjects are often gender variant. *See also* Genitals: Intersexuality; and Testicles: Castration.

Further Reading: Califia, Patrick. *Sex Changes: The Politics of Transgenderism*. San Francisco: Cleis Press, 2003; Herdt, Gilbert, ed. *Third Sex, Third Gender: Beyond Sexual Dimorphism in Culture and History*. New York: Zone Books, 1996; *International Journal of Transgenderism*. Archives 1997–2002, and electronic book collection. International Journal of Transgenderism Web site http://www.symposion.com/ijt/index.htm (accessed February 2008); Ames, Jonathan. *Sexual Metamorphosis: An Anthology of Transsexual Memoirs*. New York: Vintage, 2005; Kulick, Don. *Travesti: Sex, Gender, and Culture among Brazilian Transgendered Prostitutes*. Chicago: University of Chicago Press, 1996; Meyerowitz, Joanne. *How Sex Changed: A History of Transsexuality in the United States*. Cambridge, MA: Harvard University Press, 2002; More, Kate, and Stephen

Whittle, eds. *Reclaiming Genders: Transsexual Grammars at the Fin De Siecle*. London: Cassell, 1999; Nanda, Serena. *The Hijras of India: Neither Man nor Woman*. Belmont, CA: Wadsworth, 1999; Prosser, Jay. *Second Skins: The Body Narratives of Transsexuality*. New York: Columbia University Press, 1998; Stryker, Susan. *Transgender History*. San Francisco: Seal Press, 2008; Stryker, Susan, and Stephen Whittle, eds. *The Transgender Studies Reader*. New York: Routledge, 2006; World Professional Association for Transgender Health (WPATH). "The Harry Benjamin International Gender Dysphoria Association's Standards of Care for Gender Identity Disorders, Sixth Version," http://wpath.org/Documents2/socv6.pdf (accessed February 2008).

Aren Z. Aizura

Hair

Cultural History of Hair

Human body hair, one of our most culturally rich and visually accessible symbols, is dead matter once it is visible. Hair dies below the skin surface, within each follicle, shortly after the construction of a hair strand is complete. These "dead" hair strands make their appearance on the outer side of the dermis. The follicle, or the "root," exists about one sixth of an inch below the skin of the scalp in an adult head, and each scalp contains around 120,000 to 150,000 hair follicles. Within the follicle, each strand of hair is produced, colored, and nourished until it reaches a maximum capacity. Although biologically dead, hair is one of our liveliest cultural symbols. Within the cultural realm, hair is altered endlessly and imbued with various social meanings. While fashions and styles have shifted over time, fascination and manipulation of hair has remained constant throughout history.

Physiology of Hair

A strand of hair comprises one of the two anatomical structures of the hair system, the other being the hair follicle. The follicle looks like tiny folds within the skin. These follicles are nourished by capillaries and connective tissue with the surrounding skin. Each follicle has an arrector muscle that links the follicle to the dermis and makes the hair stand on end when an organism is frightened or stressed; this muscle has no other use. The follicle produces a hair by synthesizing keratinocytes, cells that differentiate into the external and internal part of the hair strand and that also produce keratins, which make up the bulk of the inner hair strand. Keratin is a strong protein that makes up most of the hair as well as parts of the skin and nails, and, in animals, the horns, hooves, feathers, and wool. The hair follicle also contains melanocytes, cells that contain and transmit hair color to each strand. Hair follicles also produce hormones, just like the pituitary gland or the adrenal gland. Each hair follicle has its own life cycle in humans; that is to say, people do not, like many animals, molt or shed at one time. Human hair sheds and grows continuously, for unknown reasons.

The strand of hair consists of three parts: the medulla, the cortex, and the cuticle. The medulla, or medullary canal, runs through the center of the hair; the cells that make up this structure quickly degenerate, leaving pockets of air, spaces, and gaps. In animals, this allows for heat dissipation, but the medulla has no known function in humans. The cortex composes 90 percent of the weight of the hair and is where the keratins and melanin reside. The cuticle surrounds the medulla and cortex and consists of overlapping cells that look like roof shingles. The cuticle protects the internal components of the hair. It is also the target of beauty products that purport to treat or repair damaged hair. Hair color operates by permeating the cuticle and depositing color in the cortex.

The follicle and strand operate similarly in all humans despite ethnic variations in hair texture, color, density, and speed of growth. Asians' hair grows the fastest and has the thickest strand diameter but has the lowest density (number of hairs per square inch of skin) as compared with Africans' or Caucasians' hair. Africans' hair grows the slowest and has a density in between that of Asians and Caucasians. Caucasians' hair grows faster than Africans' hair but not as quickly as Asians' hair. Caucasians' hair has the highest density. These differences in texture (and color) have been utilized throughout history to create and sustain hierarchies of beauty and to differentiate groups of people. The ways in which humans style their hair separates them from, or enjoins them to, other groups, tribes, sexes, and ages.

Symbolic Meanings of Hair

Throughout history, people have altered the style and appearance of their hair to symbolize cultural norms, social differentiation, personal attributes, spiritual states, and dissent from society. Social control, power differentials, and punishment often are enacted through hair.

Human hair distributions have been consistent since the Upper Paleolithic period, despite the fact that a key symbol of prehistoric humans is a mane of wild, unkempt hair. Thus, unkempt hair has come to stand for untamed sexuality, a lack of civilization, language, and morality. Archaeological evidence, however, suggests that humans have altered their hair since the time of the caveman. Hair regenerates itself when disease or old age is not present and survives the body post mortem. During the Victorian era, the hair of deceased loved ones was made into art objects such as pictures and jewelry. Friends and lovers also gifted their hair to each other to express affection.

While hairstyles and methods of alteration have varied across time and space, some similarities stand out across history. For example, one consistent way cultures construct an "other" from which to distance themselves is through charging the other group as being excessively hirsute. Europeans constructed Native Americans in this way, and Chinese did the same when they encountered Europeans. Some Native Americans removed their body hair and therefore had less hair then did Europeans, whose hairy appearance surprised them. Despite Native Americans' hairless norms, in the eighteenth century, tales of them always included descriptions of their hairiness. Reports of Native Americans' lack of hair have been noted to include the European's surprise at this revelation. In many cultures, monsters and other scary mythical figures are covered in hair, suggesting that hairiness blurs the distinction between human and animal.

Much of the push to remove body hair in the early twentieth century was for cultural assimilation—appearing too hairy could be associated with a less-valued ethnicity. The charge of hairiness carries with it an outsider status, a lack of morality, and a lack of civilization. Often groups consciously manipulate the power of the symbol of hairiness to convey their rejection of society or their outsider status. Hippies, feminists, and civil rights activists used their hair in such a way.

Hair is a relatively easy bodily part to manipulate and use for self-expression due to its regenerating properties. Other consistent reasons for altering hair include both an attempt to comply with culture or disavow it; impressing and attracting others; revealing social status or rank; to intimidate others; and to fight the signs of aging and degeneration. It has been suggested that hairstyles have vacillated between the two axes of conspicuous and inconspicuous and between conforming and nonconforming throughout Western history.

The formula of "opposites" may illuminate differences in hairstyles and expression. The "opposite" theory suggests that opposing sexes and opposing ideologies wear their hair opposite to one another. History supports this thesis to some extent. For example, during ancient Roman times, slaves and their masters wore their facial hair opposite one another. When free men wore beards, slaves had to be clean-shaven, and when free men did not have beards, their slaves did. In this case, beards worn by slaves signaled their lesser status. More recently, hippies wore their hair long to oppose the status quo, especially the Vietnam War, and the close-cropped military style hair. The hippie slogan "free love" expresses an untamed sexuality that gets conflated with long, wild, and unkempt hair, but was also meant to challenge societal structures and norms such as the nuclear family and capitalism.

The rule does not always hold; punks and skinheads removed their hair to convey their dissent from society, but they were also positioning themselves opposite to hippies. Further, punks often directed their hair "up" in gravity-defying styles, which contrasted with the hippies and their emphasis on natural styles that encouraged their hair down. It might be more accurate to suggest that whatever the hairstyle, its distinction from other hairstyles is part of its cultural meaning.

One of the most powerful and historically consistent uses of hair for social differentiation occurs between women and men within any given society. Differing hairstyles for women and men has been one of the most consistent uses of hair to signal social identity. American and European women in the twentieth century caused an uproar, especially among religious leaders and their followers, when they began bobbing their hair—cutting it shorter and blurring one of the visual lines between the sexes. Many laws in the United States in the colonial era named the husband as the possessor of his wife's hair and mandated that she was to defer to him to alter it in any way. A woman's long hair signaled an uncontrolled sexuality, which, in this context, suggested that her husband did not have adequate control over her. However, over the past thirty years there has been a proliferation of unisex hairstyles, and many men wear their hair long and many women wear their hair short.

Some ideas about the sexes having different hairstyles arise out of religion. Religious doctrines and ideologies often mandate that women cover their hair so as not to tempt men or display their so-called desirous nature. Currently, Muslim women cover their hair, as do some Western women in certain religious ceremonies such as marriage. Some orthodox Jewish women customarily shave their heads and, once they are married, wear wigs, which are called "*sheitel*." Men were urged to wear their hair short in both Christian and Jewish cultures from the Middle Ages on. Today, many religious leaders such as monks and nuns shave their heads completely. Some Muslim men wear turbans over their heads in public, while Muslim women often veil their heads. There are passages in both the Koran and the Bible that encourage men and women to wear their hair in styles distinctive from one another and to keep their hair fashioned in modest styles.

Politics of Hair

Revolutionaries

Political shifts influenced the hairstyles of the sexes, too. From the ancient Egyptians to the Middle Ages, hairstyles followed those of royalty. Whatever the king or queen wore set the styles for their court and influenced other members of upper-class society. Sometimes people wore their hair in direct opposition to royalty, as during the French Revolution (1789–1799), but still such styles were tied to the power associated with the king and queen. Men involved in the French Revolution used their short hair to display their disdain for the aristocracy, with their elaborate wigs and long, curled hair. French men and women displayed their patriotism by wearing their hair in simpler styles and by sometimes wearing a red ribbon around a low ponytail at the back of the neck to symbolize the beheaded royalty and aristocrats. During the period of the French Revolution, French women stopped wearing their hair in elaborate constructions and opted for plainer, less-expensive accessories. There were significant changes in fashion and hairstyles within the royal court that took place in the years proceeding and during the revolution. Napoleon wore his hair short, styled like that of a Roman emperor, setting a trend for years to come. Changes in hairstyles played a part in the American Revolution too. The Puritans, both men and women, also wore shorter hair to signal their dissent from the elaborate wigs and life of King Charles I.

The Afro

Different races and ethnic groups use their hair to express political dissent from mainstream society suggesting that the political use of hair is not a relic of distant history. Members of the Black Power movement, civil rights groups, and other African Americans of the 1960s grew out their hair into Afros—tightly curled hair that extends from the scalp forming a sphere around the head—to assert black pride, to question the values of the dominant culture, and to distance themselves from previous African American political movements that were more assimilative in nature. The Afro also asserted a new aesthetic, one that did not depend on white culture as the standard. Curly or kinky hair in these contexts symbolizes a disagreement with and contestation of social values. The Afro was part of the "Black Is Beautiful" movement that problematized racism as it affected people at the personal level. Asserting ethnic beauty standards that differed from the white norm helped create self-esteem and pride in one's appearance and heritage. The rise of the Afro was simultaneously a rejection of hair straightening. Hair straightening had been popular for women and older girls throughout the first half of the twentieth century, but the practice was seen by some as imitating whites and disregarding African norms.

The Bob

Women have equally used their hair for political purposes throughout time. The bob appeared around 1910. Women made the style popular after World War I (1914–1918), when gender roles and social and political changes swept the Western world. Yet it took the media to popularize the bob by disseminating images of women with bobbed hair such as Irene Castle (1893–1969), a famous dancer, and Coco Chanel (1883–1971). The bob symbolized a liberated woman, as it was easier to manage than the long hair worn previously. Women could manage short hair better while working, playing sports, dancing, or any other activity. Critics of the bob accused women who wore their hair in such a fashion of being too masculine and too wild. Short hair on women symbolized immoral lifestyles that could include any of "unfeminine" behaviors such as smoking, drinking, dating, and engaging in sex before marriage. Long hair on women was conflated with traditional roles for women—motherhood, wife, and homemaker. The bob took over and is an example of a hairstyle that moved from conspicuous to inconspicuous and is now considered a classic hairstyle. The bobby pin was created for the purpose of styling bobbed hair. The proliferation of short hair on women created a boom in the beauty industry and in the proliferation of beauty salons.

The Economics of Hair

The elaborate styles often worn by French and English royalty during the early modern European era required a team of hairstylists who would, of course, be unavailable to the common folk. Although, the term "hairdresser" dates back to the times of Queen Elizabeth I during the seventeenth-century England, hairdressing took form as a distinct profession during the reign of Louis XV (1710–1774) of France. His mistress, Madame de Pompadour (1721–1764), changed her hair regularly, challenging the court to keep pace. During the eighteenth century, women's hair was styled in elaborate, architectural shapes—pulled over pads, and decorated with flowers, jewels, and artful objects. As the century progressed, hairstyles became so elaborate and large that wigs had to be used so that stylists could access all angles of the hair. These stylists started hairdressing as it is known today.

Legros de Rumigny of Paris was the first to institutionalize the education of hairdressers around 1765. In 1768, he published a book titled, *Art de la Coiffure des Dames*, with illustrations of his different hairstyles. He used dolls to showcase his hair designs as well, and in 1765, he had 100 dolls and twenty-eight original drawings of hairstyles. He also mentored hairdressers and set up the first beauty school. He created a pomade out of beef marrow, hazelnut oil, and lemon essence. However, the pomade would rot in women's hair, so other products had to be developed to cover the smell (such styles were worn for a long period of time). The pejorative phrase "rat's nest" comes from the tangle of hair created by elaborate hairstyles. Hair held together with edible substances was also vulnerable to insect infestation. The problems of infestation were not just of the distant past. In 1962, in Canton, Ohio, a classmate noticed blood on the neck of a girl who sat in front of him in their high school. Upon investigation, the girl had a nest of cockroaches living in her "beehive" hairdo. The beehive, popular in the mid-twentieth century America, required similar feats of hairstyling as the bouffant of the eighteenth century—teasing the hair, piling it high, and holding it in place, often for weeks, with various pomades.

After the French Revolution, hair took on simpler forms and styles. It was not until the twentieth century that hairdressers would return with the prominence they held during the eighteenth century. The popularization of hairstylists in modernity includes one major difference: the services of a stylist were no longer available only to royalty, but democratized for much of the population in the Western world. The proliferation of the beauty industry paralleled the spread of the mass media. As the rapidity of hairstyles changed, hairdressing has become a competitive enterprise in which stylists attempt to usher in new trends, however short lived. In celebrity culture, hairdressers' status depends on who dons their styles, with actors and actresses being the ultimate advertisements. During the 1990s, the "Rachel" haircut took over the heads of women in America as they copied the long, layered look of the actress Jennifer Aniston from the television show *Friends*. Film stars have so much power that, during World War II, the U.S. Department of War appealed to Veronica Lake, who started a trend for "peekaboo" bangs that covered one eye, to wear her hair off her face so that American women would follow suit and not get injured while working in factories.

Hair Modifications

Hair has been and continues to be modified in numerous ways, from the architectural creations of the seventeenth, eighteenth, and mid-twentieth centuries to the complete removal of hair during ancient Egyptian times. Hair-coloring technologies are one of the many ways humans have, historically, altered their hair. The reasons for coloring hair are multifaceted as well and include the following: restoring natural hair color as gray hair appears, following trends and fashions, changing identities, disguising oneself, or for theatrical performances. Disdain for those who color or bleach their hair or for those who wear false hair has persisted alongside such modification practices. Altering ones "natural" hair has spurred heated debates about vanity and the nature of the self. Such debates about hair alterations often occur because of religious mores and practices. Despite criticisms, people have continued to color and alter their hair. Home hair-color kits created in the 1950s helped keep such practices a secret.

Hair Color

Hair coloring during ancient times utilized items found in nature and included henna, walnut extracts, chamomile, and other substances from animals to bugs. The Romans used walnut shells, ashes, and earthworms to dye gray hair black. Members of the royal court of Elizabeth I dyed their hair to match her red hair using sulfur powder and saffron. Lye was used by the Gaul men to bleach their hair; after stripping their hair of color, they would treat it with Woad, a blue dye, for the purposes of scaring their enemies. Legros de Rumigny, the eighteenth-century hairdresser, used powder to cover gray roots. Bleaching chemicals used in tandem with sunlight has been a hair-lightening technology since Greek styles reached Italy. It was not until the late nineteenth century, however, that synthetic chemicals were used to color hair, giving birth to our conceptualization of hair coloring today. Some groups still utilize natural products to style their hair. Punks often use egg whites and food dyes to shape their hair in gravity-defying styles and color it in unnatural hues.

From the 1950s on, acceptance for coloring hair has increased; it is estimated in the early twenty-first century that between 51 to 75 percent of American women have colored their hair at least once. In 2000, hair color was a $1 billion-a-year industry. The category "hair color" was deleted from U.S. passports in 1969 because hair color was so easily altered. In the United States, most women have their hair colored in a salon (around 64 percent), while the rest color their hair at home using hair-coloring kits. The most popular color for American women (around 80 percent) is some shade of blond. In 2002, about one out of every twelve American men colored his hair. The male hair-color industry was worth $113.5 million in 2002.

Hair color today is temporary, semipermanent, or permanent. Temporary hair color is usually a rinse that washes out after a few washings. Semipermanent and permanent hair colors use ammonia and/or peroxide to open up the hair cuticle and remove the natural color. Once the original color is removed, the new dye deposits its color in the hair. The safety of hair color is debated, but if consumer behavior is any measure, the risks do not outweigh the benefits of changing hair color.

The current hair-color industry reflects a historical fascination with hair colors and their different cultural values and meanings. Red hair is the rarest naturally occurring hair color and has been regarded with suspicion throughout the ages. Redheads have been accused of being witches by the Puritans, vampires by the ancient Greeks, or hot-tempered as colloquially spoken today. The disciple that betrayed Jesus, Judas, supposedly had red hair, too.

Dark hair is the most genetically common hair color around the world. Dark hair became the feminine ideal, replacing blond, during the seventeenth century in Europe as French artists painted women with this hair color. In modern society, dark-haired women are thought of as intelligent, sultry, and exotic as compared to blond women. Men have sought dark hair since the colloquial norm of "tall, dark, and handsome" took hold during the early twentieth century. In the early part of the Roman Empire, dark hair was the ideal because prostitutes were required to wear light "yellow" hair by either dying or wearing wigs. By the end of the Roman Empire, this trend reversed and light hair was the ideal for all women.

Blond women are considered to be less intelligent than their dark-haired peers, but most women still seek such hair color. The popularity for blond hair appears throughout history and there is no conclusive evidence as to why. Some suggest that blond hair connotes youth, since less then a quarter of born blonds maintain this color past the teen years. The "dumb blonde" stereotype appears in many television shows and movies, such as the film *Gentlemen Prefer Blondes* (1953) starring Marilyn Monroe.

Hair Straightening

Hair straightening refers to the chemical or mechanical process of breaking down the bonds of hair in order to reduce its natural curl or wave. Straight hair emerged as a widespread style in America at the turn of the twentieth century with the influx of beauty products targeted to African Americans, especially women, and other ethnic minorities, whose hair is often naturally curly. The history of hair straightening in America is tied to the history of racism, although today many people straighten their hair for reasons other than to conform to racist beauty ideals.

African-American women's attitudes toward American beauty standards has often been reflected in their hair. The prevailing beauty standard for most of America's history has been based on white, European features that include light skin and straight hair. As immigrants from southern Europe arrived in America during the early twentieth century, they too straightened their often-curly hair to blend in with the dominant culture. African American men straightened their hair in styles known as the conk between the 1920s and 1960s. Even white women of various ethnicities straightened their hair, especially during the 1960s and 1970s with the popularity of the hippie look. A popular look today is the "blow-out," wherein the hair is blown straight with a blow-dryer and assisted by a straightening gel that often contains silica. Most blow-outs are performed by professional hairdressers.

Many African Americans rejected straightened hair during the civil rights movement of the 1950s and 1960s. Although much of the early civil rights movement focused on legal and social reforms, the movement also became invested in the racial politics of beauty. The assertion that "black is beautiful" meant, among other things, the rejection of white beauty standards and the celebration of the natural texture of African American hair. During and after the civil rights movement, wearing unstraightened hair came to suggest pride in one's ethnicity and race. The Afro became a popular style, at least initially signifying a rejection of racism in American culture.

Wigs

Humans have worn wigs, or false hair, throughout history. Reasons for wearing wigs have not changed across millennia and include the following: to conceal hair loss due to disease or aging, to change appearances, for religious ceremonies or cultural celebrations, to cross-dress to disguise oneself, or for adornment. When fashions in hair require extreme styling or harsh chemicals, hair loss often results, driving many people to opt for a wig. The ancient Egyptians shaved all of their hair to combat lice and to keep cool. They wore wigs when in public, especially members of the higher classes. Prostitutes were required to wear blond wigs (or dye their hair blond) during the early part of the Roman Empire. Once women in the higher classes started coloring their hair light or donning blond wigs, the law governing prostitutes' hair was repealed.

Wigs have been constructed out of human hair, synthetic materials, animal hair, and grasses and plant matter throughout time. The human hair for wigs has historically come from those who must sell their hair for their livelihood and others, including slaves (who were forced to give their hair), dead people, and animals, usually horses. Today, China is the leading supplier of hair for wigs for the United States. China ships hair that originates in South Korea and India. Whereas hair from India is currently considered the best hair, in the late nineteenth century, hair from Paris and Italy was considered prime.

Wigs reached their literal height during the late eighteenth century, when France was the leading wig producer. Women's wigs extended several feet above their heads and required pads, frames, and moldings placed on the head to extend the wigs upwards. They were often decorated with jewels, flowers, fruits, vegetables, and even miniature furniture. Some wigs were so valuable they were included in wills and estates. Women and men practiced wig powdering during this time, devoting special rooms of the house to this practice and the mess it caused. Wigs required further architectural considerations, such as raised doorways. While not everyone could afford to wear such elaborate wigs, both men and women of various classes did wear them from the late seventeenth century to the mid-eighteenth century. Wigs were so popular that in the years 1750 to 1759, 46 percent of small-town French farmers owned them. The popularity of wigs at this time was due to consumers' belief that they provided convenience and ease that caring for one's natural hair did not. Consumers at this historical moment were being inundated with new rules of and books on civility, manners, and taste; wearing a wig simplified one aspect of their appearance.

Wigs quickly went out of favor with the French Revolution and the critique of the aristocracy and did not return en masse until the 1960s. The bouffant, the beehive, and the extremely long hairstyles of the hippies created a surge in the popularity of wigs and other false hair extensions.

Because one side effect of chemotherapy is hair loss, many insurance companies cover the cost of wigs for cancer patients.

Men have worn wigs as often as have women; eighteenth-century colonial men in America, in fact, wore wigs more often then women. They shaved their heads and donned wigs made by local wig makers. Wigs were often status symbols for men, with rich men wearing higher-quality wigs and owning a selection. Wigs lost their popularity for American men after the Revolutionary War when, once again, overt signs of wealth and social inequality were somewhat less fashionable. Today men wear toupees, partial wigs that cover bald heads, often using some of the natural hair to blend it with the false hair. Toupees have been material for comedy routines and are derisively called "rugs." The humor of the toupee results from the ease of removing it or losing it (in any harsh weather or strenuous activity) and the presumed vanity of the wearer. Toupee use has declined in recent years with advances in hair-loss technologies such as Rogaine and due to the increasing acceptance of bald men. Celebrities such as Bruce Willis and Michael Jordan have recently made baldness chic.

Humans have been and continue to be concerned with their hair in all times, places, and spaces. Altering one's hair can situate the wearer inconspicuously within a group or it can suggest that the wearer is different from all the rest. Hairstyles convey the wearer's approach to the world and whether they share the values of the culture at large or if they instead belong to some subculture. Over the past thirty years, women and men have worn their hair in similar ways, yet a division of hairstyles still persists. Most men do not wear their hair long, especially past the shoulders, and women still opt for longer hair often worn in ponytails or other various up-do styles.

The spread of hair-altering technologies has reached mass proportions. Both styling products and styling tools combine to create a multibillion-dollar hair-care industry. While most people manipulate their hair daily, hair-care professionals can be found almost everywhere. Historically, the beauty industry has provided opportunities for women and minorities to earn income. *See also* Hair: Hair Straightening.

Further Reading: Berman, Judith C. "Bad Hair Days in the Paleolithic: Modern (Re)Constructions of the Cave Man." *American Anthropologist* 101, 2 (1999): 288–304; Bryer, Robin. *The History of Hair: Fashion and Fantasy Down the Ages*. London: Philip Wilson Publishers, 2000; Corson, Richard. *Fashions in Hair: The First Five Thousand Years*. London: Peter Owen, Tenth Impression, 2005; Harvey, Adia. "Becoming Entrepreneurs: Intersections of Race, Class, and Gender at the Black Beauty Salon." *Gender and Society* 19, 6 (2005): 789–808; Kunzig, Robert. "The Biology of . . . Hair," http://discover magazine.com/2002/feb/featbiology (accessed May 2007); Kwass, Michael. "Big Hair: A Wig History of Consumption in Eighteenth-Century France." *American Historical Review* June (2006): 631–659; Leeds Craig, Maxine. *Ain't I a Beauty Queen*. New York: Oxford University Press, 2002; Peiss, Kathy. "'Vital Industry' and Women's Ventures: Conceptualizing Gender in Twentieth Century Business History." *The Business History Review* 72, 2 (1998): 218–241; Sherrow, Victoria. *Encyclopedia of Hair: A Cultural History*. Westport, CT: Greenwood Press, 2006; Synnott, Anthony. "Shame and Glory: A Sociology of Hair." *The British Journal of Sociology* 38 (1987): 381–413.

Kara Van Cleaf

Hair Removal

Humans have removed hair from both their bodies and their heads since prehistoric times. Evidence left in tombs and other artifacts that suggest hair removal—sharpened rocks and shells and even tweezers—date back to 3500 BCE. All cultures have altered their hair in one way or another, using methods as diverse as electrocuting hair follicles (electrolysis), rubbing it off with abrasive materials, burning it off with chemicals, or, the most common method today, shaving. Reasons for removing hair on the head or the body include the following of cultural and aesthetic norms or religious beliefs, the expression of individuality, as a form of punishment, to prevent disease, or in preparation for surgery or for a competitive sporting event. Despite the historically consistent practice of hair removal, an easy and permanent technology for removal has yet to be developed, and the ways hair is removed are almost exactly similar to those used prehistorically. Perhaps part of being human includes ceaselessly removing hair.

Head

Humans have removed the hair on their heads since at least as early as the ancient Egyptians. They removed their hair to keep cool and to thwart parasite infestation, such as lice, on the scalp and body. However, wealthy Egyptians wore wigs because they considered appearing bald a marker of lower status, even though the lower classes also wore wigs, though of lesser quality. In addition, Egyptian priests were required to be hairless and no hair, human or otherwise, was allowed in their centers of religious worship.

One of the most common reasons for removing the hair on the head is because of some form of religious worship, devotion, or practice. Hair removal has been practiced by monks, nuns, priests, and other religious leaders. Indian political and religious leader Mahatma Gandhi kept his head bald to embody his philosophy of simplicity and his rejection of British fashions. Many Buddhist followers, including the current Dalai Lama, keep their heads closely shaved too. For them, removing hair symbolizes the removal of vanity, the ego, and worldly connections. Religious leaders and followers who shave their heads are thought to let go of their concerns with their appearance and individuality and instead focus on their spiritual existence. Removal of hair also displays the person's separation from society. In contrast, some religions encourage followers to leave their hair untouched and uncut so as not to alter how God intended them to appear. The Rastafarians are an example of this, as were the Puritans, who were discouraged from engaging in cosmetic beautification.

Throughout history, removal of head hair has sometimes been used as a form of punishment. Hair often conveys a person's identity, rank, or personality, and removing it against their will inflicts humiliation, displays their oppression, or strips them of their power. This was especially so in ancient societies where hair was believed to be magical. Slaves in ancient Rome and Greece were required to have shaved heads as a marker of their inferior status. The Romans forced the Gauls to shave their long hair when they were conquered, and they also humiliated the early Christians by shaving their heads. Women accused of adultery in some ancient societies such as Babylon, Teutonic nations, and India were forced to remove their hair. Perhaps the largest incidence of violently forced hair removal was committed by the Nazis. They removed the hair of Jewish people as they arrived at the concentration camps to be used for industrial felt, yarn, or the manufacture of socks. The Soviets who came to dismantle the Auschwitz concentration camp found seven tons of hair in a warehouse on the premises. The Nazis also removed the beards and side locks worn by Orthodox Jews to further persecute them. Hair that was shorn from prisoners is now on display at the Auschwitz-Birkenau State Museum.

Some subcultures remove their hair for aesthetic and symbolic reasons. Some skinhead groups, subcultural groups that originally formed out of working-class British communities, shave their heads entirely to signal their rebellion against middle- and upper-class norms. While a wide variety of skinhead styles and politics now exist, skinhead men usually shave their heads and women sometimes shave parts of their head but leave bangs or fringe around their faces. Many athletes do it for practical reasons such as keeping cool, displaying their musculature, or to gain seconds in races. The bald, or closely shaven head, is currently accepted on men in almost all classes, especially as toupees have gone out of fashion and no complete cure has been found for baldness. Basketball star Michael Jordan is among those celebrities who popularized the bald look, and many men with thinning hair now opt for complete hair removal.

Baldness has a symbolic link with illness and death. Some groups in Afghanistan, Africa, and India shave their heads while they mourn the loss of a loved one. Baldness is often an outcome of chemotherapy treatments for patients with cancer. People have been known to remove their hair to support a cancer patient during treatment and recovery. Family members, classmates, and teachers of such patients usually do this. Sometimes people shave off their hair and donate it to charity to be used for wigs for cancer patients.

Somewhere between the removal of head hair and body hair lays the practice of removing hair around the hairline and the eyebrows. Court women of Tudor England did this to approach the look of Queen Elizabeth I, who removed hair at her hairline, which was thought to make her appear intelligent. The term "highbrow" now refers to anything elite or high culture. In contrast, it has been suggested that the Beatles' "lowbrow" hairstyles, hair growing down the forehead, in the 1960s ushered in a celebration of lowbrow culture—culture that appeals to and is consumed by the mass population and does not require elite education or experiences to appreciate.

Eyebrows of various widths, lengths, and colors have varied throughout history, and hair removal is often part of eyebrow maintenance. In Western culture, the "monobrow"—a continuation of one eyebrow into the next, across the forehead—has been considered unattractive, so waxing or plucking the eyebrows has been popular. Some people have removed all of the eyebrow hair and replaced it using eyebrow pencils or tattoos. During

World War II, women wore thicker eyebrows as they had less time to focus on beauty and perhaps to symbolize their strength as workers, since heavy eyebrows were considered more masculine. However, the 1950s reversed this trend for women and the heavily plucked, thin eyebrow was fashionable. The thin eyebrow did not last forever, though. In the 1980s, when women dressed in more masculine styles that included big shoulder pads, they also wore big, fuller eyebrows, as famously embodied by the model Brooke Shields.

Body

Across time and throughout different cultures, humans have altered and manipulated their body hair as much as they have their head hair. Archaeologists have found artifacts that suggest that humans used seashells to tweeze and remove body hair during prehistoric times. Men and women in ancient India and Egypt removed all of their body hair, and women from ancient Greece and Rome removed all of theirs. People from Eastern cultures, such as China, used two strings to remove body hair, and this method is still practiced today. Some cultures used chemical substances found in nature to burn away body hair. Native Americans used a caustic lye, and the ancient Turks used a mixture of arsenic, quicklime, and starch to burn off hair. Abrasive materials, such as pumice stones, have been used to rub hair off the skin. All of these methods are in use today, albeit in modified forms, and, then as now, are effective only until new hair breaks the surface of the skin.

Today, additional methods are available to remove body hair on the arms, armpits, legs, pubic region, and face. Permanent methods of hair removal include electrolysis and laser treatments. Electrolysis was invented in St. Louis, Missouri, in 1875. The procedure works by using an electrical current targeted into the hair follicle. Once the follicle receives the jolt of electricity, it is destroyed and no further hair can grow. This method is time consuming and painful, since each follicle must be penetrated by a probe and zapped. Laser therapy works similarly, with less effective results, only a laser beam instead of an electric current is used on the skin to destroy the hair follicle. The most common way of removing body hair, however, is through shaving. In 2002, $8 billion was spent on disposable razors in the United States. The majority of American women remove their leg, underarm, and facial hair, and many men shave their facial hair regularly. Increasing numbers of men are removing hair from other regions of their bodies, such as the back and pubic area.

The removal of body hair fluctuates historically. Ancient Caucasian women did not remove their body hair. When the Crusaders returned from the Middle East during the tenth century, Caucasian women began removing hair. This lasted until the 1500s, when the Queen of France, Catherine de Medici, called for such practices to stop. European and American women did not generally shave their legs or underarms between the sixteenth and nineteenth centuries, but the hairless norm for women resurfaced in the early part of the twentieth century, around 1920, nineteen years after the invention of the disposable razor. After World War I, women in America began to shave their legs in greater numbers, and today, around 98 percent of women shave their legs and underarms.

The surge in hair removal for women paralleled changes in fashion that displayed more of the body. Further, women began removing body hair more as they cut their hair shorter, gained the right to vote, and worked outside the home. Some historians and theorists argue that the co-occurrence of these trends worked to assuage fears of women taking too much of men's social powers. Hairless women offered a visual cue for sexual difference, as long hair had done previously. Hirsuteness has come to symbolize masculinity as the previous markers of it eroded with political and cultural shifts that led to some equality between the sexes. Bodily hairlessness for women and facial hairlessness for men also arose when United States was experiencing mass immigration from European countries. In fact, one way a group distances itself from others is by asserting the hairiness of the other groups. Hairlessness projected cleanliness and affluence, both of which conveyed social status and allowed for social differentiation.

Advertisers in the early part of the twentieth century could not refer to women's hair removal as "shaving" because that word connoted masculinity. Instead, they made appeals to hygiene, public appearance, and femininity. Many advertisements stressed the importance of removing hair in the privacy of one's home. Advertisers constructed hair removal as a private matter and body hair as a source of shame and embarrassment. Women were encouraged in the early twentieth century to remove body hair because such practices promoted good hygiene. Underarm hair was considered a haven for bacteria and a zone of unfavorable smells. Most girls in the West now begin removing body hair with the onset of puberty, and hairlessness of legs and underarms is the norm. Researchers have discovered that hairy women are considered masculine. Social scientists in the late twentieth century found that hairy women (with hair on the legs, underarms, and/or face) are identified as aggressive, unsociable, unfriendly, less sexual, and less moral than relatively hairless women.

Men too removed facial hair for reasons of hygiene during the twentieth century. Much of the discourse surrounding the male beard in the modern era debated the possibilities of the beard as either a protective barrier against airborne diseases or as nothing but a germ trap. In 1907, a French scientist walked with a bearded man and a clean-shaven man and then took samples from their face to test for bacteria. The sample from the bearded man had many more bacteria and items such as spiders' legs. The fear of infections, especially tuberculosis, combined with the distribution of disposable razors popularized the clean-shaven look. People today report removing hair for hygienic reasons, although it has been pointed out that often removing hair breaks the skin and can lead to infections such as folliculitis (inflammation of the follicle), especially when removal takes place somewhere public where many people are de-haired.

In addition, an increasingly popular practice today is the removal of pubic hair, although this aesthetic norm has origins as far back as ancient Egypt, where both men and women removed their pubic hair. (Women in ancient Greece removed their pubic hair to appear more "civilized," and sometimes people replaced their pubic hair with a patch of false hair known as a merkin.) After the 1960s, more Western women and men began removing their pubic hair and today a popular trend is the Brazilian wax, or the total removal of pubic hair. Although the Yanomami of South America remove all of their bodily hair for aesthetic reasons, the so-called Brazilian wax was popularized using this name as a marketing term created in New York City for the complete removal of pubic hair, except for a small strip. This look was adopted from pornography and marketed to the general public. It allows women to wear little clothing and still appear hairless. Men are increasingly removing their pubic hair too. Fashions spur the removal of hair now just as they did in the early part of the twentieth century. The more flesh that is visible, the more likely any hair growing in visible places is removed.

Some groups purposely go against hair norms to display their disagreement with society and some do it to symbolically remove themselves from society, as with monks and nuns. Some feminists, lesbians, and hippies have let their body hair grow naturally to display a contestation with the traditional markers of femininity and the beauty norms and work femininity requires. *See also* Hair: Cultural History of Hair.

Further Reading: Basow, Susan, and J. Willis. "Perceptions of Body Hair on White Women: Effects of Labeling." *Psychological Reports* 89 (2002): 571–576; Black, P., and U. Sharma. "Men are real, Women are 'Made Up:' Beauty Therapy and the Construction of Feminity." *The Sociological Review* (2001): 100–116; Bryer, Robin. *The History of Hair: Fashion and Fantasy Down the Ages*. London: Philip Wilson Publishers, 2000; Corson, Richard. *Fashions in Hair: The First Five Thousand Years*. London: Peter Owen, Tenth Impression, 2005; Hope, C. "Caucasian Female Body Hair and American Culture." *Journal of American Culture* 5 (1982): 93–99; Lewis, J. M. "Caucasion Body Hair Management: A Key to Gender and Species Identification in U.S. Culture." *Journal of American Culture* 10 (1987): 7–18; Sherrow, Victoria. *Encyclopedia of Hair: A Cultural History*. Westport, CT: Greenwood Press, 2006.

Kara Van Cleaf

Hair Straightening

Hair straightening refers to the chemical or mechanical process of breaking down the bonds of hair in order to reduce a natural curl or wave in the hair. Straight hair emerged as a widespread style in America at the turn of the twentieth century with the influx of beauty products targeted to African Americans and other ethnic minorities, whose hair is often naturally curly. The history of hair straightening in America is tied to the history of racism, although today many people straighten their hair for reasons other than to conform to racist beauty ideals.

Hair curls, kinks, or waves due to the shape of the hair follicle and the protein bonds within the hair strands. People with wavy, curly, or kinky hair have more oval-shaped follicles while those with straight hair have more circular-shaped follicles. Ethnic variations in hair include that people of African decent tend to have follicles shaped more oval in form, as compared to people of Asiatic decent, whose hair follicles and shape tend

Advertisement for Madam C. J. Walker's hair products. Courtesy of Library of Congress, LC-DIG-ppmsca-02902.

toward a circular form. To alter the shape of the hair, the bonds within the hair strands must be altered since the shape of the hair follicle itself cannot be changed. Straightening the hair is temporary—the follicle keeps producing the same shape of hair despite manipulation of the hair strands.

Methods

Methods to straighten hair work by breaking the bonds within the hair strand, which can remain broken until new hairs grow in or the hair is exposed to moisture. Hair straighteners work by either chemically or mechanically (or sometimes both) breaking down the bonds that create curls. Temporary hair straightening operates by breaking the hydrogen bonds of the hair, while longer-lasting straighteners act on the disulphide bonds. Breaking down the stronger disulphide bonds requires using alkaline solutions. Such solutions require mixing with a heavy grease or cream to protect the scalp from burns. Heated irons and combs have been used, as have caustic chemicals such as lye to straighten hair. Lye was used to create the "conk" (slang for congalene) look for African American men. Sometimes combs had to be heated to 500 degrees Fahrenheit to work properly. Oils and heavy greases would be applied to the hair and then a hot comb brushed through it. Once electricity was harnessed, flat irons were developed that dissipated heat across the hair more safely and efficiently. Women and some men have straightened, and continue to straighten, their hair, and straightened hair has been highly controversial in racial politics.

Racial Politics

Because hair is such a relatively easy body part to manipulate, and because hair is symbolically coded in both racialized and gendered ways, African American women's relation to U.S. beauty standards has often been enacted on their hair. The prevailing beauty standard for most of America's history has been based on white, European features that include light skin and straight hair. Numerous African American authors have written both fiction and nonfiction accounts of the politics of hair and beauty. For example, in Zora Neal Hurston's book *Their Eyes Were Watching God*, the hair of the main character, Janie, is straighter and less kinky than other members of the community, and takes center stage in the story. Her husband forces her to keep her hair tied up and covered, which symbolized his control over her. Upon his death, she lets down her hair and burns all her head scarves. Other writers such as Toni Morrison, in *The Bluest Eye* (1965), and, more recently, Zadie Smith, in *White Teeth* (2000), have also tackled the subject.

The history of hair straightening in African American communities follows the country's history of racial politics. One of the first female and African American millionaires, Madam C. J. Walker (1867–1919), made her fortune from creating and marketing a chemical hair straightener. She invented a hair cream called Madam Walker's Wonderful Hair Grower that was first marketed to the masses in 1905. Hair straightening was popular for women and older girls throughout the first half of the twentieth century. In many African American communities, straightening one's hair was a matter of pride that suggested one was proper and well-groomed. Straightened hair garnered the respect of the local community and was also expected by the dominant white, middle-class culture. As immigrants from southern Europe arrived in America, they too straightened their often-curly hair to blend in with the dominant culture. However, even before the civil rights movement, not all of the black community embraced hair straightening; it was seen by some as imitating whites and disregarding African features. Despite criticisms of hair straightening, such practices allowed many African Americans to set up successful businesses and achieve financial independence.

During the civil rights movement in the 1950s and 1960s, many African Americans questioned the dominant beauty standards. Although much of the early civil rights movement focused on legal and social reforms, the movement also became invested in the racial politics of beauty. The assertion that "black is beautiful" meant, among other things, the rejection of white beauty standards and the celebration of the natural texture of African American hair. During and after the civil rights movement, wearing unstraightened hair came to suggest pride in one's ethnicity and race. The

Afro became a popular style, at least initially signifying a rejection of racism in American culture. The Afro, also called "a natural," rose in popularity as some black activists rejected assimilation and advocated cultural pride, separatism, and black-identity politics. First worn by radical black activists and politically active college students, the Afro was initially highly controversial in African American communities. The appearance of the Afro on the cover of the popular black magazine *Ebony* in 1968 caused uproar from its readers. The image of Angela Davis, a radical activist and member of the Communist Party who was charged in a widely publicized murder and kidnapping case, brought the Afro international attention. Eventually the Afro spread in popularity and became an iconic part of 1970s style for the masses.

For men, the conk gained popularity in the 1920s and did not go out of mainstream fashion until the 1960s. African American men in urban centers wore the conk to appear hip and professional, yet for some black men the conk symbolized unacceptable vanity. Malcolm X famously detailed his first conk in his autobiography, as well as his decision to reject the conk and the painful process of hair straightening. James Brown's famous conk was seen as "old school," and his new hairstyle was presented to the world at about the same time as his widely influential song "Say It Loud—I'm Black and I'm Proud."

White women of all ethnicities also straightened their hair, especially during the 1960s and 1970s with the popularity of the hippie look. Currently, a popular look is the "blow-out" in which the hair is blown straight with a blow-dryer and assisted by a straightening gel that often contains silica. Most blow-outs are performed by professional hairdressers.

The development of newer technologies of hair straightening has rendered the process less painful and less toxic. Straight hair today is seen as an acceptable and desirable style for women and men of all ethnicities. It is estimated that currently two thirds of all African American women straighten their hair. In the 1990s, hair-straightening techniques became popular for Caucasian women when extremely straight hair became fashionable.

Further Reading: Ashe, Bertram D. "'Why Don't He Like My Hair?:' Constructing African American Standards of Beauty in Toni Morrison's *Song of Solomon* and Zora Neale Hurston's *Their Eyes Were Watching God.*" *African American Review* 29 (1995): 579–92; Bryd, Ayana, and Lori L. Tharps. *Hair Story: Untangling the Roots of Black Hair in America.* New York: St. Martin's Press, 2001; Cleage, P. "Hairpeace." *African American Review* 27 (1993): 37–41; Leeds Craig, Maxine. *Ain't I a Beauty Queen.* New York: Oxford University Press, 2002; Mercer, Kobena. "Black Hair/Style Politics." *New Formations* 3 (1987): 33–54; Sherrow, Victoria. *Encyclopedia of Hair: A Cultural History.* Westport, CT: Greenwood Press, 2006.

Kara Van Cleaf

Shaving and Waxing of Pubic Hair

The removal of body hair is a practice that reflects adherence to cultural dictates about both beauty and hygiene. Spanning centuries and regions of the world, both full, bushy pubic hair and completely hairless pubic regions have been the norm. In cultures where humans were primarily naked, a full display of pubic hair signaled a female's sexual maturity and ability to reproduce. Pubic hair was an erotic visual trigger and a trap for the scent of pheromones, chemicals that act as sexual attractants. In modern times, pubic hair is groomed in a range of styles.

The ancient civilizations of Egypt, Greece, and Rome, and Arab civilizations dating back to the Crusades preferred the removal of pubic hair and considered it unclean. In Muslim cultures, the goal of Islamic teachings is to cleanse the body, soul, and mind, and in order to prepare oneself for this, one must possess *fitra* (an innate human nature or natural state) which is characterized by five practices: circumcision, shaving the pubic hair, cutting the mustache short, clipping the nails, and removing the hair from the armpits. Because cleanliness is considered central to faith and to prayer in Islam, Muslims (both men and women) are expected to maintain a state of good hygiene as defined by the fitra, which includes removal of the odor-causing and odor-collecting pubic hair. The fitra is not outlined in the Koran, but rather in *hadith*, or oral traditions as passed down from the Islamic prophet Muhammad, which help to determine traditional practices of daily life. According to the fitra, a person should not let his or her pubic hair grow for more than forty days and should remove it by any means with which they feel comfortable.

In sixteenth-century Turkey, women were so fixated on pubic hair removal that there were special rooms in the public baths devoted to just this purpose, but by the early nineteenth century, it had nearly disappeared from practice. The next time pubic hair removal would surface was in twentieth-century America, but even then there were periods of time when this fashion would waiver. Second-wave feminists in the 1970s insisted on a "natural" pubic region in much the same way that they rejected the wearing of makeup. This decade in U.S. history marks a major turning point for matters of female empowerment, and women began to feel that by using makeup, grooming themselves excessively, wearing restrictive and uncomfortable clothing, and removing their body hair, they were pandering to definitions of themselves that had been delineated by men. The empowered, professionally employed, sexually evolved woman of the 1970s showed her sense of equality by presenting her body in a more natural, and arguably prideful, way than she had ever done so before. However, the evolution toward more revealing swimwear paved the way for a more dramatic range of pubic hair fashion, including complete removal.

Hair removal certainly reflects regional attitudes and trends, and in the United States, women have been coaxed into associating body hair with masculinity and uncleanliness. In 1915, the Wilkinson Sword Company, a razor manufacturer, designed a marketing campaign to convince American women that underarm hair was both unfeminine and unhygienic. Armpit hair in women has carried a stigma of uncleanliness or foreignness. The stigma associated with underarm hair has developed over time into a cultural intolerance and has extended to almost all areas of a woman's body that has any trace of hair.

The hairless genital region has become the overwhelming erotic ideal at the start of the twenty-first century, as reflected by both the number of participants in removal procedures and its prevalence in pornography. This trend was ignited in Brazil in the 1980s, when near-complete removal of pubic hair was necessary to accommodate the highly revealing thong bikini. The Brazilian wax is characterized by nearly total (with the exception of a tiny strip of hair above the vulva) removal of hair from the pubic area, including the hair on the upper thigh, the buttocks, and around the anus. It was introduced to the United States in 1987, when seven Brazilian sisters, Jocely, Jonice, Joyce, Janea, Jussara, Juracy, and Judseia Padilha, opened up a waxing salon in New York City. Bikini lines have never since been the same.

In art, the vast majority of female nudes have been depicted without pubic hair (even though men, in contrast have been represented more accurately with full and natural pubic hair). The oldest known significant female nude sculpture is of Aphrodite of Cnidus, created by Praxiteles (ca. 350 BCE); her hairless form set the standard for much of female nude representation in art. More modern examples of adult women in full, though completely hairless, nudity are *Roger Freeing Angelica* (1819) and *The Source* (1856) by French painter Jean Auguste Dominique Ingres (1780–1867).

In fact, this image of the hairless female was so prevalent that a Victorian-era scholar, John Ruskin, who was a virgin upon the time of his marriage, was so horrified and disgusted by the tuft of hair between his bride's legs that he had their marriage annulled. Even at a time when women were leaving their pubic hair full, men's expectations had more to do with representation than reality.

In the late twentieth century, the consistent representation of a hairless genital region in pornography influenced cultural expectations for the genital hairstyles of women. The removal of pubic hair exposes the female genital opening, arguably a visual sexual trigger: some speculate that a hairless genital region appeals to the male fetishistic fantasy of virginal innocence. Some enthusiasts of hairlessness suggest that it affords a heightened sensitivity to tactile stimulation, and improves the experience of oral sex for both the giver and the receiver.

Further Reading: Kiefer, Otto. *Sexual Life in Ancient Rome.* London: Routledge, 1934; Lester, Paul Martin, and Susan Dente Ross. "Body Hair Removal: The 'Mundane' Production of Normative Femininity." *Sex Roles* 52 (2005): 399–406; Licht, Hans. *Sexual Life in Ancient Greece.* London: Routledge, 1932; Manniche, Lise. *Sexual Life in Ancient Egypt.* London: Kegan Paul International, 1987; Morris, Desmond. *The Naked Woman: A Study of the Female Body.* New York: Thomas Dunne Books, 2004; Synnott, Anthony. "Shame and Glory: A Sociology of Hair." *The British Journal of Sociology* 38 (1987): 381–413; Toeriena, M., and S. Wilkinsonb. "Exploring the Depilation Norm: A Qualitative Questionnaire Study of Women's Body Hair Removal." *Qualitative Research in Psychology* 1 (2004): 69–92; Ryan, Patrick J. "Fellowship in Faith: Jewish, Christian and Muslim." American: The National Catholic Weekly; https://americamagazine.org/content/article.cfm?article_id=2925; Female Magazine. http://www.femail.com.au/brazilianwax.htm; http://www.ibiblio.org/wm/paint/auth/ingres/; http://www.jeanaugusteingres.artvibrations.com/jeanaugusteingres/index/index.php; http://www.quikshave.com/timeline.htm; http://www.understanding-islam.com/rb/mb-049.htm.

Alana Welch

Hands

Cultural History of the Hands

The human hand is seen by many as an essential component in the development of civilization and culture. While not uniquely human (technically other primates also have hands), hands display certain characteristics often associated with the distinctive development of human societies. The evolution of the opposable thumb and the dexterity that comes with it, for example, are important for a number of reasons, as are the communicative and expressive aspects of the hand, an association that can be traced as far back as prehistoric cave paintings. There are a number of important themes in cultural history related to these somewhat distinctive characteristics of the human hand. Despite their recurrence, the various meanings of and associations with the human hand also vary in different cultural contexts and epochs.

Communication and Expression

The first and one of the most important aspects of the hands in relation to culture is that they are communicative or expressive. This property is evident in the wide variety of methods of communication involving the hands. Some of these methods, such as sign language, are more formalized and are often utilized independently of speech. There are well over 100 different types of sign language across the globe, including those developed within deaf communities and independent of any spoken language, those invented in an attempt to manually represent a particular spoken language, and those developed by the hearing in situations where speaking is not possible. As with spoken languages, this wide variation is also accompanied by regional differences within specific sign languages. Sign language as a form of communication can be very expressive, representing manually even the more subtle meanings of spoken language through tones and facial expressions.

Other methods of communication using the hands are less formal than sign language and are often integrated with speech. For example, in the United States, an extended middle finger is an obscene insult, while a handshake can cement an agreement or a friendship. Gesturing, the use of the hands to communicate often as a complement to verbal communication, is usually closely integrated with other forms of body language such as facial expression and posture. The specific manner in which the hands are used during social interaction varies cross-culturally, as do the acceptable amount of gesturing and other rules governing appropriate use. Given the way that gesturing can be used to add emotion or emphasis to speech, it is often utilized in contexts such as public speaking or acting. In each of these contexts, the speaker uses gestures and other nonverbal forms of communication in conjunction with speech in order to express a particular emotion or elicit an emotional response from the audience.

The communicative or expressive properties of hands can be seen not only in the many ways that they are used to communicate and express but also in the adornment and decoration of the hands themselves. There are many different methods of adornment such as rings, henna, and tattoos, which vary widely across cultures and historical periods. In addition to the variety of methods, there are many different reasons for adornment of the hands. The specific construction and manner of wear can influence meaning. A ring, for example, can take on different meanings based on its material and construction as well as the particular hand or finger on which it is worn. In the context of U.S. organized crime, the pinky ring (a ring worn on the little finger) has symbolized power and prestige, but during the 1950s and 1960s, it was also a subtle way for gay men to identify themselves and each other. More mainstream examples in the American context include engagement rings, which usually highlight a solitary diamond; wedding bands, which are often more plain; and various wedding anniversary rings that usually include a larger number of small diamonds. Rings can even symbolize membership in a graduating class, fraternity, sorority, or trade association.

Another method of adorning the hands, commonly known as Mehndi, has been practiced by Muslims, Hindus, and Christians in India, North Africa, and the Middle East for more than 5,000 years. While there are dozens of different names for this practice depending on the region and culture, the basic technique and associated meanings are similar. A brownish-red paste is made from the henna plant and then painstakingly painted on the body, especially the hands and feet. Once the paste dries, it is removed, leaving a reddish-orange stain on the skin underneath. The designs are usually extremely intricate and are said to bring good luck, prosperity, or good fortune. Mehndi is most often associated with wedding ceremonies, a tradition that in some areas (North India, for example) has become increasingly popular. While in some cases Mehndi would be reserved mostly for the bride, it has become more common for a number of women in attendance to also receive henna designs. This increased popularity has enabled henna artists to charge higher and higher fees, even providing steady, profitable employment opportunities for women in some areas. The practice of Mehndi has even gained popularity in the United States as a semipermanent form of body modification.

A more permanent method of adorning the hands is tattooing. While tattooing has been applied to the entire body, tattoos on the hands have gained a somewhat special status. Despite the slowly growing acceptance of tattoos on other parts of the body, tattooed hands are still seen by many as signifying criminal involvement or gang affiliation. Many reputable tattoo shops have policies against tattooing customer's hands for this reason as well as for those of quality control. Most tattoo artists depend heavily on their reputations, even touching up their work free of charge as it fades. Given the amount of use and abuse hands receive on a daily basis, when tattooed they often do not heal properly or become faded and otherwise marred quickly. Thus, many legitimate tattoo artists would rather not stake their reputation on a hand tattoo that will most likely lose its original beauty and detail.

Despite this reluctance by many legitimate tattoo artists, tattooed hands are common in certain contexts. In fact, the association between tattooed hands and criminal involvement or gang affiliation is not an unfounded one. A popular tattoo among English sailors was a sparrow on the back of each hand, originally signifying a 5,000-mile journey or ensuring safe passage home. More recent meanings among the English working class include freedom from prison or fast hands in a fight. A number of underground or street organizations maintain complex codes using tattoos on the hands and other parts of the body. Many African American, Latino/a, and Southeast Asian gangs use series of numbers that may be an area code or street number signifying territory claimed by a particular group. Tattooed numbers may also be a display of allegiance, the member's rank, or symbolize the group's rules or code of ethics. For example, the Almighty Latin King and Queen Nation bases its ideology on the Five Points of the Crown: respect, honesty, unity, knowledge, and love. Another popular tattoo among Latino/a and Southeast Asian gangs consists of three dots in a pyramid shape between the thumb and index finger that stand for "i vida loca" or "my crazy life." Gang tattoos can also chronicle certain elements of an individual's personal history, such as crimes committed or time served in prison. This approach is especially important to the complex code of Russian prison tattoos, which includes small tattoos on the hands worn by career criminals to display their specialization. While tattoos can be intended as a badge of honor or to inspire fear, there are also a number of gang tattoos meant specifically to antagonize rival gangs. Such adversarial tattoos often include coded insults or threats. One common example often found on the hands is the Bloods' use of the letters CK for "Crip Killer" and, alternately, the Crips' use of the letters BK for "Blood Killer."

Training and Work

Another important aspect of human hands is their sensitivity and tactility and the way that they are used to manipulate the material world. This can be seen in the association of the hands with work and labor as well as in the learning of a skill or craft. Humans have been making and using tools for approximately 2.5 million years, behavior that has been linked to the coevolution of distinctive physical characteristics such as handedness, thumb strength, and wrist flexibility. These characteristics are essential to the ability to construct and manipulate complex tools, a quality that is unique to humans. It is common to speak of manual labor or skilled craftsmanship with machines or tools as "working with one's hands" or as "hands-on." In the U.S. context, this is often associated with a kind of pride in the work ethic of Americans as well as a certain nostalgia for working-class or blue-collar culture. Despite this pride, there are some negative stereotypes associated with working with one's hands. People in these occupations, especially those doing work requiring less training, are sometimes seen as uneducated, unintelligent, or boorish.

In addition to learning a skill or trade, further development of the dexterity made possible by the unique physical characteristics of human hands is often conducted in learning a sport. Some sports require players to catch and handle a ball under difficult circumstances: the wide receiver position in American football, for example. Other sports involve a very specific grip such as the flexibility of the wrists when holding a golf club. Many styles of martial arts involve even more rigorous training of the hands. Wrestlers of the Japanese *sumo* style toughen the palms of their hands by slapping them against a large pole repeatedly. They engage in this grueling exercise to toughen their hands in preparation for the powerful shoving that takes place during a match. Many other martial arts styles have been known to use bags filled with hard materials or wooden blocks as instruments to strengthen the hands. Martial artists practice various open- and closed-handed strikes using these instruments, attempting to strengthen different parts of the hand that can then be turned against an opponent.

While athletes and martial artists work to develop gross motor movements and hand strength, others work to refine their fine motor skills. Chinese embroidery has existed for several thousand years and requires extremely fine weaving and stitching techniques. Large rugs and blankets as well as clothing are all made of silk and woven by hand. Some of the more detailed works include hundreds of different colors of silk thread and may take up to five years to complete. One thread is split into as many as forty-eight smaller strands, a technique that requires such fine motor skills and eyesight that embroiderers are known to need breaks every fifteen to twenty minutes. Most embroiderers begin training at around seven years of age and are now required to do eye exercises to prevent damage. The European tradition of making lace by hand also requires dexterity and a sensitive touch. While Chinese embroidery is usually made in very dense, colorful patterns depicting different themes from Chinese culture, lace has an open pattern made by looping, twisting, or knotting the cotton thread, a technique that has been preserved mostly in Eastern Europe.

Of course, some of the skills related to the sensitivity or tactility of the hands are not necessarily associated with legitimate occupations and can include different forms of deception, such as sleight of hand and pickpocketing. Sleight of hand usually refers to a number of different tricks that are used to deceive an audience or victim through the speed and dexterity of the hands. Such tricks can be used to make a small object seem to disappear, in shell games, card tricks, rope tricks, and other minor magic tricks. Those who can perform tricks using sleight of hand may employ the hands to manipulate objects in deceptive ways (such as "palming" a coin) or to direct attention away from an object that is then hidden or passed to the other hand; both techniques require the use of hand and finger muscles not often applied in daily life. The proficient use of these muscles requires much practice and training, as does the skill of pickpocketing. Picking pockets usually refers to the theft of money, a wallet, or other object from the pocket of someone's pants, coat, or purse. While there are a number of techniques, some requiring an accomplice, most of them depend heavily on misdirection and the speed and dexterity of the hands. A pickpocket may bump into the victim or make some other sort of casual physical contact in order to divert their attention and, while apologizing, slip their wallet from their pocket. Often pickpockets use a newspaper or coat to cover the hand removing the wallet. A spilled drink or staged argument can also be used as distraction while the thumb and index finger are used to quickly remove the victim's wallet.

Character and Spirituality

A third characteristic of the hands is the idea that they are somehow reflective of some fundamental truth about a person's character or destiny. This characteristic can even be associated with the ways that hands are used to express religious or spiritual sentiments. The ancient practice of palmistry or chiromancy, the prediction of a person's future or exploration of certain elements of their character based on the hands, is one example of this association. Throughout history, there have been many different approaches to palmistry, each with its own specific elements. Each identifies different characteristics of the hand as signs to be interpreted. It is commonly believed that palmists look only at the length of the lines on the palm; however, palmists may interpret a person's future or character based on the size, color, texture, shape, flexibility, or other characteristics of their fingers, fingernails, the backs of their hands, and the lines or creases in their palms.

While its history is a long and interesting one, there are also a number of popular myths about palmistry. Despite the fact that texts on palmistry were brought back to Europe by Crusaders during the twelfth and thirteenth centuries and translated from Arabic into Latin, the popular belief persists that it was introduced by the Gypsies several hundred years later. Later, in the sixteenth and seventeenth centuries, English writers such as George Wharton and Thomas Hyll began to write about palmistry in an attempt to remove its lower-class and Gypsy associations. Amid a plethora of other pseudosciences, the popularity of palmistry grew, as did its rationalization. This is evidenced in a change in nomenclature from the more mystical "chiromancy" to the more scientific "chirology." Another common myth is that palmistry was banned by the Catholic Church. In fact, palmistry is mentioned in the Bible and due to its connection to medieval medicine and mathematics was considered part of the classical education required for clergy. Many myths about palmistry are linked to famous figures. During the thirteenth, fourteenth, and fifteenth centuries, numerous texts on palmistry were written and falsely attributed to Aristotle. Another popular tale has Aristotle discovering an ancient treatise on palm reading on an altar to the god Hermes. While it is likely that the ancient Greeks including Aristotle had some general knowledge of palmistry by the fourth century BCE through their contact with India and China, there is little evidence to substantiate extensive knowledge or writing on the subject. Even Julius Caesar is often said to have used palmistry to judge his soldiers and, according to one popular story, used it to reveal an imposter. However, the Roman upper classes were much fonder of astrology; palm reading was seen as somewhat beneath them. The veracity of many of these popular stories is uncertain due to the fact that the traditions of palmistry have historically been passed orally. Despite the lack of historical record, however, it is clear that people in many different cultures have believed in and practiced palm reading for thousands of years.

The hands are also important in many religious contexts. Prayer is one among many religious acts in which the hands can be important. During prayer, adherents of a range of religions may fold, clasp, or hold their hands upraised. They may kneel and lay their hands on the ground with their palms up, hold sticks of burning incense, make the sign of the cross, or hold hands with one another. The Buddhist *mudras*, or hand gestures, while not technically prayers, bear some similarity to these different practices of prayer, each supposedly imparting a specific quality to or signifying the intention of the practitioner through its incorporation in the practice of meditation. For example, in the gesture of pressing the earth, the left and right hand positions signal meditation and pressing the earth to stand for Buddha's meditations on emptiness and his overcoming of difficulties. The mudra also is a prominent symbol in Buddhist art and architecture, often featured in statues of the different Buddhas.

Hands are also important to Christian iconography. One example is the meaning attached to stigmata, or spontaneous bodily wounds supposedly representative of the wounds suffered by Jesus Christ during his crucifixion, especially on the hands. These wounds have been reported by members of the clergy and extremely devout Catholics throughout history, starting in the thirteenth century. Stigmatics, the majority of whom have been women, often experience pain, illness, and visions. One of the most famous of these women, Catherine of Siena, experienced stigmata in 1375 until her death in 1381, and is one of only a handful of women to be declared a doctor of the church. St. Francis of Assisi, another famous Catholic figure, is usually credited as the first reported case of stigmata, having experienced it in Italy during an extended fast in 1224. Although the phenomenon has been reported with some regularity since the thirteenth century, a dramatic increase occurred in the twentieth century. One of the most famous stigmatics, Padre Pio, who first experienced stigmata in 1918, is also said to have experienced physical and mental attacks by Satan. While stigmata are not a significant part of Christian art or architecture, they have become part of popular culture, inspiring a network of avid believers, numerous films, and themes for television show episodes. The most recent well-known stigmatic, Giorgio Bongiovanni, has published articles and given numerous televised speeches and interviews, including warnings about the inevitability of World War III and a link between Christianity and extraterrestrials.

Another connection between the hands and spirituality is the notion that all of the world's religions are divided into those of the Left-Hand Path and those of the Right-Hand Path. In essence, Left-Hand Path religions rely on the power of the individual self and the carnal or worldly, while the Right-Hand Path is focused on adherence to a moral code, the otherworldly, and transcendence through faith. This division is most often referenced by believers in Left-Hand Path religions in an attempt to legitimize their beliefs, as most scholars and believers in Right-Hand Path religions do not recognize Left-Hand Path forms of spirituality as true religions. This division is thought to have begun with a somewhat obscure form of Hinduism known as Tantra, whose followers believe that in addition to traditional Hindu practices, one can achieve spiritual enlightenment through rituals that involve sexual activity, the consumption of alcohol and other intoxicating substances, and animal sacrifice. The idea became popular in early twentieth century Western occult writings and later in the New Age movement. Examples of religions considered to be of the Left-Hand Path include Dark Paganism, First Church of Satan, and the Temple of Set, while most Western and Judeo-Christian religions are considered Right-Hand Path. The origin of this terminology is thought to be linked to ideas about left and right in which the left is considered evil, unlucky, dark, or abnormal, while the right is considered good, competent, or lucky. This ancient set of associations with left and right is also evidenced by ideas about handedness.

Handedness, the dominance of one hand over the other, has long been associated with character. It is fairly well known that the majority of people are more proficient with their right hand; however, there are a percentage who are left-handed (5 to 30 percent). While being left-handed has historically been associated with negative traits, right-handedness is often associated with positive ones. This is evident in a number of words and phrases that use the word "right" in reference to the law or justice, authority, and correctness. Some of the negative traits associated with left-handedness include being clumsy, awkward, unintelligent, untrustworthy, devious, or lazy. This prejudice is evident in a wide variety of words and colloquialisms, for example the expression that one has "two left feet." Negative expressions and etymological associations can be found in a wide variety of cultures and languages, appearing in classical Latin dating from the first century BCE. On the other hand, in most Latin-based and European languages, the word for "right" connotes correctness, justice, and even skill. These connotations are not restricted to Western and Latin-based languages. A number of insulting terms in Hungarian (a Finno-Ugric language) make use of the word for "left," while in Mandarin Chinese (a Sino-Tibetan language), the word for "left" also carries the meaning of impropriety or illegality.

Punishment

As they can sometimes be associated with negative traits, it is not surprising that hands have also been implicated in different methods of punishment. Many violent forms of punishment and even penal codes have been based around the axiom "an eye for an eye," a quotation from Exodus 21: 23-27 that expresses the principal of retributive justice and has roots in ancient Babylonian law. This approach to punishment is especially relevant to theft, which, according to some interpretations of this axiom, justifies the severing of a hand. Despite the seemingly harsh formulation of this principle, many religious texts, including the Talmud and Koran, seem to encourage a more moderate interpretation. In U.S. educational settings, corporal punishment was long seen as necessary to the proper discipline of children. These punishments could include being struck on the palm or back of the hand with a wooden ruler or rod and were frequently accompanied by references to the intransigence of children along with the expression "spare the rod and spoil the child." Even now, this form of punishment is still legal in certain states in the United States and is used in many others despite its illegality.

Another practice that continues despite having been outlawed in many places is torture. While there are many forms and degrees of torture, those that target the hands do so not only to inflict maximum pain but also to affect the victim's ability to use their hands later in life. Some methods of torture inflicted on the hands include forcible removal of fingernails, beating with hard objects, handcuffing in painful positions for long periods of time, dislocation of joints, burning with heat or chemicals, and crushing of bones. While these forms of punishment are inflicted on the hands by others and against the will of the victim, there are those who punish themselves through physical violence to their hands. In the world of Japanese organized crime, *yakuza*, a serious offense against their code of conduct must be righted by the removal of the first joint of one's own little finger. Any further offenses would call for removal of the next joint, and so on. Such punishment is said to be reminiscent of ancient Japan, in which a man's grip on his sword was weakened by the partial loss of a finger, leaving him vulnerable and drawing him further into the yakuza community for protection. *See also* Hands: Mehndi; and Hands: The Hand in Marriage.

Further Reading: Cryan, John R. "Banning of Corporal Punishment in Childcare, School and Other Educative Settings in the U.S." *Childhood Education* 63, no. 3 (February 1987): 146–53; Dowdey, Patrick, and Meifan Zhang, (ed.). *Threads of Light: Chinese Embroidery and the Photography of Robert Glenn Ketchum.* Los Angeles: UCLA, 2002; Fitzherbert, Andrew. *The Palmist's Companion: A History and Bibliography of Palmistry.* Lanham, MD: Rowman & Littlefield, 1992; Gattuso, John, ed. *Talking to God: Portrait of a World at Prayer.* Milford, NJ: Stone Creek Publications, 2006; Gibson, Kathleen R., and Tim Ingold. *Tools, Language and Cognition in Human Evolution.* Cambridge: Cambridge University Press, 1995; Heselt van Dinter, Maarten. *The World of Tattoo: An Illustrated History.* Amsterdam: KIT Publishers, 2005; Kaplan, David E., and Alec Dubro. *Yakuza: Japan's Criminal Underworld.* Berkeley: University of California Press, 2003; Liddell, Scott K. *Grammar, Gesture, and Meaning in American Sign Language.* Cambridge: Cambridge University Press, 2003; Lovell, Simon. *How to Cheat at Everything: A Con Man Reveals the Secrets of the Esoteric Trade of Cheating, Scams, and Hustles.* New York: Thunder's Mouth Press, 2006; Mannix, Daniel P. *History of Torture.* Glouchestershire, UK: Sutton Publishing, 2003; Roome, Loretta. *Mehndi: The Timeless Art of Henna Painting.* New York: St. Martin's Griffin, 1998; Rosenbaum, Michael. *The Fighting Arts: Their Evolution from Secret Societies to Modern Times.* Wolfeboro,

NH: YMAA Publication Center, 2002; Roth, Melissa. *The Left Stuff: How the Left-handed Have Survived and Thrived in a Right-handed World.* M. Evans, 2005.

Mike Jolley

Mehndi

The practice known as *Mehndi* (alternately referred to as *Mehendi* and *Hina*, taken from the Hindustani) refers to the temporary application of henna pigment to the skin (predominantly the hands and feet) for the purposes of adornment. Mehndi is practiced in South Asian, Middle Eastern, and North African cultures, but has more recently become popular as a form of temporary skin decoration in Western cultures.

The origins of Mehndi are difficult to conclusively fix, given competing historical accounts. Some historical evidence suggests that Mehndi skin decoration began in India, while other historians believe the Mughals introduced the practice to India in the twelfth century CE. There is also strong historical evidence that indicates that Mehndi can be traced back to the ancient Egyptian civilizations, where henna was used to mark the fingers and toes of pharaohs prior to the mummification process, in preparation for the afterlife.

Mehndi at the India Day Festival, Worcester State College. (AP Photo/Worcester Telegram & Gazette, Paula B. Ferazzi)

It is, however, generally agreed that the art of Mehndi is an ancient practice spanning a range of cultures. Intricate Mehndi designs are most often
applied to the hands and feets of brides prior to their wedding ceremonies;
however, traditions in countries such as India, Bangladesh, Pakistan, and the
Sudan also see bridegrooms decorated. In many Middle Eastern cultures,
Mehndi skin decorations are applied for a range of special occasions, including weddings and engagements, family gatherings, festivals, during the seventh month of pregnancy, and after the birth of a child.

Henna paste is used in the application of Mehndi designs for its distinctive ochre pigment. The henna is traditionally applied to the skin with
small, fine, metal-tipped jacquard bottles to achieve the necessary design
intricacies. Henna itself is derived from a plant known as the *Lawsonia
inermis*, grown in hot, arid climes such as North Africa and South Asia. Indian designs are distinctively reddish brown, however, as Arab henna artists
heat the paste prior to its application, these designs are usually darker in
color.

Mehndi designs are regarded as auspicious, hence their centrality to celebrations and ceremonies such as weddings. However, many Muslim women
in Middle Eastern cultures decorate their hands and feet with Mehndi
designs throughout the year, as Islam regards the application of henna as sacred (or "*sunnah*"). Indian Mehndi designs often include depictions of pea-
cocks (the national bird of India), elephants with raised trunks (a symbol of
good luck), and the sacred lotus flower. Mehndi wedding designs can also
include the names of both the bride and groom hidden in the intricate
design.

The designs of Mehndi decoration vary from culture to culture. Middle
Eastern Mehndi deploys floral designs that recall Arabic art. North African
Mehndi also uses floral motifs, but structured in a more geometric pattern.
Indian and Pakistani Mehndi styles often extend beyond the decoration of
the hands and feet, with paisley patterns and teardrop shapes covering the
arms and legs. In southern Asia, Mehndi designs incorporate influences
from both Indian and Middle Eastern decoration, but usually include solid
blocks of color on the fingertips and toes.

Mehndi body decoration has now become more widespread and popular
in traditional cultures, and increasingly their application is not only limited
to special occasions and ceremonies. Professional Mehndi artists have developed ready-made patterns and stencils for all parts of the body, as Mehndi
now is not strictly limited to adorning the hands and feet. Interestingly, this
expanded application of Mehndi, and the commodification of designs and
techniques in cultures where henna skin decoration has long been a tradition, has been attributed in part to the interest Western cultures have more
recently taken in Mehndi skin adornment. U.S. celebrities such as Gwen Ste-
fani and Madonna have decorated themselves with Mehndi designs, and,
given their high profiles and popular cultural influence, have made Mehndi
skin art fashionable and sought after in contemporary Western cultures.

In the last few decades in the West, tattoos (a body decoration that was
once considered the domain only of men—particularly those from the
working classes—and prisoners) have become more popular, enjoying a

decidedly mainstream fashion appeal. Given this, the introduction of Mehndi skin decoration to the West via music and film celebrities has provided an expressive, alternative form of body adornment that does not have the permanence of a tattoo, and does not involve the use of needles (or the experience of pain) in its application.

In the wake of the popularity of henna skin art in the West, Mehndi designs have become increasingly commodified in cultures beyond those that have traditionally engaged in Mehndi skin adornment, particularly in the West. This turn to a commodification of the ancient art of henna skin decoration has had complex cultural effects. Paradoxically, it could be argued that the appeal of the "exotic" to the West is what is being marketed as a saleable item, even as the West simultaneously (and actively) espouses hostility, suspicion, and fear of Middle Eastern and Asian cultures (especially in the wake of the 9/11 terrorist attacks). The taking up of henna skin art and the widespread popularity of traditional Mehndi body art in the West signifies a form of cultural appropriation, whereby Mehndi practice and designs have been absorbed into a capitalist logic of commodification and consumerist desire. In a push to answer a Western desire for the consumption and colonization of the "exotic," the practice of Mehndi is drained of its traditional meaning and cultural significance. A critical postcolonial viewpoint might see this as a kind of symbolic violence toward the cultures for whom the practice of Mehndi is central and sacred.

Further Reading: DeMello, Margo. *Bodies of Inscription: A Cultural History of the Modern Tattoo Community.* Durham, NC: Duke University Press, 2000; Polhemus, Ted. *Hot Bodies, Cool Styles: New Techniques in Self-Adornment.* London: Thames & Hudson, 2004; Roome, Loretta. *Mehndi: The Timeless Art of Henna Painting.* New York: St. Martin's Griffin, 1998.

Samantha Murray

The Hand in Marriage

The cultural history of the hand includes its deep symbolic significance in uniting individuals and families in marriage. To take another's "hand in marriage" is a concept that has long historical precedent, including in Greek and Roman antiquity and in pagan and medieval Europe.

Roman Matrimony

Manus literally means "hand" in Latin. Manus in early ancient Rome referred to one kind of *iustum matrimonium*, or marriage between two people, who were legally eligible to marry. Roman law specified who could marry based on citizenship and social status. In the early days of the Roman republic, the ceremony involved the joining of hands of the bride and groom before witnesses. Manus was also called *coemptio*, or "purchase," because the groom would pay a symbolic sum in money or goods and receive a bride in exchange. A more formal marriage ceremony involving manus was the *confarreatio*. Receiving its name from a cake of spelt (*far*) used during the ceremony, the confarreatio was presided over by Rome's most senior religious officials, the Pontifex Maximus and the Flamen Dialis, and required the presence of ten witnesses. Restricted to those whose parents had been married under confarreatio, this type of elaborate marriage ceremony was exclusive to the patrician class. Rome's Vestal Virgins were selected from girls born out of confarreatio marriage.

Paterfamilias and *Patria Potestas*

The joining of hands in a manus marriage ceremony symbolized a marital arrangement in which the legal authority *patria potestas* (explained below) was transferred from the *paterfamilias*, or patriarch, of the bride's family to the bridegroom. In Roman society, the paterfamilias was a free, male citizen who had legal authority over his own person, called *sui iuris*. Usually, not only was the eldest surviving male in the male line of a family free from another's authority, but he also had authority over every other person in the family. In a manus marriage, a paterfamilias wielded two principal kinds of authority: he held *potestas* over his wife, his children, and his children's descendents; and he held *dominium* over all property, including household slaves. In most cases, a wife who entered into a manus marriage held the same legal status as her children.

Patria potestas, according to Roman jurists, was unique among ancient societies, and a manus marriage conferred wide-sweeping authority to bridegrooms. While wives, sons, daughters, and descendents could manage property and exact transactions using monies, estates, and goods owned by the bridegroom, they could not legally own property. Any goods or monies earned or acquired by those under the authority of the paterfamilias were legally considered his property. The paterfamilias also had the authority to arrange marriages and to initiate divorces among his dependents. In the first century CE, for example, the emperor Augustus forced his stepson Tiberius to divorce from a happy marriage to marry his own daughter Julia, in hopes that Julia would bear a son by Tiberius, who would in turn be descended by blood from Augustus.

In principle, the paterfamilias held the legal power of life and death over members of his familia. The paterfamilias decided whether or not to raise or to kill, by exposure to the elements, any child who was born in his household. While this power was probably rarely executed, Roman legend also reports of fathers who killed their sons for treason. In the *Lex de Maritandis Ordinibus*, which provided legislation designed to encourage marriage, especially among the elite, Emperor Augustus also provided the paterfamilias with the explicit authority to kill a daughter caught in the act of committing adultery. Believing that male children were needed for the administration of the Roman Empire, Augustus sought through these laws to encourage the Roman elite to breed. As an incentive for women to marry and have children, the *Lex de Maritandis Ordinibus* offered the personal freedom of sui iuris to any Roman citizen woman who bore three children who survived to adulthood, and to any freed former slave who bore four children who survived. In such cases, a Roman matron could be freed by law from the manus of her husband if she married under manus.

A woman's own father could grant his daughter the freedom of legal authority over her own person before she married. In such cases, a wife retained her sui iuris status after marriage. While a woman might be free from the potestas of her husband (or, in the case of a manus marriage in which the bridegroom was still under the potestas of his father, her father-in-law), if granted sui iuris, she did not have potestas or any comparable legal power over others, including her own children. In the case of divorces, which were quite frequent in Roman society, custody of and all legal authority over the children of the divorced couple would reside with father. In a free marriage (that is, a marriage without manus), the bride's natal paterfamilias retained patria potestas. In such cases, a woman could inherit property from her natal paterfamilias. The legal transference of authority from the woman's natal to marital paterfamilias in a manus marriage could be avoided if a wife stayed away from her husband's house for three nights each year. Manus marriage seems to have fallen largely out of favor among the patrician class by the middle of the first century BCE.

Greek Matrimony

The hand was also significantly symbolic in vase paintings that depict ancient Greek marriages. The process of marriage began with an *engye*, or a verbal contract between a prospective bridegroom and the prospective bride's father or *kyrios* (legal guardian), represented in at least one fifth-century Attic vase painting by a handshake between two male parties. Part of the negotiations during the engye involved settling upon the groom a dowry for the maintenance of the bride, which would transfer back to the bride if the marriage ended in divorce or if she became a widow. The engye constituted one element in the larger process that brought about a *gamos*, or marriage, which also included the actual ritual of the wedding, the sexual union of the bride and groom, and the subsequent living together.

The Wedding

The constituent parts of the wedding ceremony are well attested in Greek literature and art. Weddings began, as did all significant undertakings in ancient Greece, with prenuptial sacrifices and offerings to the gods. Brides gave offerings of clothing and childhood toys to Artemis, the goddess of virginity and ritual transition from girlhood to womanhood, and to Aphrodite, the goddess of sexuality and human fertility. Prior to the ceremony, both bride and groom bathed themselves as a form of ritual purification using water from sacred springs and special vases. The father of the bride or groom hosted an elaborate feast in which meat from the sacrificial offerings to the gods and sesame cakes were served to the guests. Choral songs accompanied by dancing took place; the songs' lyrics praised the beauty of the bride and the excellence of the groom.

The feast was preparatory to the heart of the Greek wedding ceremony, which involved a procession by torchlight leading the bride from the house of her father to the house of the groom. A fair number of classical vases depict this procession, some of which represent the bride and groom in a chariot or cart, while others show the bride and groom on foot. This latter group of processional images typically depicts at the center of the procession the groom glancing backward toward the bride while clasping her right or left hand or wrist as an accompanying female companion pulls back the bride's veil to reveal her face. The clasping of the bride's hand or wrist symbolizes not only the essence of the ceremony itself and the transference of the bride to the groom's household, but also the sexual and domestic union that are about to take place. This is particularly clear in vase paintings in which a winged Eros appears between the bride and groom (or stands in place of the female companion as the figure who conducts the *anakalypteria*, or unveiling of the bride). Thus, the clasped hand or wrist was an iconographic marker for the entire process of the gamos.

The Kyrios

The relative agency of the male and passivity of the female in the hand/wrist-clasping images is significant because it embodies the legal status of the bride in relation to the groom. Every woman had a *kyrios*, or legal guardian, who represented her in legal cases, conducted business on her behalf, oversaw transactional exchanges involving property she owned or inherited, and arranged marriages on her behalf. In ancient Athens, a woman was allowed to have on her person only enough money to purchase a bushel of grain, since her kyrios was expected to do most financial transactions for the household. The kyrios was usually the woman's father before marriage (if he did not survive, it was usually the eldest male in her father's line), but the wedding procession ritually enacted the transference of the authority of the bride's natal kyrios to her new husband.

Pagan and Medieval Handfasting

The hand's historical significance in uniting two people into marriage is also suggested in the ancient pagan practice of handfasting. Handfasting is based on the handshake used to seal a contract. Handfasting was used in ancient Europe and survived through the medieval period, and in some places until the early twentieth century. In a handfasting ritual, a couple's wrists were bound together, often by a cord, and sometimes a knot was tied, leading to the expression "tie the knot." The hands often remained tied together throughout the ceremony, sometimes until the union was consummated. Handfasting was usually used as a betrothal ritual, signifying an agreement that the couple would be married in another season, or, in some cases, in a year and a day.

Wrist tying was also sometimes used in marriage ceremonies, and in some places, handfasting was the equivalent of a marriage ceremony performed by nonclergy. Handfasting constituted "a solemn, binding contract" that was the equivalent of marriage in the British Isles, Germany, and the United States from the sixteenth to the eighteenth centuries, and in Scotland up until the early twentieth century. In Sir Walter Scott's novel *The Monastery*, the handfasting ceremony suggested a trial marriage lasting a year and a day, leading to the popular perception that handfasting was a temporary union that could be easily ended.

Neopagans, Wiccans, and others interested in Celtic and Pagan history have revived handfasting as part of contemporary marriage ceremonies, although the practice of handfasting for betrothal has all but died out.

Further Reading: Dixon, Susan. *The Roman Family*. Baltimore, MD: The Johns Hopkins University Press, 1992; Fantham, Elaine, Helene Peet Foley, et al. *Women in the Classical World*. Oxford: Oxford University Press, 1994; Harris, W. V. "Child-Exposure in the Roman Empire," *The Journal of Roman Studies* 84 (1994): 1–22; Johnston, David. *Roman Law in Context*. Cambridge: Cambridge University Press, 1999; Oakley, John H., and Rebecca H. Sinos. *The Wedding in Ancient Athens*. Madison: The University of Wisconsin Press, 1993; Yalom, Marilyn. *A History of the Wife*. New York: HarperCollins, 2001.

Angela Gosetti-Murrayjohn and Victoria Pitts-Taylor

Head

Cultural History of the Head

Many of the distinctive features of human culture and existence have historically been associated with the human head. The story of human evolution is inextricable from changes in the shape and size of the head, brain, jaw, and other facial features. Though their exact relationship is still debated, these changes have often been linked to human intelligence and the ability to communicate using complex symbols. The abstract intelligence and methods of communication are essential to the distinctiveness of human culture and civilization; however, ideas about the human head are not significant just to the study of evolution. The head is also important in the history of Western thought, including philosophy, medicine, and psychology, and penology, and it is relevant to many different symbols and practices associated with punishment, fashion, warfare, and the display of social status.

Adornment and Display

Adorning the head is an ancient practice. Various methods of and reasons for adornment can be found in different cultures and parts of the world. Some of the materials used to adorn the head include straw, felt, plastic, leather, paper, velvet, horsehair, silk, taffeta, fur, and feathers. At times, some of these materials (beaver fur and egret feathers, for example) became so popular that the animals from which they were harvested were hunted to the brink of extinction. It is impossible to determine when people first began adorning their heads, but there are a wide variety of reasons for wearing headgear. Some reasons are practical, such as for warmth or protection, while others are to display or communicate something about the wearer to others. In fact, the use of head decoration to reveal certain personal traits has become one of its defining characteristics. Indeed, one of the earliest known hats was the skullcap worn by freed slaves during the Roman Empire to indicate their liberated status, a symbolic association that was carried over into eighteenth-century revolutionary struggles.

One common use of head adornment is as an indication of rank or status in religious or spiritual settings, such as the *mitre* in the hierarchy of the Catholic Church or the ceremonial headdresses in any number of tribal societies involving shaman or healers. Most of these headdresses are constructed of local materials that are highly symbolic and available only to a privileged few. Often the collection of materials and the construction of the headdress is highly ritualized, sometimes using rare or valuable items and involving great skill. For example, many Native American tribal headdresses were composed of items that were difficult to obtain and required careful manipulation like eagle feathers, buffalo horns, and porcupine quills. Such headdresses would be worn only for specific ceremonies and could be possessed only by the "medicine man." On the other hand, some headdresses, while also displayed for religious or spiritual reasons, are readily available and commonly worn. For example, the veil worn primarily (although not exclusively) by women in many Middle Eastern and Muslim cultures is sometimes seen as a way to maintain gender separation in everyday life, an important principle for some followers of Islam.

Hats have been fashionable for both women and men in various times since antiquity. The wearing of hats by ancient people is usually associated with rank or practical use rather than fashion, but was nonetheless popular. For example, the *fez* or *tarbush* dates back to ancient Greece and is still worn throughout the Middle East, South Asia, and some parts of Southeast Asia. With the collapse of the Western Roman Empire by the Middle Ages and the resulting proliferation of monarchies and court society, hats became even more important to the display of rank and even more varied. Economic changes associated with modernity made hats more available to those outside the royalty or aristocracy. The burgeoning urbanization of Europe also contributed to this increase in popularity and variety beginning in the Middle Ages and extending into the Renaissance. The term "milliner" originally referred to Milan-based dealers in expensive accessories during the sixteenth century, a time when ornate women's hats became particularly popular throughout Europe. For some time, millinery designated the profession of making hats for men and women; however, makers of men's hats have since come to be known as hatters or hat makers. In France, the term "*chapelier*" was used for quite some time, recently being replaced by the word "*modiste*." During times when feathers were a popular component of hats, such as in the early nineteenth century, another professional, the *plumassier*, specialized in the preparation and dying of feathers, often working closely with milliners. While in previous eras, Milan, Paris, and London each had their time as the center of hat fashion, beginning in the 1930s, New York City's department stores led the way with a variety of small-brimmed styles. Throughout the late twentieth and early twenty-first centuries, the different styles and overall popularity of the hat have varied as the fashion industry has undergone rapid changes. Although the term "millinery" is still used in the United States to refer to hat making, hat design has become less specialized and is now much more open to fashion designers of different backgrounds.

Another common use of head adornment is the indication of inclusion or solidarity. In modern times, hats are worn to support sports teams, especially by football, soccer, baseball, rugby, and hockey fans. These hats usually represent the team through displaying team colors, a logo, and/or a mascot. Rivalries can become somewhat heated based on these displays of support; however, the use of head adornment by street gangs is linked to even more violent circumstances. Street gangs wear baseball caps and bandannas to display their affiliations; these can be a source of violent conflict with rival gangs, often resulting in members being beaten, stabbed, or shot. Gangs may choose to represent membership using baseball caps or bandannas that display their gang colors or other symbolic associations, including letters that stand for different phrases meant to disrespect a rival gang or symbols that are important to their ideology. For example, since it contains a five-pointed star, a symbol often used to represent an alliance of different gangs includes caps with the Dallas Cowboys professional football team logo; these are often worn by members of the People Nation. The symbol is part of their ideology, representing love, truth, peace, freedom, and justice. Despite the deviant and often-criminal activities of street gangs, membership is a source of identity and pride for many. Their appeal to many youth has been linked to a highly structured and hierarchical set of rituals. These structured sets of beliefs usually include a credo that references principles widely accepted as affirmative. This positive veneer facilitates recruitment and helps encourage loyalty and a feeling of righteousness as well as a sense of the gang as a structured organization. Another example of this type of display is the Texas Rangers professional hockey team logo, which looks like a pitchfork pointing downward. This symbol, sometimes worn by members of the People Nation, is a disrespectful inversion of the pitchfork used to symbolize their rivals, the Folk Nation. In addition to these symbolic associations, the manner of wear may also be used to represent membership. Baseball caps may be worn tilted to the right to represent gangs affiliated with the Folk Nation or to the left to represent affiliation with the People Nation.

In addition to the many different meanings associated with hats, some forms of head decoration also serve more practical purposes. Helmets, for example, protect the head of the wearer who is engaged in warfare, sports that involve physical contact, and the operation of heavy machinery or high-speed vehicles. Helmets have been made from a wide variety of materials ranging from wood or hardened leather to different metals to high-tech fibers like Kevlar. While helmets have been made and used for centuries, they have become more specific in their function and design. For example, as heavy artillery became more common in warfare, forged steel helmets became necessary for protection against arrows or swords, as opposed to the leather or bronze that was previously sufficient. In addition to practical concerns, this specificity of design can be linked to the absorption of different kinds of energy or impact and protection against certain kinds of objects. Technological advances in the study of aerodynamics and the development of high-strength fibers such as Kevlar also have been important.

While helmets are usually linked to a specific practical purpose, they often have symbolic importance as well. While people have decorated helmets for centuries, one of the earliest known standardized traditions is called "heraldry." This tradition became standardized in medieval Europe and started as a means of identifying combatants on the battlefield. During the Middle Ages, it became much more complex, involving the standardization of different colors and symbols as a way of representing nation, family lineage, rank, and other aspects of one's identity. There is also a heraldic tradition in Japan with some differences and similarities to the European tradition. Coincidentally, these traditions began around the same time period (the twelfth century) and were initially used by aristocratic families; however, unlike the European tradition, in Japan, the coat of arms, or *mon*, bears little standardization and a much less complex design. Another difference is the gradual adoption of mon by common people, as evidenced in its current use by families and businesses. The helmets utilized by modern military forces also often carry a symbolic representation of rank as well as specific role. The U.S. military, for example, has used a system of bars or stripes in the past as well as different symbols to designate medical field personnel.

Beginning with its emergence in post-World War II California, the Hells Angels Motorcycle Club (HAMC) has used a number of different symbols inspired by the military. Though not all members wear helmets, those who do often sport a winged skull, or "death's head," an insignia that was designed and trademarked by the HAMC. This insignia, while worn on the head, also makes use of the symbolic aspects of the head itself or, in this case, the skull. Depictions of the human skull have carried a number of varying symbolic associations in different cultures and time periods. In Western culture, the skull has been used as a warning of danger or death, most commonly seen in nineteenth-century poison warnings and in popular representations of pirates. While piracy has a long history throughout the world, many of its popular representations are loosely based on the Dutch, French, and English pirates who sailed the Caribbean during the seventeenth and eighteenth centuries. One of their intimidation tactics was the flying of a flag depicting a skull, usually paired with crossbones or other threatening images. The human skull has been used for intimidation in other contexts as well including by certain units of the U.S. Marine Corps and the British army. Not all representations of the human skull are intended to be negative or intimidating. Skulls are an important aspect of the Mexican *El Día de los* Muertos, or the Day of the Dead, a celebration to honor the dead that has its origins in ancient Aztec mythology. Skull-shaped candy, toys, and decorations are all traditional parts of this holiday and are reminiscent of Halloween.

Intellect, Character, and Personality

The word "head" is often used to indicate a formal or informal leadership role, for example, "a head of state." This use of the word to indicate leadership is usually connotative of initiative and strength as well as the ability to think strategically. This connotation can be seen more generally in ideas about the physical head being the center of initiative and intelligence. The association of the human head with intelligence, character, and the individual personality is important to the history of Western thought, as is evident in the number of theories of mind and brain as well as their development into a number of sciences and academic disciplines. While many of these are actually focused on the study of the brain, the nineteenth-century pseudosciences of phrenology and craniometry both dealt with certain aspects of the head itself.

Phrenology was developed by German physician Franz Joseph Gall (1758–1828) early in the nineteenth century and popularized in the United States and United Kingdom by Johann Spurzheim (1776–1832). While phrenology acknowledged the centrality of the brain to mental activity, phrenological analysis depended on the presumption of a correspondence between the shape of the skull and certain character traits. By feeling the bumps on a patient's skull, the phrenologist attempted to determine the frequency with which each of the twenty-seven "organs" of the brain and their associated psychological traits were used. Phrenology held a tenuous position in academia and was a source of intense scientific debate throughout the nineteenth century, eventually being discredited. Despite the skepticism of some academics, phrenologists received quite a bit of business, often being consulted for advice and as a form of background check for potential employees. As in these examples, phrenology was primarily used to assess one's character traits and psychological well-being. Craniometry, on the other hand, had a different set of uses.

Craniometry can be defined as the study of the overall shape and size of the skull and face. Practitioners of this pseudoscience made a number of causal arguments about the link between these physical characteristics, evolution, race, intelligence, and criminality. Unlike phrenology, craniometry was considered much more scientifically relevant and was an important part of the physical anthropology of the nineteenth century. Several different craniometrical theories were widely accepted, and one, Pieter Camper's theory of the facial angle, was used by Charles Darwin (1809–1882) as proof of his theory of evolution. Camper (1722–1789), a Dutch anatomist and anthropologist, theorized a relationship between the angle of the face and intelligence, resulting in his hierarchical categorization of different races. This use of craniometry as a way to justify assumptions and practices based on supposed racial differences became a recurring theme in the sciences, even being cited as an influence on the eugenics movement and Nazism. This theme is also reflected in the work of Samuel Morton (1799–1851) and his followers on "cranial capacity," a theory that linked the size of the skull and brain to the intelligence of different races. Despite being discredited for a number of reasons, including blatant falsification of data to fit stereotypical notions about race, in the twentieth century Morton's work was again referenced by white supremacists and in attempts to legitimize a biological basis for racial differences. Another well-known social scientist, Cesare Lombroso (1836–1909), used craniometry in conjunction with phrenology and physiognomy (the pseudoscientific study of facial features) in his biologically based theories of criminality. Influenced by Darwinism, Lombroso claimed that criminality was inherited and that criminals were, in fact, "savages" in a "devolved" or regressed state. Lombroso's biological determinism included a racial hierarchy not unlike those mentioned above as well as a number of stereotypical assumptions about gender. While seen as important to the development of the discipline of criminology, Lombroso's theories were commonly referenced by proponents of the eugenics movement and used to justify various types of stigmatization.

Punishment and Violence

Pseudoscientific theories are not the only way that the head has been linked to stigmatization and criminality. Punishment and torture have a long history and may be focused on the head for several reasons. Many of these techniques tend to be associated with major historical events such as the Spanish Inquisition; however, a number of torture techniques involving the head are still in use.

The first reason for the targeting of the head is fairly obvious: pain. The human head contains a large number of nerve endings and vulnerable points, making it a prime target. One torture device, known as the head crusher or vice, works by slowly clamping down tighter and tighter on the head; it was often used to extract confessions in the Middle Ages. This device has a long history and was recently featured in reports of a torture manual found in a safe house used by the terrorist organization al Qaeda. Head slapping has also received attention in recent debates about whether the U.S. Justice Department's interrogation techniques actually constitute torture.

Techniques involving psychological torture may be focused on the head. Simulated drowning involves dunking the victim's head into water or pouring water down the mouth and nasal passages, triggering the gag reflex. While this technique is painful, its main purpose is to disorient victims and make them believe that they are about to be drowned. Variations on this technique were also included in the U.S. Justice Department's recent statement about the interrogation of suspects by the U.S government. Another psychological torture technique often involving the head is sensory deprivation, such as hooding. This involves removing different types of stimuli for extended periods of time; it can cause anxiety, hallucinations, depression, and other severe effects on a victim's mental state.

Additionally, torture and punishment applied to the head can be intended to designate or mark the individual, often utilizing public space to do so. Such stigmatization has been used throughout history, for example, in colonial America, where even a minor crime like stealing could result in having one's ears slit. The pillory, a device that locked the head and arms in an uncomfortable position for an extended period of time while in public, was also a common punishment in Europe and the American colonies. This device subjected the victim to public degradation as well as the physical assault of people in the local community. The visibility of these forms of punishment was intended to humiliate the offender but also as a deterrent to others who would see the grim consequences of breaking the law.

The practice of beheading also utilizes this principle of public display. Beheading dates at least as far back as the punishment of Roman citizens and was considered to be a more honorable method of execution as opposed to crucifixion. It has been used all over the world, and, while condemned by human rights organizations, is still officially practiced in a few Middle Eastern countries. Despite being considered an unnecessarily brutal form of punishment, in many contexts beheading was considered more humane than other methods. This is due to its relative painlessness when performed correctly. Throughout history, a number of different tools have been used to perform this task, including various axes and swords (sometimes in combination with a block), as well as many different versions of the infamous French *guillotine* and the less well-known German *fallbeil*. Depending on the location and historical period, beheading was sometimes reserved only for important people or aristocrats, as in England well into the eighteenth century. It could also be reserved for the commission of certain crimes, especially treason or religious dissent. In legal systems based on the attempted extraction of confessions, such as in Europe until the late eighteenth century, beheading was used as the final measure after torture, relieving the victim from pain. In a rather different context, Japanese *samurai* subjected themselves to beheading intentionally from the twelfth well into the nineteenth century. This ritual suicide, also known as *seppuku* or *hara-kiri*, was committed by these warriors as a result of a defeat or dishonor. The ritual began with an excruciating disembowelment performed by the samurai on himself with a knife. It was then completed by his quick and precise beheading by another samurai using a long sword.

The practice of head-hunting is also closely linked to ritual as well as the reinforcement of hierarchy and the capture of an enemy's soul or life force. At different times, head-hunting has been practiced all over the world, including in parts of the Middle East, Asia, ancient Europe, and by American GIs in the Japanese theater of World War II. While sometimes intended to intimidate an enemy, the ritualization of head-hunting was most intense in Southeast Asia, Melanesia, and the Amazon Basin. Different tribal cultures in these areas engaged in a wide variety of rituals related to head-hunting, including preservation, shrinking, and personal and public display, often part of a complex cosmology. The study of these ritualized practices was integral to the development of anthropology in the nineteenth century but was mostly eliminated during colonization. *See also* Brain: Cultural History of the Brain; and Head: Veiling.

Further Reading: Attard, Robert. *Collecting Military Headgear: A Guide to 5000 Years of Helmet History.* Atglen, PA: Schiffer Publishing, 2004; Carlson, Elof Axel. *The Unfit: A History of a Bad Idea.* Woodbury, NY: Cold Spring Harbor Laboratory Press, 2001; Fox-Davies, Arthur Charles. *Complete Guide to Heraldry.* Sterling, 2007; Gould, Stephen Jay. *The Mismeasure of Man.* New York, NY: W. W. Norton & Company, 1996; "The Hat Bible," http://www.hatsuk.com/hatsuk/hatsukhtml/bible/history.htm; Henschen, Folke. *The Human Skull: A Cultural History.* New York: Frederick A. Praeger, 1966; Howard, David. *The Last Filipino Head Hunters.* San Francisco, CA: Last Gasp, 2001; McCoy, Alfred. *A Question of Torture: CIA Interrogation, from the Cold War to the War on Terror.* New York, NY: Holt Paperbacks, 2006; Mannix, Daniel P. *The History of Torture.* Gloucestershire, UK: Sutton Publishing, 2003; "History of Hats," http://www.thehatsite.com/historyofhats.html; Tomlinson, Stephen. *Head Masters: Phrenology, Secular Education, and Nineteenth-Century Social Thought.* Tuscaloosa, AZ: University of

Alabama Press, 2005; Valentine, Bill. *Gang Intelligence Manual: Identifying and Understanding Modern-Day Violent Gangs in the United States*. Boulder, CO: Paladin Press, 1995.

Mike Jolley

Head Shaping

Cranial modification, or head shaping, also known as artificial cranial deformation or cranial vault modification, is a practice that purposely alters the growth of an infant's head and changes the shape of her or his skull. Methods of head molding include cradle boarding, head binding, and the use of skull-molding caps or helmets. Because infants' skulls are softer than those of adults, they are malleable, and cultures that practice head molding generally begin the process shortly after infants' birth, continuing over months or years. The practice affects not only the shape of the skull but also the face, altering the appearance of the forehead and sometimes the shape of the mandible. There are many variations on cranial modification, and the practice has been documented worldwide across a number of cultures and on all continents. Historically, it is one of the most widespread forms of aesthetic body modification and has origins that date to the Neanderthals. It was common in antiquity, and especially widespread among indigenous people in both northern and southern continents. It is still practiced in South America among isolated tribes. Evidence for a range of types of cranial modification comes from human remains as well as eyewitness accounts from early colonial settlers in the New World who exhaustively documented such practices. Anthropologists of the nineteenth century debated the purposes and generated multiple typologies of cranial modification. In the twentieth century, anthropologists linked the practices to cultural, regional, and ethnic affinities. The purpose of the practice appears to vary, but head molding consistently conveys information about a person's identity.

Methods

There are numerous methods and types of cranial modification, along with many ways of cataloging them. Nineteenth-century anthropologists created many typologies of cranial modification that sought to capture minute distinctions in the head shape they created. More contemporary anthropologists link typologies with social context and method.

Among the types that were common in South America are annular vault modification and tabular vault modification. Annular vault modification creates a conical shape to the head, directed toward the back, often by binding the head tightly with bands or straps and constricting the circumference of the head. Tabular vault modification puts pressure on the anterior and posterior of the skull, flattening the frontal and/or occipital bones and creating expansion in the parietal region. Tabular vault modification may be erect, when pressure is put at roughly a 90-degree angle at the back of the skull, or oblique, where pressure is angled about 45 degrees, parallel to the frontal bone. Tabular vault modification requires more pressure and is often accomplished with the use of boards or tablets.

The methods of cranial modification depend upon the style preferred in each group, and range from wrapping the head to applying pressure with boards. Cradle boarding is a practice of securing an infant to a board worn on the back, also used for skull modification, undertaken for example by the Mayan peoples and the Navajo. Other various apparatuses of boards tied together have been used to shape the skull. Cranial binding is performed by wrapping the head with cloth or rope in order to reshape the head, with or without a board. Head pressing, which is practiced manually, usually by the mother, is sometimes used to reshape the skull, although with less dramatic results. Tight-fitting caps of wool or other material have also been used. The procedure can begin within days of birth, and often lasts from six months to a year, although in some cases up to five years. The effects are permanent.

Anthropologists have disagreed on whether the practice is painful or difficult for infants, with some investigating the physical side effects of the practice and others suggesting that infants were not especially stressed by the practice. Some researchers suggest that the procedure may cause porotic hyperostosis (an overgrowth of bone marrow in the skull) or occipital necrosis because it changes blood flow in the area, and can affect the sinuses. It was considered objectionable by colonial authorities who occupied native lands. For example, in 1585 the ecclesiastical court of Lima, Peru, banned the practice.

Meaning

A vast range of tribal groups have practiced head shaping from ancient Egypt to pre-Columbian civilizations. The historical meanings of cranial modification are not thoroughly understood, but cranial modification has been variously undertaken for beautification, to establish elite status, and to mark group identity as well as differences. It has been pointed out that as head molding must be performed in infancy, it is not used as a rite of passage, unlike many other forms of body modification. It is used, however, to convey information about a person's identity.

Among the Tiwanaku of northern Chile, living in about 400 CE–1000 CE, cranial vault modification was accomplished by wrapping the head with cloths. It may have been used as a way to self-identify the Tiwanaku ethnicity, in contrast to other tribal groups living in the area, such as the Atacameño people. Cranial vault modification may have represented a method of affirming local identities when migration patterns brought different groups together. In archeological findings, Tiwanaku males and females were equally likely to have modified skulls. In other tribal customs, however, skull modifications were sometimes gendered.

Cranial shaping is also thought to be used to express elite status. Some Egyptian royalty, including King Tutankhamen, appeared to have modified skulls.

Contemporary Head Shaping

High-tech skull-molding helmets are currently used in Western medicine to reshape the head of an infant whose skull has been flattened or misshapen during gestation, birth, or in the first few months of life, during which time the skull can flatten simply from sleep position. The use of head-shaping helmets reflects the Western preference for round (unflattened) head shape and is aimed primarily at cosmetic concerns, but can also be used to prevent complications from skull flattening. The practice of placing infants on their backs to sleep has become more common since sleep position was linked to sudden infant death syndrome. Since then, many infants in the United States have been prescribed helmets for what are known in Western medicine as "positional head deformities."

Further Reading: Hoshower, Lisa M., Jane Buikstra, Paul Goldstein, and Ann Webster. "Artificial Cranial Deformation at the OMO M10 Site: a Tiwanaku Complex from the Moquega Valley, Peru," *Latin American Antiquity* vol. 6, no. 2 (1995): 145–164; O'Laughlin V. D. "Effects of Different Kinds of Cranial Deformation on the Incidence of Wormian Bones." *American Journal of Physical Anthropology* 123 (2004): 146–155; Torres-Rouff, Christina. "Cranial Vault Modification and Ethnicity in Middle Horizon San Pedro de Atacama, Chile." *Cultural Anthropology* vol. 43, no. 1 (2002): 10–25; Trinkhaus, Erik. "Artificial Cranial Deformation in the Shanidar 1 and 5 Neandertals," *Current Anthropology* vol. 23, no. 2 (1982): 198–199.

Victoria Pitts-Taylor and Margaret Howard

Head Slashing

Head slashing is practiced by the Hamadsha, a religious sect located in Morocco, a predominately Muslim country in northeastern Africa. The Hamadsha is a small, controversial sect made up of mainly working-class and poor men who participate in rituals that include frenzied dancing, eating cacti, drinking boiling water, and punching themselves as well as head slashing, where the head is made to bleed by cutting it with knives and blades. While they are often bloody or otherwise appear to be self-harming, such practices are aimed primarily at healing the body and spirit.

The Hamadsha identify themselves as a small brotherhood of Sunni Muslims. They are strongly male dominated and deeply conservative. The Hamadsha trace their spiritual ancestry to the Sufi sects of Islam, to ancient Mediterranean cultures, and to sub-Saharan African pagan rituals and traditions. Hamadsha practice the more mystical elements of Islam, known as Sufism, although other mystical groups of Muslims may consider them severe and marginal. Within the Hamadsha are two closely related brotherhoods known for their worship of the Moroccan saints Sidi Ali ben Hamadsha and his servant, Sidi Ahmed Dghughi, who reportedly lived around 1700 CE. It is believed that head slashing originated with these saints. When Sidi Ahmed found Sidi Ali dead, he slashed his own head with an axe in distress and mourning. Afterward, throughout his life, in prayer and mourning, Sidi Ahmed would slash his head. The Hamadsha believe that through this action, Sidi Ahmed obtained the *baraka* of Sidi Ali.

The Hamadsha practice head slashing to combat vengeful spirits—specifically, in order to cure a person who has been attacked or possessed by such spirits, which are able to take on the form of a human or animal. These spirits are called Jnun (singular Jinn). The Hamadsha believe that the Jnun can be playful and whimsical, but also vengeful and potentially harmful, possibly even evil. According to the Hamadsha, there are countless Jnun that inhabit the earth. Their existence is supported in the Koran, the Muslim holy book. Usually, the victim of a Jnun attack, referred to as the *majnun*, may have harmed a Jnun spirit and is often unaware of his transgression. The Hamadsha believe that when these spirits attack a person, they can leave their victims blinded, mute, deaf, depressed, or even partially or completely paralyzed. They can also take over and possess an individual by enacting changes in behavior and causing fainting, tremors, or speaking in tongues.

Head slashing is one part of a set of practices aimed at the diagnosis and cure of the wounded or ill self. The Hamadsha treat symptoms that Western medicine might see as symptomatic of epilepsy, schizophrenia, depression, anxiety attacks, or other psychological or physical illnesses. Since the Hamadsha believe that physical and psychological ills are often the result of a Jnun attack, the only cure is to appease the offended spirit. Family members take the inflicted person to the muqaddim, or a Hamadasha leader. The muqaddim will attempt to identify the specific Jinn who has taken possession or inflicted the individual. The muqaddim may pull on the victim's ear, read from the Koran, make an animal sacrifice, or touch his head against that of the victim. The Jinn will then identify itself and what it wants from its victim. These requests usually range from having the victim dance in a certain manner to burning a particular type of incense. If the muqaddim is unable to tell what a Jinn desires, than he will try a number of different options in order to appease the Jinn.

A healing ritual, or *hadra*, takes place wherein the possessed or ill individual, a healer, or another Hamadsha member evokes possession of a spiritual force called the *baraka*. Most often it is the healer, or an authority in Hamadsha culture and religious ideology, who takes possession of the baraka. The healer dances and enters into a trance, slashing his head with small knives or blades in order to appease the Jinn spirit. Human blood is believed to contain baraka. The blood is collected and consumed by the ill individual in order to receive the grace of the baraka. One important female Jinn, Aisha Qandisha, is said to have a thirst for blood, and head slashing is also aimed at appeasing her.

The hadra can last up to several hours and is observed by a number of men, women, and even children. In this ceremony, primarily male participants call upon the spirit of Allah, the Muslim name for God, and dance, shout, and convulse while playing fast, frenzied music. The men dance while beating themselves until they are entranced. Once entranced, they use sharp instruments and knives to slash their faces and heads. The cuts can be minor or quite deep, even reaching the skull. Occasionally, a woman may join in the dancing and may cut her head or breast. While the hadra may appear especially bloody and painful to outsiders, the experience of this trance reportedly renders participants unaware of pain, discomfort, or wounding.

In addition to healing, these practices can also signify devotion and praise. The most sacred of the hadra ceremonies occurs shortly after the Islamic prophet Muhammad's birthday. During this ceremony, the Hamadsha use axes to slash their heads in order to calm the spirit of Aisha Qandisha. The dancers then take their blood and serve it, sometimes with bread, to the ill to consume.

Head slashing is a very controversial ritual that has been both pathologized and revered. Some see head slashing as a form of self-mutilation. Such critics not only see it as a form of religious zealotry, but worry about its dangers both to those wounding themselves and to those who are being treated for possession. There are a number of medical complications that can occur as a result of head slashing; these range from infection to permanent damage, and even death. In addition, those who are given human blood to drink may become ill from its consumption. Critics of the practice also worry that the person believed to be possessed by a Jinn may have an illness that requires more conventional medical care.

Though controversial, Crapanzano believes that the techniques of the Hamadsha are a form of therapy. The Hamadsha have a high success rate, in that quite often after their rituals, the person believed to be possessed is considered cured. Further, the practices create an opportunity for group formation and social bonding, and allow individuals to experience a social acknowledgement of personal illness and self-transformation.

Further Reading: Crapanzano, Vincent. *The Hamadsha: A Study in Moroccan Ethnopsychiatry.* Berkeley, CA: University of California Press, 1973; Favazza, Armando R. *Bodies Under Siege: Self-Mutilation in Culture and Psychiatry.* Baltimore, MD: The John Hopkins University Press, 1987.

Angelique C. Harris

Veiling

The headdress known today as the veil dates back 4,000 years to the ancient civilizations of Mesopotamia. Throughout history, this item of clothing worn over the head, mostly by women, and covering the body in different

One contemporary style of hijab, or Muslim veiling, is the headscarf, which covers the hair but not the face. Courtesy of Corbis.

degrees, has incited much political contention and debate concerning the role of women, multiculturalism, globalization, and religious freedom worldwide. Veiling, almost always except in cases of fashion, ties to religious practices and customs. Today, the most common group that regularly veils includes Muslim women; most current discussions and representations of veiling are associated with Islamic countries. However, three of the world's religions, Judaism, Christianity, and Islam, include veiling practices of some sort, and all three arose from the same geographical location, the Arabian Peninsula.

Islam

Islam, which translates to mean surrender or submission, is a religion that professes a total devotion to God. It is based on the teaching of Muhammad, the prophet to whom it is believed God revealed the Koran. Islam arose in the seventh century, during which time veiling was not a religious practice but a diffuse cultural practice throughout the Arabian Peninsula. Veiling symbolized class and status. Working women could not veil, as it was often impractical. As only the upper classes could afford to keep women from working, and so veiling was seen as a luxury and privilege. As Islam spread, it enveloped regional practices of veiling. As the male elite began interpreting the Koran, the veil took on religious significance. The Koran calls for modesty of both men and women and the hadiths, stories of Muhammad's life, tell stories of his veiled wives. Both texts, the Koran and the hadiths, have both been interpreted to support the veiling of women, although they have also been cited by opponents of veiling. The passage from the Koran used most often to support veiling states that women "not display their beauty and adornments" and instead "draw their head cover over their bosoms and not display their ornament" (S. 24:31). Other passages cited in support of veiling include the following: "And when you ask them [the Prophet's wives] for anything you want ask them from before a screen (hijab)" (S. 33:53) and "O Prophet! Tell your wives and daughters and the believing women that they should cast their outer garments over themselves, that is more convenient that they should be known and not molested" (S. 33:59).

The word "hijab" refers to the diverse ways Muslim women veil. The meaning of the word "hijab" more closely approximates the English verbs to screen and to cover than it is to the verb to veil. There are different types and degrees of hijab. The burka usually covers the entire face of its wearer, leaving only a mesh screen for the eyes. The chador is the full-body dress worn by Iranian women. A nikab is a veil that covers everything under the nose and cheeks and often wraps around top to cover the forehead. Women are expected to veil because any display of their bodies, hair, or faces may incite sexual, so-called impure, feelings in men, which contradicts the Islamic tenet of modesty. Thus, Muslim women veil to protect themselves and men from a masculine, unrestrained sexuality. They also veil to show their faith in Islam and to uphold their belief in the importance of modesty and the different sex roles of men and women. Today, many young women also veil to display resistance to the West and its consumerist and colonial culture. Further, veiled women claim that the practice grants them a freedom from the stares, advances and harassment from men in public and this allows them a greater productivity and reliance on their intellect in public spheres.

Opponents of the veil claim that the practice symbolizes women's servility to men. They argue that while the Koran does state that both sexes should practice modesty, it never demands that women veil. Interpretations that see the veil as mandatory for women have been made by a male-only Islamic clergy. Critics of the veil also argue that it does not inherently signify one's commitment to Islam, since veiling predates Islam and is therefore not solely a Muslim invention. Opponents see veiling as a practice that results from beliefs that women are impure, dangerous, and second-class citizens as compared to men. Veiling is an extension of the practice of purdah, which refers to the physical separation of women from men in the home and in society. Veiling maintains such separation when women leave the home. The anti-veiling argument calls for a greater equality and sharing of space and roles between the sexes.

The veil has been fought over for at least several centuries. At the turn of the nineteenth century many Eastern, Islamic countries became critical of veiling practices and in 1899 the ruler of Egypt, Qasim Amin, called for an end to veiling and other practices identified as misogynistic. As the twentieth century progressed, many Islamic nations criticized veiling because it was not seen as civilized. To compete with Western nations and convince them of their ability for self-governance, countries such as Turkey and Iran denounced the veil. In 1936, Reza Shah Pahlavi of Iran forcibly outlawed the veil and enforced Western dress, as did his son, who followed him as shah. Westernization programs faced a great deal of opposition, and the chador, the full-body cloak, was reinstated as required dress in 1979 when the Ayatollah Khomeini came to power and installed an Islamic theocracy. Some countries such as Tunisia still outlaw veiling although not without local opposition. In Turkey, a ban on veiling in universities was repealed in early 2008.

As the West encroached more on the social life and psyche of the world in the twentieth and twenty-first centuries, Muslims have revived the hijab as a marker of identity and opposition to Western ideals. It is not uncommon to find a range of veiling practices within a family. For example, a grandmother might veil because it is tradition, the mother doesn't veil because she is a professional, and the daughter veils to resist the colonialism of the West. Many Westerners view the veil as oppressive and unjust, and politicians have used Middle Eastern countries veiling practices as justifications for occupation and invasion.

Further controversies have arisen in the Western world, where the veil has been outlawed in schools, as in France, or criticized so sharply as to stigmatize those who wear it. Jack Straw, Britain's former foreign secretary, claimed that the veil created too much "separation and difference" and that it threatened the social harmony of the nation. After the 9/11 attacks, many Muslims reported feeling discriminated against for their religious practices and dress. Some Western politicians claim that any dress that obfuscates the wearer's face of body poses a security threat.

Instead of liberating women from traditional roles, the ban on the veil in Turkey may have thwarted women's advancement and participation in society, according to those who oppose the ban. Until recently, women who choose to wear the veil in Turkey cannot participate fully in some aspects of society—they could not teach in universities, practice law in court, work for the state, or serve as elected officials in Turkey's parliament. Women who sought an advanced degree must go abroad if they wear a veil. The ban was claimed to protect the rights of the non-veiling women and to encourage a secular public life. This is just one of the many examples of the politics surrounding the veil and the status of women.

Judaism

Jewish people also practice veiling. Historically, because a woman's hair was considered to be sexually arousing, Talmudic law required that women cover their heads. Virgins did not have to veil but married women did. Often, married women shaved their heads at marriage and would then wear a veil, scarf, or a wig. Some orthodox Jewish women still wear wigs and/or scarves over their own hair. Again, as with the Islamic practices, veiling or covering the head is meant to encourage modesty and assist men with sexual restraint because, according to Judaic beliefs, a woman's hair displayed her beauty. Despite the practice of wearing a scarf, wig, or veil among conservative sects, head covering is not as widespread within Judaism as it is within Islam.

Part of the Jewish wedding ritual includes "bedeken," or the veiling of the woman by her husband. Before the ceremony, the groom covers the bride with the veil and then removes the veil at its conclusion. This custom may have come from two different biblical stories. The first story is that of Rebecca in Genesis (24:65), who veils herself upon meeting Isaac, her husband. The second is from the story of Jacob (Genesis 25:33), who was fooled into marrying the wrong woman, Leah, after working to marry Rachel for seven years. Leah was veiled and so he did not know of the mistake until after the ceremony. Popular legend suggests that by veiling the bride himself, the groom is assured the bride is his wife.

Christianity

The Christian bride wears a veil, too; it is lifted by the groom at the end of the wedding ceremony. The practice of veiling the bride is thought to originate with the Romans, who veiled brides before marriage to protect them from evil spirits or from the eyes of outsiders. It has also been suggested that the veil symbolized a protective covering for the purity of the bride. Others suggest that the veil dates back to the times when a man would throw a blanket over the woman of his choosing for a wife. Nuns, so-called brides of Christ, also wear veils as a part of their habit. They wear a white veil during their first, canonical year and receive the black veil once they demonstrate their servility and dedication to God.

Christian women wore head coverings in church up until the 1900s. A passage in Corinthians (11:3) states that women should cover their heads, but not men. This practice is seldom followed today. The Catholic Church mandated that women veil in church in 1917, but officially reversed the custom in 1983. In this tradition, veiling while in church symbolized the covering of a woman's "glory," the source of her beauty, for the sake of celebrating the glory of God. Images, statues, and sculptures of Mary, the mother of Jesus, display her veiled. Further, the Apostle Paul encouraged women to veil to display their subordination to her husband. An unveiled woman could be justifiably punished.

Removing a women's hair in both Christian and Judaic traditions and writings is considered a form of punishment. A woman's hair in all three religions suggests her sexuality, which in some way threatens the customs and beliefs of each and has been the target of control. Recently, in response to the ban on veils in France, a schoolgirl shaved off her hair so she could adhere to both the French law of no veiling and the Islamic tenet of modesty.

It is difficult to consider the history of veiling without considering the history of patriarchy. All three religious traditions view the female body as harboring dangerous temptations that must be covered so as to protect the order of things. Such views imply that men's sexuality cannot be controlled without the help of women, and yet may constitute control of women's sexuality. But as some contemporary Muslim women claim, the veil grants women a freedom to move and speak in public without being reduced to a sexual object. One of the implications of such a view is a vast difference between the sexes in regard to sexuality.

Male Veil

Despite these historical and contemporary examples, women are not the only sex that wears the veil. The Tuareg of Saharan Africa are a Muslim group in which the men veil when they reach adolescence, while the women do not. Anthropologists claim that the Tuareg men veil to maintain social distance among relatives in their matrilineal society. The veil in this society, as in the others' discussed above, symbolically creates a distance from the wearer and others.

Men in a variety of religious and ethnic traditions wear a range of head coverings. The kamilavka, for instance, is worn by Orthodox Christian monks to symbolize their separation from the common people and their unique closeness to the godly. Other examples include the biretta, fez, turban, zucchetto, and fedora.

Further Reading: Ahmed, Leila. *Women and Gender in Islam: Historical Roots of a Modern Debate*. New Haven: Yale University Press, 1992; Caldwell, Patricia. "Lifting the Veil: Shared Cultural Values of Control." *Weber Studies* 7.2 (1990); Chesser, Barbara Jo. "Analysis of Wedding Rituals: An Attempt to Make Weddings More Meaningful." *Family Relations* 29 (1980): 204–209; El Guindi, Fadwa. *Veil: Modesty, Privacy and Resistance*. Oxford: Berg, 2000; Haddad, Yvonne Yazbeck, Jane I. Smith, and Kathleen M. Moore. *Muslim Women in America: The Challenge of Islamic Identity Today*. New York: Oxford University Press, 2006; Hirschmann, Nancy J. "Western Feminism, Eastern

Veiling, and the Question of Free Agency." *Constellations: An International Journal of Critical and Democratic Theory* 5 (1998): 345–369; McCloud, Aminah. "American Muslim Women and U.S. Society." *Journal of Law and Religion* 12 (1995–1996): 51–59; Murphy, Robert. "Social Distance and the Veil." *American Anthropologist* 66 (1964): 1,257–1,274; Read, J., and J. Bartkowski. "To Veil or Not to Veil? A Case Study of Identity Negotiation among Muslim Women in Austin, Texas." *Gender and Society* 14 (2000): 395–417; Sanders, Eli. "Interpreting Veils: Meanings have changed with politics, history." *Seattle Times*, May 27, 2003; Sechzer, Jeri Altneu. "'Islam and Woman: Where Tradition Meets Modernity:' History and Interpretations of Islamic Women's Status." *Sex Roles* 51 (2004): 263–272; Shirazi, Faegheh. *The Veil Unveiled: The Hijab in Modern Culture.* Gainesville: University Press of Florida, 2001; White, Elizabeth. "Purdah." *Frontiers: A Journal of Women Studies* 2 (1977): 31–42.

Kara Van Cleaf

Heart

Cultural History of the Heart

In cultures all over the world, the human heart is thought of as more than just an anatomical organ. From antiquity to modern times it has intrigued scientists, philosophers and artists. Ideas about the heart have been vastly disseminated throughout the world for centuries through the various channels of science, philosophy and religious and artistic imagery. Even to the present day, the heart is referred to by artists and writers, is represented symbolically in religions, and used to communicate the idea of love.

The heart is the central organ of the human circulatory system. It is comprised of muscles and valves that pump blood throughout the body via different types of blood vessels. It is located in the chest between the fourth and fifth ribs and in between the lungs. In an adult, it beats an average of seventy times per minute. What is known as the beating of the heart is the sound of the muscle contracting and relaxing as it pumps the blood throughout the rest of the body.

Early Beliefs

The belief that the heart was the site of both thought and emotion was widely held in the ancient world. Rather than being defined as an organ that simply fulfilled a physical role, the heart was also believed to contain one's soul and spirituality. Because of these early views of the heart, it still represents emotional and metaphysical aspects of human life.

As early as 3000 BCE, the heart was thought to house the soul of a person. In ancient Egyptian culture, the common belief was that a person's soul and essential being were located in the heart. This belief was reflected in Egyptian rituals around death. Once a person died, the quality of their eternal afterlife needed to be determined. They could either walk with the gods in happiness or suffer eternally, and the path of their outcome depended upon a judgment of the quality of the heart. Because the Egyptians believed the heart was the site of one's being, the heart was measured, literally, to determine the fate of a person's spirit. It was extracted

A heart symbol with initials can profess two people's love for one another. Courtesy of Corbis.

and used in a weighing ritual during which the heart was placed on one side of a scale. On the other side of the scale was a feather that represented truth. This ritual determined whether or not the person's heart weighted well against truth. If it did, it was believed that the person's spirit would walk with the gods in harmony for all of eternity, but if it did not, they would suffer in perpetuity. Without this ritual of the heart, it was also believed that the deceased could not transition into the afterlife. The weighing of the heart was the only path from death to the spirit world. It should be noted that the Egyptians were interested in the heart not only as a spiritual matter, but also a medical one. They were the authors of the first known treatise on the workings of the heart; their investigations into cardiology examined the relationship between the heart and the pulse.

In ancient Greece, the heart again had both physical and spiritual importance. Around the fourth century BCE, Aristotle wrote about the heart's physical, psychological and metaphysical roles. Aristotle (384–322 BCE) described the heart's anatomy, extrapolating from observations of dissected animals and other indirect methods, and determined it to be the center of the human body and its most important organ. He also wrote that the heart, which he believed to be a three-chambered organ, was the hottest organ and provided heat for the body; this heat was what gave life. It should be noted that Aristotle's work preceded the use of human dissection, which became more widespread in Alexandria in the third century BCE, and the subsequent discovery of the nervous system.

In contrast to the present day consensus that the heart is a pump that propels blood through the circulatory system and that the brain is the organ of the mind, the Greeks had two competing theories about the roles of the heart and brain. While the encephalocentric theorists, who included the early physician Hippocrates, believed the brain is the ruling organ of the body, the cardiocentrists—among them, Aristotle and the Stoics—believed the heart to be the ruling organ of the body. Aristotle believed that the heart housed the mind, emotion and memory, and in particular, the soul.

Aristotle's cardiocentrism was partly affirmed by Galen, a Roman royal physician in the second century CE. Galen's treatise *On the Usefulness of the Parts of the Body*, a work which made advancements in the knowledge of circulation that were highly influential in the development of anatomy and cardiology, asserted that the heart was directly connected to the soul. Galen, however, diverged from Aristotle's view that the heart alone was the most important organ. While Galen believed that the heart generated "vital" blood, Galen also emphasized the liver as a producer of "nutritive" blood. Further, Galen's notion of the soul followed Plato's view of it as tripartite. Plato divided the soul into three parts, the Logos, the Thymos and the Epithymetikon. The Logos was the soul of rationality and it resided in the head. The Thymos, the source of emotion, was located in the chest, and the Epithymetikon, the soul of desire and passions, resides below the diaphragm. For Galen, not only the heart, but the liver and the brain each were the site of the soul's various functions. The heart, for Galen, was responsible for generating the body's vital life force. Galen's anatomical theories on the heart and blood, which also suggested that the body consumed blood, largely held sway until the seventeenth century.

The heart gained its greatest importance through the Greek belief that it was the site of the soul. Poets and philosophers alike pondered the human soul and its meaning. This can be seen in starting with the Greek poet Homer. He is the believed author of two influential and epic poems, *The Illiad* and *The Odyssey*. These were written between 800 and 600 BCE. In studies of literature, these two poems are praised for their poetic genius. They considered broad themes of humanity, war, and religion. In *The Odyssey*, the heart was used to convey Odysseus' emotional state and spirit. Identified as residing in the chest, it "growled" with emotions, was "troubled," and was the spiritual center that the character had to hold onto in order to maintain his spirit. The soul is identified as residing in the chest or heart, which is inscribed with the character's feelings and spirituality.

The heart had a dual role in culture because of the Greek understanding that the heart was the ruling organ of the body and the site of the human soul. The views of the ancient Greeks remained commonly held until the sixteenth century. By casting the heart as the seat of emotions and the source of body heat, the Greeks have influenced the cultural role of the heart ever since.

The Renaissance

Greek observations about the heart were commonly held in Europe until the Renaissance period. During the Renaissance, the study of anatomy was not just a physiological endeavor, but a theological one as well. While scientists sought to understand the anatomical function of organs, they also contemplated their philosophical and religious meaning. Scientists and those interested in anatomy continued to cite the heart as the source of emotions as well as behold it as a spiritual organ.

However, during the course of the Renaissance period in Europe, anatomical understandings of the heart changed. Leonardo da Vinci conducted experiments that ultimately reversed the cardiocentric ideas from antiquity. He conducted experiments on frogs in which he removed the heart and observed that the frog still retained life. However, when da Vinci removed a part of the brain, it died. He concluded that the heart was not the site of the soul because the organism remained alive without a heart, but not without part of the brain. Da Vinci's works were some of the most influential that resulted in the heart losing its anatomical position as the organ housing the source of life and being.

In the seventeenth century, another well-known scientist, William Harvey (1578–1657), studied the heart. Harvey was an English doctor who was the first to conceive of the heart as a pumping mechanism. He conducted experiments in laboratory settings and measured and observed the quantities of blood in a variety of organisms. He also observed the directions of blood flow and which chambers of the heart the blood would fill and empty from. For example, when Harvey wrapped a ligature around the bicep to stop the flow of blood to the rest arm, he observed that the lower arm would become pale. He thus concluded that there must be a system of veins and arteries that transport blood throughout the body. These experiments and observations work led to a complete change in understanding about the heart's anatomical functioning and the conceptualization of the circulatory system. Until this time, the heart was conceived of a muscle, but not as a pumping mechanism. It also was not thought of as a pumping mechanism that supplied blood to what we now know today as the circulatory system. Through his anatomical studies, he determined that the heart did not generate or make blood, but was actually a pump which expanded and contracted and allowed blood to travel throughout the body. By contracting, the heart pushed blood out of its chambers to the body through veins and arteries and then expanded to retrieve the blood as it returned. However, despite this major shift in the theory of the heart because of his work, Harvey did not challenge the metaphysical belief that the heart as the site of emotion. His contribution primarily furthered understanding of anatomical details and functioning.

While views about the anatomy of the heart changed over time, the cultural significance of the heart remained. In popular culture during this period, the heart was still thought of as the site of emotions and the organ of the soul. Related to this is the idea that the heart radiated heat into the body. Scientific language during this time also made connections between the heart and heat. For example, Harvey himself described the heart as the "sun of the body" in his writings. This referred not only to the heart as a source of life and heat, but also as a ruling, central organ—much like the role of the sun in the solar system—wherein laid the spiritual and emotional core of the human body. Artistic depictions of the heart often had the heart drawn with flames surrounding it to indicate that is was a source of body heat and the radiation of heat and emotions. A good example of such an image is that of the sacred heart of Jesus, popularized through Catholic iconography. This heart is traditionally depicted surrounded by flames and emanating great light. It was based on apparitions of Jesus said to be seen by the St. Marguerite-Marie Alacoque in the seventeenth century.

Of interest are the similarities that occurred during the Renaissance period in other parts of the world. In sixteenth-century South America, for example, the Aztecs believed the heart to be of cosmological and spiritual significance. To them, the heart was connected to and provided life for the sun god. When enemies were encountered and killed, the Aztecs held rituals to sacrifice the extracted heart to the sun god. The heart was symbolically given to the sun god and thought to ensure that the sun continued to burn. Such rituals reflected not only the centrality of the heart to the human body, but also the ideas of it producing heat.

Additionally, hearts were sacrificed in Mayan rituals and used as a blood source for offering up the life-giving liquid of blood to the gods. The Mayans believed these sacrifices were necessary for the survival of both the people and the gods. These sacrifices occurred for centuries prior to the Spanish conquests during the Renaissance period. Across the globe, the heart was infused with cultural meanings that incorporated ideas of heat and life force.

The Emotional Heart

The myth of the heart as the site of the human soul and all emotion still influences the cultural meaning of the heart today. After its anatomical function and character were no longer debated, its cultural meanings remained connected with emotion. References to the heart in popular culture are intimately bound up in ideas about romantic love. One example of this is the variety of idioms using the heart found in language. From song lyrics to poetry and literature, the word "heart" represents a whole array of emotional states. Referencing a "broken heart" represents love lost. If one's heart is given away to another person, then he/she is in love with that person. If one can "find it in their heart," they have found compassion. Because of its history, the heart is the first and foremost of body parts used to convey abstract ideas of love and romance.

Across cultures and eras, there have also been different references to the heart in imagery and the arts. Art historians have written about the popularization of the heart imagery in representing love and devotion during medieval times. In medieval paintings, love and romance were symbolized through various incarnations of heart imagery. This included both the actual organ as well as the now familiar symmetrical, red symbol. Couples were pictured exchanging hearts or one was painted offering his or her heart to another. One famous Flemish tapestry from 1400 entitled "The offering of the heart" depicted a man offering up a red heart to a woman as a symbol of his love and commitment. Additionally, wounded hearts appeared in medieval art with spears through them to indicate emotional pain. Works such as those by Italian artist Giotto di Bondone in the fourteenth century showed the heart in a variety of contexts being offered up and torn from the chest. These images were copied by many artists throughout the medieval period. Today images of a broken or wounded heart are still understood to represent pain and loss. A heart with initials is still doodled, drawn, carved and tattooed to profess two people's love for one another.

As an organ endowed with so much cultural meaning, the heart has been an often portrayed object in poetry. Poetry relies heavily on symbol and metaphor and has traditionally been a way to profess and expound on one's romantic love for another. The strong historical and cultural equations of the heart with emotions have easily been incorporated in poetry. Since antiquity, poets have commonly used the trope of the heart in romantic and philosophical expression. Sappho in the eighth century BCE pleaded for her love not to break "with great pains" her heart. William Shakespeare's famous character Romeo asks, after falling for Juliet, if his "heart had loved til now." References to hearts are ubiquitus in popular love songs.

The Spiritual Heart

The heart also symbolizes sacred aspects of humanity. A variety of religions from across the world use the symbolism of the heart. Depictions of Saint Augustine, a prominent figure in Western Christianity, most often showed him writing his book *Confessions,* the story of his conversion to Christianity. In paintings and drawings, he was most often shown holding a pen in one hand and his heart in the other, or with his hand over his heart, as in Sandro Botticelli's portrait *St. Augustine.*

The imagery of the heart is prominent in Catholic iconography. The Sacred Heart represents Jesus' physical heart and is an object of devotion for many Catholics. This heart appears in a stylized form, red with flames around it or light emanating from it. It often also has thorns wrapped around it and blood dripping. The symbol was influenced by the anatomical understandings of the heart as a pump for blood as well as the notion that the heart was a source of heat. These, paired with the associations of emotion and compassion from antiquity, are the origins of the powerful Catholic icon of divine love.

Heart symbolism is not restricted to Western religions. Hindus also use the heart as a reference point and symbol. They believe in a system of chakras located in the body. Chakras are energy points located throughout the body that, when opened up and flowing freely, will lead a person to enlightenment. Each chakra has its own symbol and is connected to a particular realm or aspect of consciousness. The one in the chest, the heart chakra, is believed to take one into the realm of relationships and compassion. Hindus believe that if one can open up their heart chakra, they are able to envision their deepest spiritual self.

Buddhism also refers to the heart. One of the central tenets of Buddhism is the desire to achieve a "cool mind and a warm heart." The heart represents compassion in Buddhism, which is believed, when paired with clarity of mind, to be the highest form of consciousness. Here again, the heart is representative of an abstract notion of divine compassion and love.

In Chinese spirituality, the heart is also the central organ of the body. It is believed to be the king of all organs in the body and the site of "true knowledge," according to the Chinese philosopher Confucius. His ideas about the heart, from the sixth century BCE, are central to Confuscian thought. According to him, if the heart is right and in order, so too are the rest of one's body and senses. He emphasized the connection between purity of heart and beauty of character.

The Symbol

More than just a body part referenced in language and imagination, the heart is a drawn symbol that does not reflect the actual anatomical shape of the organ. This drawn symbol of the heart is a widely known image that conveys the idea of love, unity and compassion.

The symbol of the heart is a powerful icon made up of two rounded curves that come to a point at the bottom and is typically drawn in red. The color is rooted both in the heart's anatomical relationship to blood, but also in the historical relationship to emotion and passion. The origins of the symbol's shape, however, are not agreed upon. Some believe it to be more similar to the actual shape of a cow's heart, which would have been more accessible to humans in ancient times. Others locate its origin in the shape of an ancient seed that was associated with sexuality and love. Still others locate its origins in the leaf of an ancient plant that symbolized eternal love. One symbol dictionary cites its beginnings in the Ice Age and claims it to be a mixture of ancient symbols indicating togetherness and fire.

Despite being unable to pinpoint its actual origins, the heart symbol is one of the most universally recognized symbols in the world. It is used in a variety of ways in popular imagery, including carvings in tree trunks uniting lovers' initials, bumper stickers proclaiming a love of anything from cats to trucks, and tee shirts with the popular claim to love New York. Perhaps one of the most famous uses of the symbol of the heart is seen in the holiday of Valentine's Day. This holiday originated in ancient Rome and is believed to be associated with a feast involving the celebration of Lupercal, a fertility god. Love notes would be exchanged on this day, which was on the fifteenth of February at the time. The celebration continued through Christian times, but became more associated with the death of St. Valentine, which occurred on the fourteenth of February. The later Christian tradition of the holiday involved the choosing of marriage partners on the eve of the holiday. Around 1800 in England, small cards or trinkets with quotes professing love or affection became popular gifts to a chosen special someone. These valentines started as homemade cards, but by the 1830s and 1840s were made and sold commercially. The most common symbol for Valentines was the heart, widely and universally implemented to communicate the holiday's central theme of love and romance.

The heart symbol is widespread in popular culture today. In tattooing, the heart is a popular image choice, and is the center of one of the most iconic tattoos in culture: the red heart with "MOM" written in a banner over it. Other images may include hearts with wings, the Sacred Heart of Catholicism, or a heart with the name of the beloved.

Further Reading: Best, Charles, and Norman Taylor. *The Living Body: A Text in Human Physiology.* New York: Holt, Rinehart and Winston, 1961; Blair, Kirstie. *Victorian Poetry and the Culture of the Heart.* Oxford: Oxford University Press, 2006; Bremmer, J. *The Early Greek Concept of the Soul.* Princeton, NJ: Princeton University Press, 1983; Budge, E. A. Wallis, translator. *The Egyptian Book of the Dead.* New York: Dover, 1967; Godwin, Gail. *Heart.* New York: HarperCollins, 2001; Jager, Eric. *The Book of the Heart.* Chicago: University of Chicago Press, 2001; Keele, Kenneth. *Leonardo da Vinci's Elements of the Science of Man.* New York: Academic Press, 1983; Rush, John. *Spiritual Tattoo: A Cultural History of Tattooing, Piercing, Scarification, Branding, and Implants.* Berkeley, CA: Frog, 2005; http://www.heartsymbol.com.

Laura Mauldin

Hymen

Surgical Restoration of the Hymen

Hymen replacement surgery—also known as hymenoplasty, hymenorrhaphy, hymen restoration, hymen reconstruction or revirgination—is described in the medical literature as a mildly invasive procedure that does not require hospitalization. In most cases the hymen is reconstructed by pulling together, and suturing, the remnants of the hymenal ring. The "repair" takes four to six weeks to heal completely. In some cases, however, what remains of the hymenal tissue is insufficient for reconstruction and thus plastic surgery techniques are employed in order to create a hymenal ring from vaginal mucosa.

Hymenoplasty is a controversial medical procedure increasingly practiced in the West, but most often associated with women from cultures in which virginity is considered to be a *sin qua non* for marriage. In such cultures, rituals designed to prove a bride's virginity are performed before marriage and on the wedding night. These range from obtaining a certificate of virginity from a medical practitioner or "virginity inspector," to showing blood-stained cloths or sheets to family members, friends, or neighbors after defloration has taken place. Medical practitioners in the United States claim that they most often perform the procedures on women from Latin American, Middle Eastern, and some Asian countries. These women, it is claimed, are likely to be rejected by future husbands or families, or, in extreme cases, to become victims of violence or even homicide if they are found not to be virgins prior to marriage. Lack of evidence of virginity is, in some cultures, regarded as legal grounds for the dissolution of a marriage. Hymen reconstruction is not, however, a procedure that is undergone solely by women wishing to restore the virginity that is expected of them prior to marriage. If popular magazine articles are to be believed, there are women who purchase new hymens as anniversary presents for partners to whom they did not loose their virginity, as well as women who simply want to experience the "loss of virginity" at a point in life where they are better equipped to enjoy it.

Hymen restoration has been criticized on a number of grounds. For those for whom abstinence until marriage is a religious imperative, hymen repair is considered a deception. Consequently, the procedure is allegedly illegal in most Arab countries, which is not to say that it is not practiced. Some feminists have argued that since virginity in women is valued in masculinist cultures in which women are regarded as the property of men, hymenoplasty perpetuates patriarchal values and forms of social relations. A claim sometimes associated with this position is that hymen restoration constitutes a form of female genital mutilation. However, such an association is rejected by others who argue that hymen reconstruction does not in anyway mutilate the genitals, and that the risk of physical, psychological, and sexual complications is far less than in clitoridectomy. Instead, defenders of the practice argue that insofar as hymen reconstruction could be thought of as an example of ritualistic surgery—that is, surgery performed for the fulfilment of a person's need rather than a response to their medical condition—it is more accurately compared to cosmetic surgery. From a clinical perspective, critics have argued that since hymen replacement is not a procedure that is taught in medical residencies, there is the possibility that it will be poorly performed and lead to unnecessary complications. Similarly, some gynaecological surgeons have argued that hymen repair is a bogus procedure, since it cannot actually restore virginity.

Attempts to produce the appearance of an intact hymen and thus of virginity are by no means new. For example, midwives have been known to disguise a broken hymen with a needle and thread, sometimes using membrane material from goats and other animals, and in early twentieth-century Japanese culture, it was allegedly not uncommon for plastic surgeons to sew a piece of sheep's intestine into the vagina shortly before a wedding. In a range of cultural contexts and historical epochs, women have also inserted into their vaginas blood-filled vessels of various sorts designed to break upon contact with the penis. Suppositories made from plant material that irritates the vaginal wall have also been used to stimulate blood flow, as have leeches.

Further Reading: Apesos, Jame, Roy Jackson, John R. Miklos, and Robert D. Moore. *Vaginal Rejuvenation: Vaginal/Vulvar Procedures, Restored Femininity.* New York: LM Publishers, 2006; Drenth, Jelto. *The Origin of the World: Science and the Fiction of the Vagina.* London: Reaktion Books, 2005; Matlock, David. L. *Sex by Design.* Los Angeles: Demiurgus Publications, 2004.

Nikki Sullivan

Jaw

Surgical Reshaping of the Jaw

Surgery of the jaw is called *orthognathic* surgery from the Greek word *orthos*, for "straight" and *gnathos* for "jaw." Orthognathic surgery is performed to straighten out a crooked maxilla (upper jaw bone) and/or mandible (lower jaw bone) and/or crooked teeth. Some orthognathic procedures are classified as reconstructive and others as cosmetic. Males and females tend to have differently shaped jaws and beauty ideals of the jaw are sex-specific. Some transsexual women (women who were born male, but identify and live as women) use jaw surgery to feminize their faces. In nations where Anglo-European ideals of facial beauty dominate, orthognathic surgery is advertised to people of Asian descent as a way to "soften" their ethnic features. This strategy is controversial, as it raises the issue of acceptance and exclusion on racial grounds. Beauty ideals in Japan and Korea also devalue the facial structure that orthognathic procedures are designed to modify.

Sexual Difference and Beauty Ideals of the Jaw

All cosmetic jaw procedures aim towards similar ideals of beauty. For both sexes, the symmetry between left and right sides of the face, including symmetry between the right and left sides of the jaw, is important. Beauty ideals suggest that the jaw should be properly proportioned to the rest of the face. The jaw should not be recessive, or too prominent. Instead, it should work in harmony with the other features to lend a sense of balance to the face. Compared to men, women are expected to have a round jaw. Men should have a square jaw relative to women. The jaw should be more prominent in men than in women. In men, a prominent jaw creates a strong look. In women, it is considered ugly when the jaw is the most prominent feature of the face.

Racialized Ideals of the Beautiful Jaw

Historically, the jaw has been important to the practice of physiognomy. Physiognomy, which dates to Ancient Greece and was popular in Europe in the eighteenth and nineteenth centuries, is the practice of reading an individual's personality according to their facial anatomy. On the basis of the racialized significance of facial parts like the jaw, physiognomists have constructed a hierarchy between the so-called "races." Anglo-European facial type was said to be the most evolved, and all "others" were judged inferior in comparison. The jaw structure of African people was constituted as "evidence" of the alleged barbarism of African people simply because their jaws tend to be set on a steeper angle than that of Anglo-Europeans. Physiognomy has now been criticised as a racist pseudoscience.

According to orthognathic surgeons, a sharply angled jaw makes the face appear flat, wide and square. This feature is devalued in nations where Anglo-European ideals of facial beauty are dominant. It is also devalued by Japanese and Korean standards of facial beauty. In Western nations like Australia and the United States, orthognathic surgery is marketed to people of Asian descent as an "Asian procedure," along with "Asian blepharoplasty" (double-eyelid surgery) and nasal bridge augmentation. People of Asian heritage in Asia and other continents undergo orthognathic surgery to modify what is perceived as an overly angular jaw. It is not clear that these patients wish to erase their ethnic heritage. Cosmetic surgeons and their patients argue that "Asian" procedures are designed to soften, rather than erase the patient's ethnic heritage. Critics of this position point out the fact that Western nations have a history of interpreting facial anatomy in racist ways. Critics also question why it is that cosmetic surgery is not designated with a racial descriptor whenever the target market is "Anglo-European."

Surgical Procedures on the Jaw

Some orthognathic (jaw) procedures are classified as reconstructive because they aim to restore normal function to the jaw area. Others are classified as cosmetic because the goal is to improve the appearance of the patient's face. However, it is often the case that reconstructive procedures also improve the appearance of the face. Some cosmetic procedures can alter facial function. Dental implants, a cosmetic procedure that replaces one or more missing teeth, can also correct speech difficulties relating to the missing tooth. Hence, the line between reconstructive and cosmetic procedures is not as clear as this common distinction implies.

Maxillary osteotomy and/or mandibular osteotomy are often performed to correct a patient's bite. Osteotomy is the name given to any surgical procedure that involves shaving down bine tissue. The term "bite" refers to the way that the top and bottom jaw are positioned in relation to one another when the mouth is closed. For both aesthetic and functional reasons, it is important that the top and bottom jaws meet neatly, so that there is no large gap between them.

As the teeth are anchored in the jaw, it is sometimes necessary to modify the jaw structure in order to correct the position of the teeth. Mentoplasty (surgery of the chin) is often carried out in conjunction with jaw reshaping procedures. If it is deemed necessary to increase the size of the jaw itself, a jaw implant can be placed inside the lower lip. If teeth are missing and conventional tooth replacement techniques like a removable denture or dental bridge are inadequate, an implant can be surgically embedded in the jaw to accommodate screw-in false teeth.

Transsexual women who can afford the procedure often undergo mandibular angle reduction surgery. The shape of the male jaw can hinder a transsexual woman's ability to integrate into society without her transsexual status being noticed. There are general differences between male and female facial anatomy. Males tend to have wide jaws that are square at the back. Compared to males, females generally have round jaws. However, some males do have round jaws and some women, square jaws. During mandibular reduction, an incision is made, most often in the gums, and the mandible (jaw bone) is shaved down using a bone-contouring saw. This procedure, which aims to round off the jaw, is often performed in conjunction with procedures to reduce the height and width of the jaw and reduce the masseter muscles (used for chewing). These procedures are painful and expensive but they do help relieve the anxiety associated with a transsexual person's fear of not passing.

Further Reading: Kaw, Eugenia. "Medicalisation of Racial Features: Asian American Women and Cosmetic Surgery." *Medical Anthropology Quarterly* 7 (1993): 74–89; Lee, Charles S. "Craniofacial, Asian Malar and Mandibular Surgery." http://www.emedicine.com/plastic/topic427.htm (accessed March 2007).

Gretchen Riordan

Labia

Labiaplasty

Labiaplasty (or labioplasty) is the term used to refer to the surgical modification of the labia minora and/or labia majora. It is derived from the Latin *labia*, meaning "lips" and the Greek *plastia*, meaning "to mold." Labiaplasty, which, according to plastic surgeons, is performed for both functional and aesthetic reasons, can involve the reduction of "elongated" labia (sometimes referred to as "labial hypertrophy"), the modification of asymmetrical labia, and the removal of "hyper-pigmented" parts of the labia minora. Labial reduction is most commonly performed using one of two techniques: "direct labia excision," or "V-wedge resection." Labia excision, which is sometimes described as a contouring technique, involves the removal of excess tissue from the free edge of the labia, using a scalpel or a laser device. "V-shaped wedge resection technique" involves removing a V-shaped area of labial tissue and then suturing the edges of the excision. The former procedure is more often employed when the elimination of hyper pigmentation found at the edge of the labia is desired. Other procedures often performed concurrently include: the reduction or removal of excess prepuce skin surrounding the clitoral hood, the smoothing out of overly wrinkled labia minora via collagen injection or autologous fat transplant, and the removal of fatty tissue and/or excess skin from the labia majora and/or mons pubis.

Given the growing demand for such modifications, it is important to consider some of the factors that may have contributed to women's desire to undergo procedures that are largely cosmetic, generally expensive, sometimes painful, and, like all surgery, involve risks. One of the most common explanations is that whilst conformity to culturally prescribed and approved forms of female genitalia is essential to female gender attribution—to being positioned as and taking up the position of "woman"—female genitalia has not, until relatively recently in the West, been openly displayed. This situation is changing as a result of ever-more revealing clothing (in particular swimwear and underwear), the popularization of pubic hair removal, increasing exposure to nudity in magazines, on the internet and in film and television, increased consumption, by women, of heterosexual pornography, and campaigns advising women (for political and/or medical reasons) to familiarize themselves with their own bodies. More often than not, when female genitalia are represented, in particular in pornographic texts, they are rendered ideal through the use of techniques such as lighting, airbrushing, Photoshopping, and so on. In short, one rarely sees images of large labia minora outside of medical texts.

Whilst the "winged butterfly," as it's sometimes referred to, may be held in high regard in Japan, it is perceived as unattractive, rather than a sexual delicacy, in contemporary Western cultures such as the United States, the United Kingdom, and Australia. If we are to believe the plethora of material currently available on labiaplasty, ideally labia minora are small, symmetrical, consistently pale in color, and remain, at all times, neatly tucked away inside the labia majora. Insofar as aesthetic procedures such as labiaplasty are primarily designed to achieve this ideal, they tend to (re)shape female genitalia in homogenizing ways, thereby reproducing limiting and limited gender norms and further pathologizing corporeal difference. Moreover, the notion of an ideal or perfect vulva achievable through surgery is, as feminist critics have noted, founded on (and reproduces) the long-held idea that female genitalia (and by association, female sexuality) are inherently excessive, unruly, improper, even dangerous ("loose lips sink ships"). The self-doubt that women sometimes feel as an effect of such historical constructions serves the cosmetic industry well: labiaplasty becomes the solution to "labial hypertrophy," a condition largely created in and through the development of procedures to reduce the size of the labia and the sense of shame and/or sexual inhibition associated with "unsightly" genitalia. Consequently, some feminist critics suggest that rather than enhancing women's bodies and thereby their sense of self, labiaplasty, and the rhetoric which shapes its practice, invokes and generates medicalized norms which ultimately construct female embodiment as forever lacking, forever in need of improvement. Femininity thus becomes, by definition, that which if forever caught in labyrinthine cycles of (com)modification.

Although what is understood as cosmetic genital surgery may not yet be as popular in non-Western countries, Western women are not alone in arguing that genital modification can result in more attractive genitals and in enhanced sexual pleasure. This then raises questions regarding the differential status, both legal and social, of cosmetic procedures such as those discussed, and female circumcision, a term used to refer to heterogeneous practices ranging from the nicking of a particular part of the vulva, to the removal of labia minora and majora and the suturing of the vaginal opening. Currently in much of the Western world, female circumcision, or female genital mutilation (FGM) as it is referred to in legislative terms, has been criminalized. Whilst exceptions do exist, in much anti-FGM legislation the excision or "mutilation" of the whole or any part of the labia majora, labia minora or clitoris, is something to which one cannot consent since "mutilation"—the rendering imperfect of a natural and essential part—is, by definition, an irrational act. But despite this, labiaplasty (and other related procedures) is not regarded as an illegal practice, nor as one to which women cannot, be definition, consent: indeed, if one is to believe the statistics, the number of women choosing to undergo such procedures has increased exponentially in the last two decades. This seems to suggest that the modification of female genitalia is not in itself problematic, at least not in the dominant Western imaginary. This has led some to question why we regard some forms of genital modification as mutilatory acts of oppression, and others as freely chosen enhancements whose effects are liberatory. A cultural relativist position would question what are the social, ethical, and political effects of presuming that practices common to us, framed as they are in the rhetoric of consumer capitalism, are qualitatively different from (or even the polar opposite of) practices we associate with non-Western "others." These are not questions that can be answered here, but they are being explored in detail by critics keen to avoid presuming their own constitution of self (of gender, sexuality, pleasure, and so on) to be the ideal human state.

Further Reading: Braun, Virginia. "In Search of (Better) Sexual Pleasure: Female Genital 'Cosmetic' Surgery." *Sexualities* 8:4 (2005): 407–24; Matlock, David. L. *Sex by Design*. Los Angeles: Demiurgus Publications, 2004; Sullivan, Nikki. "'The Price to Pay for Our Common Good:' Genital Modification and the Somatechnologies of Cultural (In)Difference." *Social Semiotics* 17:3 (2007).

Nikki Sullivan

Legs

Cultural History of Legs

The human leg has many parts, including the basal segment, the femur or thighbone, the tibia or shinbone, and the smaller tibia. While legs have the main purpose of movement for humans of all cultures, they are treated differently based on gender, social ranking, and age within societies around the world and throughout history. Humans, birds and apes (occasionally) walk bipedally, but bipedal mobility is nonetheless symbolic of humanness. The way people walk can reveal their mood, personality, emotional, physical, and even social status. For example, a tired, wounded soldier would have a different walk from a prostitute trying to get a client. Legs have been infused with a variety of symbolic meanings related to gender and sexuality and have been referenced in literature and fashion, as well as playing a part in music, fine art, and medical advancements.

Adornment and Clothing

While clothing and fashion styles have changed dramatically over centuries, legs have been adorned, protected and sexualized by stockings, garters, shinguards and other coverings. According to legend, the knighthood was started in the early 1300s after English King Edward the Third danced with the Countess of Salisbury and she lost a garter on the floor. To decrease her shame, he put the garter on his own leg.

In sixteenth and seventeenth-century Europe, both male and female members of the royal courts adorned their legs. For example, in the court of Louis XII, the King's male pages wore red and yellow stockings, one color on each leg. In 1718, fashion for legs appeared to be more ornate and obvious, and this was the same time as the hoop skirt became extremely popular. To have silk stockings at that time was affordable only by the wealthy. By the 1800s, men were wearing long pants with no stockings. Women's legs in the Victorian period were usually concealed under layers of skirts, and high ankle boots. The use of the word "limbs" was used carefully because of the arousing nature of the word at this time. In the twentieth century, Western women's clothing revealed more of the legs, and stimulated a revival in leg hair removal, a practice that has ancient origins.

In ancient Greece, the soldiers dressed for battle in leg guards of metal or bronze from the ankle up to the knee. Roman soldiers often wore only a "greave" on the right leg. The protection for the Japanese Samurai warriors was different; the majority of the armor was made from bamboo and some metal for the torso. Militaries have had to adapt the protection of the legs with the kind of war, which has changed many times since ancient Greece. For example, in medieval Europe, high boots called "cothurnes" were worn by hunters to protect the foot and calf. There were also upperleg coverings made of leather or metal called "cuisse" and a lower portion known as "greaves." The metal armor was designed to be worn over chain mail or clothing, and was attached to the leg with a strap. In the Americas, cowboys wore leather coverings over the pants called "chaps" that provided further protection while riding horses and bulls. Chaps, or *chaperajos*, were first used by the Spanish settlers of Mexico, often made from the hides of buffalo. Mexicans designed leather britches in the early nineteenth century, and full-length britches of leather were worn by Texans during the middle of the century.

Many of the San Francisco mine workers who wore canvas or burlap pants when they worked in the goldmines had large irritated areas on their thighs and upper legs. On May 20, 1873, the German designer Claude Levi Strauss and his tailor David Jacobs received U.S. Patent No.139,121. This was for the pants known so commonly today as "jeans." Strauss' pants not only covered the legs for safety but have become the most famous and common pants in history, while also providing comfort for the legs with no chaffing.

Hair Removal

Body hair removal has ancient origins. In ancient India, Egypt, Greece and Rome, it was common for women to remove all body hair; in India and Egypt, men removed theirs as well. Chinese hair removal was accomplished through the employment of two strings; elsewhere, as in Native America, caustic agents were used, like lye. Caucasian women borrowed the practice of hair removal from Middle Easterners during the Crusades; for centuries later, however, European women did not remove their leg hair, until the practice was revived in the nineteenth century.

It is fashionable and common today for women in Western countries to remove the hair from the legs, whether permanently with lasers, or temporarily with razors and depilatories. In the twentieth century, the legs became more visible in fashion, since women's clothing became more revealing of the thigh, calf and ankle. Young children often have light leg hair, rarely noticeable. The appearance of the shaved leg in women may suggest a desire to echo this youthful appearance. When shorter skirts and sheer stockings became fashionable, the leg hair of women began to be removed. Companies such as Gillette and Schick made the razor available as an inexpensive vehicle to smooth, hairless legs. The gender assigned look of slim, hairless legs has become synonymous with female, while the hairy and muscular leg is often associated with the male gender assignment. In response to the gendering of body hair, some Western feminists, homosexual, bisexual, and heterosexual women have chosen not to alter their bodies in this way. The "natural" or unshaven look was coded in the late twentieth century as suggesting an alternative, feminist standard of beauty.

Music and Fine Art

In nineteenth-century Tibet, the human femur, which is also known as the thighbone, was used to make a trumpet called a "Rkang Dung." These musical instruments are also made of metal for louder ensemble performances. The bones used from the deceased were wrapped carefully with wire, usually brass, with an added mouthpiece at the end of the bone. They are often decorated with white coral. These instruments are on display in the United States at the National Music Museum. Also known as "Rkang gling," these "leg flutes" are played using the left hand by monks and shamans for various rituals in Boen and Buddist monasteries. Tibetian monks, or "yogi," have been seen playing these musical femur instruments for centuries.

The history of fine art is overflowing with images of human legs, mimicking the fashion, social and surrealistic images of people and their legs. One of the most obvious and well-known references in fine art to the human leg is the term known as "Contrappasto" which means "opposite" or "counterpoise" in the Italian language. This term refers to way a subject being drawn or painted is standing, with their weight on only one leg, and the other leg being slightly bent at the knee. This way of standing affects the mood of the subject, giving a more relaxed and less mechanical pose to the figure. Beginning with the Greeks, this artistic technique has been used to show the mood of the person being painted or sculpted by the positioning of the legs. The Italian Renaissance, a movement responsible for many of the greatest art and artists of the last five hundred years, is full of examples of "contrappasto."

One of the most famous and earliest examples of this is Donatello's bronze sculpture "David." Another artist, who is responsible for the schooling of great artists such as Leonardo and Botticelli, is Andrea del Verrocchio. He used this method of posing the figure in a way that gave more life to the sculpture in his work as well. This is clearly visible in his painting *Baptism of Christ* painted in the 1400s. More recently the technique could be seen in work by the French artist, Aristide Maillol. His sculptures "Nymph" in 1930 and "Harmony" in 1940 are excellent examples of "contrappasto" with the female figure showing only one leg bent and the neck turned. The bronze sculpture by Maillol, "Venus with a Necklace" is a classic example of the shifted weight on one leg.

The Greeks in the fifth century BCE and the painters and sculptors of the Renaissance are credited for the birth and rebirth of this technique. However, it is so widely used by artists today that the untrained eye is unconsciously jaded to the relaxed stance of a person with their leg bent, their body relaxed, and their head tilted to the side. Numerous paintings, as well as sculptures, have explored the social and emotional issues around the loss of legs, and amputation. One powerful painting by Flemish painter Pieter Bruegel entitled *The Beggars* depicts four poor beggars who have lost their legs. The desperation in the faces points to their lack of the freedom to move about on both legs, forcing them to ask for help, money, and kindness from others. This situation can be a fact of life for many who lose their legs due to amputation. The first known illustration of amputation is credited to Hans von Gerssdorff, in 1517.

The famous Belgian surrealist painter, Rene Magritte, is a well known surrealist painter. His 1953 oil-on-canvas painting *The Wonders of Nature* portrays two figures in an amorous pose, with human legs, but with the upper bodies of oversized fish.

Amputation and Loss of the Legs

Many people have lost one or both of their legs or portions of them due to illness, war or accident. Amputation is performed on some patients with infections in the lower leg, those whose injuries have begun developing gangrene, or who suffer diabetic ulcers of the feet and legs. Millions of soldiers throughout history have also lost limbs due to war injuries. Early surgeries on the battlefield often meant death, but as medics became more trained, the casualties due to amputation diminished. The prosthetics available to the amputees have also become more high-tech, for both military and civilian patients. The ancient wooden "peg leg" and hook associated with pirates and seamen was replaced in 1858 by Douglas Bly. He invented and patented the "anatomical leg" for amputees. After World War I, the American Prosthetics and Orthotics Association was assembled to organize the development of prosthetics. For the leg, there are two basic types of prosthesis. For those who are amputated below the knee, a "transtibial prosthesis" and when the leg is amputated above the knee there are "transfemoral prosthesis." Prosthetic legs have changed over the years to be aesthetically attractive and technically strong and dependable.

Some amputees have become highly successful, famous, or influential in fields that seem to depend upon having two legs. Emmanuel Ofosu Yeboah, a man born with a deformed right leg, is originally from Ghana. He decided that in order to try and change the viewpoints of those in his country who thought less of people with a disability, he would ride 600 kilometers on a bicycle across Ghana. An American man, Clayton Bates, lost his leg as a teenager and still managed to have a career as a tap dancer. He was so successful that he appeared on the *Ed Sullivan Show*, and numerous stage musicals, television shows and in motion pictures. Tony Christiansen, from New Zealand is another example of physical achievement despite the lack of legs. Despite having lost his legs when he was nine in an accident near a railway, he has a black belt in Tae Kwon Do, is a gold medal-winning athlete, and has climbed Mt. Kilimanjaro in Africa. Not all legless people have been able to use their handicap in this way, however. Disability activists have underscored the difficulties of everyday mobility for amputees and others who do not have the use of legs, and have argued for greater accessibility in terms of a "built environment" that is sensitive to physical diversity.

While amputation for many presents a set of complex physical and psychological challenges, for a small number of people it is a deeply held, although often secret, desire. A rare but provocative psychological phenomenon, "Amputee Identity Disorder," also called "apotemnophilia" and "body integrity identity disorder," refers to a deeply felt need of people with healthy legs (or arms) to become amputees, usually of the legs but sometimes of the arms. Amputee Identity Disorder, which is still being developed as a diagnostic category in psychiatry, came to the attention of the world in 1997, when Scottish surgeon Robert Smith removed the healthy leg of patient Kevin Wright, a man who had requested the surgery because of his almost lifelong desire to be an amputee. Smith reportedly operated on a similar patient two years later. After the hospital, Falkirk Royal Infirmary, received global attention for the surgery, the institution banned future surgical treatment of patients like Wright. However, Smith maintains that surgical removal of the leg is sometimes necessary for such patients, who may otherwise resort to self-amputation.

Another form of leg modification is limb-lengthening surgery. Some people, often those born with dwarfism, voluntarily undergo surgical procedures that lengthen their legs. Professor Gavriil Abramovich Ilizarov was one of numerous doctors to experiment with surgical lengthening of the human legs. The basis of his procedure is simple, but not quick or easy: the patient's legs are broken below the knee. While the leg heals, a process that generates bone growth, a rod is inserted and gradually extended, instigating a lengthening process of the bones. The practice is highly controversial: it can be painful, can take several years, and is most successfully performed on children, who are still in the process of growing. There are many reasons for this surgery to be performed or desired, although achieving social normalcy for people with various forms of dwarfism is regarded as the primary concern. There are also reports of voluntary "leg stretching" in Asian countries. The desired height for certain schools and companies for their employees is often higher than the natural height of the applicants.

Myth, Legend, and Religion

Many cultures have their own ways of celebrating and using the legs. In a Japanese ceremony devoted to prayer for stronger legs, very large sandals made of straw are paraded down the streets in Fukushima to a shrine. On the Solomon Islands of Ulawa and Malaita, common figures were historically made using the human leg and animal or shark bodies. Another symbol known as "the Three Legs of Mann" is used as the national emblem of the Isle of Man, located in the Irish Sea. Many Manx sailors found this symbol to be a popular tattoo, usually on the right leg. The flag features the "Trinacria" which is three legs that are joined at the upper thigh and slightly bent at the knee. The word "trincaria" means "triangular" and in Sicily it is used to reference the three coasts of that area which were called

"Trincaria" centuries ago. The history of this symbol cites numerous origins; the sun's path across the sky, pagan worship, and the spokes of a wheel. A similar figure is the "fylfot" which is four legs instead of three and aesthetically resembles the swastika used in Nazi Germany. It was used in worship of Aryan solar gods. The three-legged symbol was also used on the coins of the Norse King Cuaran in the tenth century.

Literature

The English language has slang, jargon, humor, literary references and poetry dedicated to the human leg. Many words in the English language are synonyms or slang for the leg. For example "gam" is a slang word for leg in certain circles, while "pillars," "shafts," "stems," "stilts" and "props" are commonly used slang words for legs by many African Americans. The slang "to leg it" means to walk quickly away, while "leg over" can imply sexual intercourse.

George Trevelyan, the English historian and writer said; "I have two doctors, my left leg and my right leg." This was his way of communicating the importance of exercise, and the need to stay healthy. Legs cannot only prove to be a mode of transportation and freedom, but can be the vehicles to better health. The American author Henry David Thoreau, in his 1862 prose entitled "Walking," writes, "When sometimes I am reminded that the mechanics and shop-keepers stay in their shops not only all the forenoon, but all the afternoon too, sitting with crossed legs, so many of them—as if the legs were made to sit upon, and not to stand or walk upon—I think that they deserve some credit for not having all committed suicide long ago." During the nineteenth century, Honore de Balzac also wrote about legs in his "Theorie de la Demarche" or "Theory of Walking."

William Shakespeare's play, *The Merchant of Venice*, has a character named Lancelot who voices an internal and conflicted monologue and mentions his legs as a mode of escape. "Certainly my conscience will serve me to run from this Jew my master. The fiend is at mine elbow and tempts me, saying to me 'Gobbo, Launcelot Gobbo, good Launcelot' or 'good Gobbo' or 'good Launcelot Gobbo, use your legs, take the start, run away." Shakespeare's play Romeo and Juliet is also frothed with references to the human leg. In the famous love story, Juliet Montague's Nurse talks to her about her choice of lovers. Shakespeare writes, "Well, you have made a simple choice. You know not how to choose a man. Romeo! No, not he, though his face be better than any man's, yet his leg excels all men's, and for a hand and a foot and a body, though they be not to be talked on, yet they are past compare." Then, later in the play, the character Mercutio tries to get his best friend Romeo's attention. Complaining that Romeo doesn't hear him, Meructio tries to arouse his interest by describing Rosaline's beauty, including her eyes and lips, but also "by her fine feet, by her straight legs, by her trembling thighs, and by the regions right next to her thighs." Poetry is also filled with references to the human leg. One poet, Mark Halliday, wrote a poem entitled "Legs" in a collection of prose called *Selfwolf*, published in 1988. Halliday describes the poem as a "symptom" of the end of his marriage. His desire for something new and forbidden, the attractive legs of his neighbour, distracted him from the current state of his emotions. *See also* Hair: Hair Removal; and Limbs: Limb-Lengthening Surgery.

Further Reading: Brenton, Jean. *Instruments de musique du monde*. Paris: Editions de la Martinière, 2000, and New York: Harry N. Abrams, 2000, p. 108; Grizzly, Buck. "History of Chaps," http://www.gunfighter.com (accessed February 26, 2008); Kirkup, John. *A History of Limb Amputation*. New York, NY: Springer Publishing, 2006; McPherson, Stephanie Sammartino. *Levi Strausse*. Kirkup, John. *A History of Limb Amputation*. Lerner Publishing Group, 2007; Morra, Joanne, and Marquard Smith. "The prosthetic impulse: From a posthuman present to a biocultural future." Cambridge, MA: MIT Press, 2006; Riley, Richard Lee. *Living with a Below-Knee Amputation*. Thorofare: Slack, 2006; Tiggemann, Marika; Christine Lewis. "Attitudes Towards Women's Body Hair: Relationship with Disgust Sensitivity." *Psychology of Women Quarterly* 28 (2004): 381.

Margaret Howard

Limbs

Limb-Lengthening Surgery

Limb-lengthening surgery is available for people with dwarfism, predominantly children, who wish to extend their arms and legs to increase their height. It involves breaking the limbs and inserting a rod, which can then be gradually extended as the bone heals to lengthen the limbs. The origins of this procedure date back to the early 1900s, but the operation became more widely available in the 1980s and continues today, despite considerable controversy.

As the line between medical and cosmetic procedures has increasingly blurred in American culture, deeming the natural body a project to be perfected with surgery, simultaneous activism by the disability rights movement has called the desire for "normal" bodies into question. At the center of this culture clash is the controversy over extended limb-lengthening surgery (ELL) for people with dwarfism. Though originally intended for correcting limb-length discrepancies, such as withered limbs from polio, ELL gained particular attention when first used in the late 1980s to lengthen the limbs of people with achondroplasia, hypochondroplasia, and cartilage-hair hypoplasia, all genetic differences resulting in degrees of dwarfism.

Because ELL entails gradual bone regrowth, this process can take several years, best if done before or during adolescence. Varying in technique, ELL is achieved by breaking the arm and leg bones, resituating them with pins attached to an external frame, and gradually elongating the frame, allowing the bone to regenerate over time to fill in the break. ELL has high costs in terms of money, time, and physical pain, but successful surgery can add as much as eleven inches to some patients, increasing their abilities as well as concealing their dwarfism. However, the condition causing dwarfism is in no way cured and may still cause orthopedic complications later on.

ELL has become particularly controversial in both the community of little people, who criticize ELL as a cosmetic effort to become more "normal," as well as among bioethicists, who question whether children should be put through such an arduous, often painful process. ELL was an appreciated development by some, but its cultural reception remains far from certain.

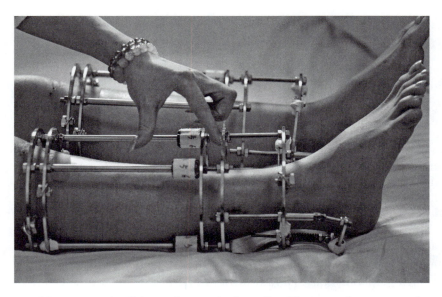

Leg-stretching surgery in China to be two inches taller. The procedure was used as an elective procedure in China before it was banned. The Health Ministry banned the procedure except as treatment for damaged bones or uneven limbs caused by injury, tumors, or other deformities. (AP Photo/Elizabeth Dalziel)

Though the first efforts at limb-lengthening began in the early 1900s, Vittorio Putti's 1921 device, the "Osteoton," caused the first swell in this research. These early devices consisted of either pins or wires inserted into the bone fragments and attached to an external frame, constantly stretching the limb through a compressed spring. Despite the abundant complications, research continued, as World War II revived interest in ELL. This led to a new era of developments, following F.G. Allan's technique of using a screw to stretch the frame, providing control over the rate of growth that a spring frame had not offered. In the early 1970s, H. Wagner's device, shortly followed by a similar Italian innovation called "the Orthofix," allowed patients to walk with crutches while undergoing ELL, which made both devices widely popular among North American orthopedic surgeons who valued patient mobility.

The 1951 innovations of G. Ilizarov in Russia, made prevalent by Dr. Dror Paley in 1986 when he brought the Ilizarov technique to North America, helped ELL become the controversial topic it is today by using ELL for people with dwarfism. With his keen understanding of the biology of lengthening, Ilizarov's technique of using a ring fixator, a steadier device for holding bone fragments in place with stainless steel pins, allowed for a more reliable, controlled bone growth with fewer complications. He also slowed down the lengthening process to 1 mm/day and combined ELL with calisthenics, leaving the device on until the bone had regained its strength. Further developments continue around this technique, but this remains the "Ilizarov Era," as his technique has been so foundational to current ELL practices.

Much of the resistance to ELL stems from the disability rights movement, which encourages people with disabilities to take pride in their differences. The disability rights movement began in the 1960s, led by Ed Roberts in Berkeley, California. After fighting for his own access needs as a student with polio at the University of California, Roberts founded the first Center for Independent Living in 1972, providing a core site for creating a community, fighting for social access and equality. After making some legal gains in the 1980s and 1990s, most notably the Americans with Disabilities Act, the disability rights movement continues to rally around increasing access while working to change social attitudes that deem disability as in need of cures and pity.

Linked with the larger disability rights movement, little people have increasingly come to identify with their height, taking pride in their difference and challenging the exclusionary norms that define taller statures as beautiful. The organization Little People of America has taken a stance that children should not undergo the surgery unless it is a medical necessity, which is rarely the case as ELL tends to weaken the bones and increase the risk of arthritis. ELL has divided the community, as those who opt for ELL are criticized for trying to hide their congenital difference and maintaining narrow conceptions of beauty. However, those opting for the surgery argue its practicality, as the extra height they gain will greatly ease their everyday lives as long as society is structurally intended for people of taller stature.

ELL encourages people to question what lengths they are willing to put their child through to help make them appear more normal. Because this surgery is most successful in youth, it puts particular pressure on parents, who must assess whether their child is capable of making the decision for themselves or else choose on their behalf. This debate has been taken up in bioethics, in particular by the Hastings Center's Surgically Shaping Children Project, which examined ELL along with other normalizing surgeries. On the one hand, parents want to do everything they can to help their child's chances for success, but on the other hand, they do not want to suggest to the child that there is something wrong with their appearance just because of their genetic difference. Though the debate continues, there has been some general consensus among scholars that whether or not ELL should be done, it must be put off until the child is mature enough to participate in the decision.

In the midst of these wider debates, several people who underwent ELL have shared their stories. In particular, Gillian Mueller was one of the first in the little people community to speak openly about undergoing ELL, stimulating much discussion. These narratives further complicate the picture, as the range of experiences shows how different ELL can be for each patient, causing some excruciating pain while others mild aches, and providing some with huge improvements in quality of life while leaving others more disabled after the surgery. The ELL controversy has become even more complex since the 1994 discovery of the gene for achondroplasia, allowing for prenatal testing to eliminate dwarfism altogether, indicating that the relationship between the little people community and biomedicine grows more fraught, a tension that will not be easily resolved.

Further Reading: Little People of America Web Site, http://www.lpaonline.org; Moseley, C.F. "Leg Lengthening: The Historical Perspective." *The Orthopedic Clinics of North America* 22: 4 (1991): 555–561; Parens, Erik, ed. *Surgically Shaping Children: Technology, Ethics, and the Pursuit of Normality.* Baltimore, MD: The Johns Hopkins University Press, 2006; Paterson, Dennis. "Leg-Lengthening Procedures: A Historical Review." *Clinical Orthopaedics and Related Research* 250 (1990): 27–33.

Emily Laurel Smith

Lips

Cultural History of Lips

The facial lips are highly sensitive moveable organs that serve integral functions in eating and speaking. In most cultures, the lips are also used in kissing. Possibly because of their association with kissing and other pleasurable intimate activities (such as oral sex), the lips are a site of beauty and sensuality for many. As such, cultures the world over and throughout history have developed techniques to accentuate and enhance the lips. These techniques range from temporary and fanciful, such as adding color or shine to the lips with lipsticks and glosses, or semi-permanent and invasive such as lip stretching and surgical augmentation. In spite of the seemingly universal preference for full lips, large lips have historically been stereotypically associated with people of the African diaspora. It was once believed that the fleshier lips of Africans were a visible signal of their underlying animal nature, just as the thin, defined lips of Europeans were thought to be emblematic of a gentler, more refined nature. The stereotypes of the big-lipped African became a cornerstone of American minstrelsy, and black-faced characters with exaggerated red lips have been used in a variety of media throughout the nineteenth and twentieth centuries to represent savage Blackness and evoke fears or poke fun at Black stereotypes.

The Biology of Facial Lips

The facial lips are a pair of fleshy, moveable protuberances whose primary functions include food intake and articulation in speech. The lips contain a high concentration of nerve endings, making it a highly sensitive tactile sensory organ. For infants, this makes the mouth a viable tool for exploring their surroundings. The sensitivity of the lips also makes stimulation of the lips highly pleasurable for many.

The skin of the lips has far fewer layers than the skin of the rest of the face, and is much thinner and more delicate than the surrounding tissue. Lip skin does not contain melanocytes, pigment producing structures found in the skin covering the majority of the body, or sebaceous glands, which produce a layer of oil to protect the skin. The implications of this are twofold. Because the skin of the lips is so comparatively thin, blood vessels can be seen through the skin, thus giving the healthy lip its characteristic pinkish color, especially in lighter-skinned individuals. Similarly, in colder temperatures or if a person isn't getting enough oxygen, the lips can take on a bluish hue. Also, as the lips do not lubricate themselves naturally, they often require extra care to maintain their smoothness and suppleness—especially in harsh climates or extreme conditions. Lip balms, glosses, and certain lipsticks are used to this end.

Lipstick

Lipstick is an emollient, pigmented cosmetic applied to the facial lips. Some of the oldest known predecessors of modern lipstick were manufactured by ancient Egyptians and Mesopotamians, using any number of natural substances such as semiprecious jewels, plant extracts, iodine, and even pulverized insects as pigments. Their primary use was to beautify the lips. Today, lipsticks are generally crafted from standardized chemical pigments using a variety of oils, waxes, and other unguents as bases. While their primary function is to add color to the lips, various lipsticks can be formulated to protect, soften, or even artificially plump the lips.

The wearing of lipstick serves a variety of cultural purposes. For some, wearing lipstick is a marker of passing from girlhood to womanhood, as in the West lipstick is largely worn by women of reproductive age. Lipstick also is thought to accentuate the mouth and emphasize its sensuality and its ability to give and receive tactile pleasure. Because of the mouth's association with sensuality and sexuality, for some lipstick is associated with an admission of sexual activity or with women of questionable repute. Because of its association with femininity, beauty and female sexuality, it is also an indispensable prop for most female impersonators and drag queens.

It's no accident that lipstick is associated with youth, femininity, and sensuality. Generally speaking, women with higher levels of estrogen tend to have fuller lips. Additionally, the lips of younger women tend to appear brighter in color, as older skin renews at a much slower rate, thereby dulling its natural color. Studies have shown that lipstick actually tricks the eye into perceiving the wearer as having fuller lips, which, some scientists suggest, serves as a cue to the wearer's youth, health, and attractiveness.

Lip Enhancement and Augmentation

There are some for whom the use of lipsticks, glosses and other cosmetics to accentuate the mouth's femininity and beauty are not enough. Such people may resort to a variety of surgical and non-surgical lip enhancement techniques to add to the lips' fullness, smoothness, and suppleness. Lip enhancement surgeries are on record in the West at least as early as 1900. Many surgeons initially tried injecting paraffin into the lips to add to their fullness, but achieved no lasting results. Since then, silicone and collagen have been popular options for lip enhancement procedures. While collagen is still in use, silicone had fallen out of favor for this procedure by the 1980s.

Collagen is a naturally occurring protein found in human and animal skin. The collagen used for lip enhancement injections is typically extracted from cowhides. While it can achieve an aesthetically pleasing result, bovine collagen can trigger an allergic response in some individuals. Also, because collagen occurs naturally in the skin, it is readily absorbed by the body. As such, collagen injections must be repeated every one to three months for a consistent effect. In recent decades, dermatologists have developed collagen injection formulations that make use of collagen either derived from the patient's own skin or from the skin of cadavers. These injections tend not to trigger allergic reactions; however they are absorbed by the body quite rapidly.

Similar to patient-derived collagen injections, fat transfer is another popular lip enhancement procedure. In a fat-transfer operation, fat is harvested from a "donor site," a place on the patient's body where an excess of fat exists (the part of the leg just inside the knee is a popular place for many). The fat is then clarified to remove impurities and either emulsified and injected into a recipient site, or cut into strips and surgically inserted into the recipient site. While the technique can achieve a very natural look and feel, the body tends to reabsorb its own fat cells quickly. Thus, the procedure would need to be repeated every few months.

In addition to these organic compounds, there are several synthetic compounds currently used in lip augmentation procedures. Most popular among them are Gore-Tex, Radiance and Restylane. Gore-Tex, the same synthetic polymer used to waterproof a variety of clothing, shoes and outerwear, is used as a permanent-yet-reversible surgical implant to fill out lips and repair other soft tissues. Gore-Tex implants (including Softform and Advanta) come in thin flat or tubular strips that are cut to size and are surgically inserted into the lips. Although convenient because of its one-time insertion and easy surgical removal, some have reported extended post-operative healing times and many find that the implant can be palpated through the skin. Both Radiance and Restylane are synthetic solutions that are injected into the lips. Such synthetic compounds tend to achieve longer-lasting results than organic injectables, as they are not readily absorbed by the body. However, if the lips are built up too quickly with such compounds, patients have been known to report lumps and nodules of varying sizes, some of which require surgical removal. Use of such injectables to augment the lips still requires several visits.

Lips and Racialization

In spite of the seemingly universal aesthetic preference for fuller lips, there apparently exists a fine line between "full" and "too full." Especially in the West, that line tends to coincide with racial boundaries. Specifically, too-full lips have long been a characteristic stereotypically associated with peoples of the African diaspora. In 1784, Germany's leading anatomist Samuel Thomas von Soemmering published "Über die körperliche Verschiedenheit des Mohren vom Europäen (Concerning the physical differences between the Moor and the European)," which served as the definitive reference regarding the black/African body well into the nineteenth century. According to his studies, based on observations of living persons and the dissection of several cadavers, those of African descent were said to have larger bodies and exaggerated fleshy body parts as opposed to the finely shaped, aesthetically preferential features of the European. The African (or Moor) was described as having more grossly cut, roughly hewn features than his or her European counterparts, which according to reigning theories of physiognomy at the time, was suggestive of a baser, more animal—perhaps even criminal—nature.

Like phrenology, nasology and other pseudosciences once heavily relied upon, physiognomy is no longer considered scientifically or socially valid. In spite of this, studies suggest that people still link particular social or mental temperaments with particular facial features. Several studies have shown that people tend to associate higher levels of negative behaviors such as criminality, ignorance and laziness with more exaggerated stereotypically African facial features—fuller lips and broader noses being the most prominent. One study even showed that people may recall exaggerated stereotypically black facial features in a perpetrator of a violent crime, regardless of whether or not the suspect possessed these features. This was true irrespective of the viewer's own race or racial attitudes. Again, lips and noses were the key features of interest.

The association of particular physical features with stereotypical negative behaviors has been so ingrained into the historical American psyche that an entire theatrical convention—the minstrel show—was formed around it. The minstrel show is a pre-Vaudeville, U.S. theatrical invention. Arguably the first uniquely American theatrical creation, minstrel shows consisted of a variety of skits designed to mock African American stereotypes, from demeanor to appearance. Early minstrel show actors were all Caucasian. In order to achieve the desired theatrical effect, minstrels wore what has come to be called "blackface" in addition to their costumes. Blackface, as the name would suggest, consisted of a black base (often using charcoal or the ash from burned cork) being used to darken the skin, along with the use of bright red lipstick to exaggerate the size and shape of the lips. The big, red lips of minstrels have become an internationally recognizable hallmark of the genre.

Outside of minstrelsy, a number of jokes, gags and turns of phrase rely on or make use of the cultural association of exaggerated lips and savage Blackness for their humor. Well into the twentieth century, numerous cartoons have made use of characters with exaggerated red or white lips to play the role of the comical or ignorant savage, often including other stereotypical trappings of primitivism such as laziness, lack of social graces, having a bone through one's nose, a plate in one's lip, and even mock cannibalism. Throughout the eighteenth, nineteenth, and twentieth centuries, these same features and their associated settings were reproduced in dolls and playsets, knick-knacks, paintings, drawings, wall hangings, banks, and all manner of collectable kitsch. Considered a cornerstone of American memorabilia by many, such items are still highly sought after as collectibles both in the United States and abroad. The big, black-faced, red-lipped savage was still a popular theme in toys, collectibles, and even the occasional advertisement in Japan at least as recently as the late-1990s. The collection and use of such images was a central theme in Spike Lee's 2000 film, *Bamboozled*.

The association of too-full lips with negative black stereotypes is not without irony. Interestingly, many studies suggest that what is "normal" or "average" among white American (or European) women is often not what white women or men would consider to be the most beautiful or ideal. Aesthetic studies reveal that most Caucasians have an aesthetic preference for lips that are thicker than what is statistically average among that group. This is mirrored in the fact that the lips of most Caucasian models are significantly thicker than the lips of the average Caucasian woman in the general population. Further, these same studies suggest that white models are more likely to have what are considered "ethnic" features than African American models are to have "Caucasoid" features.

Lip Stretching and Piercing

In addition to lipsticks, glosses and other topically applied adornments for the lips, people have employed a variety of other techniques to accentuate or otherwise beautify the lips. Namely, many cultures across time and place have employed some sort of lip piercing technique to enhance or bejewel the lips. While the image of a woman with a plate in her lip or particular facial piercings may evoke images of savagery and barbarism in the popular conscious mind, many different groups have made use of similar techniques, and several have achieved and currently enjoy widespread popularity with youth the world over.

Among the most controversial and perhaps stereotyped of body modifications are the practices of lip stretching and plate wearing. Historically, the practice was widespread among various tribal groups in sub-Saharan Africa, the American Northwest, and the Amazon basin, among others. However, lip stretching and plate wearing in sub-Saharan Africa are perhaps the most familiar to the Western mind. This is likely due at least in part to the fact that many African lip stretching practices have been documented on film and in photograph, while many of the other tribes to practice lip stretching did so largely before the advent of the photograph or the video camera. The conflation of lip stretching, plate wearing and African-ness are all evidenced by the various pop culture caricatures of the black African savage, dancing, grunting, adorned with a bone in the nose and a plate in the lip (such as used in cartoons and comic strips well into the twentieth century). In actuality, the person receiving the plate/being stretched, the age at which it occurred and the cultural significance of lip stretching varied across groups.

For example, among the Ubangi and Sara groups in Chad, the lip stretching process began almost immediately after birth for girls. Unlike many other tribal groups, the Ubangi and Sara tended to stretch both the upper and lower lips (as opposed to just the lower, as is done by the majority of other tribal groups known to adhere to the practice). While once widespread, lip stretching has not been in widespread practice among these groups since the mid-twentieth century.

Among the Surma (aka Suri) and Mursi of what is currently known as Ethiopia, stretching of the lower lip is reserved for girls of marriageable age. Among these tribes, the stretching process is generally begun by the mother, and starts around the age of fifteen. Among the Surma and Mursi, not only does a stretched lip signify that a girl is available for marriage, engaged or married, but for many women it serves as a sense of ethnic pride and a way of distinguishing themselves from nearby tribes. This practice is still widespread among these tribes today.

Initially, a sharp object is used to make a small incision in the lip to be stretched. After the incision is made, a relatively small piece of jewelry, ranging from a few millimeters to a few centimeters, is placed into the incision. The incision is then generally allowed to heal around the inserted jewelry item for anywhere from a few days to several years. After the incision has healed for a culturally appropriate period of time, the incision is stretched further by inserting progressively larger pieces of jewelry into the initial opening. As the incision in the lip becomes progressively larger, often-ornate pieces of bone, clay, wood, or stone are inserted to keep the incision open. Using this technique, the facial lips can be stretched to accommodate a piece of jewelry up to several inches in diameter.

While lip stretching remains a "primitive" practice in the minds of many, the practice has been adopted by Westerners enthusiastic about indigenous forms of body modification, some of whom have been called modern primitives. Most body piercers in the West perform lip stretching either using traditional methods—beginning with a small lip piercing and using a tapered needle to stretch the piercing to the desired size—or by cutting a larger incision in the lip and inserting a relatively large piece of jewelry into the incision. In spite of the underlying tribal affiliations popularly associated with lip stretching, people of all races and social backgrounds can now be seen wearing modern lip plates. Such body modifications are especially popular among modern primitive and urban punk subcultures, among others.

In addition to lip plates, a variety of other lip piercings have gained popularity in the West. Lip piercings can be placed anywhere around the mouth, making for a virtually limitless number of possible piercing sites and combinations. The actual smooth surface of the lip itself, however, is rarely pierced. Although endless piercing possibilities exist, several particular styles have become popular enough to have their own names and associated techniques. For example, a "labret" is a piercing placed in the labret—the flat surface just beneath the lower lip. A small bar is placed into the piercing. A flat disk between the lip and gums holds the piercing in place inside the mouth, and a small metal or acrylic ball is usually visible on the outer part of the piercing. A "vertical labret" describes a curved barbell, inserted vertically at the labret, which is visible both at the labret and just between the upper and lower lips. A "snakebite" is the term used to describe a set of two piercings, one at each side of the lower lip. The "Monroe" is an off-center piercing, placed just above the upper lip. When a labret stud or similar piece of jewelry is worn in this opening (as is customary), it is quite reminiscent of

Marilyn Monroe's infamous mole—hence the name. *See also* Fat: Fat Injections; Lips: Lip Stretching; and Skin: Cultural History of Skin.

For Further Reading: All About Lip Augmentation Web site. Lip Implants and Soft Tissue Augmentation Materials. http://www.lipaugmentation.com/lip_implants.htm (accessed November 2007); Nordqvist, Christian. "Attractive women tend to have higher oestrogen levels." Medical News Today Web site. http://www.medicalnewstoday.com/articles/32924.php (accessed December 2007); Oliver, Mary Beth, Ronald Jackson II, Ndidi N. Moses, and Celnisha L. Dangerfield. "The Face of Crime: Viewers' Memory of Race-Related Facial Features of Individuals Pictured in the News." *Journal of Communication* 54, 1 (2004): 88–104; Russell, John. "Race and Reflexivity: The Black Other in Contemporary Japanese Mass Culture." *Cultural Anthropology* 6, 1 (1991): 3–25; Schiebinger, Londa. "The Anatomy of Difference: Race and Sex in Eighteenth-Century Science." *Eighteenth Century Studies* 23, 4 (1990): 387–405; Sutter Jr., Robert E., and Patrick Turley. "Soft tissue evaluation of contemporary Caucasian and African American female facial profiles." *The Angle Orthodontist* 68, 6 (1998): 487–496; Turton, David. "Lip-plates and 'The People Who Take Photographs:' Uneasy Encounters Between Mursi and Tourists in Southern Ethiopia." *Anthropology Today* 20, 3 (2004): 3–8.

Alena J. Singleton

Lip Enlargement

The term "lip enlargement" can refer to any of the practices and procedures used to alter the lips in an attempt to create the appearance of large, full lips. More specifically, lips may be enlarged through surgical reshaping (for example, a lip "lift"), nonsurgical injections of filler materials, surgical implantation of synthetic substances, or widely available topical applications. Cultural representations of cosmetic surgery as exaggerated or disfiguring often center on inflated lips to symbolize "overdoing it," as in the 1996 film *The First Wives Club*. Despite the often-farcical portrayal of lip enlargement, Western cultures continue to idealize full lips. According to recent polls, American actress Angelina Jolie is said to have the "sexiest" lips among celebrities, and cosmetic surgeons report that prospective lip enlargement patients often specifically request "Angelina Jolie lips."

Practices designed to enlarge the exterior surface of the lips, or to present the appearance of larger lips, have existed in a range of societies and time periods. In ancient Egypt, people painted their lips with henna and other plant dyes. Traditional tribal practices in places as distinct as Africa and the Amazon have included the introduction of various substances (such as wooden disks) to enlarge upper or lower lips Traditional methods of lip enlargement generally involve the introduction of successively larger disks of wood or clay into a piercing on the lip. Over time, the lip stretches to accommodate this disk or plate.

In Africa, some tribes in Ethiopia, Chad, and elsewhere use disks to stretch both lips and earlobes. This practice is most common among adolescent women, and is seen as a preparation for marriage and adulthood. Disks may be made of clay or wood, and their insertion into the body is seen as serving aesthetic purposes.

In South America, lowland indigenous tribes, especially those in the Amazon River region, traditionally enlarged both lips and earlobes with disks made of light wood, which were painted and decorated. Although in some historical periods both women and men enlarged their lips with the use of disks, today this practice is associated with men and can be part of their rites of passage into adulthood. Enlarged lips are associated with masculinity and verbal skill (in speaking and singing), and the use of disks is most common among high-status tribesmen. The Kayapó and Suyá are among the tribes maintaining this tradition in the Amazon region.

Today, both surgical and non-surgical methods are available for those (mostly women) who aspire to dominant cultural ideals that perceive full, defined lips as conveying an impression of health, youth, sensuality, and beauty. According to plastic surgeons, the ideal lips have: a well-defined border around the vermillion or dark part of the lip; a "cupid's bow" (indentation in the center of the top lip); are horizontally symmetrical; and have a larger lower than upper lip.

Cosmetic lip enlargement falls into the category of cosmetic procedures referred to as "minimally invasive." The most common technique for lip enlargement is the injection of a substance into one or both lips. The two most common injectable fillers are collagen and the patient's own fat. While collagen is a protein produced by humans, most collagen used for cosmetic procedures is a type of bovine collagen, which was approved for cosmetic injection use by the Food and Drug Administration in the early 1980s. In addition to being used for lip enlargement, collagen is also used to fill facial wrinkles. In this lip enlargement procedure, collagen is injected into the corners of the patient's mouth, sometimes with lidocaine or another mild anesthetic mixed in to dull pain or discomfort. Sedation and general anesthesia are not typically used in lip enlargement procedures.

As an alternative to collagen, or for those who are found to be allergic to that substance, a patient's fat may be harvested from the abdomen, buttocks, or another part of the body using the equipment employed in liposuction procedures (a large needle with a suction pump). The fat is then injected into the corners of the lips. Local anesthesia is generally used in this procedure. Besides collagen and natural fat, other injectable fillers may be used to enlarge lips, including donated human tissue, silicone (which many surgeons do not recommend because it can leak into other tissues), Restylane (hyaluronic acid), Alloderm (made from donated skin tissue), or Fibril (gelatin mixed with the patient's blood). The procedures associated with these products are similar to the injection of collagen or fat.

Collagen and fat injections have temporary effects; for this reason, surgeons often "overfill" the lips, as the swelling begins to reduce almost immediately. Collagen's effects are generally said to last three to four months. Fat injections supposedly last longer than collagen injections, but are also not permanent. People who choose to undergo these procedures are informed of the temporary character of their effects, and often choose to undergo regular "touch-up" injections indefinitely.

A more permanent, though reversible, alternative to injectable fillers is the insertion of implants into the lips (upper, lower, or both). The most common substance used to make lip implants is Gore-Tex, a synthetic polymer that is available in strands/threads or a hollow tube known as Soft-Form. Generally, implants are inserted through incisions at the corners of the mouth in two pieces to avoid a reduced range of motion in the lips. The procedure is usually performed with local anesthesia, often in a doctor's office. Patients sometimes experiment with temporary lip augmentation methods first before moving on to permanent (though removable) implants. As with any implant, there is a danger of the body rejecting lip implants or of the insertion site becoming infected.

Another surgical option is a lip lift, which reduces the amount of skin between the bottom of the nose and the top of the lip and allows more of the red part of the lip (known as vermillion) to be visible. There are also other means of reshaping the lips surgically, such as the so-called V-Y lip augmentation, which reshapes the top lip in order to expand the surface area of the vermillion. These procedures are usually performed on an outpatient basis with local anesthesia. As with surgical implants, these are more permanent alterations when compared with collagen or other injected substances.

In recent years, nonsurgical lip enlargement products, collectively known as "plumpers," have emerged. These topical applications often work by irritating the lips, causing temporary swelling. The active ingredients in these substances may include: cinnamon, ginger, menthol, pepper extracts, and vitamins such as niacin or Vitamin B6. These products are marketed with claims to enlarge lips temporarily; some claim to have effects that last several hours. Most lip plumpers come in the form of lipsticks or lip glosses, applying color in addition to their supposed lip-fattening properties. These products are marketed explicitly to women along with other cosmetics. (*See also* Lips: Lip Stretching).

Further Reading: Cohen, Meg, and Karen Kozlowski. *Read My Lips: A Cultural History of Lipstick*. San Francisco: Chronicle Books, 1998; Klein, Arnold William. "In Search of the Perfect Lip: 2005." *Dermatologic Surgery* 31 (2005): 1,599–1,603.

Erynn Masi de Casanova

Lip Stretching

Lip stretching is a practice in which a hole made in one or both facial lips is stretched, often to very large sizes, by the insertion of various objects of successively larger sizes. Historically, the practice was widespread among various tribal groups in sub-Saharan Africa, the American Northwest, and the Amazon basin, among others. While some tribes have used lip stretching as a marker of feminine beauty and an announcement of a woman's marriageability, among other tribes lip stretching was reserved for men of a particular age and rank. While still practiced today among some aboriginal groups, the practice of lip stretching has transcended its tribal affiliations and has become more common among some Western subcultures. Variations on traditional lip stretching practices are now seen in piercing and body-modification parlors across the globe.

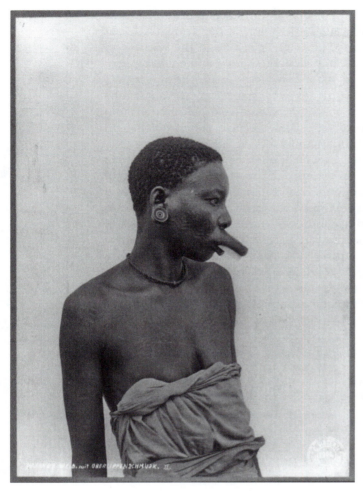

Lip stretching of a Makonki woman, Mikindani, Tanganyika. Courtesy of Library of Congress, LC-USZ62-88316.

Historical Context

The historical record bears significant, concrete evidence of lip stretching among tribal populations in three major geographical areas—various parts of sub-Saharan Africa, the American Northwest, and parts of Brazil. Among the tribal groups who have historically practiced lip stretching, each has done so among varying social subgroups for a variety of reasons.

In spite of the varying cultural significance of lip stretching, the methods for stretching one's facial lips are remarkably similar across contexts. Initially, a small incision is made in the lip to be stretched. After the incision is made, a relatively small (ranging from a few millimeters to a few centimeters) plate-, rod-, or plug-shaped piece of jewelry is placed into the incision. The incision is then generally allowed to heal around the inserted jewelry item for anywhere from a few days to several years. After the incision has healed for a culturally appropriate period of time, the incision is stretched further by inserting progressively larger pieces of jewelry into the initial opening. As the incision in the lip becomes progressively larger, often-ornate pieces of bone, clay, wood or stone are inserted to keep the incision open. Anthropologists and archaeologists have documented that one's lip can be stretched to accommodate a piece of jewelry up to several inches in diameter.

Africa

Although the traditional methods of lip stretching are remarkably similar across cultural contexts, the sub-population subject to lip stretching, the stage of life at which the process began, and the reasons for doing so varied widely across groups. For example, among the Ubangi and Sara groups in Chad, the lip stretching process began almost immediately after birth for girls. Unlike many other tribal groups, the Ubangi and Sara tended to stretch both the upper and lower lips (as opposed to just the lower, as is done by the majority of other tribal groups known to adhere to the practice). While once widespread, lip stretching has not been in widespread practice among these groups since the mid-twentieth century. The practice's decline in popularity is thought to stem in part from modernizing influences and increasing contact with the West and other cultural groups that do not engage in the practice.

Among the Surma (aka Suri) and Mursi of what is currently known as Ethiopia, stretching of the lower lip is reserved for girls of marriageable age. Among these tribes, the stretching process is generally begun by the mother, and starts around the age of fifteen. Among the Surma and Mursi, not only does a stretched lip signify that a girl is available for marriage, engaged or married, but for many women it serves as a sense of ethnic pride and a way of distinguishing themselves from nearby tribes. This practice is still widespread among these tribes today. Interestingly, in addition to carrying their original cultural meanings, it has been suggested that among these tribes the practice persists in large part because it has become a "cultural attraction" of sorts. As these groups have become well known for their lip stretching practices, they are known to attract professional photographers, curious tourists looking for an "authentic experience," and even television and film crews. Allowing themselves and their rituals to be filmed or photographed has become a source of income and security to many Mursi and Surma, among others.

American Northwest

Many tribal groups in the American Northwest were known to have practiced lip stretching of some sort. Lip-stretching practices among the Tlingit, Haida, and Tsimshian are well documented, and evidence of the practice has also been documented among the Haisla, Haihais and Heiltsuk, although to a lesser extent. Amongst these tribes, lip stretching was prescribed for all girls born into the tribe. Slaves or servants that had been captured from neighboring tribes in times of war were not subjected to this practice. The lower lip was initially pierced at first menstruation. Anthropologists widely believe that for the tribes of the American Northwest, the size of the plate or plug worn in the lower lip tended to be proportional to the girl/woman's social status. The higher one's social status, the larger and more ornate the plate or plug. It would follow, then, that slaves or servants would be exempt or even barred from this practice, as they had no social status. Their lack of a plate signified their identity as "outsider." While this process was almost exclusively the domain of women, anecdotal evidence suggests that a few men of very high rank and social prestige may have also sported stretched lower lips.

Amazon Basin

In sharp contrast to the aforementioned groups, the Suya and Kayapo of the area now known as Brazil restricted lip stretching to men. In these cultures, a male child's lip was pierced at birth. Through his early childhood, a male Suya or Kayapo child would likely be seen wearing feathers and/or brightly colored strings hanging from this piercing. The piercing was not stretched until the boy was socially acknowledged as having left his mother's side and entered the realm of men. The piercing was stretched to increasingly large diameters as he advanced in age, marries, and has children. Although lip stretching is still practiced among these groups, it is far less common than it was in decades and centuries past thanks in part to decreased cultural isolation and greater contact with industrialized societies.

Western Adaptations

While lip stretching remains a "primitive" practice in the minds of many, the practice has been adopted into the cannon of Western subcultural body modification. Many experienced body piercers are skilled in "modern" lip stretching techniques. Most piercers in the West perform lip stretching in one of two ways.

The first, and arguably least painful, way to perform a lip stretching is to begin with a small lip piercing and use a tapered needle to stretch the piercing so as to accommodate a successively larger piercing. Once the piercing has been given sufficient time to heal, the process is repeated until one's lip has been stretched to the desired size.

The second common method for performing lip stretching in the West is to create an opening in the lip either by cutting an incision with a scalpel or using a specialized tool to punch a hole through the flesh (much as would be done if hole-punching a sheet of paper). A relatively large piece of jewelry can then be placed into this opening and allowed to heal. While this method allows for the stretcher to wear larger pieces of jewelry faster, this method is highly painful and carries an increased risk for tearing, scarring, and injury or damage to the mouth, teeth, and gums.

Health Risks

The risks associated with lip stretching or wearing large lip plates or plugs include oral and facial pain, tooth loss, periodontal disease, and permanent difficulties with eating, drinking, and speaking.

Further Reading: Abbink, Jon. "Tourism and Its Discontents: Suri-Tourist Encounters in Southern Ethiopia." *Social Anthropology* 8, 1 (2000): 1–17; Moss, Madonna. "George Catlin Among the Nayas: Understanding the Practice of Labret Wearing on the Northwest Coast." *Ethnohistory* 46, 1 (1999): 31–65; Mursi Online. "Lip Plates and the Mursi Life Cycle." http://www.mursi.org/life-cycle/lip-plates (accessed July 2007). Seeger, Anthony. "The Meaning of Body Ornaments: A Suya Example." *Ethnology* 14, 3 (1975): 211–224. Turner, Terence. "Social Body and Embodied Subject: Bodiliness, Subjectivity, and Sociality Among the Kayapo." *Cultural Anthropology* 10, 2 (May 1995): 142–170; Turton, David. "Lip-plates and 'The People Who Take Photographs': Uneasy Encounters Between Mursi and Tourists in Southern Ethiopia." *Anthropology Today* 20, 3 (2004): 3–8.

Alena J. Singleton